Marriage & Death Notices

from

Barbour and Henry

Counties, Alabama

Newspapers

1846-1890

Compiled by:

Helen S. Foley

Southern Historical Press, Inc.

Please direct all correspondence and orders to:

www.southernhistoricalpress.com
or
SOUTHERN HISTORICAL PRESS, Inc.
PO BOX 1267
375 West Broad Street
Greenville, SC   29601
southernhistoricalpress@gmail.com

ISBN #0-89308-658-4

Printed in the United States of America

Contents

MARRIAGES

FOREWARD

Marriage and death notices and events about people appearing
in the newspapers were compiled from available papers on file at
the Barbour and Henry County Courthouses, the Eufaula Carnegie
Library, and the Alabama History and Archives. Newspapers con-
taining no items were deleted. Notices are as brief as possible,
giving all the family history, date and name of the newspaper in
which they appeared. Entries are not limited to Southeast
Alabama, but were compiled from anyplace as they were found in
the papers. However, the greater part of the data is from Barbour and surrounding counties.

Many marriages were performed in Georgetown, Georgia, just
across the Chattahoochee River from Eufaula, and was known as
the "Gretna Green" of Southeast Alabama. Early records of
Georgetown were destroyed by fire in 1921.

The first marriage in Barbour County was that of Daniel
McCall, father of Hart McCall, once tax collector of this county,
to Miss Mary McDaniel, which took place in 1822. The couple,
with their parents and friends had to go nearly to Franklin on
the Chattahoochee, to find a person authorized by law to perform
the marriage ceremony. This was done by William Beauchamp, a
magistrate of the residence of Gen. Wm. Irwin, who was for many
years a state senator of Henry County, and for whom the town of
Eufaula was first named, Irwinton.

The above marriage taken from a speech delivered in Clayton
on the fourth of July, 1876, by Green Beauchamp, Esq., who was
present at the marriage. (From: Eufaula Tribune's Historical
Progress Edition, Thursday, Dec. 5, 1940).

THE EUFAULA DEMOCRAT
1846

E. C. Bullock, Editor and John Black, Publisher.

Wed. July 8, 1846
Married in Eufaula on Wednesday last, by Rev. Mr. Heard, Mr.
Joseph Saulsbury to Miss Mary Kennon, all of Eufaula.

Wed. Sept. 2, 1846
Married on the 18th inst., at Enon, by Rev. Armstrong, A. D.
Cleckley, Esq., to Miss Ann Caroline, daughter of William and
Mary Cox.

Wed. Oct. 14, 1846
Married in Eufaula on the 10th inst., by Rev. J. A. Heard,
Dr. N. J. Moore, of Henry County, to Miss Rebecca E. Penson, of
Dallas.

Wed. Nov. 25, 1846
Married in Eufaula on the 17th inst., by Rev. J. A. Heard,
Dr. C. W. Snow to Miss Emily E., daughter of Allen Lovelace, Esq.

Married at Cannandagua, N.Y., on Sept. 24th, by Rev. O. C.
Daggett, Mr. D. Danforth to Miss Francis E., daughter of the
Rev. E. B. Coleman.

Wed. Dec. 9, 1846
Married in Geneva, Ala., on the 1st inst., by Rev. E.
Albritton, R. J. Newell, Esq., of Georgetown, Ga., to Miss
Caledonia, daughter of Asa Alexander, Esq.

Married on the 1st inst., by Rev. R. C. Smith, Jas. L. Pugh,
Esq., to Miss Sarah Serena, daughter of Col. Jno. L. Hunter, all
of Eufaula.

THE EUFAULA DEMOCRAT
1847

S. G. Cato, Editor and John Black, Publisher.

Wed. June 16, 1847
Married in Barbour County on the 20th inst., by Benj.
Gardner, Esq., Mr. Hansford D. Price to Miss Sarah Cunningham.

Wed. July 7, 1847
Married on the 1st inst., at the home of Alex. McMillan, by
Thos. Cargile, Esq., Mr. A. T. Trawick to Miss Margaret McMillan,
all of Barbour County.

Wed. Sept. 22, 1847
Married in Eufaula on Thursday last, by Rev. O. R. Blue, Mr.
John Black to Miss Mary Billings.

THE EUFAULA DEMOCRAT
1848

S. G. Cato, Editor and John Black, Publisher.

Wed. Jan. 5, 1848
Married in Dallas County, Ala., on Dec. 29th, by Rev. W. H.
Merideth, J. G. McLean of Eufaula, to Miss Susannah Smyly,
daughter of Capt. Jno. Smyly of Dallas County.

Wed. Jan. 19, 1848
Married in LaGrange, Ga., on 12th inst., by Rev. Jno. E. Dawson, Col. Eli S. Shorter, of Eufaula, to Miss Marietta Fannin, of the former place.

Wed. Jan. 26, 1848
Married in Barbour County, Jan. 16, 1848, on board the Steamer Emily, by Squire Lewis, Mr. Jas. J. Murphy, to Miss Elizabeth Ann Skipper, both of Henry County, Ala.

Wed. Feb. 2, 1848
Married on 20th inst., in Wynton, Ga., by Rev. J. Boring, Rev. O. R. Blue, of Alabama Conference, to Miss Ann E., daughter of Gen. Nicholas Howard.

Wed. May 3, 1848
Married in Eufaula on 26th inst., by Rev. Zachariah Thomas, Mr. Wilhelm Bort to Miss Sarah Ann Bethena Heidt, all of Eufaula.

Tues. July 25, 1848
Married in Clinton, Ga., on 18th inst., Reuben C. Shorter, Jr., of Wetumpka, Ala., to Miss Caroline Billingslea of the former place.

Tues. Aug. 1, 1848
Married on the 28th ult., by Rev. Brown, Mr. Jno. Green to Miss Martha McClendon, all of Randolph County, Ga.

Tues. Dec. 5, 1848*
Married on 23d ult., in Pike County, by Rev. M. A. Patterson, Mr. N. Montross Hyatt, of Eufaula, to Miss Sarah Emeline, daughter of H. Hobdy, Esq., of Pike County.

THE EUFAULA DEMOCRAT
1849

Tennent Lomax, Editor and John Black, Publisher.

Tues. Jan. 23, 1849
Married on Jan. 16th by Rev. Wm. H. Van Doren, Mr. Geo. W. McGinty to Mrs. Elizabeth C., daughter of Allen Loveless, Esq.

Tues. Feb. 20, 1849
Chas. Burton and Elizabeth Nichols of Boston were married in Albany on the 15th.

Tues. Mar. 6, 1849
Married by Hon. B. C. Landsdale, at the home of Artemus Ward, on 21st inst., Mr. Amos Hicks to Miss Elizabeth Ward, eldest daughter of Mr. West Ward, all of this county.--Abbeville, Henry County, 22d Feb. 1849.

Tues. Mar. 13, 1849
Married at Thomasville, Ga., 25th of Feb., by Rev. S. Potter, Hon. Daniel McCrimmon, of Abbeville, Ala., to Miss Mary Ann, daughter of Rev. I. L. Potter of the former place.

Tues. May 15, 1849
Mr. Tennent Lomax, Esq., and Miss Sophia H. Shorter were married by Rev. Mr. McIntosh on the 19th inst., at the home of Gen. R. C. Shorter in Eufaula.

*Tennet Lomax, Editor and John Black, Publisher.

Mr. Orastus Bell and Miss Elizabeth Taylor were married by
M. B. Wellborn, Esq., on 13th inst., at the home of Mr. A. B.
Holliman in Eufaula.

Tues. June 5, 1849
Married on 27th of May, 1849, in Barbour County, by Rev.
Appleton Haygood, Mr. A. V. McAlister to Miss Nancy, the daughter
of Mr. J. Lolless, of the former place, and late of Muscogee
County, Ga.

Tues. July 3, 1849
Married on 28th ult., in Glennville, by Rev. Scales, L. L.
Cato, Esq., to Miss Martha J. Richardson.

Tues. Dec. 18, 1849
Married on 4th inst., by Rev. Malone, Mr. H. B. Fitts to
Miss Elizabeth Oliver, all of Eufaula.

Tues. Dec. 25, 1849
Married on 19th inst., at the home of J. N. Copeland, by
Rev. L. C. Harrison, Mr. Theodore Dent, of Tuscaloosa County, to
Miss Virginia D. Cannon, youngest daughter of Capt. S. R. Cannon.

THE EUFAULA DEMOCRAT
1850

Alpheus Baker, Jr., Editor and John Black, Publisher.

July 2, 1850
Married in Barbour County, on 26th of June, by Rev. Ware,
Mr. Jno. L. Roberts to Miss Sarah, daughter of Wiley Oliver, Esq.,
of this county.

Married in Bentonville, Coffee County on 9th June, at the
home of Judge G. T. Yelverton, by Rev. Mr. Moses W. Helms, Robt.
Tilman Esq., to Miss Sarah E. Grimes, all of Coffee County, (Ala).

SPIRIT OF THE SOUTH
1850

P. T. Sayre & E. C. Bullock, Editors and John Black, Publisher &
Proprietor.

Dec. 3, 1850
Married on 26th ult., at the home of Mr. Jno. E. Dennard,
by Rev. S. Dennard, Mr. Thos. S. Seals and Miss Matailda Dennard,
all of Barbour County.

Dec. 10, 1850
Married on 3d inst., in Eufaula, by Rev. Jno. H. Dawson,
Robt. R. Howard, Esq., of Columbus, (Ga.) and Miss Mary Louise
Flournoy, daughter of Maj. Thos. F. Flournoy.

Dec. 24, 1850
Married at LaGrange, Ga., on 17th inst., by Rev. Otis Smith,
Mr. Cullen A. Battle, of Eufaula, and Miss Georgia Florence
Williams, of the former place.

Also, at the same time and place, R. J. Morgan, Esq., and
Miss Mary H. Battle.

Dec. 31, 1850
Married on 26th inst., by Rev. Mr. McIntosh, Mr. Richard
Morris to Miss Elizabeth, eldest daughter of Thos. Cargile, Esq.,

all of Eufaula.

SPIRIT OF THE SOUTH
1851

P. T. Sayre & E. C. Bullock, Editors and John Black, Publisher & Proprietor.

Feb. 4, 1851
Married on 29th ult., in Eufaula, by Rev. Mr. Mathews of Cuthbert, Maj. Samuel D. Irvin and Miss Julia A. Cargile, daughter of Thos. Cargile, Esq.

June 17, 1851
Married on Tuesday last, by Rev. Mr. McIntosh, Mr. A. A. Raleigh to Miss Hariet Lewis, all of Eufaula.

SPIRIT OF THE SOUTH
1855-1856

Nov. 6, 1855
Married on 21st ult., near Spring Hill, Barbour County, by J. M. White, Esq., Mr. Jas. T. Robinson to Miss Margaret A. Lang.

Married on 30th of Oct., by Elder A. Van Hoose, Mr. Wm. H. Locke, of Eufaula, to Miss Ann J. Sylvester, of Barbour County.

Jan. 22, 1856
Married in Catoosa County, Ga., on 10th inst., by Rev. J. B. Frost, Mr. Thos. J. Coxwell, of Barbour County, to Miss Sarah Jane, daughter of Col. Spencer Riley, of the former place.

Mar. 11, 1856
Married on 4th inst., by D. A. Bush, Esq., Mr. Benj. Morris, of Patrick County, Va., to Miss Rozanna, daughter of Wm. Blair, Esq., of Barbour County, Ala.

INDEPENDENT AMERICAN
(Published Troy, Pike County, Ala.)
1855

E. B. Arms, Proprietor & Publisher; D. J. L. Cunningham & A. N. Worthy, Editors.

Wed. Aug. 1, 1855
Married on 27th of May 1855, by W. S. Clary, Esq., at the house of Alsey Durham, Mr. Manassa T. Wilson to Miss Margaret Durham, all of Pike County.

Wed. Aug. 15, 1855
Married on the 21st ult., at the Baptist Church in Troy (Ala.) by Rev. Mathew Bishop, Columbus J. L. Cunningham, Esq., Associate Editor of the American, to Miss Harriet E. Hamilton, formerly of Abbeville, S.C.

Wed. Aug. 29, 1855
Married on 23d inst., by Rev. Matthew Bishop, at the home of Robt. H. Johnson, in this place, Mr. L. Waltz, of Montgomery, to Miss A. J. Cooper.

Wed. Sept. 3, 1855
Married on 15th ult., by Jas. Folmar, Esq., Jas. P. Small and Miss Rocksy Ann Hines, all of Pike County.

Married near Midway, (Ala.) on 23d ult., by Rev. Joel Sims, Maj. J. W. Mabry and Miss Mary Ann Calloway.

Wed. Sept. 12, 1855
Married at the home of Mr. Jas. Jordan, on the 6th inst., by Jno. R. Wilson, Esq., Mr. Jno. Taylor and Miss Sarah Ann Jordan.

Married on the 6th inst., at the home of E. Davis, by Jason Tyson, Esq., Mr. Nathan J. Ellis to Miss Edeth E. Whittington, all of Pike County, Ala.

Wed. Sept. 19, 1855
Married on 12th inst., at the home of Mrs. Ann E. Benbow, by Rev. Jno. S. Holmes, Mr. Grover Hall, of Milton, Fla., to Miss M. A. Benbow, of Pike County, Ala.

Married on the 6th of Sept., by F. B. Hurley, Esq., Martin M. Burks to Miss Martha J. Sanders, all of Pike County.

Married on the 10th inst., by Jno. R. Wilson, Esq., Mr. Jno. D. Blair to Miss Mildred Underwood.

Married on the 13th inst., by Jno. R. Wilson, Esq., Mr. J. W. Weaver to Miss Margaret Stone.

Married on the 30th ult., by W. S. Cleary, Esq., Mr. Jordan Griggs to Miss Rebecca Davenport, all of Pike County.

Wed. Nov. 14, 1855
Married on the 8th inst., at the home of Mr. Jno. Allen, by Jason Tyson, Esq., Mr. Geo. W. Grimes to Miss Sarah A. E. Allen, all of Pike County.

Wed. Nov. 21, 1855
Married at Millville in Butler County, (Ala.) on the 8th of Nov., by Jas. A. Thagard, Esq., Mr. Wilson J. Tisdale, of Pike County, to Miss M. C. Odom, of Butler County.

Married at the home of Mastin E. Berry, on the 15th inst., by J. G. Brooks, Esq., Mr. W. J. Braswell to Miss Margaret C. Berry, all of Pike County, Ala.

Married on the 3d of Oct., by Rev. Mr. McCarty, Mr. Julius C. Philips to Miss Ann E. Leftwich, all of Macon County, (Ala.).

Married on the 9th inst., near Union Springs, Macon County, Ala., by Rev. J. T. S. Park, Mr. Duncan Graham of Helicon, Ala., and Miss Jane E. Bond, second daughter of W. B. Bond, of the former place.

Wed. Dec. 6, 1855
Married on 28th of Nov., at the residence of Mr. W. H. Manning, by Jason Tyson, Esq., Mr. Jno. S. J. Veazley to Miss Elizabeth J. Manning, all of Pike County, Ala.

Wed. Dec. 12, 1855
Married on 29th of Nov., at the home of Mr. Wm. D. Tisdale, by I. J. Brunson, Esq., Mr. Jno. F. Hamilton, of Covington County, Ala., to Miss Elizabeth R. Tisdale, of Pike County, Ala.

Married at the home of W. C. Brooks, on the 4th inst., by Jno. R. Wilson, Esq., Mr. Reuben H. Lane to Miss Mary C. Brooks, all of Pike County, Ala.

Wed. Dec. 26, 1855
Married at the home of Mr. Saunders in this county, on the

20th inst., by U. S. Jones, Esq., Mr. Wm. D. Bragg, Upson County, Ga. to Mrs. Amanda Carter.

Married on 18th inst., near Notasulga, (Ala.) by Rev. C. S. Burks, Mr. Jno. Greathouse, of Tallapoosa County, Ala., to Miss Jane Elizabeth Calloway, of Macon County, Ala.

Married recently in Coweta County, Ga., Mr. Tench, Attorney at Law, to Mrs. Rebecca A. Lomas, of Notasulga.

INDEPENDENT AMERICAN
1856

Sam'l. M. Adams, Proprietor & Publisher.

Wed. Jan. 9, 1856
Married on 2nd inst., by Rev. A. N. Worthy, Shep. Ruffin, Esq., of Elba, (Ala.) to Miss Nancy C. Mullins, of Pike County.

Married on 3d inst., at the residence of Wm. A. Gibson, by Jason Tyson, Esq., Mr. Wm. H. Manning to Miss Martha Ann Simmons, all of Pike County, Ala.

Married on 3d inst., by Rev. A. N. Worthy, Mr. Wm. L. Simmons to Miss Georgia Williams, all of Pike County, (Ala.).

Wed. Jan. 16, 1856
Married on 25th of Dec., by B. F. Beverly, Mr. Darling Pitman, of Troy, to Miss Theodocia M. Wilder.

Wed. Jan. 23, 1856
Miss Jeanie Hicks, daughter of Judge Hicks, was married on the 10th ult., at the residence of Chief Jno. Ross, at Taleanah, in the Cherokee Nation, to Mr. Stepler, brother-in-law to the Chief.

Wed. Jan. 30, 1856
Married at the home of Irby Wynne, on the 24th inst., by Jno. R. Wilson, Esq., Mr. Samuel Y. Tompkins to Miss Francis A. E. Wynne, all of Pike County, Ala.

Wed. Feb. 13, 1856
Married on 7th of Feb., 1856, at the home of Mr. E. P. Salter, by Rev. J. J. Cumbie, Mr. Jno. R. Pennington to Miss Martha Williams, all of Bughall, Ala.

Wed. Mar. 5, 1856
Married at the home of Wm. Merritt in Bradly County, Ark., on 20th of Jan. 1856, by Rev. J. B. White, Mr. Jno. H. Brooks to Miss Jane L. Merritt.

Married on 18th of Feb., at the home of Mr. Whigham, by Rev. B. H. Banks, A. J. Smith to Miss M. V. Whigham, all of Pike County, Ala.

Married on 12th of Feb., at the home of Mr. Smith, by Rev. B. H. Banks, Mr. J. B. Whigham to Miss Jalaney Jane Smith, all of Pike County, Ala.

Wed. Apr. 16, 1856
Married on the 13th inst. by Rev. A. N. Worthy, Mr. Lewis A. Livingston to Miss Sarah A. House, all of this place.

Married on 20th of Mar., by Rev. W. D. Atkinson, Mr. Jno. A. Patridge, of Merriwetter (Meriwether) and Miss Sarah J. Whatley, of Harris County. (Georgia counties).

Wed. May 28, 1856
    Married on 20th inst., at the Baptist Church in Troy, by
Rev. A. N. Worthy, Mr. Newton Franklin Jones, of Auburn, Ala.,
to Miss Martha E. House, of this place.

    Married on 1st inst., by Rev. G. R. Tally, Mr. Henry L.
Gibson to Miss Mary E. Ballard, all of Pike County.

EUFAULA EXPRESS
1858-59

Jas. H. Butt, Editor and Jno. A. Burton, Publisher.

Thurs. Nov. 18, 1858
    Married on 16th inst., at the home of Col. Jas. L. Pugh, by
Rev. Evander McNair, Wm. A. McTye, Esq., to Miss Terese W. Hunter
all of Eufaula.

Thurs. Dec. 23, 1858
    Married on 2nd inst., by Rev. McNair, Col. H. B. Hill, of
Clayton, to Miss Jane Porter of this city.

    Married on 21st inst., by Rev. L. P. Golson, Fern M. Wood,
Esq., Editor of the Clayton Banner, to Miss Sallie Roquemore,
all of Barbour County.

Thurs. Dec. 30, 1858
    Married near Clayton on 16th inst., by Hon. J. S. Williams,
M. K. Shelby to Miss Adeline Warren, all of Barbour County.

Thurs. Jan. 6, 1859
    Married in Barbour County, Ala., at the home of the bride's
father, on 29th of Dec. 1858, by Jno. M. White, Esq., Mr. Jno. P.
Scott and Mary E. Sterns.

Thurs. Jan. 13, 1859
    Married at the home of the bride's father near Clayton, on
the 6th inst., by B. Williams, Esq., Mr. Z. Bush to Miss Sophrona
A. DeBose, all of Barbour County.

Thurs. Jan. 27, 1859
    Married at the home of P. A. Sapp, Esq., on the 25th inst.,
by Rev. L. C. Harrison, Gen. Thos. Flournoy to Miss Ellen Baker,
all of this city.

Thurs. Feb. 3, 1859
    Married on 1st inst., by Rev. W. M. Motley, Mr. Jas. H.
Evans to Miss Angelina Patterson.

Thurs. Mar. 10, 1859
    Married on 3d inst., by Rev. E. McNair, Mr. M. D. Oliver,
of Eufaula, to Miss Parrie E., daughter of Col. R. G. Ricks, of
Clay County, Ga.

Thurs. May 5, 1859
    Married in Apalachicola (Fla.) on 18th inst., at the home
of the bride, by Rev. Simson Peter Richardson, Capt. Andrew W.
Wing to Miss Enily (Emily?) Louisa Stuart, of that city.

Thurs. June 23, 1859
    Married on 14th inst., by Rev. Evander McNair, J. M.
Buford to Mrs. M. C. Wallace, eldest daughter of the late Dr.
W. L. Cowan.

Married in Eufaula on 8th inst., by Rev. Jas. S. Paullin, Mr. Jas. M. Stanford, of Ga., to Miss Sarah E. Scott, of this city.

Married in Quitman County, Ga., on 16th inst., by Rev. E. McNair, J. T. Smith, Esq., to Miss Margaret Saulsbury, all of Barbour County.

Thurs. July 7, 1859
Married at the home of the bride's father in Stewart County, Ga., on 30th of June, by F. Cowan, Esq., Mr. Edmond E. Glover, of Barbour County, to Miss Sarah J. Sims.

Thurs. Oct. 6, 1859
Married on 29th ult., by David Bush, Esq., Mr. Thos. J. Brown to Miss Eliza Redman, all of Barbour County.

SPIRIT OF THE SOUTH
(Published in Eufaula, Ala.)
1859

July 12, 1859
Married on the 10th inst., by S. H. Dent, Esq., Mr. Green B. Lunsford and Miss Clementine A. Black, all of Barbour County, Ala.

THE CLAYTON BANNER
1860

Jas. E. Golson & Jeff Bufford, Editors.

Thurs. June 28, 1860
Married on the 21st., at the home of Mr. J. M. Lampley, in Louisville, by Rev. A. D. Campbell, Mr. J. F. Harrison to Miss A. T. Anglin.

Thurs. July 12, 1860
Married on July 10th at the home of Mr. R. C. Redding, by Rev. L. F. Dowell, Mr. J. C. Holmes and Mrs. Sallie E. Rice, all of Barbour County.

Thurs. July 26, 1860
Married on 12th inst., at the home of Jno. O. Brant, by R. E. Brown, Esq., Jno. S. Johnson, of Randolph County, Ga., and Miss Sarah Brant, of Barbour County, Ala.

Thurs. Sept. 20, 1860
Married on 5th inst., at the home of the bride's mother, by R. E. Brown, Esq., Mr. Jno. C. Williams and Miss Sarah McDonald, all of Barbour County.

THE HENRY COUNTY REGISTER
(Published in Abbeville, Alabama)
1867

J. M. B. Kelly and E. R. Quillan

Sat. May 11, 1867
Married in Montgomery, (Ala.) at the home of the bride's father, by Rev. A. C. Barron, on the 1st inst., Mr. Thos. J. Scott to Miss Mary A., eldest daughter of Rev. Jno. B. Taylor.

Married on 10th inst., in the Probate Office in Abbeville, Henry County, Ala., by Hon. M. B. Green, Mr. Joseph C. Singleton and Miss Martha A. Little, both of Barbour County.

1869

Sat. Jan. 16, 1869
    Married on the 14th inst., at the home of the bride's father in Henry County, Ala., by C. J. Reynolds, Esq., Mr. T. A. Helms to Miss Sallie Westmoreland.

Sat. Apr. 3, 1869
    Married on 1st inst., at the home of the bride's father, Jno. C. Holly, Jr., to Miss Mary Murphy, by Rev. C. L. McCartha.

Sat. May 8, 1869
    Married on 2nd inst., at the home of Mrs. A. Skipper, by Z. W. Laney, Esq., Mr. W. J. G. Skipper to Miss M. C. Wood.

    Married on 2nd inst., at the home of the bride's mother, by Rev. Geo. P. Kincey, Mr. H. W. Arnold to Miss S. A. Grace.

Sat. Nov. 13, 1869
    Mr. Jno. Raborn and Mrs. Amy Perser were married in Marion County, Alabama recently.

1870

Sat. Apr. 16, 1870
    Married on the 12th inst., in Fort Gaines, Ga., by Robt. Peterson, Esq., Mr. Chas. S. Kincey to Miss Emeline Arnold, all of Henry County, Ala.

Sat. Aug. 27, 1870
    Married on 24th inst., at the home of T. A. Trawick, Esq., by Rev. C. L. Dobbs, Mr. Frank McLellan and Miss Rebecca Kirkland all of Henry County.

Sat. Oct. 15, 1870
    Married at the home of the bride's father on the 13th inst., by Rev. A. L. Martin, Mr. Seymour Kirkland & Miss Sallie Black-lidge, all of Henry County.

THE BLUFF CITY TIMES
(Published in Eufaula, Ala.)
1869

J. M. Macon, Editor and John Post & J. M. Williams, Proprietors.

Thurs. Dec. 2, 1869
    Married at the home of the bride's mother, near Clayton, on Nov. 16th, by Rev. J. Stratton Paullin, Mr. L. B. Bush to Miss Fannie Johnson, all of Barbour County.

    Married at the home of the bride's mother on the 28th of Nov., by Rev. J. Stratton Paullin, Mr. Augustus Robson to Miss Calista Pynes, and Mr. D. H. Blair to Miss Mary A. Pynes.

Thurs. Dec. 16, 1869
    Married at the M. E. Church in Clayton on Nov. 30th, by Rev. W. H. Ellison, Mr. Richard Williams to Miss Mary E. Lane.

1870

Thurs. Dec. 23, 1870
    Married at the home of the bride's father in Barbour County on Dec. 14th, by Elder J. Stratton Paullin, Mr. H. J. Williamson and Miss Mary Bishop.

Also, on Dec. 16th, at the same time, Joseph M. White, Esq., to Miss Grace Cowart.

Thurs. May 12, 1870*
    Married on 10th inst., at the home of the bride's father, by B. B. Fields, Esq., Jno. W. Gibbons to Miss Mary E. Dillard, all of Barbour County.

Thurs. June 9, 1870
    Married on June 7th at the home of the bride's uncle, Mr. W. E. Barnett, Mr. Aaron Davis of Bainbridge, Ga., to Miss Henrietta Shebeiner, of Eufaula.

Thurs. June 30, 1870
    Married at the home of the bride's father, Dr. Wm. H. Thornton, in Eufaula, by Rev. M. B. Wharton, G. L. Comer, Esq., and Miss Laura V. Thornton.

Thurs. Aug. 18, 1870
    Married at the home of the bride's father near Evergreen, (Ala.) by Rev. Thos. Ansley, Jno. Bascom Miller to Miss Nancy Preslar. - Evergreen (Ala.) Observer.

Thurs. Aug. 25, 1870
    Married on Tuesday last, at the Presbyterian Church in Eufaula, by Dr. Robinson, Capt. Yancey Dean and Miss Callie Simpson.

Thurs. Oct. 27, 1870
    Married at the Baptist Church in Cuthbert, (Ga.) on Oct. 25th, by Rev. M. B. Wharton, Dr. Chas. E. Estes, of Eufaula, and Miss Willie R. Thornton, of Cuthbert, Ga.

Thurs. Nov. 3, 1870
    Married on the 31st inst., at the home of the bride's father, by Rev. J. J. Robinson, Mr. Chas. F. Sporman, of Eufaula, and Miss Vassie L. Andrews, of Barbour County.

Thurs. Dec. 1, 1870
    Married at the home of the bride's father in Eufaula, on the 24th inst., by Rev. A. W. Barnett, Miss Mattie Tillman to Mr. W. H. Burnett, of China Grove, Ala.

Thurs. Dec. 15, 1870
    Married at the Presbyterian Church in Eufaula, on the 8th of Dec., by Rev. Dr. J. J. Robinson, Miss Maggie S. McKay and Mr. Chas. S. McDowell, both of Eufaula.

Thurs. Dec. 22, 1870
    Married on Dec. 21st by Rev. Dr. J. J. Robinson, at the home of Ex-Gov. Jno. Gill Shorter, Dr. P. D. L. Baker and Mrs. S. B. Battle, all of Eufaula.

1871

Thurs. Jan. 5, 1871
    Married in Eufaula on Dec. 25th, 1870, at the home of the bride's father, Mr. T. D. Patterson, by Rev. J. A. Briggs, Mr. F. N. Craddock, of Lawrenceville, (Ala.) and Miss Carnelia Patterson.

*Edited and published by J. M. Macon and M. A. Sheehan.

Thurs. Jan. 19, 1871
     Married at the Episcopal Church in Eufaula on Jan. 17th, by
Rev. J. C. Davis, Mr. Eugene Brown, of Sumter County, S. C., and
Miss Sarena Hoole, daughter of B. J. Hoole, of Barbour County.

     Married on 27th ult., at Augusta, Ga., Mr. W. S. White, of
Clayton, and Miss Marion Richards, of the former place.

Thurs. Feb. 2, 1871
     Married in Georgetown, Ga., on 26th of Jan. 1871, Mr. Jno.
Sheets and Miss Babe Merritt, both of this place.

Thurs. Feb. 9, 1871
     Married in Clayton (Ala.) at the home of the bride's father,
Feb. 1st., by Rev. J. Stratton Paullin, Mr. Jno. D. Godwin, of
Eufaula, and Miss Mary A. McNab.

     Married on 12th inst., at the home of the bride, by Rev.
Wm. H. Ellison, Dr. Jno. R. Barr to Miss Lizzie Hamiter, all of
Barbour County.

Thurs. Feb. 16, 1871
     Married on 12th, by Rev. W. N. Reeves, Mr. D. A. Perryman
and Mrs. M. A. Pippin, all of this city.

Thurs. Mar. 23, 1871
     Married at the home of Dr. J. W. Drewry in Eufaula, on the
16th inst., by Rev. A. J. Briggs, Mr. J. J. Creyon to Miss
Maggie Burtz, all of Eufaula.

     Married on Sunday at the home of Mrs. Coleman in Clayton,
(Ala.) by Rev. J. S. Paullin, Mr. W. H. Williams and Miss Sallie
O. Ventress. - Clayton Courier.

Thurs. May 30, 1871
     Married in the Baptist Church in Eufaula, Ala., by Rev. M.
B. Wharton, on 23d inst., Miss Alice Keils and Mr. Malcolm
McNair, all of this city.

     Married in the Baptist Church in Clayton, on 29th inst., by
Rev. J. S. Paullin, Miss Emma D., daughter of Jno. A. Foster,
Esq., of Clayton, and Mr. J. Edmund Toole, of LaGrange, Ga.

Thurs. May 4, 1871
     Married at the home of the bride's mother on the 20th of
Apr., 1871, by Rev. Mr. Gwin, pastor of the Baptist Church in
Montgomery, (Ala.) Merrill A. Sheehan, Esq., and Miss Bettie P.
McRae, all of Montgomery.

Thurs. May 11, 1871
     Married at the Church of the Holy Redeemer in Eufaula, on
10th of May, by Rev. Father Savage, Mr. Marcena R. Parker, of
Mobile, to Miss Alida M. Couric of Eufaula.

     Married in Walton County, Fla., at the home of Mrs. Turbin,
by Rev. W. Potts Harrison, W. Henry McCullough, of Antrim,
Ireland, to Miss Lizzie McLean.

Thurs. July 20, 1871
     Married at St. George's Church, London, on 17th of June,
Capt. Van Buren Bates, A Kentuckian, who served in the Confederate army, and Miss Nora Swan, a Nova Scotian.

Thurs. Sept. 28, 1871
     Married this morning at the home of the bride's father by

Rev. J. C. Davis, Mr. Theodore Pruden and Miss Alice M., daughter of Mr. Jas. Ross, all of Eufaula.

Thurs. Oct. 19, 1871
      Married in Eufaula on 12th inst., by Rev. A. J. Briggs, Mr. E. B. Young, Jr., and Miss Mamie B., daughter of Mrs. Flora A. Jennings, late of New Orleans.*

Thurs. Nov. 2, 1871
      Married at the home of the bride's father in Americus, Ga., on the 24th inst., by Rev. Samuel Anthony, Mr. Jno. D. McCormick, of Eufaula, Ala., and Miss Sallie, daughter of Dr. S. B. Hawkins, of Americus.

Thurs. Nov. 9, 1871
      Married in the Presbyterian Church by Rev. J. J. Robinson, on the 31st ult., Miss M. S. Allen, of Eufaula and Mr. W. D. Danforth of Augusta.

Thurs. Nov. 23, 1871
      Married in Twiggs County, Ga., on the 14th inst., by Rev. H. Bunn, Mrs. E. J. Albritton to Mr. Thos. Glover.

      Married in Eufaula on the 22nd at St. James Church, by Rev. J. C. Davis, Miss S. C. Bullock and Mr. J. A. Dobbins, all of Eufaula.

Thurs. May 18, 1871
      Married in Pensacola, Fla., on May 4th, by Rev. J. Augustus Pace, Pastor of the M. E. Church South, Mr. J. W. Gingles to Miss Fannie Hutchinson.

Thurs. Nov. 14, 1871
      Married on 7th inst., at the First Baptist Church in Eufaula, by Rev. M. B. Wharton, Miss Annie Shorter, daughter of Hon. Eli S. Shorter, to Col. A. H. Leftwick, of Baltimore. Attendants: Mr. Wm. A. Shorter, Miss Alice Leftwick, Mr. A. T. Leftwick, Miss Annie Fannin; Mr. S. B. Toney, Miss Lizzie McNab; Mr. J. G. Powers, Miss Anna G. Thornton; Mr. R. C. Shorter, Miss Susie Threewitts; Mr. J. G. Pope, Miss Eddie Williams; Mr. J. Reeves, Miss Sallie McKleroy; Mr. Townsend, Miss Mollie Hyatt; Dr. W. P. Copeland, Miss Tadie Bray; Mr. A. A. Couric, Miss Sallie Boykin; Mr. J. C. McKenzie, Miss Maggie McTyer; Master C. C. Shorter, Miss Dellie Shorter; Master Eli. S. Shorter, Miss Emmie Kalb.

Thurs. Dec. 21, 1871
      Married in the Baptist Church in Eufaula on the 20th by Rev. M. B. Wharton, Mr. A. A. Couric and Miss S. S. McKleroy, all of this city.

1872

Thurs. Jan. 4, 1872*
      Married at the home of the bride's father, Mr. J. L. Tillman, in this city, on the 30th of Dec., by Rev. A. W. Barnett, Mr. Geo. M. Morris, of South Carolina, and Miss E. J. E. Tillman, of Eufaula. *Edited and Published by J. M. Macon.

Thurs. Jan. 25, 1872

*Nov 2nd paper: Miss Mamie B. Jennings was the daughter of the Late Joseph B. Jennings.

12

Married in the First Baptist Church of Eufaula, by Rev. W. N. Reeves, on the 18th inst., Rev. J. S. Paullin, Pastor of the Baptist Church at Clayton, to Miss Emily S. McKleroy, of Eufaula.

Married in Cuthbert, Ga., by Rev. A. B. Campbell, Mr. W. H. B. Price, of Eufaula, to Miss Mollie M. Smith, of Cuthbert.

Thurs. Feb. 8, 1872
       Married in Grace Church in Clayton, Ala., on 6th of Feb., by Rev. J. C. Davis, of Eufaula, Miss Sarah B., daughter of Gen. H. D. Clayton, to Mr. A. M. Walthour, all of Clayton.

Thurs. Feb. 15, 1872
       Married in Eufaula, Ala., on 8th inst., by Rev. E. M. Bounds, Capt. H. L. Wheeler, of Concord, Mass., to Miss Addie L. Bliss, of Burlington, Vermont.

Thurs. Mar. 28, 1872
       Married at the home of the bride's father in Eufaula on 26th inst., by Rev. M. B. Wharton, Pastor of the Baptist church of Louisville, Ky., Mr. Geo. H. Estes and Miss Anna G. Thornton, daughter of Dr. W. H. Thornton, all of this city.

Married recently at the home of the bride's father in Eufaula, by Rev. W. N. Reeves, Miss Olivia C. Price and Mr. C. C. Skillman, of Kentucky.

Thurs. Apr. 18, 1872
       Married at St. James Church on 16th inst., by Rev. J. C. Davis, Dr. W. P. Copeland, of Eufaula, and Miss Mollie Flewellen, daughter of Col. Jas. T. Flewellen.

EUFAULA TRI-WEEKLY NEWS
1874

Jno. Black & Son, Proprietors.

Thurs. Jan. 1, 1874
       Married on 30th ult., at the home of the bride, by E. M. Bounds, Mr. Neil McLeod and Miss M. Laura McLeod, both of Barbour County.

Thurs. Jan. 22, 1874
       Married on 18th inst., by Rev. Martin, at the home of the bride's father, Mr. Edward Ennis and Miss Josephine Pittman, all of Henry County, Ala.

Sat. June 13, 1874
       Miss Ella Butler, daughter of Mr. Wm. Butler of Jackson County, Florida, was married to Capt. T. H. Moore, on Thursday.

Thurs. Nov. 21, 1874
       Married in Glennville, Ala., at the home of the bride's father, Maj. Wm. Dawson, on 19th inst., Mr. Thos. P. Graves, of Eufaula, and Miss Florence Dawson.

Tues. Dec. 8, 1874
       Mr. Willie K. Bell, formerly of Eufaula, but now a resident of Americus, Ga., married Miss Lula Felder, of Americus, on the 3rd inst.

EUFAULA NEWS
1875

13

Tues. Jan. 19, 1875
    Morgan H. Smith and Miss Fannie Nunn were married in
Autaugaville, (Ala.) recently.

Sat. Mar. 6, 1875
    Mr. Silas Stern and Miss Clara Meyers were married in New
York on the 28th ult.

Sat. Apr. 3, 1875
    Married in Cokesbury, S. C. on Mar. 30th, 1875, Dr. A. W.
Barnett, of Eufaula, and Miss Adela A. Conner, of the former
place.

Thurs. Apr. 29, 1875
    Married at the home of Mr. W. J. Cox, on the 17th inst.,
by Rev. E. M. Bounds, Mr. J. E. Pucci and Miss Lizzie Moore, all
of Eufaula.

    Married in the Church of the Most Holy Redeemer, on 29th
inst., by Rev. D. Savage, Mr. Danl. Rowett and Miss Mary Colby,
all of Eufaula.

Mon. June 14, 1875
    Mr. Jno. L. Hogan and Miss Minnie E. Rynehart were married
at St. Luke's Church in Columbus, (Ga.) last Thursday.

    Also, Mr. Randolph M. Mulford and Miss Emma Hill were
married at the Episcopal Church on Thursday.

THE HENRY COUNTY REGISTER
(Published in Abbeville, Ala., by Merrill A. Sheehan)
1875

Fri. Jan. 8, 1875
    Capt. A. A. Cassady of this county and Miss Addie Norton
were married in Bullock County recently.

Fri. Jan. 15, 1875
    Mr. Jas. M. Martin, of Abbeville, and Miss Callie Morris,
of Clopton, were married at the home of the bride's father
yesterday.

    Married on the 14th inst., at the home of Mr. Irwin Hix, in
Abbeville, by Z. W. Laney, Esq., Mr. Gater Moring and Miss
Camilla McMillan, all of Henry County.

Fri. Jan. 22, 1875
    Married on 21st inst., at the home of the bride's father,
by Rev. A. L. Martin, Mr. W. Oscar Crumley and Miss Clifford
West, all of Henry County.

Fri. Jan. 29, 1875
    Mr. Adam Heisel and Miss Georgia Lindley were married in
Eufaula on the 20th inst., by Rev. J. J. Robinson.

Fri. Feb. 5, 1875
    Mr. Joel Porter and Miss Lula Green were married yesterday
by Rev. Sims, at the home of Judge M. B. Green, of Abbeville.

Fri. Feb. 26, 1875
    Mr. Frank Austin and Miss Mollie Williams, both of Abbeville,
were married at the home of the bride's uncle, in Clay County,
Ga., on the 18th inst.

Fri. Mar. 5, 1875
Mr. Geo. C. Sansbury and Miss Ida Windham, of Dale County, (Ala.) were married on the 18th ult.

Married at the house of the bride's mother, by Rev. Benj. Herndon, on the 28th ult., Mr. Wm. Fails and Miss Matilda Money, all of Henry County.

Fri. Mar. 19, 1875
J. Wilson Goff and Miss D. Jane Bird were married in Dale County recently.

Also, Wm. Standford and Miss Pandora M. Dowling. - Ozark Star.

Fri. Apr. 30, 1875
Chas. F. Fields and Miss Emma Lylvester were married on the 15th inst.* *From Marriage Records, Barbour Co., (Ala.), p. 190, Chas. R. (Robinson) Fields and Mary E. Sylvester married on 4-15-1875.

Married on the 21st inst., Shady Crockett and Miss Mary Mims, both of Henry County.

Fri. June 25, 1875
Wm. Linn, Jr., and Miss Jennie Dawkins, daughter of R. H. Dawkins of Henry County, were married at the home of the bride's father on 24th inst.

Fri. Oct. 15, 1875
Mr. E. A. Saunders and Miss Lizzie Martin were married at the home of the bride's father, Rev. A. L. Martin, of Abbeville, on the 7th inst.

Fri. Oct. 29, 1875
Mr. E. E. Hudson and Mrs. Alsy Wells were married on the 24th inst.

Also, Mr. Hiram Barron and Mrs. Catherine Ward, on the same day, all of Henry County.

Wm. A. Bishop, Esq., and Miss Mary Cowan, both of Clayton, (Ala.) were married on the 20th inst.

Fri. Nov. 12, 1875
Mr. Thos. Holland, Jr., and Miss Theresa Kirkland were married by C. S. Kincey, at the home of the bride's mother on the 4th inst.

Fri. Nov. 19, 1875
Married at the home of the bride's father, by Rev. G. Patterson, on the 14th inst., Mr. A. H. B. Davis and Miss Salome Penuel, daughter of C. B. Penuel, Esq.

Also, on the 14th inst., by Harris Gamble, Esq., Mr. D. W. Merritt and Miss Martha Smith, all of Henry County.

Fri. Nov. 26, 1875
Mr. Isaac Smith and Miss Senie Thomson were married by Elder Robt. Blan, on the 14th inst., at the home of the later in Pike County, (Ala.). - Troy Enquirer.

Fri. Dec. 10, 1875
Probate Judge Jones (Judge Wiley E. Jones) of Barbour County, and Miss Fannie Dent, daughter of Jno. H. Dent, of Cave Springs, Ga., were married on 31st ult., at the home of the

bride's father.

Mr. Jno. B. Ward and Miss Nora Newman were married last Tuesday at the M. E. Church by Rev. A. L. Martin. Attendants were: Walter Stokes with Miss Mattie Price; Wm. Martin with Mary Kennedy; Ed. West with Laura Appling; Ed. Oates with Lizzie Kennedy; Thos. Solomon with Nettie Appling; Millard Owens with Mollie Solomon; Eugene Sheehan with Maggie Oates; Willie Stokes with Johnnie Skipper; Lee Stokes with Emma Price; Jas. Ward with Mattie Stokes.

Harry C. Copeland and Sallie E. Hardy, daughter of Jno. Hardy, of Jasper County, Ala., (Ga.?) were married recently. Both formerly of Eufaula, (Ala.).

Married at the home of the bride's father on the 1st inst., Mr. Luther Searcy and Miss Alice Whitehurst, both of Henry County.

Fri. Dec. 17, 1875
Married on the 12th inst., by Hon. J. B. Appling, at the home of the bride's father, Mr. A. R. Clark and Miss Talula Guilford, daughter of Mr. G. H. Guilford, all of Henry County.

Also, on the same day at Lawrenceville, by Rev. Cumbey, Noah Hutto and Miss Mollie Price.

Also, on the 9th inst., by Rev. Cumbey, Mr. Wm. Jerkins and Miss Mary McClellan.

Fri. Dec. 24, 1875
Married on the 21st inst., at the home of the bride's father, by Rev. C. Smith, Dr. W. J. Lee of Haw Ridge, Ala. and Mrs. Mollie E. Price, of Abbeville.

Rev. Emmett Solomon and Miss Manie Allen were married at Wetumpka, (Ala.) on the 15th inst.

THE HENRY COUNTY REGISTER
1876

Fri. Jan. 21, 1876
Mr. W. S. Whitehurst and Miss R. A. Scott were married at Abbeville on the 15th inst., by Z. W. Laney, Esq., all of Henry County.

Also, on the same day by Hon. J. B. Appling, Mr. J. W. Haughton and Miss Vina Roney.

Fri. Mar. 24, 1876*
Married at the home of Mrs. Holland, by Hon. J. B. Appling on the 21st, Mr. W. T. Kirkland and Miss Charity J. Skein. (* E. B. Jordan, Editor).

Fri. Apr. 21, 1876
Married on the 10th inst., by Rev. L. R. Sims at the home of Mr. Geo. T. Roberts, Mr. C. T. Sanders and Miss Jane Ayres.

Fri. June 9, 1876
Married at the home of the bride's father in Lawrenceville, (Ala.) on June 1st, by Hon. Jno. B. Appling, Wm. L. Kelly and Miss Malissa Holly.

Fri. Sept. 29, 1876
Rev. E. M. Bounds and Miss Emma Barnett were married in Eufaula a few days ago.

Fri. Oct. 13, 1876
    Mr. Geo. W. Denard and Miss John H. Gilmore were married at
the home of the bride's mother near Shorterville in Henry County,
by Rev. L. R. Sims on Oct. 3d, 1876.

Fri. Nov. 17, 1876*
    Mr. Henry Stroder and Miss Mary Warren were married on
Tuesday last, by Z. W. Laney, Esq. (*S. A. Fackler, Publisher).

THE EUFAULA WEEKLY TIMES
1877

R. D. Shropshire, Editor; M. A. Sheehan & J. T. Brown, Publishers.

Thurs. May 3, 1877
    Dr. F. L. Constantine and wife, of Birmingham, (Ala.)
recently celebrated their golden wedding.

Thurs. May 24, 1877
    Married in Montgomery on the 16th inst., by Rev. H. String-
fellow, Mr. Edward F. Doughtie, formerly of Eufaula, and Miss
Sarah Jones Farley, of Montgomery.

Thurs. May 31, 1877
    Married on May 16th, at the home of the bride's father, by
Rev. W. H. Patterson, Mr. J. S. Cade and Miss Annie Smart, all
of Barbour County.

Thurs. June 14, 1877
    Married at the Catholic Church in Atlanta, Ga., on the 6th
inst., by Father Quinlan, Mr. H. E. Williamson, formerly of
Eufaula, and Miss Lizzie Lynch, of Atlanta.

    Married at Midway, Ala., June 7th, 1877, by Rev. Jere S.
Williams, Capt. E. L. Jenkins and Miss Mattie M. Baker.

    Married at the home of the bride's parents near Eufaula, on
13th inst., by Rev. Josiah Bancroft, Mr. Wm. L. Bass, of Macon,
Ga., and Miss Lizzie J. Doughtie, of Eufaula.

Thurs. July 26, 1877
    Ex-Lieutenant Gov. Stockdale, and Miss Elizabeth Schleicher,
daughter of Congressman Schleicher, both of Texas, were married
in Washington on Tuesday.

Thurs. Aug. 30, 1877
    Thos. C. Lester, of South Carolina, was married in Union
Springs, (Ala.) on the 21st inst., to Mrs. C. M. Griswold, of
the latter place.

Thurs. Sept. 20, 1877
    Married in Houston County, Ga., on 21st ult., Gus Riley, of
Houston County, and Miss Mattie Calloway of Macon, Ga.

Thurs. Sept. 27, 1877
    Married on the 25th inst., by Rev. Dr. Robinson, at the
home of the bride's mother, Mr. W. E. McCormick and Miss Lizzie
Beauchamp, all of Eufaula.

Thurs. Oct. 25, 1877
    Married on 16th inst., at the home of the bride's mother,
Mrs. Bettie Cook, by Rev. S. T. Fuller, Mr. W. O. Johnson and
Miss Hatchie, daughter of the late Maj. Hatch. - Hamilton (Ga.)
Journal. (The parents of the bride formerly lived in Eufaula.)

17

Mr. James C. Griffin and Miss Nannie M. Anderson were married in Lafayette (Ala.) on the 16th inst.

Thurs. Dec. 20, 1877
Married at the home of the bride's father, on 10th inst., Mr. Walter White to Miss Margaret A. Parker, all of Barbour County. - Clayton Courier of 15th.

Married on 20th of Nov., by Rev. J. S. Paullin, at the home of the bride's father near Louisville, Ala., Elder Wm. H. Norton to Miss Emma M. McKenzie.

Mr. Z. T. Byrd and Miss Henrietta McNeese were married at the home of the bride's father near Eufaula, on Thursday, by Rev. T. A. Johnson, all of Barbour County.

Thurs. Jan. 3, 1878
Married in Eufaula Dec. 30th, at the home of Mr. E. Kuttner, Mr. L. W. Peeples and Miss Lula Allen, both of Dawson, Ga.

Married at the home of the bride's father in Barbour Co. by Rev. D. Rogers on Dec. 20, 1877, Mr. Wm. West and Miss Marguerett E. Hawkins.

Thurs. Jan. 10, 1878
Married at the home of Mrs. M. J. Whitworth, near Breekville, Miss., by Rev. W. C. Black, Mr. J. Z. Gaston, formerly of Eufaula, to Miss M. G. Caston, of Madison County, Miss.

Thurs. Jan. 31, 1878
Married on 27th inst., at Malone's Church, near Eufaula, by Rev. T. A. Johnson, Mr. M. A. Vining, of Barbour County, to Miss S. E. Averett, of Chattahoochee County, Ga.

Thurs. Apr. 11, 1878
Married at the Baptist Church, by Rev. O. F. Gregory yesterday, Mr. J. Thomas Walker and Miss Lilia Bell, both of Eufaula.

Thurs. July 4, 1878
Married on 26th inst., at the home of the bride's parents near Midway, Ala., by Rev. W. H. Norton, Dr. W. U. Morton to Miss Weltha M. Feagin.

Married in Columbus, Ga., on 19th ult., at the home of J. W. Pease, Esq., by Rev. Jno. P. Margart, Frank M. Margart, of Batesville, Ala., to Miss Nilla Norman, of Union Spring, (Ala.).

Thurs. Aug. 1, 1878
Married July 30th at the home of the bride's mother, Mrs. S. E. McNeill, by Rev. J. J. Robinson, D. D., Mr. T. W. Givens and Miss Angie McNeill, all of Eufaula.

Married at the home of A. D. Williams, in Russell County, Ala., by Rev. J. W. Solomon, on 24th inst., Jno. R. Hayes and Miss Eddie C. Williams, both of Barbour County.

Thurs. Aug. 8, 1878
Mrs. Melissa J. Lyons was married yesterday at her home in Eufaula to Mr. Clem. Clayton.

Thurs. Oct. 17, 1878*
Mr. Will L. Bryan, of Selma, (Ala.) and Miss Ida McNab, of Clayton, were married in Clayton on Monday. (*Jas. T. Goode, Editor).

Thurs. Oct. 24, 1878
      Married in Eufaula at the Presbyterian Church on the 22nd
inst., by Rev. J. J. Robinson, Miss Mattie, daughter of Capt.
W. C. Wallace, of Eufaula, and Mr. Wallace McPherson, of Atlanta,
(Ga.).

Sat. Oct. 26, 1878
      In Georgetown, (Ga.) on Thursday last, Mr. LeGrand Guerry
was married to Miss Fannie, daughter of R. G. Morris, Esq.

      On Tuesday last, at the home of the bride's father, by Rev.
Crook, Miss Sallie E. Cawthon was married to Mr. J. D. Johnson,
all of near Eufaula.

Tues. Nov. 5, 1878
      Miss Sarah Jane Rollins was married to D. F. McCrany, Esq.,
on the 24th ult., in Barbour County.

Thurs. Nov. 21, 1878
      Married near Eufaula, by Rev. J. Bancroft, on the 19th inst.,
Mr. Eugene Persons to Miss Betty Henry.

Thurs. Nov. 28, 1878
      Married at the Baptist Church in Eufaula on Tuesday, Mr.
Lucius J. Richardson and Miss Emma Kolb, dau. of Mr. Reuben
Kolb, of Eufaula. Attendants were: Mr. J. C. McKenzie and Miss
Lizzie Wellborn; S. T. Barnett and Miss Anna Sylvester; Jno.
Thornton and Miss Ida Bloodworth; Eli S. Shorter, Jr., and Miss
Mary Davis; Phil. McKay and Miss Annie Fannin; Reuben F. Kolb
and Miss Mamie Rhodes.

Thurs. Dec. 5, 1878
      Married on 28th of Nov. in Cuthbert, Ga., Mr. N. A. Smith
of Spring Hill, (Barbour County) and Miss Eland Easly, of
Cuthbert.

      Married yesterday at the Presbyterian Church in Eufaula, by
Rev. Dr. J. J. Robinson, Mr. Charley Jackson and Miss Sallie
Hart, daughter of Capt. H. C. Hart. (Marriage Records in Court
House, Clayton, Ala.: Chas. W. Jackson and Sallie R. Hart,
married 12-4-1878).

Thurs. Dec. 19, 1878
      Married at the Presbyterian Church in Union Springs, (Ala.)
by Rev. F. B. Webb, on Dec. 11th, Mr. A. J. Pittman and Miss
Mary C. Foster, daugher of Dr. Jas. M. Foster, all of Union
Springs. - Union Springs (Ala.) Herald.

THE TIMES AND NEWS
1879

Published in Eufaula, Ala., by Eufaula Publishing Co., J. T.
  Goode, Editor.

Thurs. Jan. 2, 1879
      Married at the home of Mr. J. W. Comer, Esq., in Barbour
County on 16th of Dec., Mr. J. W. Thornton, of Midway, (Ala.)
to Miss Sallie McCormick.

Thurs. Jan. 9, 1879
      Married on Thursday last, by Esq. McRae, Mr. Alex Dashinger
to Miss Mary Moore, all of Barbour County.

Tues. Jan. 14, 1879
Married at the home of the bride's father, on the 9th inst., by Rev. W. H. Patterson, Mr. M. F. Davis and Miss Willie Sheally, all of Barbour County.

Married on the 2d inst., by Mr. J. E. Smith, Mr. Daniel Harrell and Miss Emma Craft. (Georgetown, Ga.).

Thurs. Jan. 16, 1879
Married on 18th of Dec., 1878, at the home of the bride's mother near Glennville, Ala., by Rev. J. E. Owens, Mr. J. M. Jones and Miss Emma Davis.

Sat. Jan. 18, 1879
Mr. Henry Finny, of Jones County, Ga., and Miss Tommie Crowell, of Troy, Ala., were married in the Episcopal Church in that city on 15th inst.

Married at the home of the bride's uncle, Mr. Bellingroth, in Atlanta, Ga., by Rev. J. H. Martin, Mr. Patten Tallman, of Hatchechubbee, Ala., and Miss Mary DeLacy, a sister of Mayor DeLacy, of Hatchechubbee.

Tues. Jan. 28, 1879
Married on 22nd inst., in Seale, Ala., at the home of Judge Simon O'Neal, the bride's grandfather, by Rev. J. C. Cook, of Columbus, Ga., with Mr. W. R. Wright, of Talliafore, Ga., to Mrs. Fannie Kennedy, of Seale.

Thurs. Feb. 6, 1879
Married at the home of the bride's father in this county on the 29th, Dr. Green B. Battle, son of Dr. Thos. W. Battle, to Miss Minnie Fitzgerald, daughter of Mr. Jas. Fitzgerald. -Lumpkin (Ga.) Independent.

Tues. Feb. 11, 1879
Dr. Alex L. Hamilton and Miss Eudora A. Moore were married Feb. 6th in the Chapel of Andrew Female College, (in Cuthbert, Ga.) by Rev. Howard McGehee.

Mr. Reuben Mitchell, of Opelika, (Ala.) and Miss Birdie Wood, of Eufaula, were married at the home of the bride's mother, Mrs. Fern Wood. Attendants were Master Hunter Roquemore and Marie Wood, sister of the bride.

Thurs. Mar. 1, 1879
Married at the home of the bride's uncle, Mr. Wash McRae, near Louisville, Ala., on 27th of Feb., by Rev. Mr. Read, Mr. Benj. Brock and Miss Mollie McRae.

Tues. Mar. 25, 1879
Mr. Cul. Stephens, of Eufaula, and Miss Sallie Stephens, of Dawson, Ga., were married in Eufaula Sunday by Rev. W. N. Reeves.

Wed. Apr. 23, 1879
Mr. Geo. P. Keys and Miss Sallie A. Menefee were married in Auburn, (Ala.) on the 13th inst.

Sat. Apr. 26, 1879
On the 16th near Benton, (Ala.) Mr. R. S. Leslie and Miss L. C. Trott were married.

Wed. Apr. 30, 1879
Mr. A. J. Carver, Jr. of Eufaula, Ala., and Miss Ellie E.

Rogers, daughter of Judge Harrison Rogers, of Dawson, Ga., were
married at the Baptist Church last evening, by Rev. J. A. Ivey.
Attendants were: Messrs. Warren F. Dent and A. D. B. McKenzie,
of Eufaula; W. A. James, L. R. Rogers, G. M. Roberts and E. C.
Paschal, of Dawson. Misses Bettie Tharpe, Macon, Ga., Carrie
Stewart, Americus; Susie Morris, Georgetown, Ga.; Carrie Hill,
of Terrill County, (Ga.); Nora Allen and Dixie Cheatham, of Dawson. Ushers: Messrs. J. D. Laing and C. E. Holliday. Organist
was Mrs. J. H. Guerry. - <u>Dawson</u> (Ga.) <u>Journal</u>.

Sat. Jan. 11, 1879
       The Rev. Mr. Glenn and Mrs. Cassady, relict of the late
Rev. John Cassady, were married in Barbour County a few days
hence. (Court House Records: Jas. W. Glenn and Mary P. Cassady
were married 1-9-1879).

Tues. May 6, 1879
       Married at the First M. E. Church in Atlanta, (Ga.) last
Wednesday, Mr. Wm. W. Austell, son of Gen. Austell, and Miss
Idolene Lochrane, daughter of Judge O. A. Lochrane, all of
Atlanta.

Tues. May 13, 1879
       Mr. Chas. H. Bradshaw and Mrs. Jane Powers of Schley (Ga.)
were married last Friday.

Thurs. May 22, 1879
       Mr. Geo. W. Cook, of Montgomery, Ala., and Miss Elvie
Dawson of Columbus, (Ga.) were married in Columbus on Tuesday
last.

Sat. May 24, 1879
       Mr. A. A. Cassady, of Louisville, Ala., was married a few
days since, to Miss Wood, of Fla.

Thurs. May 29, 1879
       Married at the Episcopal Church in Eufaula, on May 28th, Mr.
Joseph P. Hull, formerly of Nashville, Tenn., but now of Eufaula,
to Miss Hattie E. Kincey, eldest daughter of Mrs. W. J. Kincey,
of Eufaula, by Rev. J. C. Davis.

Thurs. June 5, 1879
       Mr.-R. W. Prior and Miss Ida Harris, of Athens (Ala.) were
married on the 3rd inst.

Sat. June 7, 1879
       Prof. D. M. Calloway and Mrs. H. H. Nance, both of Selma,
(Ala.) were married on the 3d inst.

Wed. June 11, 1879
       Married on 3rd inst., at the home of the bride's father, by
Rev. T. A. Johnson, Mr. T. B. Jones and Miss America Vining, all
of Barbour County.

Tues. June 17, 1879
       Mr. W. H. Donally and Miss Sarah E. Jackson, of Henry
County, were married on the 8th inst.

       Col. Sam C. Williams, of Atlanta, and Miss L. J. Reese, of
Macon, were married in the latter city on Tuesday.

Thurs. June 19, 1879
       Mr. E. H. Devency, of Philadelphia, and Miss Nellie Hood,

21

daughter of Judge Hood, of Cuthbert, (Ga.) were married on the
11th inst.

Wed. July 2, 1879
Mr. R. A. Tarver and Miss Nettie Becker, of Montgomery, were
married in that city on Monday last.

Thurs. July 3, 1879
Mr. J. B. Yelverton and Miss Mary S. Kirksey, both of Newton, (Ala.) were married on the 18th ult.

Wed. July 9, 1879
Miss Bertha Kuttner, daughter of Mr. Edward Kuttner, of
Eufaula, and Mr. Morris S. Barnett, of Bainbridge, Ga., were
married by Rev. A. Mayers in Eufaula on the 6th inst.

Thurs. July 10, 1879
Married on 9th inst., at St. James Episcopal Church in
Eufaula, by Rev. W. C. Hunter, Mr. Norris N. Curtis, of Columbus
(Ga.) and Miss Pat Wellborn, of Eufaula.

Mr. Arthur Bingham, of Talladega, (Ala.) and Mrs. B. A.
Lanhorne, of Montgomery, were married on the 8th inst.

Also, Mr. Phillip C. Tant, of Augusta, (Ga.) and Miss
Louise M. Smith of Montgomery. - Montgomery (Ala.) Advertiser.

Mr. W. H. Huntley, of LaGrange, (Ga.) and Miss Ida Richardson, of Marietta, (Ga.) were married at Kimball House in Atlanta,
on the 6th.

Tues. July 15, 1879
Mr. Willis M. Ball and Miss Fannie E. Leverette were married
in Tallahassee, (Fla.) on Wednesday last.

Miss Fannie Snodgrass, junior editor of the Scottsboro (Ala.)
Herald, and Mr. Frank King, of Louisiana, were married on the
9th inst.

Wed. July 23, 1879
Mr. Gustan B. Owens and Miss Mary Skipper, both of Henry
County, (Ala.) were married on the 15th inst.

Mr. A. P. Herrington, of Albany, Ga., and Miss Camilla
Ogletree, of Georgetown, Ga., were married on the 16th at the
home of the bride's father, Mr. Samuel R. Ogletree, of the latter
place.

Sat. July 26, 1879
Mr. Herbert C. Hill and Miss Lizzie Pope, both of Jasper
County (Ga.) were married on Wednesday last.

Thurs. July 31, 1879
Mr. Francis B. Clark, of Mobile, (Ala.) and Miss May Banks,
of Montgomery, were married on Tuesday last.

Sat. Aug. 2, 1879
Mr. H. H. Epping, Jr., of Columbus, Ga., and Miss Dora
Flournoy, of Russell County, Ala., were married Tuesday last, at
the home of Mrs. Early Hunt, of Wynnton, near Columbus.

Married at Ft. Gaines, (Ga.) on the 24th ult., Mr. M. W.
Helton to Miss P. E. Whatley.

Also, on the same day, Mr. Bradley to Miss Moody, both
couples from Alabama.

Wed. Aug. 13, 1879
    Mr. Geo. Nason and Miss Minnie Pryor were married in Mobile,
(Ala.) on Tuesday.

Thurs. Aug. 14, 1879
    Dr. J. E. Westmoreland and Miss Ida Cartright were married
recently in Limestone County, Ala.

Sat. Aug. 16, 1879
    Mr. Jas. Martin and Miss Belle Scott, both of Union Springs,
(Ala.), were married on the 12th inst., in Athens, Montgomery
County, (Ala.).

Wed. Sept. 10, 1879
    Rev. S. S. Collins and Mrs. Georgia Childs were married in
Pike County, (Ala.) on the 2nd inst.

Sat. Sept. 13, 1879
    Married in Clayton (Ala.) the 10th inst., at the home of
the bride's father, Col. H. M. Tompkins, by Rev. D. B. Waddell,
Mr. Walter S. White, High Sheriff of Barbour County, and Miss
Mary B. Tompkins.

Thurs. Sept. 18, 1879
    Mr. W. H. Hooker, of the Opelika (Ala.) Times, and Miss
Nora Fuller were married at Salem, Lee County, (Ala.) on Wednesday.

Thurs. Sept. 25, 1879
    Mr. Henry Bostwicx (Bostwick?) and Miss Mary Barber were
married in the Episcopal Church in Columbus, (Ga.) on Thursday
last.

Thurs. Oct. 9, 1879
    Mr. and Mrs. Austin C. Cargill, of Eufaula, celebrated the
twenty-fifth anniversary of their wedding Wednesday.

Sat. Oct. 11, 1879
    Dr. Lou O'Neal, of Talbotton, Ga., and Miss Annie Slaton,
of Auburn, Ala., were married in the latter city on the 7th.

Tues. Oct. 21, 1879
    Mr. Edward F. Noble and Miss Lucy Micou were married on
Tuesday last at Tallahassee, Ala.

Tues. Oct. 28, 1879
    Mr. Jesse W. Rankin, of Atlanta, (Ga.) and Miss Fannie G.
Lamar, of Macon (Ga.) were married in the Baptist Church in
Macon on Wednesday night.

Wed. Oct. 29, 1879
    Married on 22 inst., at the home of the bride's father, by
Rev. W. H. Patterson, George W. Sparks, Esq., and Miss Sallie E.
Castello, all of Barbour County.

Wed. Nov. 5, 1879
    Married at the First Baptist Church in Montgomery, (Ala.)
on the 21st, Mr. Thos. W. Hannon and Miss Emilie B. Littlepage.

Thurs. Nov. 6, 1879
    Mr. Soule Redd, of Columbus, Ga., and Miss Nellie Haile,
daughter of Col. E. Haile, of Russell County, Ala., were married
on Saturday last.

Mr. D. F. Sessions and Miss Fannie Culver, daughter of Maj. I. F. Culver, all of Bullock County, (Ala.) were married on Thursday last.

Thurs. Nov. 13, 1879
Mr. R. E. Williams, of Union Spring, (Ala.) and Miss Mattie Johnson, of Greenville, (Ala.) were married on the 4th inst.

Also, Dr. C. H. Franklin, of Union Springs, and Miss Lou Banks, of Hurtville, (Ala.) married on the 5th inst.

Sat. Nov. 14, 1879
On the 4th, in the Presbyterian Church at Bainbridge, (Ga.) Rev. J. T. McBryde, the pastor, and Miss Ada Dickinson were married.

Thurs. Nov. 20, 1879
Mr. Adam R. Smith and Miss Fidelia Whetstone, of Coosa County, (Ala.) were married on the 6th inst.

Also, the same place and day, Mr. Thos. Smart and Miss Laura Wilson were married.

Tues. Nov. 25, 1879
Jno. W. Cobb, son of Gov. (R.) Cobb, was married at Helena, (Ala.) on the 5th inst., to Miss Susan Dunnman.

Mr. Thos. W. Terry and Miss Mary Kennedy were married in Talladega County, (Ala.) last week.

On the 12th inst., S. H. Pitts, of Russell County, Ala., and Miss P. A. Jones, of Muscogee County, Ga., were married.

Tues. Dec. 2, 1879
Married at the home of the bride's father in Troy, Ala., on the 27th ult., by Rev. S. A. Pilley, Mr. Alex. C. Edmondson, of Eufaula, and Miss Ella Brantley.

Mr. Chas R. Pendleton, of the Valdosta (Ga.) Times, was married last Wednesday to Miss Sallie Peoples.

Sat. Dec. 13, 1879
Married at the home of the bride's father, Rev. Junius Jordan, on the 11th inst., by Rev. R. B. Crawford, Mr. H. E. Jordan and Miss E. Lee Jordan, all of Eufaula.

Tues. Dec. 16, 1879
Dr. A. J. Boyd, of Troy, Ala., and Miss Neaty Langley, of Greenwood, Fla., were married at the latter place on the 3d instant.

Thurs. Dec. 18, 1879
Mr. Frank Bush and Miss Rosa Norwood, of near White Oak Springs, (Barbour County) were married by Jno. Williams, Esq., last Sunday.

Married at the First Baptist Church in Eufaula on the 16th inst., by Rev. M. M. Wamboldt, Mr. J. Edward Fitzgerald, of Columbus, Ga., and Miss Mary C. Davis, of Eufaula. Attendants were: Mr. J. E. Duskin and Miss Laura Sylvester; Mr. C. L. Rhodes and Miss Ida Bludworth; Mr. J. C. McKenzie and Miss Florence Rhodes; Mr. W. A. Davis and Miss Alice Fitzgerald. Ushers, Messrs. R. M. Jennings and R. H. Walker.

Sat. Dec. 20, 1879
Mr. Fox Henderson and Miss Sallie E. Wilkerson were married

in Troy, (Ala.) on the 11th.

Tues. Dec. 30, 1879
     At the home of Mr. Isaac Wells on the 14th inst., by Robert
James, Esq., Mr. W. T. McGehee and Miss Julia A. Wells were
married, all of Barbour County.

THE TIMES AND NEWS
1880

Tri-Weekly published in Eufaula, Ala., A. A. Walker, President.

Sat. Jan. 3, 1880
     Mr. J. Eason Oliver and Miss Lucy Pye were married at the
home of her step-father, Mr. Colson Guilford, in Quitman County,
Ga., by J. E. Smith, Esq., on 30th ult.

Thurs. Jan. 8, 1880
     Married at the home of the bride's mother in Eufaula, on
Jan. 6th by Rev. M. M. Wamboldt, Jos. Sawyer and Miss Ellen
Fredrick. (From Marriage Record, Clayton Court House: Jos. E.
Sawyer and Ellen Fredirek, married 1-6-1880).

     Married at the home of the bride's father, at Juniper,
Talbot County, Ga., on 7th inst., by Rev. Geo. T. Chandler of
Americus, Mr. Robt. W. Williamson of Eufaula, and Miss M. Eugenia
Chandler of the former place. Attendants: Phil McKay and Miss
Sallie Chandler; S. T. Barnett and Miss Eva Paschal; J. D. Hough
and Miss Callie Wheatley; J. W. Wheatley, Jr. and Miss Minnie
Paschal.

Tues. Jan. 13, 1880
     Mr. E. R. Kincey, formerly of Eufaula, and Mrs. Mattie
Watts were married in Selma on the 8th inst. - Selma (Ala.)
Times.

     Married at the home of the bride's father in Barbour County,
on 8th inst., by Rev. J. Stratton Paullin, Rev. Z. T. Weaver and
Miss Mattie J. Russell.

Tues. Jan. 27, 1880
     Married yesterday, Col. Wm. H. Chambers and Miss Mollie
Gordon, by Rev. A. M. Wynn, at the home of the bride's aunt, Mrs.
Abercrombie, in Russell County, Ala. - Columbus (Ga.) Times.

Thurs. Jan. 29, 1880
     Married at the home of Mr. Price, on the 25th inst., by
A. M. McLendon, Esq., Mr. Wm. Taylor and Miss Emma Ellet, all of
Barbour County.

Thurs. Feb. 26, 1880
     Married on the 19th inst., at the home of the bride's
father, by Rev. T. A. J. Hawkins, Mr. A. A. Adams and Miss Abby
Wood, all of Barbour County.

Tues. Mar. 2, 1880
     Married in Clayton, Ala., on 26th ult., by Rev. Wm. K.
Norton, Mr. Thos. C. Norton and Miss Sarah Jane McKraney.

Sat. Mar. 13, 1880
     Married recently at the home of the bride's father, by R.
T. K. James, Esq., Mr. Wade H. Tate and Miss Sallie Brigham, all
of Barbour County.

25

Sat. Apr. 3, 1880
      Mr. Wm. H. Bowdon and Miss Willie Evans, of White Oak
Springs, (Barbour County) were married Thursday at Georgetown,
Ga.

Thurs. Apr. 10, 1880
      Married at the home of the bride's mother, in Eufaula, on
Apr. 8th, by Rev. J. J. Robinson, Rev. M. McN. McKay, of Griffin,
Ga., and Miss Minnie McDowell.

Sat. May 15, 1880
      Married at the home of the bride's father, in Troy (Ala.)
on the 13th inst., by Rev. T. H. Stout, Mr. O. Worthy and Miss
Sallie McKenzie, all of Troy. Attendants were: J. G. Carroll
and Miss Allie Murphee; Alex. McKenzie and Miss Ida Wiley; C. J.
Knox and Miss Mary Tullis; Ira Lampley and Miss Minnie Holley;
Randolph Brown and Miss Annie McKenzie.

Tues. Apr. 13, 1880
      Married on the 11th inst., in Georgetown, Ga., by Jno.
Moore, Esq., Mr. J. T. Brown and Miss Effie E. McLeod, both of
Eufaula.

Thurs. May 20, 1880
      Miss Augusta Lamar was married at Oxford, Miss., on Wednes-
day last, to T. H. Heiskell, Esq., a lawyer of Memphis, Tenn.

Thurs. June 10, 1880
      Mr. C. W. Guice, of Eufaula, and Miss Susie M. Juhan, of
Macon, Ga. were married at Macon on the 7th inst.

Tues. June 22, 1880
      Married at the home of the bride's mother on the 15th inst.,
by Rev. W. H. Patterson, of Eufaula, Mr. Hugh F. Melton and Miss
Genie Balkcom, both of Quitman County, Ga.

Thurs. June 24, 1880
      Married at the M. E. Church in Eufaula, on the 23rd, inst.,
by Rev. R. H. Rivers, Mr. J. E. Duskin and Miss Mary A. Williford,
all of Eufaula. Attendants were: E. B. Tullis and Miss Annie
Jennings; J. L. Harrison, of Georgetown, Ga., and Miss Carrie
Malone; H. Lampley and Miss Annie Carter, of Florence, Ga.;
Eugene Martin and Miss Cornelia Barnett; Robt. F. Nance and Miss
Fannie Williford; M. L. Duskin and Miss Addie Martin. Ushers
were Messrs. W. W. Flewellen and Ed. Martin.

Thurs. Sept. 9, 1880
      Mr. Wm. G. Hamilton and Miss Lizzie Veal, both of Eufaula,
were married in Georgetown, Ga., last Monday. (The Eufaula
Times and News, Tri-Weekly, W. D. Jelks, Proprietor).

Fri. Oct. 15, 1880
      Mr. Wm. N. Raney and Miss Julia Thornton were married at
the Baptist Church in Eufaula Wednesday. Attendants were Mr.
Geo. Raney and Miss Mamie Rhodes; Mr. D. F. McCall and Miss
Retta Thornton; Mr. E. S. Shorter and Miss Sallie Toney; Mr. E.
R. Ross and Miss Addie Martin; Mr. J. K. Battle and Miss Laura
Sylvester; Mr. Ira W. Lampley and Miss Ida Bludworth. Ushers:
L. W. Weedon and John W. Bray.

Fri. Oct. 22, 1880
      Mr. H. A. Hayes, of Greenwood, Fla., and Miss Blanch V.
Powell, of Cuthbert, Ga., were married by Dr. A. L. Hamilton, in

26

Cuthbert on the 20th inst.

Wed. Nov. 3, 1880
     Mr. Marion Creel and Miss Emma Walker, both of Henry County,
(Ala.) were married in Georgetown, Ga., on Monday, by Rev. W. P.
Jordan.

Thurs. Nov. 11, 1880
     Mr. W. A. Hill, of Quitman County, Ga., and Miss Fannie
Mitchell of Hamilton, Ga., were married at the latter place
last Thursday.

     Married in Macon, Ga. on the 4th inst., Mr. C. M. Williams,
of Eufaula, and Miss Clifford E. Spain, of Macon. Attendants
were: Mr. Jas. Spain and Miss Lucia Ethridge; Mr. Alex McKenzie
and Miss Tochi Williams; Mr. W. D. Williams and Miss Hattie
Harris; Mr. L. W. Weedon and Miss Annie Powers.

     Married on the 7th inst., at the home of Mr. T. M. Fedrick,
by Rev. T. A. Johnson, Mr. P. O. Fedrick and Miss Roxie A.
Robinson, all of Barbour County.

     Mr. Dan T. Sheehan and Miss Abbie Woodruff, of Eufaula, were
married in the Catholic Church, by Father Savage on the 9th inst.

Fri. Nov. 12, 1880
     Mr. W. G. Cawthon, of Barbour County, and Miss C. J.
Williams were married at the home of the bride's mother in Henry
County, (Ala.) by Rev. Jere S. Williams, on the 10th inst.

Fri. Nov. 26, 1880
     Married in Cuthbert, Ga., yesterday, Judge W. L. Clark and
Miss Laura Dews.

Thurs. Dec. 2, 1880
     Mr. Wiley A. Cargill and Miss Jimmie F. Moore were married
by E. J. Moore, Esq., on last Sunday at the home of Mr. Lafayette
Moore, in Quitman County, Ga.

Thurs. Dec. 9, 1880
     Married at the home of Mr. Alexander McGehee on the 5th
inst., by Rev. Junius Jordan, Mr. Edward B. James and Miss Annie
E. McGehee, all of Barbour County.

Fri. Dec. 10, 1880
     Married at Midway (Ala.) on Tuesday last, Mr. Mac Caldwell
and Miss Feagin. (From The Clayton Courier, Dec. 18th: Mr. M. J.
Caldwell and Miss Isophene Feagin).

     Married at the home of A. A. Raleigh, in Eufaula on yester-
day, by Rev. W. H. Patterson, Mrs. A. E. Battle and Mr. T. K.
Mullins, of Troy, Ala.

Thurs. Dec. 16, 1880
     Married at the home of Hugh McLean in Barbour County, on
Sunday last, Mr. Daniel W. Creel to Miss Amanda Strickland.

     Married on the 1st at Mrs. Pruett's Hotel in Midway, (Ala.)
by Rev. W. S. Rogers, Mr. C. C. Blackwell and Miss Ella Feagin.
Attendants were: Mr. M. J. Caldwell and Miss Venie Feagin; Mr.
Lamar King and Miss Phenie Feagin; Mr. Geo. Hall and Miss Loudie
Feagin.

Fri. Dec. 17, 1880
     Married near Eufaula on Tuesday last, by Rev. Father Savage,

Mr. Lary O'Byrne and Miss Lillis Bates.

Married in Cuthbert, Ga., yesterday, Mr. Arthur Hood, Jr. to Miss Leila Green.

Thurs. Dec. 23, 1880
Mr. A.J. Thornton, of Montgomery and Miss Helen Alcott, of Atlanta, (Ga.) were married on the 14th inst.

Mr. W. F. Wilkinson, editor of the Prattville (Ala.) Signal, and Miss Ida McConaughy, of Shelby were married on the 8th inst.

THE CLAYTON COURIER
1880

Published in Clayton, Alabama by Edgar R. Quillin.

Sat. Aug. 14, 1880
Married at the home of Dr. M. Warren, Aug. 6th, by J. S. Paullin, Mr. J. M. Lampley of Louisville, (Ala.) to Mrs. Sue Borders.

Sat. Oct. 9, 1880
Married on the 23d of Sept., at the home of the bride's father, by Rev. Baxter Greer, Mr. Dickson L. Blair to Miss Bettie Turner, both of Barbour County.

Sat. Oct. 16, 1880
Miss Daisy L. Withers, daughter of Gen. J. M. Withers, of Mobile, was married in Atlanta to Mr. C. L. Humphries, of Mobile, on Wednesday last at one o'clock, and the bride died at 7 o'clock the same day.

Sat. Nov. 13, 1880
Married on Nov. 7th at the home of the bride's mother in Bullock County, (Ala.) by Rev. J. S. Paullin, Mr. B. C. Martin to Miss Hattie M. Pearson.

Sat. Nov. 20, 1880
Married at Robeson's Mill on Monday last, by Rev. Jesse Robeson, Mr. G. D. Helms to Mrs. Julia Ann McCrackin, all of Barbour County.

Married on Sunday last at the home of the bride's mother, by Rev. R. B. Crawford, Mr. Mason Norton, son of the M. E. minister at Clayton, to Miss Willie Petty, the daughter of Charley Petty.

Sat. Nov. 27, 1880
Married at the home of the bride's father, near Eufaula on Wednesday last, Mr. Thos. Ventress, of Clayton, and Miss Ida Fields.

Sat. Dec. 4, 1880
Married at the home of the bride's mother, on Thursday last, by Rev. J. S. Paullin, Mr. Duncan McRae to Miss Mary McRae, all of Barbour County.

Sat. Dec. 11, 1880
Married on Thursday last, by Jas. H. Walker, Esq., Mr. Jesse Dasinger to Miss Lou Catherine Davis, all of Barbour County.

Sat. Dec. 18, 1880
Married on the 8th inst., at Perote, Ala., Mr. W. A. Hixon

to Miss Lavonia Braswell.

Mr. A. W. Weaver and Mrs. Elizabeth Britt were married by Rev. Z. T. Weaver at the home of Mr. Enoch Mills, in Barbour County, on the 16th inst. The bride is the mother of Mr. Jno. T. Britt, of Clayton.

THE EUFAULA WEEKLY BULLETIN
1881

J. D. Hoyl, Proprietor.

Sat. Mar. 5, 1881
Mr. G. Gunby Jordan and Miss Lizzie B. Curtis, both of Columbus, Ga., were married at the Episcopal Church in that city. -Columbus (Ga.) Enquirer-Sun.

Married in Philadelphia, Pa., on the 2nd inst., Mr. Isaac Steuerman, of Eufaula, Ala., and Miss Nettie Fernberger, of the former city.

Married at the home of the bride's mother in Eufaula on the 2nd inst., by Rev. R. H. Rivers, Mr. Walter Andrews and Miss Mary Roberts, all of Eufaula.

Mr. Lorenzo Woodruff and Miss Jennie Ferguson, both of Montgomery, (Ala.) were married at the Methodist Church in that city on Thursday last.

Sat. Mar. 12, 1881
Mr. Thos. L. Yarrington and Miss Lula F. Harris were married in Jacksonville, Fla., on the 22nd ult.

Sat. Mar. 19, 1881
Mr. J. M. Dixon and Miss Rachael Payne were married on the 1st inst., near Skipperville, Dale County, (Ala.).

Mr. Jas. W. Simonton was married Thursday in Brooklyn, N.Y., to Miss Mary E. Bronson Walbridge.

Married at the Methodist Church in Eufaula on the 15th inst., by Rev. Dr. R. H. Rivers, Mr. P. Penn Watson, of Penn's Store, Va., and Miss Addie Martin, daughter of Capt. and Mrs. Jno. O. Martin, of Eufaula. Attendants were: Mr. P. C. Penn, of Penn's Store, Va., and Miss Eva Martin; Mr. M. C. Rhodes and Miss Emma Hyatt; Mr. C. R. Ross and Miss Lucie Flewellen, of Cuthbert, Ga.; Mr. W. A. Davis and Miss Laura Sylvester; Mr. C. C. Shorter and Miss Lucia Etheridge, of Macon, Ga.; Mr. R. Y. Garrett, of Columbus, Ga., and Miss Sallie Toney; Mr. C. A. Caldwell, of Macon, Ga., and Miss Emmie Goode, of Georgetown, Ga.; Mr. A. D. B. McKenzie and Miss Carrie Malone; Mr. J. I. Meares, of New York, and Miss Minnie Bray; Mr. E. C. Estes, of Columbus, Ga., and Miss Alice Shorter; Mr. J. K. Battle and Miss Katie Bray; Mr. J. W. Bray and Miss Corneille Barnett.

Sat. Mar. 26, 1881
Mr. Chas. C. Irby, of Eufaula, and Miss Mollie E. Pratt, of Cuthbert, Ga. were married on the 15th inst., in Harris County, Ga., at the home of the bride's sister.

Sat. Mar. 26, 1881
Mr. Mathias Sapperfield and Miss Ida Herring, both of Eufaula, were married last Sunday in Georgetown, Ga.

Sat. Apr. 9, 1881
Married on the 5th inst., by Justice McLendon, Mr. Alfred K.

Dickinson and Miss Mary C. Hinchey, all of Eufaula.

Sat. Apr. 16, 1881
Mr. Lennard Hendericks, of Ft. Smith, Ark., and Miss Darthula Hardie of Montgomery, (Ala.) were married in the Presbyterian Church in Montgomery on Wednesday. The groom is a lawyer whose parents reside in Talladega. (Ala.).

Married on the 10th inst., at the home of the bride's parents in Barbour County, Mr. J. M. Smith and Miss Lydia Berry, by Rev. R. B. Lee.

Married on Tuesday, at the home of the bride's father, Mr. Geo. H. Slaughter, in Barbour County, Mr. Jno. J. Willis, of Echo, Dale County, (Ala.) and Miss Fannie E. Slaughter.

Sat. Apr. 23, 1881
Married Thursday at the First Baptist Church in Eufaula, by Rev. M. M. Wamboldt, Mr. Ed. T. Long, of Columbus, Ga., and Miss Mamie C. Rhodes, of Eufaula. Attendants were: Mr. Jamie Rhodes and Miss Minnie Long, of Hurtville, Ala.; Mr. L. W. Redd, of Columbus, Ga. and Miss Florence Rhodes; Mr. J. B. Hill, of Columbus, Ga. and Miss Myra Ravenscroft of Troy, Ala.; Mr. J. C. Van Sycle, of Macon, Ga., and Miss Islay Reeves; Mr. C. H. Watts, of Columbus, Ga., and Miss Bessie Simpson; Mr. P. B. Patterson, of Columbus, Ga. and Miss Eva Martin; Mr. C. L. Rhodes and Miss Nellie Bray; Mr. C. P. Hardaway and Miss Sophie Holt; Mr. L. J. Simpson and Miss Alice Shorter; Mr. W. M. Bray and Miss Gena Berry. Fairy Guides of the bridal train: Misses Malanie Dean and Laura Long. Ushers: S. T. Barnett and C. D. Martin.

Married in the Catholic Church on Apr. 19th, 1881, by Rev. Father Crowley, Mr. Robt. Cherry and Mrs. Marie F. Brady, all of Eufaula.

Married on the 18th inst. at the home of the bride's sister, Mrs. Samuel Spencer, in Baltimore, Md., Mr. H. L. Hull, of Opelika, Ala., and Miss Sallie Benning, of Columbus, Ga., the daughter of the late Gen. Benning.

Sat. Apr. 30, 1881
Mr. J. R. Adams and Miss Katie Cook, both of Montgomery, (Ala.) were married in the Presbyterian Church at that place on the 27th.

Married at the home of the bride's parents in Monticello, Fla., on the 27th inst., Mr. P. Butler Mays, of Eufaula, and Miss Maggie F. Simkins, of the former place.

Married in Quitman County, Ga., on the 25th inst., Mr. N. W. Halliday and Miss D. L. Stanford, of Quitman County.

Married on the 26th inst., at the Catholic Church in Eufaula, by Father Crowley, Mr. Hugh McGeeve, of Atlanta, Ga., and Miss Mary A. T. O'Byrne, of Eufaula.

Sat. May 7, 1881
Married on the 27th ult., Mr. G. W. Peterson and Miss Roxie Oakley, of Columbia, Henry County, (Ala.).

Sat. May 14, 1881
Married at the home of the bride's mother in Morgan Calhoun County, Ga., on the 10th inst., by Rev. W. H. Patterson, Rev. D. Belton Jay, of Eufaula, and Miss Annie Clayton, of the former place. The groom is the son of Mr. and Mrs. J. L. Jay, of Eufaula.

Sat. July 2, 1881
Married on June 28th at the home of the bride's father, Mr. A. J. Veal, Mr. J. C. Sheets, of Lebanon, Ky., and Miss Rosa C. Veal, by Rev. W. H. Patterson.

Mr. Geo. C. Williams, publisher of the Columbia (Ala.) Enterprise, and Miss Mattie A. Clark, were married on the 21st inst.

Sat. July 30, 1881
Mr. Thos. Malone, of Abbeville (Ala.) and Miss Carrie Barrow, of Ozark, (Ala.) were married on the 15th inst.

Sat. Aug. 6, 1881
Married at the home of the bride's parents in Eufaula on the 4th inst., by Rev. M. M. Wamboldt, Mr. W. H. Prewett and Miss Anna Roberts, only daughter of Capt. and Mrs. G. A. Roberts.

Sat. Aug. 20, 1881
Jas. Wyatt Oates, Esq., formerly of Henry County, (Ala.) and brother of Col. W. C. Oates, was married recently in St. John's Presbyterian Church, San Francisco, to Miss Mattie A. Solomon, daughter of Mrs. M. S. Solomon.

Mr. Jas. C. Bell and Miss Sallie Estes, both of Memphis were married on the 11th inst., at Versailles, Ky. The groom was formerly of Eufaula, but removed to Memphis in 1874, and is the son of Mr. R. D. S. Bell.

Sat. Aug. 27, 1881
Mr. Henry Brown, formerly of Eufaula, but for six or eight years past a resident of Americus, Ga., was married on the 20th inst., to Miss Mattie Burke, of Americus. The groom is a son of Mr. Harvey Brown, of Eufaula.

Married at White Church, near Eufaula, on Sunday last, Mr. Thos. O. Hamilton and Miss Jane Loftin, by Rev. T. A. Johnson.

Sat. Oct. 1, 1881
Married at the home of Mrs. Malone in Eufaula, on the 29th inst., by Rev. R. H. Rivers, Mr. Stephen S. Cawthon, of Troy, Ala., and Miss Hattie Lou Stewart, of Eufaula.

Married in Macon, Ga., on the 26th inst., by Matt R. Freeman, Esq., Mr. Jas. Boyle, of St. Louis, Mo., and Mrs. Nannie H. Hartman, of Eufaula.

Sat. Nov. 12, 1881
Mr. Geo. A. Whitaker, of Eufaula, and Miss Jessie Pittman, of Georgetown, Ga. were married Wednesday in Georgetown, by Rev. Peter Twitty. Attendants were: Mr. Benj. Morris and Miss Emmie Goode; Mr. J. E. Dozier and Miss Belle Goode; Judge W. A. Jordan and Miss Emma Brown; Mr. Jno. Whitaker and Miss Katie Watts. Mrs. Mary Brannon performed on the organ.

Sat. Nov. 19, 1881
Married in Georgetown, (Ga.) on last Wednesday, at the home of Dr. J. W. Mercer, by Rev. P. S. Twitty, Mr. Samuel Guerry and Miss Bealle Goode.

Sat. Dec. 3, 1881
Married on Tuesday in Georgetown, (Ga.) at the home of the bride's father, Hon. T. L. Guerry, by Rev. P. S. Twitty, Mrs. Mary Brannon to F. Morris, Esq.

Married Thursday in Eufaula, by A. C. McLendon, Esq., Mr. E. Ratler and Miss Toodle Jenkins.

Mr. Adrian P. Jordan, formerly of Eufaula, was married on the 20th inst. at Wild Wood, Sumpter County, Fla., to Miss Agnes B. Crenshaw.

Married in Eufaula on the 29th, at the home of the bride's parents, by Rev. Dr. Rivers, Mr. Andrew S. Brown, of Ft. Gaines, Ga., and Miss Mary Webb, daughter of Mr. and Mrs. Jno. N. Webb.

Sat. Dec. 17, 1881

Mr. Henry J. Sandlin and Miss Maybelle Clarke, daughter of Judge Jas. Clarke of Americus, Ga., were married at Hawkinsville, Ga., on Friday, by Rev. H. R. Felder.

Married on the 15th inst., by Rev. Dr. Martin, in Abbeville, Ala., Mr. Jas. Pittman and Miss Joe Cumings.

Married on the 15th inst., near Lawrenceville, (Henry County, Ala.) by Rev. Mr. Helms, and Mr. Alonzo Richards and Miss Abbie Woods.

Married on the 15th, by Rev. Dr. Martin, Mr. Wm. Wood and Miss Margaret Richards, of near Lawrenceville, (Henry County, Ala.).

Married on the 8th inst., near Lawrenceville, (Henry County, Ala.) by Rev. Mr. Hudley, Mr. Wm. Owens and Miss Callie Everette.

Also on the same day and place, by Rev. Mr. Malone, Mr. Jack Ray and Miss Fannie Driggers.

Sat. Dec. 24, 1881

Married in Savannah, Ga., on the 14th inst., at the home of Dr. Dudley Cox, Mr. W. A. Givins, of Tampa, Fla., to Miss Florine A. Coke, of Savannah.

Married at the home of Mr. S. T. Schreiber, in Eufaula on last Tuesday, by Rev. Dr. Rivers, Mr. H. S. Perkins, of Birmingham, Ala., and Miss Mattie King, of Eufaula.

THE CLAYTON COURIER
1881

Edgar R. Quillan, Publisher.

Sat. Jan. 1, 1881

Dr. Henry Blair, of Louisville, (Ala.) and Miss Cora Carlisle were married at the home of the bride's father near Brundidge, (Ala.) on Friday last. The groom is the son of Mr. Mike Blair, of Louisville.

Married on Thursday at the home of the bride's mother by Rev. B. D. D. Greer, Mr. Tom McTyer, of Eufaula to Miss Emily Campbell, of Clayton.

Sat. Jan. 8, 1881

Married near Elamville, (Barbour County) last week, W. H. Doster and Nancy Payne; C. W. Armstrong and Martha C. Williams, Lawson Doster and Nancy Griffin, and also S. Johnson and S. Deloach.

Sat. Jan. 15, 1881

Married on the 10th of Jan. 1881, by T. P. C. Phillips, Esq., near Elamville, Ala., Benj. H. Phillips to Mary J. Casey.

Married at the home of the bride's father at Spring Hill, (Barbour County) on the 6th inst., Mr. P. E. Florence to Miss Sallie F. Cody, the daughter of M. Cody, Esq.

Sat. Jan. 22, 1881
Married at the home of the bride's father, Dr. J. A. Reynolds, by Rev. Ellison, on Wednesday, Mr. Robt. M. Lee and Miss Annie Reynolds.

Married on Wednesday at the home of the bride's mother, Mrs. B. F. Petty, by Rev. Ellison, Miss Portia Petty and Mr. W. H. King. Attendants: Rev. B. D. D. Greer and Miss Lela Petty. Mr. Richard Petty and Miss Kate Parish. Mr. Justus Collins and Miss Lonie Green. Mr. J. E. Parish and Miss Vic Clayton. Mr. Bob T. Roberts and Miss Claudia Waddell. Mr. Jno. T. Britt and Miss Addie Ventress. Mr. A. E. Hudson and Miss Ida Parish. Mr. Tennant Stewart and Miss Sallie Fenn. Mr. Needham Lee, Jr., and Miss Hattie Dill.

Sat. Feb. 26, 1881
Married at the home of the bride's father on Feb. 16th, by M. H. Rutland, Esq., Jno. C. McLeod to Miss Mary J. Baker, all of Barbour County.

Sat. Feb. 19, 1881
Married at home of the bride's father, Mr. Geo. Poyer, of Barbour County, on the 13th inst., by Rev. Dr. Tobey, of Eufaula, Mr. Chas. Johnson, of Atlanta, and Miss Mary G. Boyer.

Sat. Mar. 5, 1881
Married at the home of Squire Oppert, on Sunday last, by H. W. B. Price, Mr. J. A. Rollins and Mrs. M. E. Ingram, all of Barbour County.

Married on the 17th of Feb. at the home of the bride's mother, Mrs. Bowdon, by J. F. Walker, Esq., Mr. W. T. Halford and Miss Margaret Bowdon, all of Barbour County.

Married on Tuesday last, at the home of the bride's father, by Rev. Dr. Ellison, Mr. G. M. Bobbitt and Miss Cynthia Crews.

Sat. Mar. 12, 1881
Married at Mt. Andrew, on the 27th ult., by J. J. S. Willis, Esq., Mr. Geo. P. Flowers and Miss Ida Johnson, all of Barbour County.

Sat. Apr. 16, 1881
Married at the home of the bride's father, Mr. Geo. Slaughter, of Barbour County, by Rev. Mr. Crook, Mr. J. J. Willis, of Echo, Dale County, (Ala.) and Miss Fannie Slaughter.

Sat. May 28, 1881
Married at the home of the bride's parents, by Rev. D. C. Crook, on the 24th inst., Mr. W. A. Cheek to Miss Carrie A. Cooper, all of Barbour County.

Sat. Oct. 22, 1881
Married near White Oak on the 13th inst., by Jno. C. Williams, Esq., Mr. W. J. Martin and Miss S. C. Atwell.

Sat. Nov. 26, 1881
Mr. Joe Miller and Miss Polly Whittington of Mt. Andrew (Barbour County) were married at Georgetown, Ga., last Wednesday.

33

Sat. Dec. 3, 1881
    Married at the home of the bride's father, W. W. Sims, on
27th ult., by Rev. R. B. Arnold, Mr. Jas. G. Dominey and Mary J.
Sims, all of Barbour County.

Sat. Dec. 10, 1881
    Married on the 4th inst., by Rev. Wm. Pritchett, Mr. Jno.
Williams and Miss Henrietta Harris.

Sat. Dec. 31, 1881
    Married at the residence of the bride's father on the 15th
inst., Mr. B. F. Gann and Miss Fannie Ward.

    Married on the 25th inst., at the home of the bride, near
Clayton, by Rev. Z. T. Weaver, Miss Lydia Williams and Jas.
Perkins.

    Married at the residence of Dr. P. R. Holt, the bride's
father, in Eufaula on the 28th inst., Mr. H. P. Blount, of
Atlanta, and Miss Loula Holt.

EUFAULA TIMES AND NEWS
1881

W. D. Jelks, Proprietor.

Thurs. Jan. 20, 1881
    Mr. F. G. Guilmartin and Miss Minnie Holly, of Troy, (Ala.)
were married on the 12th.

    Married in Georgetown, Ga., on the 12th inst., by Rev.
Junius Jordan, Mr. Eleazer Whitaker and Miss Mollie McRee, of
Quitman County, Ga.

    Mr. H. S. Edwards, of Macon, (Ga.) was married in that city
last Thursday to Miss Roxie Lane.

Thurs. Jan. 27, 1881
    Married on the 5th inst., in Eufaula, Mr. Henry T. May and
Miss Emma, daughter of J. M. Whitehead, Esq., of Greenville.
-Greenville (Ala.) Advocate.

    Married in Ft. Gaines, (Ga.) on Thursday last, Mr. Jas. W.
Sutlive and Miss Cora Holland.

Thurs. Feb. 3, 1881
    Married Wednesday at the home of the bride's father, Mr.
W. H. Godwin and Miss Eula Beckham, both of Eufaula.

    Mr. Chas. W. Joseph and Miss Mattie Jackson were married in
Montgomery on the 26th.

Thurs. Feb. 24, 1881
    Married in Fort Gaines, (Ga.) recently, Mr. T. D. Gwinn to
Miss Ella Dudley.

    Married last Thursday in Eufaula, Miss Annie Jennings and
Mr. C. J. Knox of Troy, Ala., at the home of the bride's mother,
by Rev. Dr. Rivers.

Thurs. Mar. 17, 1881
    Dr. W. R. King, of Union Springs, (Ala.) on the 5th inst.,
to Miss Nellie N. Williams, of Spring Hill, in Barbour County.

Thurs. May 12, 1881
    Married at Abbeville, (Ala.) on the 5th inst., at the home

34

of the bride's father, Maj. Jno. Bland, by Hon. Dan Gordon, Mr.
B. E. Seymore and Miss Ella Bland, both of Abbeville.

Thurs. May 19, 1881
      Married at the home of the bride's father, R. H. Dawkins,
near Abbeville, (Ala.) on the 13th inst., by Rev. A. L. Martin,
Mr. J. J. Kilpatrick and Miss Loula Dawkins.

Thurs. May 28, 1881
      Mr. D. C. N. Burkhalter and Miss Lula Hooks, of Americus,
Ga., were married recently.

Thurs. June 23, 1881
      Mr. Geo. Hubbard and Miss Mary McGilvray, all of Barbour
County, were married recently.
      Mr. J. I. Butts, of Ga., and Miss Sallie Barham, of Barbour
County, were married at Clayton last week.

Thurs. July 7, 1881
      Married by Hon. Dan Gordon at the home of the bride's mother,
Mrs. Mary Hudspeth, at Abbeville, (Ala.) on the 30th ult., Mr.
Andrew Tally and Miss Mary Hudspeth.

Thurs. July 21, 1881
      Miss Mary Lou Hoover, of Birmingham and Jas. T. Thornton,
of Columbus, (Ga.) were married recently.

Thurs. July 28, 1881
      Mr. Z. T. Parish and Miss Fannie Creel, of Henry County,
(Ala.) were married by Rev. Aaron Helms on the 23rd inst.

Thurs. Aug. 5, 1881
      Married recently at Sandy Point, Barbour County, Ala., by
Rev. Junius Jordan, Mr. Green A. James to Miss Sarah Forrest.

Thurs. Sept. 22, 1881
      Married at the home of the bride's mother near Troy, (Ala.)
Jas. E. McCormick and Miss Georgia Brown. The groom is from
Barbour County.

Thurs. Oct. 6, 1881
      Mr. C. A. Dutton and Miss Nellie J. Throcmorton, both of
Denver, were married about ten days ago. -Denver (Colo.) Tribune.

Thurs. Oct. 13, 1881
      Married last week, Mr. Chas. H. Laney of the Geneva (Ala.)
Bulletin, to Miss Belle McKinnon, of that city.

Thurs. Oct. 27, 1881
      Married in the Methodist Church on Tuesday, by Rev. Dr.
Rivers, Mr. T. C. Doughtie and Miss Carrie L. Malone, both of
Eufaula.
      This evening at the M. E. Church in Eufaula, by Rev. R. H.
Rivers, Mr. Emmett B. Tullis will be married to Miss Corneille
Barnett. Attendants will be: Mrs. Jno. Thornton and Miss Katie
Bray, Mr. Eugene Martin and Miss Julia Young, Mr. Ira Lampley
and Miss Anna Sylvester, Mr. Harman Lampley and Miss Emmie Goode,
Mr. W. Berry and Miss Annie Reese, Mr. Jno. Kendall and Miss
Alice Shorter, Mr. Jno. Bray and Miss Dell Shorter, Mr. Tom
Berry and Miss Effie Jennings, Mr. Ed Dent and Miss Gena Berry,
Mr. E. C. Bullock and Miss Hattie Barnett, Mr. W. D. Jelks and
Miss Carrie Barnett, Mr. S. T. Barnett and Miss Ida Bludworth.

Thurs. Nov. 3, 1881
Married by Rev. Jere S. Williams, at Abbeville (Ala.) on the 31st last, Mr. W. J. Smith and Miss M. J. Kirkland.

Thurs. Nov. 17, 1881
Married at the home of Jno. G. Smith, on the 14th inst., by Rev. T. A. Johnson, Mr. J. W. McElroy to Miss S. E. Cronin, all of Barbour County.

Thurs. Nov. 24, 1881
Married in Fort Gaines, Ga., Miss Annie Brown to Mr. W. C. Jenkins.

Married at the Episcopal Church in Eufaula on the 15th inst. Mr. Bob T. Roberts and Miss Claudie Waddell.

Thurs. Dec. 1, 1881
Miss Mattie Murphree, of Troy, (Ala.) was married yesterday to Jas. B. Wiley, of Birmingham.

Thurs. Dec. 8, 1881
At Leavenworth, Kansas, last Wednesday, J. G. Waples, of Texas, and Miss Mary Richards, of Kansas, were married.

Married recently in Lumpkin, Ga., Miss Sallie W. Banks and George R. Williams.

Mr. Frank W. Bowdon, of Talladego, (Ala.) was married to Miss Bessie Jefferson, of Uniontown, (Ala.) on Dec. 1st.

Married near Eufaula on last Thursday, Mr. Jesse T. DeShazo and Miss Aura Bush.

Thurs. Dec. 22, 1881
Mr. Jno. M. Mobley and Miss India McDaniel, of Smithville, (Henry County, Ala.) were married on the 15th inst.

THE EUFAULA WEEKLY BULLETIN
1882

J. D. Hoyle, Proprietor.

Wed. Jan. 4, 1882
Mr. Marion B. Clark and Miss Jennie Henley were married in Henry County, (Ala.) during Christmas week, at the home of the bride's father, by Rev. J. Henley.

Also, on the same day, Mr. Stephen Norton, of Otho, was married to Miss Aquilla Clarke, at the home of the bride's father.

Wed. Jan. 18, 1882
Married on the 12th inst., at the home of Mr. Jule Malone, near Eufaula, by Rev. Dr. Martin, Mr. Albert Manley and Miss Hazey Ward.

Wed. Feb. 8, 1882
Married at Ft. Gaines, Ga., on Monday last, by Sam F. Lewis, Esq., Mr. Ferd. J. Hartung, of Eufaula, and Miss Josie Heuer, of Ft. Gaines.

Wed. Feb. 15, 1882
Married at the home of the bride's mother, near Mt. Andrew (Barbour County) on Thursday last, by P. B. Patterson, Esq., Mr. Hillary Crew and Miss Julia Flinn. - Clayton Courier.

Wed. Mar. 22, 1882
    Married in Georgetown, (Ga.) on Monday last, by Rev. H. E.
Brooks, of Eufaula, Mr. J. E. Walters and Miss L. A. Culver, both
of near Troy, (Ala.).

Wed. Apr. 12, 1822
    Mr. P. T. Hackaby and Miss Lavenia Trotman, daughter of Mr.
Thos. Trotman of this county, were married Sunday. Both were
reared in Stewart County, (Ga.). - Lumpkin (Ga.) Independent.

Wed. Apr. 19, 1882
    Married at the home of Mr. R. S. Wynn, in Macon, Ga., on
the 11th inst. by Rev. E. W. Warren, Mr. J. A. Green, of Macon,
and Miss Emma C. Thomas, of Eufaula, Ala.

Wed. May 17, 1882
    Married at the home of the bride's mother in Eufaula, on
Tuesday by Dr. Rivers, Miss Clara Bostwick and Jos. J. Twitty,
formerly of Camilla, Ga., now of Ft. Gaines, Ga., where he is
principal of the Academy there.

Wed. June 7, 1882
    Married at the home of the bride's parents in Juniper, Ga.,
on June 1, 1882, by Rev. Geo. C. Chandler, Mr. Johnnie Sibley,
of Augusta, Ga., and Miss Sallie Chandler of the former place.
The bride is a sister of Mrs. R. W. Williamson, of Eufaula.
The groom is a brother of Mr. Wm. C. Sibley of Augusta, Ga.

    Mr. E. D. Adams and Miss Clara Hatchett, both of Ft. Gaines,
Ga., were married last Thursday in that place.

Wed. July 26, 1882
    Married at Lexington, Ky., by Rev. T. A. Tidball, D. D.,
on July 20th, Col. Samuel W. Goode, of Atlanta, Ga., to Miss
Lizzie E. Stone, of the former place. -Atlanta (Ga.) Constitution.

Wed. Aug. 2, 1882
    Married in Abbeville, Ala., by Rev. Dr. Martin, Mr. Chas.
Laney and Miss Lee, both of Abbeville.

Wed. Aug. 9, 1882
    Married in Abbeville, (Ala.) on Aug. 6th at the home of the
bride's father, A. M. Skipper, Esq., by Rev. A. S. Martin, Mr.
Wm. I. Weems and Miss Jannie Skipper, all of Abbeville.

Wed. Sept. 27, 1882
    Married in Eufaula at the Finerty House, on 25th inst., by
J. G. L. Martin, Esq., Judge Bush, of Webster County, Ga., and
Miss M. E. Clements.

Wed. Oct. 18, 1882
    Married on 10th inst., in Georgetown, Ga., by W. A. Jordan,
Mr. Lawrence Sauls and Miss Sallie Curran, both of Eufaula.

Wed. Nov. 1, 1882
    Married in the Synagogue in Eufaula on Oct. 29th by Rev. Mr.
Hecht, Mr. Henry Bloom, of Louisville, Ky., and Miss Sarah Stem,
of Eufaula. Attendants were: Miss Sarah Bernstien and Mr.
Julius Kaufman, of Florence, Ga.; Miss Minnie Bernstien and Mr.
Louis Ottensasser; Miss Freddie Heibron and Mr. Bert Scheuer;
Miss Fannie Stern and Mr. Lee Bloom, of Louisville, Ky.

    Mr. W. F. Grace, of Macon, and Miss Ida Hamilton, of Cuth-
bert, (Ga.) were married in the M. E. Church at the latter place

recently.

Dr. J. L. Jordan of Columbus (Ga.) and Miss Kate Langley, of Greenwood, Fla., were married on Tuesday at the latter place.

Mr. Eugene Q. Smith, of Montgomery, and Miss Sallie E. Flewellen, of Cuthbert, (Ga.) were married in the latter place on Wednesday last.

Mr. M. Patrick, of Tallahassee, Fla., and Mrs. Ella Dohn, of Denton, Texas, were married in Eufaula at the Finerty House, by Dr. R. H. Rivers.

Married on the 25th inst., by Rev. E. M. Whiting, at the home of the bride's father, Judge Green, Miss Amanda Green to Prof. J. F. Scaife, of Eufaula. -Fort Gaines (Ga.) Tribune.

Wed. Nov. 8, 1882
Married on the 5th inst., at the home of Mr. Mathew Vaughan, near Eufaula, by Rev. T. A. Johnson, Mr. W. T. York and Miss Jessie Chesnutt, both of Stewart County, Ga.

Married on the 1st inst., at the home of Maj. W. T. Pruett, near Eufaula, by Rev. T. A. Johnson, Mr. Clarence E. Hooks, of Stewart County, Ga., and Miss Mary Lou Hendrix, of Barbour County.

Wed. Nov. 22, 1882
Married on 16th inst., at the home of Mr. Ashley Vining near Eufaula, by Rev. T. A. Johnson, Mr. J. P. Carter and Miss Leila Vining, both of Barbour County.

Also on the 16th near Eufaula, by Rev. Junius Jordan, Mr. Jesse B. Windham and Miss Theodosia Gibson.

Col. T. H. B. Rivers, of Glennville, (Ala.) and Mrs. Laura E. Phillips, of Columbus, Ga., were married at the Rankin House in the latter city on the 14th inst.

Wed. Dec. 5, 1882
Married in Americus, Ga., on the 30th of Nov., by Rev. Mr. Cook, at the home of the bride's father, Mr. S. W. Dickson, of Eufaula, and Miss Annie Davenport, of the former city.

Wed. Dec. 13, 1882
Married on the 10th inst., at the home of Dr. T. M. Allen in Eufaula, by Rev. R. H. Rivers, D. D., Maj. W. C. Estes and Mrs. S. A. Joyce, both of Cotton Hill, Clay County, Ga.

EUFAULA TIMES AND NEWS
1882

Thurs. Jan. 19, 1882
Mr. Oliver T. Smith, of Union Springs, (Ala.) was married to Miss Katie Wood, of Selma, (Ala.).

Married at the home of the bride's father, Z. W. Laney, Esq. at Abbeville, (Ala.) by Rev. A. L. Martin, on the 17th inst., Mr. Wm. O. Long and Miss E. P. Laney.

Tues. Feb. 7, 1882
Mr. E. H. Smart, city marshal of Bainbridge, (Ga.) and Miss C. L. Waugh were married recently.

Tues. Feb. 28, 1882
Married on the 19th inst., in Henry County, (Ala.) Mr. Jas. W. Roberts and Mrs. Susan C. Radford.

Mr. Richard Dow, of Atlanta, Ga., and Miss Annie Mays were married at the home of Maj. Ball in Eufaula on last Thursday.

Tues. Mar. 21, 1882
Miss Mamie Little and Mr. H. H. McPherson were married recently at Fort Deposit, Lowndes County, (Ala.).

Tues. Apr. 4, 1882
Married at the home of the bride's mother, at Roseland, near Eufaula, by Rev. Waddell, on 28th ult., Hon. Wm. C. Oates to Mrs. Sallie A. Toney, daughter of the late Col. Washington Toney.

Tues. Apr. 25, 1882
Mr. Jas. Warren and Miss Emma Dickard, both of this place, were married by Justice W. H. Dill last Thursday.

Tues. May 2, 1882
Mr. J. M. Floyd and Miss Laura Scarborough, both of Barbour County, were married recently.

Hon. Perry C. Walker, of Evergreen, Ala., and Miss Carrie Crumpton, of Mobile, daughter of Rev. B. H. Crumpton, late of Greenville, were married Tuesday last.

Tues. May 9, 1882
Mr. Jas. K. Isbell, of Otho, Ala., and Miss Emmie Stratford, of Russell County, (Ala.) daughter of Mr. Richard Stratford, were married yesterday in Columbus, (Ga.) by Rev. Dr. J. H. Campbell. -Columbus (Ga.) Enquirer.

Tues. June 20, 1882
Married on Tuesday last at the home of the bride's father, Mr. A. W. Stokes, by Rev. Dr. R. H. Rivers, Mr. Claude C. Grayson, of Selma, Ala., and Miss Della Stokes.

Tues. July 11, 1882
Mr. Frank Stollenwerk, of Selma (Ala.) and Miss Emma Calhoun, of Greenville, (Ala.) were married at the latter place last Thursday.

Tues. July 18, 1882
Married on the 13th inst., at the home of the bride's father, Col. H. J. Irby, near Eufaula, by Rev. W. H. Patterson, Mr. C. J. Hughes, of Bartow, Fla., and Miss Fannie Irby.

Tues. Aug. 8, 1882
Married at the home of the bride's father, Mr. A. B. Starke, near Spring Hill, Barbour County, by Dr. T. W. Tobey, assisted by Rev. J. J. Porter, Miss Lula B. Starke and Rev. J. C. Porter, of Ky.

Married at the home of Mr. Offie Alston, in Hoboken, near Eufaula, on the 3rd inst., by Rev. Junius Jordan, Mr. Jno. Spurlock and Miss Annie Newman, all of Hoboken.

Tues. Aug. 29, 1882
Married in Clayton on Tuesday, Miss Elvira Campbell, of Clayton, and Mr. R. Oberly, of Camp, Ga.

Married at Ft. Browder, on the 24th inst., by Rev. A. J. Briggs, Mr. Geo. W. Pruett and Miss Viola L. Moore, all of Barbour County.

Tues. Sept. 5, 1882

Married by Mr. Mac Bush, a justice, Mrs. Robt. Hatfield to Mr. Fletcher Wilkerson, on last Sunday near Eufaula.

Married near Lawrenceville, Henry County, (Ala.) Mr. Drew Vickhurst to Miss Georgia Hendley.

Tues. Sept. 12, 1882

Married in Clayton on last Thursday, Prof. Kendrick Faulk and Miss Lillie Robson.

Tues. Oct. 17, 1882

Married at Clopton, Ala., yesterday, by Rev. R. B. Crawford, Mr. Eli McSwean, of Eufaula, and Miss Leonora Johns.

Tues. Oct. 24, 1882

Jas. Hatfield and Miss Jimmerson were married near Eufaula on Sunday.

Tues. Nov. 7, 1882

Mr. J. C. Crowell and Miss M. W. Merriwether, both of Bullock County, (Ala.) were married recently in Columbus.

Tues. Nov. 14, 1882

Married in Bullock County, (Ala.) on Oct. 31st inst., Mr. Irby J. Dunklin, of Greenville, Ala., and Miss Sallie Tompkins of Bullock County.

Married in Greenville, Ala., on Nov. 2nd, Thos. J. Peagler and Miss Ellen Dunklin, both of Greenville.

Married on the 5th inst., near Eufaula, W. A. Brazzell and Miss Sallie Smith; and on the 8th inst., J. A. Walsh and Miss Mary Cole.

Tues. Nov. 21, 1882

Married in Montgomery, on the 15th inst., Mr. N. N. Thornton, of Harris, (Barbour County) and Miss Stratford, of Montgomery.

Married in the Episcopal Church in Montgomery on Tuesday, Mr. Henry D. Clayton, Jr., of Eufaula, and Miss Jennie Allen, of Montgomery.

Married last Thursday, Mr. Bunyan Davie, of Clayton, and Miss Hattie Jones, of Troy, Ala., at the home of Judge U. L. Jones.

Tues. Nov. 28, 1882

Married in Barbour County, by Rev. Chambers, Mr. Liji Johnston and Miss Minnie Smitha.

Tues. Dec. 8, 1882

Married in Eufaula on last Saturday, by J. G. L. Martin, Esq., Mr. D. M. McLeod.

Married at the home of the bride's father, J. W. Price, on Thursday, by Rev. J. E. Chambliss, Mr. Thos. C. Johnson and Miss Lillie Price, all of Eufaula.

THE CLAYTON COURIER
1882

Edgar R. Quillin, Publisher.

Sat. Jan. 7, 1882

Mr. Geo. Holt and Miss Lula Smith, daughter of Mr. Isham Smith, were married at Midway, (Ala.) on Thursday last.

Sat. Jan. 21, 1882
Married at the home of the bride's parents by Elder J. S. Paullin, last Sunday, Mr. Van Dorn McLean and Miss Melissa Andrews.

Mr. Buck Lassiter and Miss Dixie Cawthon were married in Georgetown, Ga., on Tuesday.

Sat. Jan. 28, 1882
Married on the 19th inst., at the home of the bride's parents near Elamville, by Mr. Jas. A. Baxter, Esq., Mr. C. C. Hunt and Miss Clara McRae. (Barbour County).

Married at the home of Rev. Dr. Ellison on Sunday last, Mr. Wm. Halford and Miss Sallie Bowdon.

Married in Clayton at the home of the bride's parents on Tuesday, by Rev. Dr. Ellison, Mr. Jno. T. Britt and Miss Katie Parish, daughter of J. E. Parish, Esq. Attendants were: Mr. H. D. Clayton, Jr., and Miss Lonie Green. Rev. B. D. D. Greer and Miss Cora Munford. Mr. Frank Watkins and Miss Ludie Solomon. Mr. J. K. Quillin and Miss Sallie Fenn. Mr. J. E. Parish, Jr., and Miss Vickie Clayton. Mr. E. A. Hudson and Miss Ida Parish.

Sat. Feb. 18, 1882
Married on Dec. 1st last, at the home of the bride's parents, Mr. T. J. Green and Miss Emma Floyd.

Mr. Luke T. Atkins and Miss Sallie M. McLendon of Goodwater, Ala., were married in Columbus, Ga., on Sunday, by Justice N. L. Redd.

Sat. Feb. 25, 1882
Married at Eufaula on the 22nd inst., by Rev. Rivers, Mr. J. A. Hancock and Miss Mary Ann Barfield.

Judge Henry B. Tompkins, of Savannah (Ga.) and Miss Bessie, daughter of Hon. G. A. Washington of Nashville, were married on the 16th inst., in Nashville.

Sat. May 13, 1882
Married at the home of the groom's brother in Barbour County, on the 9th inst., by Rev. Mr. Meredith, Mr. R. G. Shehane and Miss Delphia S. Garner.

Sat. May 20, 1882
Married on the 11th inst., by P. B. Patterson, Esq., Dr. W. R. Moye and Miss Mattie Lott, all of Mt. Andrew, (Barbour County).

THE EUFAULA WEEKLY BULLETIN
1883

J. D. Hoyl, Proprietor.

Wed. Jan. 3, 1883
Mr. Ed. F. Doughtie, formerly of Eufaula, but now of Montgomery, was married on Tuesday last in the Episcopal Church at Knoxville, Tenn., to Miss Carrie Bell, of that city.

Mr. Z. W. Williams, of Barbour County, and Miss Wright, of Thomasville, Ga., were married recently.

41

Married in Eufaula yesterday at the home of Misses Chitty, by Rev. R. H. Rivers, Mr. R. A. Solomon and Miss Mack Chitty.

Wed. Feb. 7, 1883
Married yesterday in Bibb County, near Macon, (Ga.) Mr. A. S. McGregor and Mrs. Lavarre, nee Miss Jeannie G. Andrews, daughter of Dr. S. F. W. Andrews, of Macon.

Mr. N. J. Ursury and Miss Mary E. Strickland, both of Barbour County, were married last week near Mt. Andrew.

Married in the M. E. Church on the 4th inst., by Rev. M. S. Andrews, Mr. Andrew M. Webb of Eufaula, and Miss Madora Robbin Winfield, of Georgetown, Ga.

Married on Feb. 1st in Eufaula by Rev. Junius Jordan, Mr. Thos. Leroy and Miss Henrietta King, all of Barbour County.

Wed. Feb. 14, 1883
Married yesterday at the home of Mr. J. M. Spurlock, near Eufaula, by Rev. Dr. Andrews, Mr. Robt. Greer, of Eufaula and Miss Ella S. Spurlock. Attendants were: Jas. F. Green and Miss Eula Spurlock; Chas. R. Ross and Miss Lillie Drewry; Jas. M. Spurlock and Miss Laura Coleman; Chauncey Rhodes and Miss Annie Guice; Ira Lampley and Miss Gena Berry; Alex McKenzie and Miss Rheta Thornton.

Fri. Feb. 23, 1883
Married in Alabama: Near Mt. Hebron, Thos. Lee and Miss Susan Smith. Near Union, J. F. Fason and Miss Della Baines. Near West Point, Ga., Homer Hayes of Union Springs and Levie Olive. In Selma, Chas. W. Buhler and Miss Callie T. Allen. Near Macon Station, Elwood D. Davis and Miss Mary L. Collins. In Evergreen, Chapman Bettis, of Grove Hill, and Miss Ida Hill. In Calhoun County, J. R. Davis and Miss Mary Henderson. In Opelika, Mr. Benton and Miss Jennie Hurt. In Coosa County, Isaac S. Johnson and Miss Cynthia E. Suttle. In Marshall County, E. D. Loyd and Miss M. G. Loyd; also Jas. Noble and Miss Georgia Hambrick. At Echo, W. S. Coleman and Miss Lizzie Riley. At Choctaw Corner, Simeon Rodgers, of Wilcox, and Miss Maggie Privett.

Thurs. Feb. 22, 1883
Married on the 15th inst., at the Presbyterian Church, (Montgomery) by Rev. Dr. Perrie, Mr. Jno. I. Miller, of Bullock County, and Miss Velie, daughter of Mr. Alex Wilson, of Montgomery. (Advertiser and Mail, published Montgomery, Ala. and bound in with The Eufaula Weekly Bulletin).

Sun. Feb. 25, 1883
Married in Alabama: In Bibb County, Young Griffin and Mary Ann Lightsey. In Hale County, J. Brooks May and Nicjae E. Kinnaird. In Newberne, Dr. Lucius D. Webb and Miss Sallie C. Brown. In Lawrence County, W. R. Harris and Miss Martha Ash; also, Uriah Johnson and Miss Sarah Gay. In Greene County, Jas. Spencer and Miss Josephine Gosa. (Advertiser and Mail, published Montgomery, Ala. and bound in with The Eufaula Weekly Bulletin).

Wed. Mar. 21, 1883
Miss Jessamine Wood, daughter of Rev. Jesse Wood, formerly of Barbour County, was married recently in California, to Mr. Robt. A. (Allen) Green. The bride's father is editor of the Chico (Calif.) Daily Enterprise.

Married on Mar. 14th by Rev. Sale De Mendes, in New York at the home of the bride's brother, Mr. Phillip Bernstein, of

Eufaula, Ala., and Miss Flora Harrison, of New York.

Wed. Mar. 28, 1883
Mr. and Mrs. Shadrack Mims, of Prattville, Ala., celebrated
the fiftieth anniversary of their marriage on Thursday last.

Wed. June 13, 1883
Married at the home of the bride's parents in Eufaula, Mr.
W. D. Jelks and Miss Alice K. Shorter, daughter of Maj. Henry R.
Shorter.

Wed. June 27, 1883
Married recently, Mr. Eugene Granberry, of the editorial
staff of the Columbus (Ga.) Enquirer-Sun, and Miss Lotta Cropp,
of Columbus.

Wed. July 11, 1883
Mr. T. D. Semple and Miss Rosa Gunter, both of Montgomery,
were married last Thursday at the home of the bride's father in
that city.

Wed. Aug. 1, 1883
Mr. Jefferson Pipkin and Miss Bynum, both of Barbour County,
were married on the 18th inst.

EUFAULA TIMES AND NEWS
1883

W. J. Jelks, Proprietor.

Tues. Jan. 1, 1883
Married in Eufaula last afternoon, W. C. Germany and Miss
Annie O. Bagby both of Union Springs, (Ala.).

Tues. Jan. 23, 1883
Married on the 18th inst., by R. S. Lee, Esq., McNaughton
Nolen and Mary Berry, all of Cotton Hill in Barbour County.

Married at Georgetown, (Ga.) on Wednesday, by Rev. J.
Menefee, of Columbia, Mr. Hamp (H.P.) Purcell and Miss Bobbie
Kaigler.

Married at Lawrenceville, (Ala.) Mr. Robt. Walden and Miss
Lela Hendly.

Married Thursday at the home of Maj. J. M. Buford in
Eufaula, by Rev. J. D. A. Cook, of Americus, Mr. Robt. C. Jelks,
of Atlanta, and Miss Willie Cowan of Union Springs.

Tues. Jan. 30, 1883
Married on the 18th inst., by A. B. Bush, Mr. E. M. Johnson
and Miss Lula Harper, all of Cotton Hill.

Mr. Ed. McDonald and Miss Eloise Powell were married in
Cuthbert on Wednesday.

Married in Union Springs, (Ala.) on Wednesday, Mr. C. B.
Chapman and Miss Jessie Strickland, both of that city.

Tues. Feb. 6, 1883
Married Thursday at the home of R. J. Woods, Esq., of
Eufaula, by Rev. M. S. Andrews, Mr. Jno. M. Kendall and Miss
Sallie W. Jennings, both of Eufaula. Attendants were: Mr. Will
M. Bray and Miss Effie Jennings; Mr. Tom D. McGough and Miss
Florrie Kendall.

Tues. Feb. 13, 1883

Married in Bullock County on Saturday, Mr. Joe Nix, of Clayton, and Miss Bethune.

Married yesterday at the First Baptist Church in Eufaula, by Rev. J. E. Chambliss, Mr. Ernest L. Brannon and Miss Florence Rhodes, both of Eufaula. Attendants were: Mr. Chas. R. Ross and Miss Katie Bray; Mr. W. R. Pratt, of Montgomery, and Miss Bessie Simpson; Mr. E. T. Long and Mrs. E. T. Long; Mr. Chancey L. Rhodes and Miss Eva Martin; Mr. Simpson R. Foy and Miss Laura Sylvester; Mr. Robt. H. Walker and Miss Sophie Holt. Ushers: Mr. Alex. McKenzie and Mr. Eugene Martin.

Tues. Feb. 20, 1883

Married at the home of Dr. J. W. Mercer, in Georgetown, Ga. on Thursday, by Rev. S. P. Twitty, of Cuthbert, Ga., Mr. J. E. Dozier and Miss Emmie Goode.

Married in Galveston, Tex., on Jan. 31st, Rev. G. W. Briggs to Miss Annie E. Wood. The groom was formerly an Alabamian, and resided for a time in Eufaula, when his father, Rev. A. J. Briggs filled the pastorate. In 1877, Waverly, as his boyhood friends called him, was transferred to the Texas Conference.

Tues. Feb. 27, 1883

Married Thursday near Clayton, Prof. P. P. Anderson to Miss Emma Bailey.

Tues. Mar. 13, 1883

Married Wednesday at the home of the bride's father, Andrew M. McAllister, Esq., near Eufaula, by Rev. T. M. Lowery, Mr. Jesse F. Stallings, of Greenville, Ala., and Miss Ella C. McAllister.

Tues. Apr. 2, 1883

Mr. Sieg. P. Sterne, former Eufaulian and brother to Messrs. Silas and Gabe Sterne, will be married on the 10th to Miss Alice J. Hart, at Woodville, Miss.

Tues. Apr. 24, 1883

Married in Columbus (Ga.) Tuesday, by Rev. A. B. Campbell, Mr. Jos. G. Moore, of Birmingham, and Miss Sallie M. Billings, formerly of Eufaula, daughter of Jno. D. Billings.

Married at the home of the bride's father, Jno. M. Bludworth, Esq., in Eufaula, by Rev. Father Fullerton, Mr. J. E. Sapp and Miss Ola Bludworth.

Married at the home of the bride's father at Spring Hill, Barbour County, on the 18th of Apr., by Rev. Ritchie J. Briggs, Mr. Jno. M. Alston to Miss Willie Briggs.

Tues. May 1, 1883

Married yesterday at the home of the bride's father, Capt. Jno. O. Martin, of Eufaula, by Rev. M. S. Andrews, Mr. E. C. Bullock and Miss Eva Martin.

Tues. May 8, 1883

Married near Eufaula on Apr. 29th, by Rev. T. A. Johnson, Mr. Jesse Whitehurst and Mrs. Mary A. Dunnaway.

Tues. May 22, 1883

Married at Skipperville, by Elder C. S. Pellam, Mr. Lewis Dixon and Miss Sallie Price, all of Dale County, Ala.

Tues. May 29, 1883
Married on the 20th inst., at the home of the bride's step-
father, Mr. M. B. Patterson, of Barbour County, by T. P. C.
Phillips, Esq., Mr. J. H. Williams and Miss Emma Guice.

Tues. July 3, 1883
Married at Abbeville, Ala., on June 26th, at the home of
the bride's uncle, Hon. Wm. C. Oates, by Dr. A. L. Martin, Mr.
David Thurman, of Gordon, Ala., and Miss Mamie Long, of Abbeville.

Married recently, Miss Mary Nunnelee, of Tuskaloosa, Ala.,
and Mr. Jno. A. Keith, of Tenn. She is a sister of editor
Nunnelee of the Tuskaloosa Gazette.

Mr. Jno. W. Whiddon and Miss Lucy J. Johnson, both of Henry
County, (Ala.) were married on the 24th of June.

Married at the home of Mr. J. R. Cawley, in Seale, (Ala.)
by W. A. L. Tucker, on the 24th, Mr. J. P. Cawley and Miss J. M.
McGee.

Tues. July 17, 1883
Married at the First Baptist Church in Eufaula on Wednesday,
by Rev. J. E. Chambliss, Mr. Thos. Geo. Berry and Miss Retta
Thornton, daughter of Mrs. W. H. Thornton. Attendants were: Mr.
Eugene C. Martin and Miss Gena Berry; Mr. Jno. T. Berry and Miss
Bessie Simpson; Mr. Clement C. Shorter and Miss Julia Young; Mr.
Walter T. Berry and Miss Willie May Cox; Mr. Samuel T. Barnett
and Miss Delle Shorter; Mr. Eli S. Shorter and Miss Laura Syl-
vester; Mr. Edward T. Martin and Miss Effie Jennings; Mr. Lucien
J. Walker and Miss Lillie Drewry. Flower girls: Miss Laurie
Comer, Hattie McKleroy, Mollie Couric and Willie Robinson.

Married at the Methodist Church in Eufaula on Thursday, by
Rev. Mark S. Andrews, Mr. Eugene C. Martin and Miss Gena Berry.
Attendants were: Mr. and Mrs. Thos. G. Berry; Mr. Ed. T. Martin
and Miss Delle Shorter; Mr. Sam T. Barnett and Miss Laura Syl-
vester; Mr. Clarence D. Martin and Miss Julia Young; Mr. J. T.
Berry and Miss Willie May Cox; Mr. E. Y. Dent and Miss Effie
Jennings; Mr. R. E. L. Martin and Miss Nannie Dent; Mr. Walter
T. Berry and Miss Adele Martin. Ushers: M. B. L. Guice and Mr.
S. B. McTyer.

Married recently, Mr. Homer B. Urquhart, of Birmingham, and
Miss Mollie H. Johnson, of Loachapoka, Lee County, (Ala.) at the
latter place. Mr. Urquhart is the son of Rev. Dr. Urquhart of
Eufaula.

Tues. Aug. 21, 1883
Married at the home of the bride's father, on Aug. 8th, by
Rev. J. W. Parker, Mr. S. D. Jernigan, of Rusk County, Tex., and
Miss S. B. Scheffer, of Ozark. -Ozark (Ala.) Star.

Married at the home of the bride's grandfather, Rev. C. A.
Bass, in Brundidge, Ala., on the 28th ult., by Rev. A. S. Dick-
son, Rev. T. H. Windham, of Dale County, (Ala.) and Miss Ida
Stephens, of Pike County. -Ozark (Ala.) Star.

Tues. Sept. 4, 1883
Married in Georgetown, Ga., recently, Mr. P. L. Helms and
Miss Mary Peeples, both from Barbour County.

Married at Headland, Ala., on the 2nd inst., by Rev. A. L.
Martin, Alderman Chas. F. Sporman, of Eufaula, and Miss Mattie
M. Price, of Abbeville.

Tues. Sept. 11, 1883
Married at the home of Mr. L. B. McCrary, in Georgetown, Ga., on the 1st of Sept., Mr. R. A. Wheeler and Miss Alice Godwin, daughter of Mr. W. C. Godwin, all of this city. -Americus (Ga.) Republican.

Married on Sunday at the home of the bride's mother in Eufaula, Miss Julia Heilborn and Mr. Moses Lowenthal, of Columbus, Ga., Rabbi Strauss officiating.

Tues. Sept. 18, 1883
Mr. Robt. Moulthrop, Jr., and Miss Katie Moss, both of Eufaula, were married at the Brown House in Macon, (Ga.) on Wednesday.

Married by A. B. Bush, Esq., on the 13th inst., Mr. Samuel D. Houston and Miss Lula Flowers, all of Cotton Hill. (Barbour County).

Tues. Oct. 23, 1883
Miss Callie McKenzie was married to Mr. Uriah C. Vinson at Georgiana, Ala., last week.

Mr. R. W. A. Wilda of Birmingham, and Miss Fiquet, of Tuskaloosa, were married in Louisville, (Ky.) recently.

Married at the home of the bride's father, Mr. L. Hinson, by Rev. T. H. Stout, on Thursday, Mr. Willie Bennett and Miss Mary Hinson, all of Clayton. -Clayton Courier.

Tues. Oct. 30, 1883
Mr. Tom Jamison and Miss Mollie Corbitt were married on the 18th inst. (Lawrenceville, Ala.).

Mr. Samuel Bowdon, of Gordon, (Ala.) and Mrs. Emma Hampton, daughter of Capt. Jno. N. Webb, of Eufaula, were married on Friday, by Rev. Dr. Andrews.

Mr. Daniel C. Farmer, of Macon, Ga., and Miss Sallie J. Phelps, of Cuthbert, were married Thursday at the home of the bride's father, Mr. D. K. Phelps, Rev. T. M. Lowery, of Eufaula officiating.

Tues. Nov. 6, 1883
Mr. J. A. Flowers and Miss Fannie Lewis were married near Lawrenceville, (Henry County, Ala.) on last night.

Married at the residence of Mrs. N. C. Blackman, on Sanford Street, in Eufaula yesterday, by Rev. W. H. Patterson, Mr. F. M. Patterson and Miss Mattie Livingston, both of Eufaula.

Mr. Jno. H. Leitner and Miss Nettie Shade were married in Columbus, (Ga.) recently.

Tues. Nov. 13, 1883
Mr. Jno. S. Jemison, editor of the Alabama Law Journal, was married to Miss Margie Allen at LaFayette, Ala., on the 7th inst.

Mr. J. P. Long and Miss Estelle Davie were married at Cowikee, (Barbour County) on Nov. 8th, by Rev. A. J. Briggs.

Married Wednesday at the home of the bride's father, Mr. R. G. Morris, Mr. Robt. C. McGinty, of Florence, and Miss Susan A. Morris, of Georgetown, (Ga.) by Rev. P. S. Twitty.

Married Thursday at the home of the bride's father, Capt. Jno. H. Bass, in Glennville, Dr. J. T. Dejarnette, of Eaton, Ga., and Miss Mamie Bass, of Glennville.

Married in Eufaula on the 8th inst., by Dr. T. A. Johnson, Mr. A. F. Benton and Miss M. J. Fredrick.

Married at the home of the bride's father, Mr. J. M. Thornton, Sr., in Batesville, (Ala.) last Wednesday, Mr. Robt. J. Fields and Miss Sallie Thornton.

Married recently at Camilla, Ga., Mr. L. P. Freeman and Miss Emma Bostwick. The groom is from Talbottom, (Ga.). Miss Bostwick formerly lived in Eufaula, and among her attendants were Miss Mattie Walker and Mr. C. W. Oliver, of Eufaula.

Tues. Nov. 20, 1883
Married at the home of the bride's mother near Eufaula, on the 15th inst., by Dr. T. A. Johnson, Mr. T. J. Smith and Miss Alice Eley, all of Barbour County.

Married at the residence of the bride's father, Mr. Geo. W. Williams, at Star Hill, (Barbour County) last Tuesday, by Rev. Mr. Rogers, Mr. C. A. Saunders and Miss Mary Williams.

Tues. Nov. 27, 1883
Mr. A. P. Greene, of Buffton, and Miss Bailey, of Americus, Ga., were married last week. -Fort Gaines (Ga.) Tribune.

Gov. L. Heston Snead and his bride, nee Miss Lizzie Christian, of Lynchburg, Va., are visiting friends in Eufaula.

Tues. Dec. 11, 1883
Mr. Eli S. Shorter, of Eufaula, and Miss Wileyna Lamar, of Macon, were married Dec. 6th, by Dr. A. J. Battle. Attendants were: Col. C. C. Shorter, Eufaula, with Miss Alberta Lamar, Macon; W. D. Lamar, Macon, with Miss Adele Shorter, Eufaula; Dr. J. D. Battle, Eufaula, with Mamie Rankin, Atlanta; E. T. Martin, Eufaula, with Miss Mary Lou Bacon, Macon; S. T. Barnett, Eufaula, with Miss Aurie Hall, Macon; D. F. McCall, Union Springs, with Miss Ida Holt, Macon; Julian Price with Miss Josie Clisby, both of Macon; D. C. Turrentine, Eufaula, with Miss Carrie Johnston, Macon; Cullen Battle, Macon, with Miss Hallie Wharton, Atlanta; Harmon Lampley, Eufaula, with Miss Lizzie Anderson, Macon.

Married at the residence of the bride's mother, Mrs. Sinquefield, on Tuesday last, Mr. L. Reynolds and Miss Carrie T. Sinquefield, Rev. A. S. Borders officiating. -Clayton Courier.

Married near Ft. Browder, Barbour County, at the home of the bride's father, Dr. Russell, on 29th of Nov., Mr. Thos. E. Whigham and Miss Carrie Russell, by Rev. Baxter Greer.

Tues. Dec. 18, 1883
Married in Eufaula at the home of the bride's aunt, on Dec. 12th, by Rev. D. C. Hunley, Mr. S. L. Bryan of Cottondale, Fla., to Miss Fannie E. Blackburn of Eufaula.

Tues. Dec. 25, 1883
Married at the residence of the bride's father, J. P. Scott, Esq., in Russell County, Ala., on Dec. 20th inst., by Dr. T. J. Johnson, Mr. J. W. Mangum to Miss Ada Scott.

Jas. B. Byrd, Esq., married near Ozark recently to Miss Lizzie Harris. -Ozark Star.

Mr. Reuben C. Kennington and Miss Addie C. Powell were married in Georgetown, (Ga.) on Sunday by Rev. M. L. Albritton, both from Eufaula.

Col. G. G. Locke, of Albany, Ga., and Miss Evelyn Irwin, of

Ft. Gaines, were married recently.

Also, W. C. Grimsley to Miss Emma Cooper. -<u>Fort Gaines</u> (Ga.)
<u>Tribune</u>.

Mr. Geo. Omen and Miss Julia James married recently. Also,
Mr. Ed. Murdock and Miss Clem Cooper were married. -<u>Cuthbert</u>
(Ga.) <u>Appeal</u>.

THE CLAYTON COURIER
1883

Sat. Nov. 24, 1883
    Married by T. P. C. Phillips, Esq., at his residence on the
11th inst., Mr. L. D. Chambers and Miss Gertie Brown, both of
Clio, (Ala.).

    Married at the home of the bride's father, at Louisville,
(Ala.) by Jas. Lang, Esq., on Sunday last, Mr. D. B. Snider, of
Pike County, (Ala.) and Miss C. R. Veal.

Sat. Dec. 8, 1883
    Married on Tuesday of last week, at the residence of the
bride's mother near Louisville, by Jas. A. Baxter, Esq., Mr. Wm.
A. Helms and Miss Jimmie Smith.

    Married at the residence of the bride's father near Elam-
ville, (Barbour County) on the 25th of Nov., by T. P. C. Phillips,
Esq., Mr. J. M. Smith and Miss Phaney Kennedy.

Sat. Dec. 22, 1883
    Married at the home of the bride's father, Elisha Lasiter,
on Wednesday, by Rev. Dr. Ellison, Mr. Ed Turner and Miss Mary
Lasiter.

Sat. Jan. 5, 1884
    Married on the 29th ult., at the home of Mr. S. M. Duffel,
near Lodi, (Barbour County) by J. F. Walker, Esq., Mr. Albert
Powell, of Skipperville, and Miss Mollie Zorn.

Sat. Jan. 19, 1884
    Married on Thursday at the home of Mr. Alex McKinnon, Mr.
Dixon and Miss Nancy McKinnon.

Sat. Jan. 26, 1884
    Married at Shorterville, (Henry County, Ala.) on Jan. 17th,
by Rev. D. Rogers, Jas. F. Walker, of Barbour County, to Miss
Clara A. Rogers, daughter of the officiating minister.

Sat. Feb. 9, 1884
    Mr. W. M. Lightner, formerly of Alabama, and Miss Belle
Robinson, of Schulinburg, Texas, were married on the 18th.
-Moravia, Lavaca County, Texas, Jan. 28, 1884.

    Col. H. J. Irby and Miss Jennie Crawford were married at
the home of the bride's parents near Eufaula on Sunday.

Sat. Mar. 15, 1884
    Married at the home of the bride's father, Mr. J. E. Parish,
on Thursday, by Rev. Mr. Sanders, Mr. Robert Simonton and Miss
Lizzie Parish.

Sat. June 28, 1884
    Married at the bride's home on 22d of June, Mr. Daniel A.
McGilvary and Mrs. Julia A. Floyd, Rev. Baxter Greer officiating.

48

Married at the Grace Episcopal Church on Wednesday, by Rev.
DeB. Waddell, Henry O. Bassett, of Pensacola, Fla., and Miss
Mittie Kendrick, daughter of Prof. Kendrick of Clayton.

Sat. July 19, 1884
    Married by Justice T. P. C. Phillips, at his residence on
July 10th, Mr. Wm. Whitehurst and Miss Nancy Cockreaw, all of
Barbour County.

EUFAULA WEEKLY TIMES AND NEWS
1884

Tues. Jan. 8, 1884
    Married at the bride's mother in Russell County, on the
26th of Dec. 1883, by Rev. T. A. Johnson, Mr. Geo. W. Hendrix to
Miss Sallie Lou McReili.

Tues. Jan. 15, 1884
    Mr. Lee Smart and Miss Annie Whigham, of Barbour County,
were married on Thursday.

    Married at the residence of G. M. Jordan, by Rev. J. S.
Jordan, S. W. Goldsmith of Stone Mountain, Ga., to Miss C. L.
Price, of Barbour County.

Tues. Jan. 22, 1884
    Married at the home of the bride's father, Capt. J. B.
Thomas, of Jernigan, Ala., by Rev. J. A. Howard, of Seale, Mr.
O. T. Howard, of Eufaula, and Miss Betty Thomas.

Tues. Jan. 29, 1884
    Married at the residence of the bride's father, Mr. D. J.
Peacock, at Hilliardsville, Ala., on the 24th inst., by Geo. L.
Fleming, Esq., Mr. J. A. Campbell and Miss Annie Peacock.

    Married yesterday in Eufaula, at the home of Mr. J. W.
Sheally, Miss Pinkie Sheally and Mr. Stark Perry, of Bullock
County. Mr. W. M. and B. L. Perry attended the wedding.

Tues. Feb. 5, 1884
    Married at the residence of W. S. Cox, near Smithville, on
Jan. 24th, by Rev. J. W. Menefee, Mr. R. A. Cox and Miss Lilla
G. Wingate. -Columbia (Ala.) Enterprise.

    Married at the Methodist Church yesterday, by Rev. Dr.
Andrews, Mr. Wm. W. Flewellen and Miss Willie May Cox. The
attendants were: E. T. Martin and S. T. Barnett, ushers. Mr.
J. M. Thornton and Miss Julia Young; S. P. Foy and Miss Kate
Henry; J. A. Sylvester and Miss Mabel Kendall; C. C. Shorter and
Miss K. Johnston; Ralph Johnston and Miss Julia McRae; Phil
McKay and Miss Anna Sylvester; A. H. Flewellen and Miss Julia
Coleman.

Tues. Feb. 12, 1884
    Married in Tuskaloosa, (Ala.) on the 6th of Feb., Miss
McEachin to Mr. William Fitts.

    Mr. Ephraim Oates and Miss Pink Saunders were married on
the 5th inst., at the residence of Mr. E. A. Saunders, Rev. A. L.
Martin officiating. -Abbeville Times.

Tues. Feb. 19, 1884
    Mr. Joseph N. Haley, of Eufaula, and Miss Augusta L. Shu-
mate, of Early County, Ga., were married at the home of the
bride's parents on yesterday.

49

E. W. McLendon, of Cottontown, (Ala.) and Miss Sophie
McMillen, of the same place, were married there Wednesday.

Mr. A. J. Carver, formerly of Eufaula, was married in
Dawson, Ga., on the 12th inst., to Miss Dixie Cheatham. -Macon
(Ga.) Telegraph.

Tues. Feb. 26, 1884
        Married at the Baptist Church Thursday, Mr. Wm. A. Davis
and Miss Laura Sylvester, by Rev. J. E. Chambliss and Rev. W. N.
Reeves. Attendants: Mr. Chauncey Rhodes, Miss Anna Sylvester;
Mr. J. A. Sylvester, Miss Jennie Davis; Mr. C. C. Shorter, Miss
Ida Bludworth; Mr. Sam Woods, of Savannah, Miss Augusta Lee, of
Greensboro, Ala.; Mr. E. T. Martin, Miss Lula Rainer, of Union
Springs; Mr. and Mrs. W. Flewellen.

Tues. Mar. 4, 1884
        Mr. Geo. Raney, formerly of Eufaula, married Miss Heath, of
Tuskegee, (Ala.) on last Sunday. Mr. Geo. Cotton acted as best
man.

Married at the residence of Mr. T. B. Jones, on 2nd inst.,
by Rev. Dr. T. A. Johnson, Mr. J. D. Woods, of Quitman County,
Ga., to Miss Mattie Vining, of Barbour County.

Tues. Mar. 11, 1884
        Married at the home of the bride's brother, Mr. J. D. God-
win, in Eufaula, yesterday, by Rev. J. E. Chambliss, Miss
Missouri Godwin was married to Judge Garland H. Pryor, of Gains-
ville, Georgia.

Mr. Wm. Oliver, formerly of Eufaula, now of Miss. was
married in Abbeville, (Ala.) yesterday to Miss Dora Calloway.

Tues. Mar. 18, 1884
        Announcement is made of the approaching marriage to Mr.
Chas. Simmons, of Eufaula, to Miss Sarah Dottenheim, of New York,
the event is to take place on Apr. 6th.

Mr. E. F. McKenzie, of Baton Rouge, La., was married Tuesday
in Louisville, Ala., to Miss Lena A. Lampley, daughter of J. A.
Lampley, by Rev. T. H. Stout. The groom is the son of Capt. B.
B. McKenzie, formerly of Barbour County.

Tues. Apr. 1, 1884
        Married at the home of the bride's father, Mr. B. J. Davis,
near Lawrenceville, (Ala.) last Wednesday, Mr. Moran Garet, of
Skipperville, and Miss Sarah Davis.

Married yesterday at the Baptist Church by Rev. Dr. Chamb-
liss, Mr. Edward B. Freeman and Miss Nettie Locke, daughter of
Mrs. W. H. Locke. Attendants: Mr. Sump McTyer and Miss Lula
Locke; Mr. Will Grimes and Miss Ella Locke; Mr. Phil McKay and
Miss Anna Sylvester; Mr. Will Ross and Miss Lillie Drewry; Mr.
Walter Berry and Miss Jennie Lewis, of Perote; Mr. J. R. Barr
and Miss Anna Guice; Mr. Tom Kirksey and Miss Gaitra Brown, of
Hurtsboro; Mr. Will Locke and Miss Minnie Long, of Hurtsboro.

Tues. Apr. 22, 1884
        Married last Tuesday at the M. E. Church in Seale, (Ala.)by
Rev. DeB. Waddell, Mr. J. Boykin Billups, of Pensacola, Fla., to
Miss Madeleine Lewis, of Seale. -Russell (County) Register.

Mr. Chas. A. Smith and Miss Rosa B. Crane were married in
Columbus, (Ga.) on the 16th. They left for a short trip to
Henry County, Ala.

Mr. D. B. Malone, of Savannah, and Miss Annie Powers, daughter of Col. Virgil Powers, of Macon, were married in the Mulberry Street M. E. Church in Macon, (Ga.) on Thursday.

Married at the Baptist Church last night by Rev. Dr. J. E. Chambliss, Mr. Frank Woodruff, of Columbus, Ga., and Miss Ida C. Bludworth, of Eufaula. Attendants: Mr. C. B. Woodruff and Miss Anna Sylvester; Mr. Jno. Peabody, Jr., and Miss Nellie Bray; Mr. D. A. Joseph and Miss Sallie Peabody; Mr. P. B. Patterson and Miss Mamie McGough; Mr. C. L. Davis and Miss Adele Shorter; Mr. S. P. Jones and Miss Annie Barschall; Mr. E. S. Faber and Miss Katie Bray; Mr. A. C. Young and Miss Effie Jennings. Prof. Van Houten presided at the organ.

Tues. Apr. 29, 1884
Mr. Colbert Price, of Eufaula, was married on the 23rd inst., at Aberdeen, Miss., to Miss Callie R. Kidd, of that city. They reached Eufaula yesterday, accompanied by Mr. Ernest Corker, of Eufaula, an attendant at the wedding.

Mr. Geo. E. Smith, of Columbus, Ga., was married to Miss Rosa L. Saunders yesterday at the home of her parents in Henry County, (Ala.) by Rev. H. Urquhart. Attendants: Miss Annie McDaniel, Mr. Z. Smith; Miss Mamie Reaves, Mr. L. Smith; Miss Mamie Bates, Mr. Frank Sanders; Mittie Sanders.

Mr. Geo. T. Brown and Miss Mollie Jones, of Columbia, (Henry County, Ala.) were married at that place last Wednesday.

Tues. May 6, 1884
Miss Maude Manning, daughter of Chief Justice Manning, of La., and G. W. Compton eloped from Alexandria, La., on Saturday, and on reaching Galveston disclosed that they were married. -Special from Marshall, Texas.

Mr. A. C. Mitchell, Jr., of Eufaula, and Miss Annie Dawson Snyder, of Atlanta, were married there on Wednesday, by Bishop Pierce.

Tues. May 20, 1884
Married yesterday, Mr. Ed. P. Blair, formerly of Eufaula, now of Mansfield, La., and Miss Laura Ramser, of Eufaula, by Rev. W. N. Reeves.

Mr. Peter Marshall Brown and Miss Jennie Beecher Bass were married at St. Luke's Church in Columbus, Ga., last Wednesday.

Tues. June 10, 1884
Married at Pine Level Church, on the 1st of June, last, by Rev. B. C. Bennett, Mr. Jno. Helms and Miss Mary Jane Phillips, all of Barbour County.

Married at Midway, Ala., on Sunday, Mr. Emmett Lamar, son of Mr. H. G. Lamar, of Barbour County, and Miss Christian, of the former place.

Tues. July 8, 1884
Married last Tuesday, near Batesville, (Barbour County) by Rev. W. H. Patterson, Mr. J. B. Cunningham, of Memphis, Tenn., and Miss M. E. Castellow, of Batesville.

Tues. Aug. 19, 1884
The marriage of Mr. David Ottensosser, of Eufaula, and Miss Bertha Bodenheimer, of New York City, is announced for the 28th inst.

Married at Apalachicola, Fla., on Thursday last, Mr. Tom Allday and Miss Freddie Woodruff, of Eufaula.

Tues. Sept. 9, 1884
Married on the 3rd inst., at the residence of Mr. A. C. Cargill, by Rev. Dr. J. E. Chambliss, Mr. Orlando J. Cargill and Miss Anna Girkie, all of Barbour County.

Tues. Sept. 16, 1884
Mr. A. U. Grouby was married last week to Miss Jennie Skipper, all of Abbeville.

Charley Lancey, of Abbeville, (Ala.) married Miss Adams, of Fort Gaines, (Ga.).

Married Thursday, Miss Sallie, daughter of Senator Jas. L. Pugh, to Mr. Albert Elliot, of York, Pa.

Tues. Sept. 23, 1884
Mr. D. C. Adams, of Fort Gaines (Ga.) and Miss Lucy Wood, of Columbus, were married Wednesday last.

Married at the residence of the bride's grandmother, Mrs. D. C. Williams, by Rev. T. Y. Ramsey, Jr., on Sept. 11th, 1884, Dr. Chas E. Goodwin and Miss Sallie McLean, all of this city. -Sentinel, Grenada, Miss.

Tues. Sept. 30, 1884
Mr. Scott Helms and Miss Fanny Campbell were married recently by Jas. A. Baxter, Esq. -Clayton Courier.

Sarah, daughter of Mr. and Mrs. Henry Bernstein, is to marry Julius Kaufman, on Wednesday, Oct. 15, 1884, at their residence, 827 Sixth St., Louisville, Ky.

Tues. Oct. 7, 1884
Married in Montgomery on the 1st inst., by Rev. Mr. Taul, Mr. N. C. Duffie, of Eufaula, and Miss Ophelia McDuffie, of Montgomery.

Rev. Mr. Williams, pastor of the Glennville M. E. Church, was married to Miss Claude Glenn, of Glennville, last Wednesday.

Tues. Oct. 14, 1884
Mr. Joshua Burtz and Miss M. Warren, both of Eufaula, were married Sunday at the residence of the bride's mother, by Dr. W. N. Reeves.

Tues. Oct. 28, 1884
Mr. Jas. Lewis, of White Pond, (Barbour County) and Mrs. Laura Hubbard, of Clayton, were married Thursday. -Clayton Courier.

Married at the residence of Mr. and Mrs. Loyd, in Atlanta, Mr. W. D. Williamson and Miss Kate Clark, sister of Mr. Peter F. Clark. The groom is the son of Mr. H. E. Williamson, Sr., and brother of Mrs. E. J. Black and Mr. R. W. Williamson, of Eufaula. Rev. Father Kirsch officiated.

Tues. Nov. 4, 1884
Mr. J. J. Brown and Miss Lula Barron, both of Eufaula, were married yesterday.

Tues. Nov. 18, 1884
Hon. Thos. W. Sadler, of Prattville, (Ala.) was married on Friday to Miss Mamie Bowen, of Autauga County, (Ala.).

W. C. Gissendaner and Miss Phillips, both of Henry County, (Ala.) were married a few days ago. -Abbeville (Ala.) Times.

Tues. Nov. 25, 1884
Mr. Jordan W. West, of Ft. Gaines, (Ga.) and Miss Annie Lou Puckett, of Coleman Station, Ga., were married on the 19th inst., by Rev. John West.

Married at Hillardsville, Tuesday, by Rev. W. H. Patterson, Mr. A. L. Smart, son of W. W. Smart, of Eufaula, and Miss Mollie Cotton, of Hilliardsville, (Ala.).

Tues. Dec. 2, 1884
Married at Hilliardsville, (Ala.) last 25th, by Rev. Scott, Mr. W. B. Goff, of Bryon, Ga., and Miss Lucy Cotton.

Tues. Dec. 9, 1884
John Corbitt and Miss Cassa Hill, of Lawrenceville (Ala.) were married last Sunday. -Abbeville (Ala.) Times.

Jim Batchelor and Miss Jesse Jones, both of Lawrenceville, (Ala.) were married last week.

Prof. A. N. Hawkins and Miss Nannie J. Worthington were married in Abbeville, (Ala.) last Wednesday.

Rev. Edgar M. Glenn was married at Forkland, Ala., to Miss Mary J. Arrington, of Forkland.

Mr. J. T. Young and Miss Laura Powell, both of Briar Hill, Pike County, Ala., were married at Georgetown, Ga., yesterday.

Miss Annie Walton, of Eufaula, was married at the residence of Mr. Geo. Singer, to Mr. L. H. McLaughlin, of Florida, on Wednesday.

Tues. Dec. 16, 1884
O. M. Hill and Miss Lula J. Jones, both of Henry County, (Ala.) were married at Lawrenceville Wednesday. -Abbeville (Ala.) Times.

Mr. Sam H. Solomon, of Clayton, and Miss Lina Bell Threadgill, of Union Springs, (Ala.) were married Tuesday, by Rev. W. K. Motley. Attendants: Dr. J. P. Martin and Miss Thacher Walker; Mr. Frank Watkins and Miss Callie Law; Mr. Cody Thomas and Miss Worman; Mr. Geo. Peach and Miss Sallie Walker; Mr. Fred Worman and Miss Belle Solomon; Mr. Jas. Cowan and Miss Fanny Solomon; Mr. Seab Ramser and Miss McLeod.

Tues. Dec. 23, 1884
Mr. Wm. Eley and Miss Fannie Sheally, both of this county, were married Thursday last, by Rev. T. A. Johnson, at the residence of the bride's father, Mr. J. W. Sheally, near Eufaula.

Tues. Dec. 30, 1884
Mr. Willie Dickson, of Atlanta, and Miss Olie Valette, of New York, were married in New York on Christmas Day. Both formerly of Eufaula.

Married at the residence of the bride's parents, Mr. and Mrs. J. T. Kendall, last evening, Mr. Chas. R. Ross and Miss Florie Kendall, by Rev. E. M. Bounds. Attendants: Mr. Henry A. Young and Miss Mamie McGough; Mr. S. A. Ramser and Miss Julia McRae; Mr. J. L. Ross and Miss Leila Felder, of Americus, Ga.; Mr. Ira Lampley and Miss Julia Young; Mr. Jas. T. Kendall, Jr., and Miss Sarah Ross; Mr. W. J. Ross and Miss Marie Belle Kendall.

1885

Tues. Jan. 6, 1885
Married at the residence of the bride's brother, Mr. K. D.
Nance, by T. P. C. Phillips, Esq., on Christmas Day, Mr. Thos. D.
McKnight, of Dale County, (Ala.) and Miss Lydia Nance, of Barbour
County. -Clayton Courier.

Married at the home of the bride's father, at Lawrenceville,
in Henry County, (Ala.) on Dec. 18th, 1884, by Rev. A. L. Blizzard, Dr. J. I. Darby, of Columbia, (Ala.) and Miss Levonia Hill,
of Lawrenceville. -Columbia (Ala.) Enterprise.

Married on the 25th of Dec. at the residence of the bride's
father near Midway, (Ala.) by Rev. Dr. A. C. Hundley, Mr. E. B.
Bismarkes to Miss Lula Harrison.

Married at the residence of the bride's parents in Eufaula
on Sunday last, by Rev. M. S. Andrews, Mr. Chas. E. Cory and Miss
B. Alice Evans, all of Eufaula.

Tues. Jan. 13, 1885
Married at the home of the bride's brother, Mr. G. W. Jack-
son, of Barbour County, Miss Mollie Jackson to Mr. Chas. E.
Moore, of Madison, Ga., by Rev. W. H. Patterson.

Mr. Walton Hill, of Montgomery, and Miss Alice Fitts, of
Tuscaloosa, were married in the Episcopal Church in Tuscaloosa
on Tuesday last.

Tues. Feb. 10, 1885
Mr. Henry Rice and Miss Florence Ellis were married at the
home of the bride's father in Quitman County, (Ga.) last Wednesday.

Miss Van Hilliard, daughter of Hon. Henry W. Hilliard, is
to wed tonight to Mr. Eugene Spalding, son of Rev. Dr. Spalding,
formerly pastor of the second Baptist Church in Atlanta.

Married on the train between Eufaula and Union Springs
yesterday, Mr. Robt. Moulthrop, Sr., and Mrs. Sallie Dobbins,
both of Eufaula, Rev. W. N. Reeves officiating.

Married Wednesday in Albany, Ga., Mr. A. S. J. Henderson,
of Dawson, (Ga.) and Miss Annie Mayo, by Rev. Geo. W. Mathews.

Tues. Feb. 17, 1885
Gen. Al. Roberts of Austin, Tex., and Miss Jennie Burgess,
of Va., were married recently. The groom was raised in Barbour
County, and is a nephew of Capt. G. A. Roberts, of Eufaula.
-Washington, Jan. 28.

Tues. Feb. 24, 1885
Married yesterday at the home of Mr. G. A. Whittaker in
Georgetown, Ga., by Rev. F. A. Branch, Mr. Geo. E. Hines, of
Athens, Ala., and Miss Kate Watts, daughter of the late Thos. A.
Watts, of Eufaula.

Usher Thomason, son of the late Hon. Oscar Thomason, of
Madison, (Ga.) and Miss Flora Fowler, daugher of M. B. Fowler, of
Covington, Ga., were married at the latter place on the 14th of
Feb.

Tues. Mar. 3, 1885
Married on last Sunday at the home of the bride's parents,
at Cureton's Bridge, Mr. Dan Slaughter, of Barbour County, to
Miss Camilla Cureton, by Rev. A. L. Sellers. -Columbia (Ala.)

Enterprise, 26th.

Married yesterday at the home of Mr. R. C. Walker, in
Eufaula, by Rev. W. H. Patterson, Mr. J. R. Smith, of Georgetown,
Ga., and Miss Loula F. Cory, of Eufaula.

Tues. Mar. 10, 1885
    Married in San Saba, Tex., recently, Mr. Wallace Willing
and Miss May Baker.

Tues. Mar. 17, 1885
    Married at the home of the bride's parents in Clayton, Ala.,
by Rev. W. S. Rogers, Rev. A. L. Blizard and Miss Mollie S.
Quillin. Attendants: J. K. Quillin with Miss V. V. Clayton; E.
C. Thomas with Miss Helen Clayton; Fred Norman with Miss Mamie
Capers; W. C. Petty with Miss Pearla McRae; Ed. Nix with Miss
Fannie Solomon; Rev. B. D. Greer with Miss Lizzie Jones. The
bride is the daughter of Editor E. R. Quillin. The groom is
pastor of the Baptist Church at Columbia, Ala.

Tues. Apr. 7, 1885
    Col. Milton A. Smith and Miss A. E. Posten were married
yesterday at the home of the bride's parents in Barbour County.

    Mr. N. J. Oakley, of Columbia, Ala., and Miss Johnnie Daffin,
of Ft. Gaines, Ga., were married at the latter place on the 26th.

    Edward Mabry and Miss Ella Morgan, of Eufaula, were married
in Texas recently. -Austin County News.

Tues. Apr. 14, 1885
    Married on 9th inst., in the Methodist Church in Americus,
Ga., Mr. Phil McKay, of Eufaula, Ala., and Miss Leila Felder, of
Americus, by Rev. T. M. Lowery, pastor of the Presbyterian Church
in Eufaula. Attendants: Dr. A. Goodwin, of Eufaula, with Miss
Brinson, of Americus; Mr. Jno. W. Bray, of Eufaula, with Miss
Spear, of Americus; Mr. H. A. Young, of Eufaula, with Miss Prince,
of Americus; Mr. Tommie Felder with Miss Ray, both of Americus;
Maj. Lucien Walker, of Montgomery, with Miss Harris, of Ft.
Valley; Mr. Tom Burney with Miss Trammell, of Dalton, Ga.; Mr.
H. D. Clayton, of Eufaula, with Miss Frazer of Union Springs,
Ala.; Mr. C. R. Ross and wife, of Eufaula; Mr. H. Lampley with
Miss Marie Belle Kendall, of Eufaula; Mr. Parker, of Americus,
with Miss Shaw, of Cuthbert.

    Mr. W. A. Bellamy, Sheriff of Russell County, (Ala.) and
Miss Fanny Bickerstaff, of Seale, (Ala.) were married yesterday
in the Baptist Church of Seale.

Tues. May 5, 1885
    Married in Lumpkin, Ga., last Wednesday, Miss Ida Grace and
Dr. F. B. Gregory, of Stewart County, (Ga.).

    Married in Montgomery on Thursday, at the home of the
bride's father, Jno. W. Shepherd, Esq., by Rev. Dr. Stingfellow,
Mr. Alexander Knowles and Miss Roberta Shepherd. -Montgomery
(Ala.) Advertiser, of 1st inst. The groom was raised in Barbour
County, and is a brother of Frank Knowles, of Eufaula.

Tues. May 26, 1885
    The marriage of Miss Frances Strasburger, of Montgomery, to
Mr. Leopold Plant, of London, England, will take place at the
Temple in Montgomery, May 27th.

    Mr. Fred S. Singer, of Lumpkin, Ga., formerly of this city,
and Miss Annie Hightower were married on the 20th inst., in the

M. E. Church in Lumpkin, by Rev. J. S. Jordan.

Tues. June 2, 1885
    Mr. Frank Boykin, of Montgomery, and Miss Ellen Walker, of
Suspension, Bullock County, (Ala.) were married last Wednesday.

Tues. June 9, 1885
    Married at the home of Mr. Thos. S. Smart, of Barbour County,
on Wednesday, by Rev. J. B. Cumming, Miss Emma Smart and Mr. Jno.
T. Grubbs, of Louisville, (Ala.).

Tues. June 16, 1885
    Mr. Jno. Z. Solomon married on the 2nd inst., in Ochesee,
Fla., in Jackson County, to Miss Eva Lidden.

Tues. June 23, 1885
    Mr. M. W. Wimberly, of Greenville, and Miss Jimmie Ware, of
Opelika, were married in Opelika Tuesday last.

    Mr. Allison Lockwood, of Mobile, and Miss Mary Saunders, of
Va., were married Wednesday last at Verbena, (Ala.).

Tues. June 30, 1885
    Married on 24th inst., in Verbena, (Ala.), Mr. J. F. Thorn-
ton and Mrs. Sallie H. Jackson, daughter of the late Capt. Henry
C. Hart.

    Married in Sumner, Ga., on 22nd inst., Mr. C. S. Williams,
of Dawson, Ga., and Miss Emma Johnson, daughter of the Rev. Dr.
T. A. Johnson, of Barbour County.

    Married at Selma (Ala.) at the Baptist Church, Mr. Isaac
R. Eshew and Miss Minnie Goodwin, both of Selma.

Tues. July 14, 1885
    Married at the residence of the bride's father, S. R. Ogle-
tree, Esq., in Georgetown, Ga., Mr. Edgar Oliver and Miss Carrie
Ogletree, by Rev. W. H. Patterson.

Tues. July 21, 1885
    Mr. Thos. J. Barney, of Macon, Ga., was married to Miss
Franziska Settegast, of Coblenz, Germany, in Augusta, Ga., on
Monday last. The bride is a sister of Mrs. Jas. Barrett, of
Augusta.

Tues. Aug. 4, 1885
    Married recently at Jacksonville, Ala., Otto Agricola and
Miss Katie Hamlin, daughter of Probate Judge Hamlin, of Gadsden,
Ala. Also Frank Cottrell and Miss Pickens, all of Gadsden.

    Miss Eva Cuckler and Mr. Thos. E. Daniel were married in
Atlanta on the 28th inst.

Tues. Aug. 18, 1885
    Mr. Robt. Dueweis and Miss Stella Stokes, of Smithville,
(Ga.) were married in Americus, Ga., by Rev. Dr. Mann on Tuesday.

Tues. Sept. 1, 1885
    Mr. Arthur Small McIver, of the Tuskegee News, and Miss
Maggie Fraser, of Sumpter C. H., South Carolina, were married at
the latter place on the 20th inst.

    Mr. Cage Doughtery and Miss Maggie Dufel, of Eufaula were
married Wednesday, by Rev. Loveless. Mr. Doughtery came to
Eufaula from Virginia several years ago.

Tues. Sept. 8, 1885
Married on 3rd inst., at the office of Justice A. M. McLendon, Mr. J. F. Howland and Miss Phinnie Hooten, all of Barbour County.

Fri. Sept. 25, 1885
Mr. J. B. Dryer and Miss Alice Griggs were married in Tuskegee last Wednesday.

Fri. Oct. 16, 1885
Married on Wednesday at the home of the bride's parents in Eufaula, by Rev. Dr. G. A. Nunnally, Mr. Jno. W. Huddleston and Miss Fannie Bayne.

Married yesterday at the Arlington (Hotel in Eufaula), by Rev. G. A. Nunnally, D. D., Mr. Henry H. Parker and Miss Ella Locke, both of Eufaula.

Mr. Jno. Hasselton and Miss Fanny May Miller, both of Montgomery, were married at the Adams Street Baptist Church in that city on Thursday, by Rev. Dr. Wamboldt.

Fri. Oct. 23, 1885
Mr. T. M. Crumption and Miss W. L. Stoddard, of Benton (Ala.) were married on Sunday last.

Mr. C. A. Sheally and Miss Bessie Meriwether, both of Bullock County, were married on the 14th inst.

Married at the home of Mr. Jno. Green, father of the bride, on 15th inst., by Rev. W. H. Patterson, Mr. Francis M. Gray and Miss E. Fannie Green, both of Quitman County, Ga.

Fri. Nov. 6, 1885
Married at Forkland, Green County, (Ala.) on Nov. 3d, S. A. Powell, of Batesville, to Miss Elberta DeMoville, Rev. Mr. Glenn officiating. Attendants were: Barlow DeMoville and Miss Lucy Cochran, of Tuscaloosa; C. C. Shorter and Miss Lidie Gary, of Meridian, Miss.; J. D. Bell and Miss Lucy Lockett, of Forkland; Turner D. Patterson and Miss Nellie Guild, of Tuscaloosa.

Mr. C. F. Rankin, of Brewton, (Ala.) and Miss Susie Martin, of Union Springs, were married on Thursday last.

Married at the home of Col. and Mrs. Sterling B. Toney yesterday, Mr. Sidney S. Muir and Miss Sarah L. Burge, by Rev. Mr. Minneqerode. Attendants were: Misses M. Louise, Anna, and Hallie Louise Burge and Mamie Johnston; best man friend of the groom, Mr. Harvey A. Dudley, and Mr. Robt. Moore. Ushers were Mr. Lewis Burret, Mr. Henry Smith and Mr. S. White. -Louisville (Ky.) Commercial, 28th.

Fri. Nov. 13, 1885
Mr. W. M. Hurst, druggist of Opelika, and Miss Mittie Robertson, of Gold Hill, Lee County, were married on the 10th inst.

Thurs. Nov. 26, 1885
Mr. Sherwood Swanson and Miss Mattie Corsey, both of Tuskegee, were married at West Point, Ga., last Wednesday.

Thurs. Dec. 3, 1885
Mr. W. L. O'Neal, of Columbus, Ga., and Miss Johnnie McLeod, of Hurtsboro, (Ala.) were married on the 28th ult.

Mr. E. D. Clenny and Miss Mollie Corbitt were married

recently near Lawrenceville, Henry County, (Ala.).

Thurs. Dec. 10, 1885
Mr. J. B. Lovelace, of Marion, (Ala.) and Mrs. Mary A. Parker, of Montgomery, were married in Tuskegee on Thursday, by Rev. M. B. Wharton.

Prof. A. M. Kelly and Miss Lula Murphy, both living near Abbeville, were married last Saturday.

Mr. Donald McDonald, of Montgomery, and Miss Hennie Pope, of Mobile, were married in the latter city last Tuesday. On the same day, Mr. Chas. N. Stanton and Miss Ella Weems, both of Mobile, were married by Bishop O'Sullivan.

Thurs. Dec. 17, 1885
Mr. Forbes Liddell, of Montgomery, and Miss Myra Ravenscroft, of Troy, (Ala.) were married Monday.

Mr. W. Frank Watkins and Miss Parrie Hill, both of Clayton, were married at the M. E. Church in Clayton on 10th inst., by Rev. C. B. Pilley. Attendants were: Mr. I. L. Watkins with Miss Mary Clayton; Mr. Jeff Quillin with Miss Mattie Stephens; Dr. Phil. Martin with Miss Vic Clayton; Mr. A. H. Thomas with Miss Mary Vickers; Mr. Dan Mabry with Miss Ada Gary; Mr. Jim Nix with Miss Weetie Warren; Mr. Will Ross with Miss May Parish; Mr. Fred Norman with Miss Carrie Mabry; Mr. Ed. Parish with Miss Mary Foster; Mr. Walter Petty with Miss Pearl Foster; Ella Parish and Iola Mabry.

Thurs. Dec. 24, 1885
Mr. Willis D. Holland, of Shelby County, (Ala.) and Miss Mollie V. Gilmer, of Selma, were married in that city last Wednesday, and in the same city and the same day, Mr. A. B. Butler and Miss Annie Dainwood, also, Mr. Frank Cater, of Montgomery, and Miss Bettie F. Coleman.

Miss Willie Harris, of Tuskegee, and Mr. A. B. Vandergrift, of Montgomery, were married on Wednesday.

Miss Della Attaway, of Tuskegee, and Mr. W. A. McKenney, of Hearne, Texas, were married Wednesday.

Married at the home of the bride's mother in Borumville, Dec. 13, Mr. Wm. M. Mitchell and Miss Naomi Key, by I. P. Cheney. (Russell County, Ala.).

Miss Della Massey, daughter of Hon. Chas. F. Massey, and Hon. Alex. H. Thomas were married in Fort Gaines, Ga., on Tuesday.

Mr. Tom Maybin and Miss Gussie Camp were married on the 20th at Clopton, Dale County, (Ala.). Also, on the same day and place, Mr. Benj. J. Lindsey and Miss Jordan, of Texas, were married.

Hon. J. M. Carmichael, of Ozark, was married a few days ago to Miss Emma Beard, of Elba, (Ala.).

Married at the home of the bride's father, by Rev. A. L. Martin, on the 20th inst., Mr. O. T. Hutto and Miss Rosa McLendon. -Abbeville (Ala.) Spirit of the Age, 23d.

Married at the home of the bride's parents in Eufaula yesterday, by Rev. W. H. Patterson, Mr. Frank Stevens and Miss Lula Clark.

Thurs. Dec. 31, 1885
Married in Birmingham on Christmas Day, Wm. Oppendyke, of

Wheeling, and Miss Sarah Thomas, of Birmingham, by Rev. D. I. Purser.

Mr. W. J. Holleman, of Eufaula, and Miss Annie Roland were married in Columbus, (Ga.) on the 26th inst., by Rev. J. W. Howard.

Married on the 24th inst., at the home of the bride's parents in Midway, (Ala.) by Rev. W. H. Patterson, Rev. R. T. Goodrum, of Thomaston, Ga., and Miss Ida Lee Jordan.

Married on the 24th inst., at the home of the bride's brother Mr. L. E. Irby, in Eufaula, by Rev. W. H. Patterson, Mr. H. R. Lewis, of Inverness, Bullock County, (Ala.) and Miss Lula Irby.

THE EUFAULA DAILY TIMES
1886

Sun. Jan. 3, 1886
Mr. J. W. Pollard, of New Berne, Ala., and Miss Bennie Thompson were married at the home of the bride's parents in Union Springs, (Ala.) last Thursday.

Mr. Robt. E. Sheehan, of Eufaula, and Miss Mary E. Holland, of Abbeville, (Ala.) were married in Abbeville on the 31st ult.

Tues. Jan. 5, 1886
Married at the home of the bride's father on 31st of Dec., at White Pond, (Barbour County) Mr. Monroe Adams and Miss Eugenia Creel, by Squire Williams.

Wed. Jan. 6, 1886
Married at her mother's home in Barbour County, by Rev. R. B. Lee, on Thursday last, Mrs. Lydia Weaver and Mr. H. J. Pipkins, of Henry County, (Ala.).

Thurs. Jan. 7, 1886
Mr. R. H. Camp, of Talladega, Ala., and Miss Ada Edmonds, of Franklin, Ky., eloped on New Year's Day and were married in Richmond, Ky.

Married at the home of the bride's father, Col. A. C. Mitchell, in Glennville, (Ala.) Mr. Thos. Reynolds, Jr., of Montgomery, and Miss Mollie Mitchell.

Wed. Jan. 13, 1886
Hon. Geo. P. Harrison, of Opelika, and Mattie Ligon, of Tuskegee, were married yesterday at the latter place.

Married in Quitman County, Ga., Mr. Jno. Going, of Columbus, Ga., and Miss Maud Railey, on Jan. 12, 1886.

Sat. Jan. 16, 1886
Married on the 10th inst., by Rev. A. L. Blizzard, Mr. Andrew Whiddon and Miss M. E. Barnes, (Henry County, Ala.).

Tues. Jan. 19, 1886
Mr. Dan M. Weston, late of Eufaula, and Miss M. J. Gatewood, of Old Spring Hill, in Barbour County, were married in Georgetown on 17th inst., by Esq. Lewis.

Wed. Jan. 20, 1886
Mr. Dan. M. Weston, late of Eufaula, and Miss M. J. Gatewood, of Old Spring Hill, in Barbour County, were married in Georgetown on 17th inst., by Esq. Lewis.

Thurs. Jan. 21, 1886
    Married on 17th inst., at the home of Mr. M. V. Capps, by
Rev. A. L. Blizzard, Mr. Wm. Murphy and Miss Janie Capps.
-Abbeville (Ala.) Spirit of the Age.

Fri. Jan. 22, 1886
    Miss Clara Quintard, daughter of Bishop Quintard, and Prof.
B. Lawson Wiggins will be married at Sewanee on Wednesday. The
groom is professor of Latin and Greek in the University of the
South at Sewanee. -Montgomery (Ala.) Advertiser.

    Florence, Jan. 20 - W. C. Campbell and Mrs. Mary C. O'Neal,
both of Florence, were married today. The bride is a daughter
of Gov. O'Neal.

Sat. Jan. 23, 1886
    Mr. B. P. Garner and Mrs. Callie Ezell, both of this place,
(Ozark, Ala.) were married on Sunday last. -Ozark Star, 20th.

    Mr. Angus P. Ingraham, of Ft. Gaines, Ga., and Miss Carrie
Wood, of Lafayette, Ala., were married on Tuesday last.

Sun. Jan. 24, 1886
    Mr. F. B. Vann and Miss Katie Brannon were married in Seale,
Russell County, (Ala.) last Thursday.

Thurs. Jan. 28, 1886
    Capt. J. B. Cox, of Troy, (Ala.) and Miss Mary A. Herndon
were married in New Orleans a few days since.

Sat. Jan. 30, 1886
    Miss Kate Gaston and Mr. E. P. Rentz will be married at
Union Point, Ga., on Feb. 4th.

Sun. Jan. 31, 1886
    Mr. Paul A. Floyd and Miss Maggie Schmidt, both of Demopolis,
(Ala.) were married at the Episcopal Church of that place Thursday.

Wed. Feb. 3, 1886
    Married yesterday at the home of the bride's mother, Mrs.
S. A. Toney, at "Roseland", near Eufaula, Dr. C. H. Bradford, of
St. Louis, and Mrs. Carrie H. Cochran.

Thurs. Feb. 4, 1886
    Mr. J. L. Ward, of Abbeville, (Ala.) and Miss Lilla Phipps,
of Hardwicksburg, (Henry County, Ala.) were married on the 26th
ult.

    Mr. Ezekiel A. Hudson, of Eufaula, and Miss Mamie E. Jackson
were married at the home of the bride's parents in Montgomery
today.

Fri. Feb. 5, 1886
    Married at the Catholic Church on Feb. 4th, by Rev. Father
Fullerton, Mr. D. C. Tully, of Lockport, N. Y., and Miss Lizzie
Eagan, of Eufaula.

Thurs. Feb. 11, 1886
    Mr. Berrin Saunders and Mrs. A. F. Catching were married at
Shorterville, (Henry County, Ala.) on the 2d inst.

Fri. Feb. 12, 1886
    Mr. L. P. Arthur, of Shellman, Ga., and Miss Mattie Kaigler,

of Georgetown, (Ga.) were married on Wednesday at the home of
Hon. R. J. Reynolds in Henry County, (Ala.).

Dr. J. M. Saddler and Miss Etta Key were married at the
Episcopal Church in Uniontown, (Ala.) on Tuesday last.

Sun. Feb. 14, 1886
        The marriage of Mr. Jas. Solomon and Miss Pearl Reynolds,
niece of Hon. R. J. Reynolds, all of Henry County, (Ala.) took
place this morning at the home of Mr. Reynolds, near Abbeville.

Wed. Feb. 17, 1886
        Mr. Geo. J. Montgomery and Miss Ella Hurston, both of
Montgomery, (Ala.) were married in that city on Monday last.

Sat. Feb. 20, 1886
        Mr. E. W. Barr and Miss A. E. Pullins, both of Selma, (Ala.)
were married in that city on Wednesday.

Tues. Feb. 23, 1886
        Mr. Thos. Coleman and Miss Eulah White were married at the
home of the bride, near Salem, Lee County, (Ala.) on Thursday
last.

Fri. Feb. 26, 1886
        The marriage of Mr. Geo. B. Davis and Miss Sallie Davis
took place yesterday at the First Baptist Church in Eufaula.
The ushers were Messrs. Jamie Rhodes, and Jeff Davis. The
attendants were: Mr. P. B. McKenzie with Miss Abbie Ogletree;
Mr. W. H. Jones with Miss Jennie Davis.

Married at the home of the bride's parents near Eufaula on
the 24th inst., by W. H. Patterson, Mr. Frank Martin and Miss
Ella A. Dobbins.

Fri. Mar. 5, 1886
        Married at the home of the bride's father at Clopton, Ala.,
Mar. 3rd, 1886, Hon. W. H. Lawson to Miss Jennie L. Steagall,
daughter of Dr. W. C. Steagall.

Sun. Mar. 7, 1886
        Mr. E. Farrier and Miss Flora Ivey were married in Montgo-
mery on Thursday.

Sat. Mar. 13, 1886
        Mr. Andrew Braxton and Miss Ida Hightower were married in
Bullock County, (Ala.) on the 7th.

W. C. Granger and Miss Annie C. Darden, and also, Mr. W. H.
Harrison and Miss Visa Granger, all of Granger, in Dale County,
(Ala.) were married recently.

Thurs. Mar. 18, 1886
        Mr. Jno. H. Ketchum, of the Blount County News, in Blounts-
ville, Ala., was married last Sunday at Hanceville, (Ala.) to
Miss Lizzie Ashwander.

Wed. Mar. 24, 1886
        Mr. Wm. J. Graves and Miss Sarah Wade, of Marion, (Ala.)
eloped on Monday last and were married in Columbus, Ga.

Mr. Jas. Jones and Miss Alice McClusky, both of Tallassee,
(Ala.) eloped last Sunday.

Fri. Mar. 25, 1886

Mr. J. T. Lackland, lawyer of Grove Hill, Ala., and Miss
Alice M. Berry, daughter of Mr. W. W. Berry, of Russell County,
(Ala.) were married last Wednesday at the home of the bride's
parents.

Fri. Apr. 9, 1886
Married Apr. 8th at the home of J. E. Duskin, Mr. Wm. C.
Grimes and Miss Francis E. Williford, all of Eufaula. The groom's
father lives in Stewart County, Ga.

Thurs. Apr. 15, 1886
Married at the home of Dr. Dozier, the bride's father, in
Quitman County, (Ga.) yesterday, by Rev. P. S. Twitty, Mrs. Jas.
H. Hill, of Bronwood, Ga., and Miss Willie L. Dozier.

Sat. Apr. 17, 1886
Mr. J. F. Hooper and Miss Nellie Gray were married in the
Presbyterian Church in Selma, (Ala.) on Thursday.

Mr. Jesse Wood and Miss Alice C. Tison, of Eyre Villa, near
Dentz, Butte County, Calif., celebrated their silver wedding on
Apr. 16th. They were married in Barbour County.

Married at Sing Sing, New York, on the 15th inst., Mr. Geo.
B. Burbank of Sing Sing, and Miss Emma Hyatt, all of Eufaula.

Sun. Apr. 18, 1886
Married at the home of Hon. R. J. Reynolds near Abbeville,
on Apr. 11th, Mr. Jno. W. Lingo and Miss Sallie Ward, both of
Henry County, (Ala.).

Wed. Apr. 21, 1886
W. H. Hooker, editor of the Opelika Times, and Miss Effie
Sims, of Grantville, Ga., were married at Grantville on Sunday,
by Dr. W. S. Brady.

Fri. Apr. 23, 1886
Mr. F. S. Persons and Miss Kate M. Abrams were married at
the Baptist Church in Greenville, (Ala.) last Thursday.

Mr. R. Stout, of Montgomery, and Miss Zemula Vass, of Mobile,
were married Wednesday at the latter city.

Wed. Apr. 28, 1886
Rev. Mr. Crawford Jackson, of Stewart Circuit, was married
at Cuthbert, (Ga.) yesterday to Miss Hernie Sherman, by Rev.
Jas. Key.

Sun. May 2, 1886
Mr. J. A. Daniels and Miss M. F. Wilkes, of Barbour County,
were married in Clayton on Thursday last.

Sat. May 8, 1886
Married on May 6th, 1886, at the home of the bride's mother
in Eufaula, Dr. Egbert B. Johnston and Miss Lula K. Bedell, by
Rev. Loveless.

Sun. May 9, 1886
Mr. L. F. Dixon and Miss Electra Smith were married in the
Methodist Church in Opelika, (Ala.) Thursday.

Wed. May 12, 1886
Mr. Allen J. Driver and Chook Frederic were married last
evening in LaFayette, Chambers County, (Ala.).

Married at the home of the bride's parents in Clayton on
May 9, 1886, Mr. Wyley Williams of Columbus, Ga., and Miss
Victoria Clayton, daughter of Gen. and Mrs. Henry D. Clayton.

Fri. May 14, 1886
Mr. A. E. Dudley and Miss J. E. Dudley, of Lowndes County,
were married in Cuthbert, Ga., yesterday. -Montgomery Advertiser.

Sat. May 15, 1886
Married at the home of Mr. A. B. Johnson, May 14, 1886, by
Rev. E. L. Loveless, Mr. Douglas L. Guerry, of Eufaula, and Miss
Laura L. Johnson, of Arlington, Ga.

Sun. May 16, 1886
Married at the home of Mr. J. D. Peters, father of the
bride, on 9th inst., Mr. E. H. Murdock to Miss Emma Peters.

Tues. May 18, 1886
Married in Georgetown, (Ga.) on Sunday, at the home of the
bride's parents, Mr. J. W. Thompson, of Eufaula, to Miss Minnie
Graddy.

Wed. May 19, 1886
Married at the home of the bride's parents in Metropolis,
Ill., on May 12, 1886, Mr. Chas. E. Veal, of Eufaula, and Miss
Nettie R. Peter, Rev. L. W. Thrall officiating.

Thurs. May 20, 1886
Mr. J. Colbert Price and Miss Ella Hudgins, of Corinth,
Miss., were married in that city on last Tuesday.

Sat. May 22, 1886
Mr. Horatio Vaughn and Miss Sallie McCartha were married in
Newton, (Dale County, Ala.) on Sunday last. -Ozark Star.

Thurs. May 27, 1886
Mr. and Mrs. Evan P. Howell, of Atlanta, (Ga.) will celebrate
their silver wedding on the 5th of June.

Sun. May 30, 1886
Mr. Wm. Bodeford and Miss Mollie Richardson, of Lee County,
(Ala.) were married on Friday, by Justice Wooten.

Fri. June 4, 1886
Mr. W. B. Long and Miss Nancy Hinson were married recently
by H. L. Lisenby. -Abbeville (Ala.) Age, 1st.

Rev. Dr. R. H. Rivers and Mrs. Rivers will celebrate their
golden wedding in Louisville, Ky., where Rev. Rivers has a church.

Sat. June 19, 1886
Married at the home of Mr. R. C. Walker on June 17th, by
Rev. W. H. Patterson, Miss Anna Cory, of Eufaula, and Dr. Wm. P.
Walden, of Cotton Hill, Ala. (Note: In the next issue of this
paper the above item was corrected to read as shown.)

Thurs. June 24, 1886
Married last night at the home of the bride's mother in
Eufaula, Mr. Jno. H. Hagerty, formerly of Cincinnati, now of
Eufaula, and Miss Nora Homer.

Wed. July 7, 1886
Married yesterday at the home of the bride's father, Mr.

Jacob Ramser in Eufaula, Mr. Joe Crawford, of Tallahassee, formerly of Eufaula, and Miss Anna Ramser. The couple left for
Waelder, Texas.

Fri. July 9, 1886
    Married at the home of Mr. G. W. Johnston, of Georgetown,
(Ga.) yesterday, Mr. A. M. Pournell, of Hague, Fla., to Miss
Belle Widener, of Georgetown.

    Married at the Methodist Church at Summerfield, Mr. R. T. S.
Bell, of Pratt Mines, and Miss Lucy Jackson, daughter of Dr. F.
W. Jackson, of Dallas County, (Ala.). Attendants were: Mr. R. W.
Jackson and Miss Alice Cory; Mr. Chas. Strider and Miss Eva Mae
Vaughan; Mr. Robt. Poole and Miss Ellie Hudson.

Wed. Aug. 11, 1886
    Miss Verna Hartman, of Columbus, and Mr. Michael Mechaca,
of New Orleans, were married in the former city on Monday.

Sat. Aug. 14, 1886
    Miss Buena V. Kendricks of Clayton and Mr. Cameron Dow, of
Pensacola, Fla., were married at Clayton on Thursday.

Tues. Sept. 7, 1886
    Mr. Earnest McCarty, of Midway, son of Rev. McCarty, and
Miss Tallulah Davis, of Prattville, will be married next Thursday.

Wed. Sept. 8, 1886
    Mr. Berthold Scheuer, of Eufaula, and Miss Lillie Denzer,
were married yesterday in New York at the Metropolitan Opera
House.

Fri. Sept. 17, 1886
    W. E. Danzey and Miss Nannie Baker of Henry County, (Ala.)
were married at Fort Gaines, (Ga.) last Sunday.

Wed. Sept. 22, 1886
    Maj. Wm. McDaniel was married last Sunday to Miss Laura
Powell at the residence of the bride's uncle at Clopton, (Ala.).

Thurs. Sept. 23, 1886
    Miss Lillie G. Lightfoot, daughter of the late Col. N. N.
Lightfoot, and Mr. Sterling P. Bradley, son of Hon. J. F. Bradley, were married last Tuesday, all of Abbeville, Ala.

Fri. Sept. 24, 1886
    Mr. A. G. Forbes and Miss Clara DeWitt, of Montgomery, were
married Wednesday.

Sun. Sept. 25, 1886
    Mr. Whitfield Dill, now of Chelsea, Mass., and Miss Leona
Hightower, of Texas, were married two weeks ago, and are now in
Clayton visiting old friends. Mr. Dill and his wife were both
raised at Clayton.

Thurs. Sept. 30, 1886
    Mr. A. R. Adams and Miss Melindy M. Jernigan, both of
Belcher, in Barbour County, were married at the home of Mr. J. C.
Deshazo yesterday, by Dr. E. L. Loveless.

Thurs. Oct. 7, 1886
    Married on Sept. 30th, 1886, at the home of the bride's
father, near Hardwicksburg, by Rev. D. Rodgers, Mr. H. T. Miller

and Miss S. A. Roberts. -Abbeville (Ala.) Age.

Mr. W. G. McMakin, of Bartow County, Ga., and Miss Laura A. Coleman, of Glennville, (Ala.) were married on the 30th ult., at the former home of Mrs. Spurlock of Eufaula, at Maple Hill, Ga., by Rev. G. S. Tumlin, pastor of the Baptist Church at Marietta, Ga. (Note: In the next issue of the paper this item was corrected to read as above.)

Married at the home of the bride near Headland, Sept. 29th, by Rev. G. S. Stanton, Mr. Jno. Smith and Mrs. Martha Locke. -Abbeville (Ala.) Age.

Fri. Oct. 22, 1886
Married on the 17th inst., at the home of Rev. J. W. Malone, Col. R. M. Hardwich, of Hardwicksburg, and Miss Ella Foster, of Georgia. -Abbeville (Ala.) Age.

Tues. Nov. 2, 1886
Married at the home of the bride's parents in Georgetown, (Ga.) on Sunday, by Rev. Dr. Reeves, of Eufaula, Mr. J. D. Martin and Miss Sallie Jackson.

Thurs. Nov. 4, 1886
Married at the home of the bride in Eufaula, last night, by Father Fullerton, Mr. Geo. Sangree to Miss Charlotte James.

Fri. Nov. 5, 1886
Miss Eula Spurlock, of Eufaula, was married Wednesday to Dr. W. A. Johnson, of Rome, Ga., in Georgetown, (Ga.) by Rev. Lewis. Attendants were: Mr. Ralph Williams and Miss Abbie Ogletree.

Sun. Nov. 7, 1886
Married at the home of the bride's father, W. H. Castellow, on Nov. 3d, 1886, Mr. J. H. Hillhouse, of Worth County, Ga., and Miss Orie Castello.

Tues. Nov. 9, 1886
Married at the residence of Mrs. J. N. Bowdon, in Eufaula, on yesterday, by Rev. Dr. Loveless, Dr. E. H. Locke, of Troy, (Ala.) to Mrs. Lou Cawthon.

To be married at the Presbyterian Church in Eufaula this afternoon, by Rev. F. B. Webb, of Union Springs, Miss Leila Stow, daughter of Mr. E. Stow, and Mr. B. A. Beach, of Columbia, (Ala.). Attendants: Miss Stella Massey and Mr. Moody, of Columbia; Miss Sallie Ross and Mr. Jas. Rhodes; Miss Marie Belle Kendall and Mr. C. O. Locke; Miss Dell Martin and Mr. W. F. Locke; Miss Eva Beach and Mr. Jno. Hayes, of Columbia; Miss Florrie Jennings and Mr. C. H. Beach; Miss Jennie McRae and Mr. Willis Berry; Miss Fannie McRae and Mr. E. Stow, Jr.

Tues. Oct. 16, 1886
Mr. R. E. L. Martin and Mrs. Susie Powers are to be married in Eufaula today at the home of the bride's mother, Mrs. Jennings, by Rev. Dr. Spaulding.

Thurs. Nov. 28, 1886
Married on the 14th inst., near Headland, by Rev. G. S. Stanton, Mr. B. L. Herring and Miss E. L. Harrison. -Abbeville (Ala.) Age.

Sat. Nov. 20, 1886

Married on Tuesday last, at the home of the bride's father, Maj. Jno. Bland, by Esq., Lancy, Mr. Kay and Mrs. Ella Seymore. Mrs. Seymore was the relict of Barney Seymore. -Abbeville (Ala.) Times. (Note: Nov. 25th paper contained additional data to make the above item read as shown).

Married in Augusta, Ga., on Nov. 16th, by Rector C. C. Williams, Miss Sallie V. Catteville, of Augusta, to Mr. H. C. Cunningham, of Steam Mills, Ga.

Thurs. Dec. 2, 1886
Miss Lila Allen, daughter of Gen. and Mrs. W. W. Allen, of Montgomery, was married in that city yesterday to Mr. Albert Sidney Lyons.

Sun. Dec. 5, 1886
Married at the home of the bride's mother near Louisville, Ala., by Rev. C. M. Shepperson, on Nov. 25th, Mr. Chas. Jones and Miss Ada Shipman, both of Barbour County. -Clayton Courier.

Thurs. Dec. 9, 1886
Married in Eufaula yesterday at the home of the bride's mother, Mrs. Roxana Wellborn, by Rev. Dr. G. A. Nunnally, Mr. J. E. Griffin, of James, Ala., and Mrs. L. S. Wellborn.

To be married today at the Presbyterian Church in Eufaula, Miss Minnie Bray, only daughter of Hon. Wells J. Bray, to Mr. B. Lloyd Guice. Attendants: Mr. Tandy Guice and Miss Kate Daniels, of Boston; Mr. L. McDowell and Miss Nellie Bray; Mr. G. W. Whitlock and Miss Katie Bray; Mr. Jno. W. Bray and Miss Ida Guice; Mr. Chas. L. Bray and Miss Stella Massey; Mr. Joseph W. Bray and Miss Annie McCormick; Mr. P. B. McKenzie and Miss Ellie Richter; Mr. W. H. Foy and Miss Anna Guice; Mr. Geo. Beauchamp and Miss Lillie Drewry; Mr. J. E. Long and Miss Bessie Simpson. Ushers: Wm. Bray, Henry Young, S. B. McTyre, and F. W. Bray.

Tues. Dec. 14, 1886
Geo. A. Dawson, of Louisiana, and Miss Alice Lemon, of Washington, were married in Indiana on Nov. 27th.

Thurs. Dec. 16, 1886
Dr. J. A. Balkum, of Henry County, and Miss Hattie Byrd, of Cold Springs, Tex., were married at the latter place on Dec. 8th inst. -Abbeville (Ala.) Age.

Wed. Dec. 22, 1886
Married last Sunday in Georgetown, Ga., at the home of Mr. R. G. Morris, by Rev. F. A. Branch, Mr. Joe Winslet to Miss Nellie Schenck, all of Quitman County.

Married on the 16th inst., at the home of the bride's parents near Shorterville, by Rev. A. L. Martin, Mr. J. H. Andrews, of Thomaston, Ga., and Miss Theodosia Perryman. -Abbeville (Ala.) Age. (Note: In the next issue of the paper this item was corrected to read as above.)

Married on the 19th inst., at the home of the bride's father, Mr. Jno. H. Spivy of near Abbeville, Miss Ella Spivy and Prof. G. B. Weaver, of Ellaville, Schely County, Ga. -Abbeville (Ala.) Age.

Thurs. Dec. 23, 1886
Rev. Mr. Dannelly and Miss Stevens, both of Louisville, (Ala.) were married in Georgetown, (Ga.) yesterday.

Miss Clara Swanson was married in Midway, (Ala.) on Wednesday to Mr. Pryor Hall.

Fri. Dec. 24, 1886
Mr. Jas. H. Laborous, of Abbeville, (Ala.) and Miss Janie Parmer, of Midway, (Ala.) were married yesterday.

Tues. Dec. 28, 1886
Mr. M. W. Roberts and Miss Rena Carr, both of Clopton, Henry County, (Ala.) were married at Georgetown, Ga. recently.

Fri. Dec. 31, 1886
Married at the home of the bride's father, Mr. Thos. J. Reeves, on Wednesday, by Rev. Junius Jordan, Miss Minnie E. Reeves, of Barbour County, and Mr. Asa A. Williams, of Henry County. Attendants were: Mr. A. McA. Williams and Miss Foy Reeves; Mr. Clarence Howell and Miss Lou Posten; Mr. Zeke Smith and Miss Mamie Posten; Mr. DeLacy Smith and Miss Queen Harvell.

1887

Fri. Jan. 7, 1887
Macon, Ga., Jan. 5 - Secretary Lamar and Mrs. Henrietta Holt, widow of the late Gen. A. S. Holt, were married in this city this morning at the home of the bride, by Rev. Wm. Park. They will visit Mrs. Mays, the daughter of Mr. Lamar, and Mrs. Jas. Ross, his sister, in Oxford, Miss., before going to Washington, D. C.

Married at the home of the bride's mother near Abbeville, (Ala.) on Jan. 2d, Mr. Jas. J. Tiller and Miss Lizzie Holley, by Z. W. Laney, Esq. -Abbeville Age.

Sat. Jan. 8, 1887
Mr. A. W. Holley, of Ft. Gaines, (Ga.) and Miss Jennie E. Holmes, of Henry County, (Ala.) were married Thursday at the residence of Mrs. Mike Holmes, by Rev. Dr. Martin, of Abbeville.

Tues. Jan. 11, 1887
Mr. J. M. Blackman and Miss Mary Anna Davis, of near Eufaula, were married a few days ago.

Miss Amanda Tilley and Mr. Tom McEachern were married Sunday, by Rev. Coffin. (Stewart County, Ga.).

Thurs. Jan. 13, 1887
Married at the home of the bride's father, Mr. Jas. Balkcom, of Quitman County, Ga., by Rev. T. H. Stout, on Jan. 12, 1887, Mr. Daniel J. Woolbright, of Terrell County, Ga., to Miss Mattie E. Balkcom.

Fri. Jan. 14, 1887
At the residence of the bride's father, Dr. H. M. Weedon, in Eufaula, by Rev. Crawford, on last evening, Capt. J. R. Barr was married to Miss Annie Weedon. Attendants: W. C. Swanson, of Clayton, and Miss Bell Weedon, of Ga.; H. A. Young, of Anniston, and Miss Ida L. Skinner, of West Ala.; Hamp Weedon and Miss Julia Teague, of Montgomery; E. Y. Dent and Miss May Weedon, of Ga.; Chas. H. Beach and Miss Nellie Beall Dent; A. E. Barnett and Miss Julia Young; Jas. L. Ross and Miss Nunie Weedon; J. E. Long and Miss Nannie Beall Dent. Ushers: Masters Hubert Weedon and Louis Dent. Flower Maids: Misses Annie and Mabel Young.

Sat. Jan. 15, 1887

Married at the Baptist Church in Columbia, (Ala.) on the
12th inst., Mr. G. L. Campbell, of Tuskegee, and Miss Nora W.
Davis, daughter of Mr. Jno T. Davis, of Columbia. Attendants:
W. W. Campbell, of Americus, and Miss Berta Davis; W. G. Campbell
and Miss Julia Oglesby; J. N. Wilson, of Marianna, Fla., and Miss
Flora Campbell, of Tuskegee; J. D. Watson, Eufaula, and Miss Ida
Wright, Tuskegee; J. S. B. Crossman, Columbus, Ga. and Miss Ella
Cody; R. F. Howard, Tuskegee and Miss Lizzie Thompson; M. N.
Christian and Miss Eva Beach. Ushers: W. H. Christian and J. W.
Espy.

Tues. Jan. 18, 1887
        Married at the residence of D. H. McGilvary, near Clayton
on the 9th inst., by Justice Jno. C. Williams, Mr. Malcolm
McCraney to Miss Rachel A. Floyd. -Clayton Courier.

        Married at the home of Mr. Chambers near Louisville, (Ala.)
on Tuesday last, by Rev. J. L. Mathison, Mr. Jack McRae and Miss
Texanna Chambers. -Clayton Courier.

Wed. Jan. 19, 1887
        Mr. Jno. W. Drewry, of Eufaula, and Miss Annie McDonald,
daughter of Mr. J. J. McDonald, of Cuthbert, Ga., will be
married today in Cuthbert, by Rev. Dr. Branch.

Sat. Jan. 22, 1887
        Married at the home of the bride's mother, Mrs. Carroll, in
Barbour County, a few days since, Miss Lula Carroll and Mr. J. W.
Bush, by Rev. R. B. Lee.

Tues. Jan. 24, 1887
        Married on the 19th inst., at the home of the bride's
father, Mr. Winston Andrews in Elamville, Barbour County, by
Rev. B. C. Bennett, Mr. Bartow Mills to Miss Joe Andrews.

Tues. Feb. 1, 1887
        New York, Jan. 27. - Miss Elizabeth Ballart and Mr. John
Henry were married last evening by Rev. Wm. Sparger, pastor of
the Beth Elohim, on State St., Brooklyn, N.Y.

Wed. Feb. 2, 1887
        Married yesterday at the home of the bride's mother, Mrs.
Mattie Manson, in Eufaula, by Rev. Dr. Nunnally, Miss Mattie
Manson and Mr. Green Sapp, of Ft. Gaines, Ga.

Thurs. Feb. 3, 1887
        Miss Annie Lou Moore, of LaFayette, (Ala.) and Mr. Hardy,
of Chipley, Ga., were married on the 29th ult.

        Married at the home of the bride's father, Mr. Thos. Crozier,
near Cotton Hill, Clay County, Ga., on Jan. 27th, by Rev. T. H.
Stout, Mr. Jno. S. Standley, of Clay County, to Miss Mattie E.
Crozier.

        Chicago, Feb. 1. - Miss Van Zandt and August Spies were
married today by proxy, the groom being represented by his
brother. A suburban justice of the peace officiating.

Sat. Feb. 5, 1887
        Married at the home of the bride's mother, Mrs. Frank
Stewart, near White Oak Springs, (Barbour County) on Feb. 3d,
by Rev. P. P. Winn, of Clayton, Miss Sallie J. Stewart and Mr.
Thos. Eford, of Clayton. Attendants: Mr. Sanford Reaves and
Miss Emmie Hammett; Mr. Eford and Miss Alice Stewart.

Wed. Feb. 9, 1887
	Married at the home of the bride's father at Lodi, (Barbour County) on last Thursday, by Justice Williams, Miss Lula Seaborn to Mr. J. W. Harris.

Thurs. Feb. 10, 1887
	Married last Sunday at the home of the bride's father, Dan'l J. Melvin, Esq., of Hardwicksburg, (Henry County) by Rev. Martin Armstrong, Miss Donie Melvin to Mr. Alex. Ham, of near Columbia, (Ala.). -Abbeville (Ala.) Age.

	Married at the residence of the bride's mother, Mrs. F. A. Jennings, last evening, by Rev. Dr. Crawford, Miss Florrie Jennings to Mr. Chas. Beach.

Sat. Feb. 12, 1887
	Married at the home of the bride's father, Jas. M. Lanier, near Georgetown, Feb. 9th, by Rev. Stout, Mr. Haywood L. Bland and Miss Jennie Lanier, both of Quitman County, Ga.

Fri. Feb. 18, 1887
	Married at the home of the bride's father, Mr. J. J. Carter, of Eufaula, yesterday, by Rev. Dr. Crawford, Miss Nellie Carter and Mr. E. W. Dixon, of Eufaula.

Sun. Feb. 20, 1887
	Married at Hilliardsville at the home of the bride's mother on the 17th inst., by R. K. Bedell, Esq., Mr. J. W. Barnes and Miss Elizabeth Calhoun, both of Henry County.

Tues. Feb. 22, 1887
	Married at the Huguley House, Eufaula, on yesterday, by Rev. Dr. Nunnally, Miss Kate Huguley to Mr. Arthur Riley.

Wed. Feb. 23, 1887
	Editor C. C. DuBose, of the Shelby (Ala.) Chronicle, and Miss Anna B. Robertson, of Indianapolis, Indiana, were married recently at the latter place.

	Married yesterday at the home of the bride's mother in Eufaula, by Rev. Father McCormick, Mr. J. H. Brady, of Columbus, Ga., to Miss Carrie McLeod. Attendants: Mr. H. C. Holleman and Miss Hattie Stevens; Mr. Jas. Holmes and Miss Nellie Stevens.

Thurs. Feb. 24, 1887
	At the Baptist Church this afternoon, Mr. Harmon Lampley and Miss Islay Reeves, daughter of Rev. W. N. Reeves, will be married by Rev. Dr. Nunnally. The attendants: Mr. Chas. Henderson, of Troy, and Miss Anna Sylvester; Mr. J. M. Thornton, Jr., and Miss Addie Noble, of Anniston; Mr. S. R. Foy and Miss Kate Durr, of Montgomery; Mr. Walter Berry and Miss Lily Moss, of Athens; Mr. E. Y. Dent and Miss Clara Toney; Mr. Chas. Mercer and Miss Bessie Simpson; Mr. C. L. Rhodes and Miss Anna Baker; Mr. Jno. Bray and Miss Lily Drewry; Dr. Albert Goodwin and Miss Ida Toney; Mr. Johnnie Reeves and Miss Janie Reeves. Best man: Mr. Ira Lampley. Ushers: Mr. Sump McTyer, Mr. Geo. Whitlock, Mr. Geo. Beauchamp, and Mr. Fred Bray. Flower girls: Misses Mittie McNab and Lillian Richardson. The pages: Masters David and Jerry Reeves.

Sat. Feb. 26, 1887
	Married at the home of the bride's father, on last Thursday, (Dale County) by Rev. A. Dowling, Mr. W. A. Scaift and Miss Nora Cox. -Ozark (Ala.) Star.

Sun. Feb. 27, 1887
Mr. J. M. T. Bush and Miss Teana Chambers were married at the home of I. H. Chambers, near Louisville, (Ala.) on Feb. 22d, 1887.

Thurs. Mar. 3, 1887
Mr. W. A. Huguley and Mrs. M. A. Bussey were married at Finerty House in Eufaula last evening, by Rev. W. N. Reeves.

Thurs. Mar. 10, 1887
Mr. Geo. H. Murray, theatrical agent of Philadelphia, was married on Feb. 3d to Miss Viola Carnes, of the same city.

Married on Mar. 8th at the home of the bride's parents, by Jas. Orr, Esq., Mr. Jno. T. Parmer, of Eufaula, to Miss Sallie J. Sims, of White Oak Station, in Barbour County.

Wed. Mar. 16, 1887
Miss Bessie Simpson, of Eufaula, and Mr. C. H. French formerly of Boston, now of Eufaula, were married in Georgetown, Ga. yesterday.

Sat. Mar. 19, 1887
Mr. J. T. Chapman, of Acree, Ga., and Miss Jannie Bowdon, of Clayton, Ala., were married at the home of the bride on Thursday.

Thurs. Mar. 31, 1887
Married at the Frazier Hotel at Columbia last Wednesday, Mr. Jas. A. Bowdon and Miss Sue Wood, both residents of Columbia, (Ala.). -Abbeville (Ala.) Times.

Tues. Apr. 12, 1887
Mr. Chas. D. Dickinson and Miss Nellie Coyen were married on Dec. 11th last, has just been made public. Both of Atlanta, Ga. -Constitution.

Dr. S. A. Holt, of Eufaula, and Miss Ida Toney were married today at the home of the bride, "Roseland", near Eufaula.

Wed. Apr. 13, 1887
Mr. Oliver E. Smith, of Gainesville, Ala., and Miss Minnie B. Threefoot, of Mobile, were married at the St. Francis Street Baptist Church on Thursday. Rev. J. S. Rencher, of the Methodist Church, officiating.

Fri. Apr. 15, 1887
Mr. Thos. H. Clark, of The Montgomery Advertiser, and Miss Carrie Marks were married Wednesday.

Married at the home of Mr. Calvin Stevens, in Eufaula, on the 14th inst., by Rev. Jos. Hundley, Mr. Wm. Shirley to Miss Nancy Thomas, of this city.

Tues. May 3, 1887
The marriage of Miss Minnie Lee Bustin and Mr. Chas. Edward Wellborn, both of Birmingham, is announced to take place in the near future. Mr. Wellborn was formerly of Eufaula.

Wed. May 4, 1887
Married at the home of the bride's father, Mr. Green C. Beckham, in Eufaula, yesterday, by Rev. Junius Jordan, Mr. Edgar Sylvester to Miss Ella Beckham.

Thurs. May 5, 1887
    Marriage license Saturday were issued to Mr. Jno. A. New-
berry and Miss Nicey Logan, of Dothan, (Ala.). -<u>Abbeville</u> (Ala.)
<u>Age</u>.

Wed. May 18, 1887
    Mr. Tom Bennett and Miss Mittie Chitty were married on the
11th inst., in Henry County, (Ala.).

Wed. June 1, 1887
    Married on the 29th inst., at Georgetown, Ga., by A. A.
Lewis, Esq., C. J. Rollins and Ella J. Gibbons, the daughter of
Mr. J. W. T. Gibbons, of Cotton Hill, (Barbour County).

Fri. June 3, 1887
    Col. S. W. John of Selma, (Ala.) was married in Montgomery
Wednesday to Miss Rosa Clisby.

Sat. June 4, 1887
    Dr. J. M. Orr, of Union Springs, (Ala.) was married on
Thursday last to Miss Mattie Lee.

Fri. June 10, 1887
    Married at the residence of the bride's mother near Eufaula,
yesterday, Mr. J. A. McLeod, son of Mr. Aleck McLeod, to Miss
Addie Martin.

Tues. June 14, 1887
    The announcement is made of the approaching marriage of Col.
Dan. Rice, of Cincinnati, and Mrs. M. C. Robinson, of Lavaca
County, Texas.

Sun. June 20, 1887
    Mrs. I. M. P. Henry, of the <u>Greenville Advocate</u>, was recen-
tly married to Mr. Albion Ockenden, of Little Hampton, England.

Sun. June 26, 1887
    Married at Troy, Ala., on 16th inst., Dr. W. A. Smart and
Miss Lizzie Jones, daughter of the late U. L. Jones, and sister
of Mrs. B. Davie, of Clayton. -<u>Clayton Courier</u>.

    Mr. Berry Lott and Miss Florence Griggs, of near Buckham,
Pike County, (Ala.) were married at Georgetown, Ga., on Wednesday
last. -<u>Clayton Courier</u>.

Tues. June 27, 1887
    Mr. Will Johnson, of South Carolina, and Miss Emma Lewis,
of Eufaula, were married in Georgetown, (Ga.) yesterday.

Thurs. June 30, 1887
    Mr. Ezekial Stokes and Miss Fannie L. Bridges were married
on 26th inst., at the home of Robt. McKnight, Esq., who officiated. -<u>Abbeville</u> (Ala.) <u>Age</u>.

Fri. July 1, 1887
    Banks Winter, the minstrel, was married to a Huntsville,
Ala., belle, Miss Clara Newman, on Wednesday.

Wed. July 6, 1887
    Married near Belcher, Ala., on Sunday, by Rev. R. B. Lee,
at the home of Mr. Jno. McIlvane, Mr. E. W. Wright and Miss
Eufala Hall.

71

Fri. July 8, 1887
     Yan Phon Lee, of Fragrant Hill, China, and Miss Elizabeth
Maud Jerome, of New Haven, Conn., were married on July 6th, at
the home of the bride's mother, by Rev. Dr. Twitchell, of Hartford.

Fri. July 15, 1887
     Married yesterday at the home of the bride's father, Dr.
H. M. Weedon, in Eufaula, by Rev. Dr. Crawford, Miss Mary N.
Weedon to Mr. Jas. L. Ross.

Wed. July 20, 1887
     Washington, July 17. - Mr. Wm. H. Lamar will wed Miss
Jennie Lamar, daughter of the Secretary of Interior, in Macon,
Ga., on the 21st of July.

     Miss Mollie Garfield, daughter of the late President Gar-
field, is soon to marry Mr. T. Standly Brown, who was private
secretary to the President.

Wed. Aug. 17, 1887
     Mr. J. F. Stallings, of Greenville, (Ala.) was married
yesterday at Tubb, (Barbour County) to Miss Belle McAllister,
daughter of Capt. A. M. McAllister.

Thurs. Aug. 18, 1887
     Married at the home of the bride's parents on the 14th
inst., by J. R. Freeman, Esq., Mr. J. H. Walker and Miss Emma
Autman. -Abbeville (Ala.) Age.

Thurs. Aug. 25, 1887
     Married on Sunday last at the home of the bride's parents
near Cureton's Bridge, by W. A. Hicks, Esq., Mr. Frank Parker
and Miss Nellie Elmore. -Abbeville (Ala.) Age.

Sun. Aug. 28, 1887
     Married on Sunday last at the home of the groom's father,
by Rev. Mr. Schramme, Mr. Monroe Cooper and Miss Annie Oliver.
-Clayton Courier.

Fri. Sept. 2, 1887
     Mr. B. M. Williford and Miss Lula Christian were married at
the home of Mr. Thompson, near Eufaula on Thursday, by Rev. J. W.
Boyd.

Sat. Sept. 3, 1887
     Mrs. Rebecca Driscoll, of Ky., and Joseph Douglas eloped to
Indiana.

Fri. Sept. 9, 1887
     Married at the home of the bride's father, Mr. Jno. Moore,
near Hatcher's Station, Ga., on Sept. 7th, by Rev. T. H. Stout,
Mr. Wm. M. Guerry, conductor on the C. R. R., to Miss Viola
Moore.

Thurs. Sept. 15, 1887
     Mr. J. Bose Dell and Miss Georgia E. Daniels were married
at the home of the bride's parents in Newton, Dale County, (Ala.)
recently. -Abbeville (Ala.) Age.

Fri. Sept. 16, 1887
     Capt. J. G. Smith, of Birmingham, and Mrs. Hightower, of
this place, were married yesterday.

Thurs. Sept. 22, 1887
    Married at the National Hotel yesterday, by Rev. W. H.
Patterson, Miss Mamie Hendrix to Mr. J. N. Franklin, both of
Barbour County.

Tues. Oct. 11, 1887
    Announcement is made of the approaching nuptials of Mr. L.
Ottensosser, our former townsman, with Miss Fannie Lesser, of
Syracuse, N. Y., on Oct. 18th.

Thurs. Oct. 13, 1887
    Married yesterday, Dr. Henry Brannon and Miss Anna Guice at
the home of the bride's mother in Eufaula, by Rev. Pickard.

Fri. Oct. 14, 1887
    Announcement is made of approaching marriage of Miss
Henrietta L. Brown to Hon. Jno. D. Roguemore in Malden, Mass.,
on the 26th of this month.

Sat. Oct. 22, 1887
    Married at the residence of Mr. and Mrs. T. J. Jackson, of
Girard, (Ala.) yesterday, their daughter, Miss Grace, to Mr.
Charlie Browne, of Eufaula, by Rev. J. B. Cummings.

    Married Thursday last at the home of Mr. J. B. Garland, the
bride's brother, Mr. R. A. Stratford to Miss Mattie Persons, by
Rev. Mr. Mason. All of Barbour County.

Thurs. Oct. 27, 1887
    Mr. J. E. Long and Miss Nannie Dent, daughter of Capt. S. H.
Dent, were married last night at the M. E. Church in Eufaula.
Attendants: Mr. P. B. McKenzie and W. T. Berry, ushers. Mr. Jas.
T. Kendall, Jr., and Miss Lee Frazer, of Union Springs; Mr. Geo.
Beauchamp and Miss Gussie Young, of Columbus; Mr. Will Simpson,
of Montgomery, and Miss Emmie Frazer, of Union Springs; Mr. Tom
Davis, of Montgomery, and Miss Annie Dent; Mr. Henry Young, of
Anniston, and Miss Lula Crisp, of Americus; Mr. Charlie Mercer
and Miss Maggie Peterson, of Greensboro; Mr. Will Allen, of
Montgomery, and Miss Nellie Dent; Mr. J. L. Ross and Mrs. Ross;
Mr. Hugh Dent and Miss Fannie Long, of Hurtsboro; Mr. Jesse Long,
Hurtsboro, and Miss Louise Dent; Mr. E. Y. Dent and Miss Callie
Law, of Union Springs; Mr. W. H. Foy and Miss Julia Young.
Flower girls: Misses Carrie Dent and Queen Long, of Hurtsboro.

Sat. Oct. 29, 1887
    Dr. Bounds, of St. Louis, Mo., was married last Tuesday at
Washington, Ga., to Miss Hattie Barnett, a niece of Dr. A. W.
Barnett, of Eufaula.

Fri. Nov. 4, 1887
    Mr. Chas. L. Perry and Miss Neva W. Fussell were married at
the home of the bride's parents in Eufaula on yesterday, by Rev.
E. W. Spaulding.

Wed. Nov. 9, 1887
    Mr. Eugene Blackman and Miss Ida M. Thompson were married
at the home of Mr. J. D. Andrews in Eufaula on Sunday last, by
Rev. W. L. Pickard.

Wed. Nov. 16, 1887
    Married near White Pond (Barbour County) on the 13th of
Nov., at the residence of Mrs. Holly, Mr. J. O. Holly and Miss
Alice Jones.

Thurs. Nov. 17, 1887
      Maj. Alfred O'Brien, of Louisiana, and Mrs. Mattie J.
Thomas, of Eufaula, niece of Mrs. N. H. Seals of this city, were
married on the 10th inst., at Mrs. Seals' home, by Rev. Dr.
Johnson, of East Nashville.

Sat. Nov. 19, 1887
      Mr. A. P. Hays and Miss Susie Walker, of Columbia, (Ala.)
were married last week.

Thurs. Nov. 24, 1887
      Married yesterday at Perry, Ga., Mr. P. B. McKenzie to Miss
Claude Hill, of that city. The ceremony took place in the
Baptist Church, by Rev. B. F. Tharpe, of Perry. The attendants:
F. L. McKenzie, of Mobile, and Miss Jean Davis, of Perry; H. C.
Holleman, Eufaula, and Miss Florine Cox, of Perry; John Holtz-
claw, of Perry, and Miss Abbie Ogletree, of Eufaula; W. F. Har-
well, Eufaula, and Miss Nora Duncan, of Perry; Geo. Cotton, of
Eufaula, and Miss Marianna Jones, of Ft. Valley; R. L. Mayes, of
Guerryton, and Miss Stella Duncan, of Perry; R. D. Powell, of
Eufaula, and Miss Minnie Norwood, of Perry; L. F. Cater, of Perry
and Miss Mamie Holtzclaw, Perry; S. B. Brown, of Ft. Valley, and
Miss Nettie Hook, of Perry; R. L. Morris, of Georgetown, and Miss
Lerie Tharpe, of Perry. Ushers: W. G. Riley, A. B. Davis, L. M.
Paul, and Will Brunson, Jr.

Sun. Nov. 27, 1887
      Married on 22nd inst., at Glennville, Ala., Mr. J. B. Harris
and Miss Sue Blasingame.

      Hon. David Clopton will be married to Mrs. Clement C. Clay
on the 28th of this month.

Wed. Nov. 30, 1887
      Married on the 27th inst., at the home of Wm. Fillengame,
Miss Margaret Fillengame, both of Barbour County.

Thurs. Dec. 8, 1887
      Rev. Lesrie P. Lathram and Miss Vida M. Hill, of Lawrence-
ville, (Henry County) were married on last Thursday.

Fri. Dec. 16, 1887
      Married yesterday at the home of Mr. J. M. Thornton, Sr.,
near Eufaula, by Rev. W. H. Patterson, Mr. Julian Sanders, of
Barbour County, and Miss Laila Engram.

Sat. Dec. 17, 1887
      Married Thursday, by Judge Parker, Mr. Horn, of Clopton,
(Ala.) and Mrs. N. J. Palmer, of Newton. -Ozark Star.

      Married recently at the home of Mr. J. L. Grace, near Ozark
(Ala.) by J. O. Godwin, Esq., Mr. Wright Glenn and Miss Maud
Grace. -Ozark Star.

Sun. Dec. 18, 1887
      Married on Wednesday at the home of Mr. H. Oppert, Esq.,
and by him, Mr. Henry Faulk and Miss Emma Bellflower. -Clayton
Courier.

      Married on Thursday last, at the home of the bride's father,
Mr. S. F. Lightner, by Rev. Mr. Mathinson, Mr. Linard Davis and
Miss Susan Lightner. -Clayton Courier.

Thurs. Dec. 22, 1887

The announcement is made of the approaching marriage of Dr.
W. H. Robertson and Miss Mary Foster, daughter of Chancellor
Foster, to take place on Dec. 28th, at the home of the bride in
Clayton.

Sat. Dec. 24, 1887
    Married at Midway Church, near Georgetown, (Ga.) Dr. A.
Mason Raines and Miss Perry Gay, of Quitman County, (Ga.) and Mr.
J. W. Boyett and Miss Essie Methvin, of Clay County, (Ga.) by
Rev. W. H. Patterson, of Eufaula.

THE EUFAULA WEEKLY TIMES AND NEWS
1887

Thurs. Jan. 13, 1887
    Married at White Pond (Barbour County) on Sunday, at the
home of Mr. Daniel Shirley, Mr. J. J. Smith and Miss Francis
Shirley, by Mr. Nathan Williams, J.P.

Thurs. Feb. 18, 1887
    Albany, Ga., Feb. 10. - Married at the home of the bride's
father, Dr. Bun Lundy, of Chickasawhatchie, Terrell County, on
the 9th inst., Miss Blanch Lundy to Mr. Emmet a. Aicardi, of
Selma, Ala., by Rev. F. A. Branch, of Dawson, Ga.

Thurs. Dec. 15, 1887
    Capt. W. R. Graham and Miss Nellie Speight, of Ft. Gaines,
Ga., were married Thursday in the M. E. Church.

    Married on Wednesday by Rev. J. A. Wynne, Mr. J. D. McRee
and Miss Christian McRae. -Clayton Courier.

    Union Springs, (Ala.) Dec. 7. - Mr. Jas. L. Banks, of
Birmingham, formerly of Union Springs, and Miss L. Lee Frazer,
of Union Springs, daughter of Judge Sidney T. Frazer, were
married in the M. E. Church in this city today, by Rev. Dr. J.
D. A. Cook, of Macon, Ga. The attendants were: Mr. W. W. Wilker-
son, of Birmingham, and Miss Emmie Frazer, of Union Springs.
Ushers: Messrs. T. S. Frazer and D. R. McCall, of Union Springs,
Dr. J. L. Watkins, Montgomery, and T. S. Forbes, of Birmingham.

1888

Thurs. Jan. 26, 1888
    Miss Minnie Reese, of Montgomery, will be married this
afternoon to Mr. W. E. Richardson, of Mobile, Ala.

    Married yesterday in Atlanta, Ga., at the Second Baptist
Church, by Rev. J. B. Hawthorne, Miss Lena Calloway and Mr. F.
Arthur Hooper, of Cuthbert, Ga. The attendants were: Miss Winnie
McCarthy and Mr. Hooper Alexander; Miss Sallie Nunnally and Mr.
T. H. Northern; Miss Maud O'Keefe and Mr. Robt. L. Maye, of
Cuthbert; Miss Jennie Davis, of Eufaula, and Mr. T. Ed Ryals, of
Macon; Miss Lizzie Hillyer and Mr. E. C. Calloway; Miss Mamie
Calloway and Mr. Jno. Gunn, of Cuthbert.

    Mr. Alpheus Baker, Jr., was married to Miss Cassie Sanders
at Tub, Ala., last evening, by Rev. Father McCormick. (Barbour
County marriage).

Thurs. Feb. 2, 1888
    Mr. J. R. Price and Miss Mollie Wilson, both of Barbour
County, were married last Tuesday, by Rev. R. B. Lee.

Thurs. Feb. 9, 1888

Mr. Jno. McLendon, of Fort Gaines, (Ga.) was married Friday at the home of the bride's parents in Eufaula, to Miss Sallie, daughter of Mr. J. H. Evans.

Mr. Geo. M. Murphey was married at the home of the bride's parents (Henry County) on Tuesday, to Miss Delia, daughter of Mr. M. V. Capps. -Abbeville (Ala.) Age.

Married yesterday at Abbeville, by Z. W. Laney, Esq., Mr. Frank Hogen and Miss Annie, daughter of Mr. Geo. Lewis. -Abbeville (Ala.) Age.

T. M. Skipper and Miss Birdy Espy, of Henry County, (Ala.) were married recently.

Thurs. Feb. 16, 1888
Married Thursday at Auburn, Ala., by Rev. Mr. Frazier, Mr. Reuben Kolb, of Eufaula, and Miss Pearl Hollifield.

Mr. Whires, *late of New Orleans, but now of Albany, Ga., and Miss Mary Ryan, of Quitman County, Ga., were married yesterday in the Catholic Church in Eufaula, by Rev. Father McCormick. (*From Marriage Record, Clayton Probate Office: Mr. F. White and Mary Ryan, married Feb. 13, 1888).

Thurs. Mar. 15, 1888
Atlanta, Ga., Mar. 8. - Married today at the home of the bride's father, Col. Bill Bonnell, Mr. Jas. T. Nisbett, Jr., and Miss Alice Bonnell.

Married at the home of the bride's father in Eufaula last night, by Rev. R. B. Crawford, Mr. J. C. Cobb and Miss Ann D. Garret.

Thurs. Apr. 5, 1888
Mr. R. S. Roddenbery, of Georgia, and Miss Abbie Ogletree, of Eufaula, will be married today by Rev. Mr. Pickard, at the home of Dr. and Mrs. A. Ogletree.

Thurs. Apr. 12, 1888
Married last night at the Methodist Church in Eufaula, by Rev. Dr. Crawford, assisted by Rev. Mr. Mason, Miss Julia Young and Mr. A. E. Barnett. Attendants were: Mr. W. H. Foy and Miss Marie Belle Kendall; J. T. Kendall, Jr., and Miss Beale Barnett; W. T. Berry and Miss Julia McRae; L. W. Foy and Miss Ellen Barnett; C. G. Barnett and Miss Nellie Beall Dent; M. S. Roberts and Miss Mamie McGough; S. H. Dent, Jr. and Miss Lula Kendall; C. P. Roberts and Miss Jennie McRae; G. A. Beauchamp and Miss Lucy Glenn; Frank Crawford and Miss Carrie Dent. Flower girls were Louise Dent and Ruth Barnett. Ushers: J. E. Long, C. R. Ross, J. R. Barr, J. L. Ross and J. M. Kendall

Thurs. June 14, 1888
Miss Mattie Bowden, formerly of Eufaula, was married recently in Birmingham to H. B. Morse.

Thurs. Aug. 2, 1888
Mr. J. B. Wilson, of Aberfoil (Bullock County) and Miss Florence B. Paullin were married at the home of Mr. M. W. Britt in Midway (Ala.) recently.

Thurs. Aug. 16, 1888
Columbus, Ga., Aug. 9. - Judge F. C. Sloppy, *of Opelika, (Ala.) and Miss Susan A. French, of Columbus, were married today. (*Correction of groom's name: Frederick C. Slappy. From

Muscogee County Court House, Office of the Probate, Columbus,
Ga. Recorded in Book "J", p. 353.)

Miss Sallie Flournoy, daughter of Mr. S. J. Flournoy, of
Eufaula, and Mr. Thos. Irby, of Anniston, were married today at
the Episcopal Church in Eufaula, by Rev. Beard, of Birmingham.
Attendants: Mr. Jas. R. Roberts and Miss Rosser Flournoy; Mr.
Phares Coleman and Miss Carrie Cochran, Mr. Sherod Smith was
best man and ushers were T. W. Toney, W. T. Flournoy, C. A. Locke
and C. L. Bray.

Married yesterday in Eufaula at the home of Mr. A. A. Couric,
by Rev. A. J. Battle, of Macon, assisted by Rev. Robt. J. Willingham, of Chattanooga, Mr. B. L. Willingham, of Macon, (Ga.)
and Mrs. M. S. Perkins, daughter of the late Gov. Jno. Gill
Shorter.

Married yesterday at the home of the bride's father at White
Oak (Barbour County) by Rev. T. H. Stout, Mr. Jas. C. Ventress
and Miss Willie E. Blair.

Thurs. Aug. 23, 1888
Married yesterday at the home of the bride's father, Dr.
J. J. Mason, in Wynnton, (Ga.) by Rev. R. H. Harris, Mr. Jno. C.
Chenny and Miss Kate Mason. -Columbus (Ga.) Enquirer.

Thurs. Aug. 30, 1888
Mr. Abb Napper and Miss Sarah Saunders, of near Barnes X
Roads, Dale County, (Ala.) were married in Ft. Gaines, (Ga.) on
Tuesday. -Abbeville (Ala.) Times.

Thurs. Oct. 11, 1888
Married at the home of the bride's parents in Dawson, Ga.,
yesterday, by Rev. B. W. Davis, Mr. Will F. Locke, of Eufaula,
and Miss Lily B. Rodgers.

Thurs. Oct. 18, 1888
Mr. R. F. Nance, of Barbour County, and Miss Rosa Belle
Scott, of Petersburg, Va., are to be married at the Washington
Street M. E. Church at the latter place on the 17th inst.

Thurs. Nov. 1, 1888
Mr. Dunbar Lamar, of Beech Island, S. C., and Miss Annie
Black, daughter of the late Hon. Geo. R. Black, of Sylvania, Ga.,
were married yesterday.

Also, Mr. Carey Lamar, of Beech Island, S. C. and Miss Anna
Baker, of Sylvania were married at a double wedding. The grooms
are brothers, the brides are cousins. -Augusta, (Ga.) Chronicle.

Mr. Miles McCoy and Miss Leona Euford were married near
Balkum on Thursday. -Abbeville (Ala.) Age, 30th.

On Sunday Jas. J. Tiller and Miss Ella Galloway were
married. -Abbeville (Ala.) Age, 30th.

THE EUFAULA DAILY TIMES
1888

Thurs. Aug. 9, 1888
Married in Eufaula yesterday, Miss Carrie L. Mabry, daughter
of Col. J. W. Mabry, and Mr. Chas. Edward Nix, all of Clayton.

Wed. Oct. 24, 1888
Mr. G. Walker Williams and Miss Sarah Bryan were married
yesterday at the home of G. L. Houston, in Barbour County.

Fri. Nov. 16, 1888

Hon. W. F. Wilkerson, of Autauga County, (Ala.) recently married Miss Eva, daughter of Rev. Dr. and Mrs. E. L. Loveless.

Tues. Nov. 20, 1888

Married at the residence of the bride's mother on last Sunday, by Rev. Father McCormick, Mr. Jas. Baker and Mrs. M. A. Hancock, all of Eufaula.

Fri. Nov. 23, 1888

Married on the 15th of Nov., at Lodi (Barbour County), Mr. Berry Jowers and Miss Emma Stricklin, both of Barbour County, by J. D. Williams, J.P.

Mr. S. R. Foy, of Eufaula, and Miss Carrie Treutlen were married in Washington last Tuesday.

Tues. Nov. 27, 1888

Married at the home of the bride's parents near Headland, (Ala.) Dr. W. P. Hardwick of Headland, and Miss Emma B. Price, daughter of Dr. J. E. Price, on the 20th inst., by Rev. P. P. Wynn.

Married yesterday at the residence of the bride's father, Maj. Lamar Cobb, Miss Olivia N. Cobb and Mr. Wm. C. Davis, son of Rev. J. C. Davis, formerly of Eufaula, now of Athens, Ga. -Athens (Ga.) Banner, 22d inst.

Sat. Dec. 1, 1888

Married in Georgetown, Ga., recently, Mr. Eugene Gibbons and Miss Sarah Griffin, both of Henry County, (Ala.).

Tues. Dec. 4, 1888

Married at the home of the bride's father in Barbour County yesterday, Mr. T. A. Griffin, Mr. W. C. Taylor and Miss Nellie Griffin, by Rev. Junius Jordan.

Sun. Dec. 9, 1888

Mr. Jno. Crozier, of Spring Vale, and Miss Sudie Keese, of Benevolence, were married at the home of the bride's father, Mr. E. H. Keese, by Rev. E. A. Keese.

Wed. Dec. 11, 1888

Married on Thursday last, at the residence of the bride's father, near Eufaula, Miss Foy Reeves and Mr. J. D. Ferrell, of Sneads, Fla.

Thurs. Dec. 13, 1888

Married Dec. 6th at Lawrenceville, (Henry County) Mr. L. C. Clark, of Cotton Hill, and Miss Mamie Price, daughter of Irwin Price, by Rev. Sellers. The groom is the son of Mr. Warren Clark of Barbour County.

Sat. Dec. 15, 1888

Mr. Wm. Grace and Miss Willie Douglas were married near Hatchechubbee on Thursday last, by Rev. J. Jordan.

Sat. Dec. 22, 1888

Married recently at the home of the bride's father in West End, Mr. A. P. Rice and Miss Mannie Maund, of Columbia, by Rev. E. M. Knowles. -Columbia (Ala.) Enterprise.

Married at the residence of the bride's parents, by Rev. E. M. Knowles, Mr. Albert Williams and Miss Angorona (Sister) Koonce, daughter of W. C. Koonce. -Columbia (Ala.) Enterprise.

Sun. Dec. 23, 1888
     Married on the 16th of Dec., Mr. Jno. D. King and Miss
Lizzie Dunsford, by G. B. James, Esq.

     On the same day, Mr. Z. B. Hughes and Miss Henrietta Wells
were married, all of Beat 16, (Barbour County).

THE CLAYTON COURIER
1888

E. R. Quillin, Publisher.

Sat. Dec. 15, 1888
     Married at Ft. Gaines, Ga., on Tuesday last, Mr. T. C. Helms,
of Louisville, Ala., and Mrs. O'Coner, of Ft. Gaines.

     Married Tuesday, Col. H. L. Martin, of Ozark, and Miss Maud
Roberts, of Elba. (Ala.).

Sat. Dec. 22, 1888
     Married Tuesday at the home of E. R. Quillin, by Rev. J. I.
Ayres, Mr. J. B. Judson, of Pulliam Washington Territory, and
Miss Kansas Helms, daughter of T. C. Helms, of Louisville, Ala.

EUFAULA WEEKLY TIMES AND NEWS
1889

Thurs. Jan. 10, 1889
     Bangor, Me., Jan. 4. - Miss Helen Hamlin, of this city, and
Mr. Edward Hamlin, of Boston, were married here last evening.

     Pomona, Cal., Jan. 2. - Daniel Hamilton, of Cucamonga, and
Allice G. Brigham were married recently at Prescott, Ariz.

     Mr. Homer Dickinson, of Atlanta, and Mrs. Florence R. Bran-
non, of Eufaula, were married yesterday at the home of the bride's
father, Mr. C. Rhodes, by Rev. W. L. Pickard.

     Married at Haw Ridge last week, Mr. J. D. Heath and Miss
Sallie Jones, also, Mr. Joe king and Miss Amanda Clark, and Mr.
Jno. Seay and Miss Florence Armour, and Mr. J. J. Warren and Miss
Willie Dunnaway. -Ozark Star.

Thurs. Jan. 17, 1889
     Married near Eufaula on the 9th inst., by Rev. T. H. Stout,
Mr. Norman Roberts, of Georgia, and Miss Nellie Baldwin, of
Barbour County.

     Married last Sunday at the home of the groom's father, Mr.
Thos. Stovall, in Eufaula, by Dr. R. S. Crawford, Dr. J. F.
Stovall and Miss Minnie F. Desha, both of Gainesville, Fla.

     Married at the home of Judge W. M. Gatewood on Jan. 10th,
by Rev. Geo. E. Brewer, Mr. R. E. Lindsey and Miss Emmie Gatewood, of Jernigan, Ala.

Thurs. Jan. 24, 1889
     Married yesterday at the home of Mrs. Z. Daniel in Eufaula,
by Rev. W. L. Pickard, Mr. Jas. E. O'Brien to Miss Lila Godwin.
Attendants were Mr. M. J. O'Brien, of Columbus, Ga., and Miss
Lizzie Daniel; Mr. Henry C. Holleman and Miss Annie Daniel.

     Married last Sunday at the home of Wm. Hall, in Barbour
County, Jas. Leroy and Miss Ida Hall, by Esq. G. B. James.

On Sunday last Mr. J. R. Chandler and Miss Francis Kelly plighted their troth, (for the second time) by Rev. Wm. Bruner. -Columbia (Ala.) Enterprise.

Married in Louisville, Ala., recently at the home of the bride's father, Mr. J. A. Lampley, by Rev. J. H. Douglass, Mr. J. A. Norris and Miss Della Lampley.

Thurs. Jan. 31, 1889
Rev. H. R. Schramm and Miss Laura Turner will be married today at Shady Grove, in Mobile County, Ala.

Married at the home of the bride's parents, Mr. Jno. Walker, of Columbia, (Ala.) and Miss Pet Clendinen, by Rev. I. F. Betts.

Thurs. Feb. 7, 1889
Mr. L. L. Thomas and Miss Ida J. Bush were married at Belcher last Sunday, by S. H. Driggers, Esq.

Thurs. Feb. 14, 1889
Married on the 6th inst., at the home of the bride's father, Mr. Marshall Culbreth, of Randolph County, Ga., by Rev. Jno. Martin, Mr. Dan B. Methvin, of Quitman County, Ga., to Miss Lena Culbreth. -Cuthbert (Ga.) Liberal.

Married recently at the home of Mrs. R. E. Carroll, the bride's mother, near Eufaula, by G. B. James, Esq., Mr. G. B. King to Miss Rossie E. Carroll.

Married last Sunday, by Mr. Jas. Orr, at the home of the bride's mother, near White Oak, Miss Catherine McLeod to Mr. W. P. Tiller.

Married at Belcher on Friday last, by Rev. Lee Ray, Mr. Martin Miller to Winnie Baker.

Thurs. Feb. 28, 1889
Married on Feb. 21st, by Rev. Dr. Stout, Mr. Charlie Fenn to Miss Iola Sims, great-granddaughter of the late Rev. Joel Sims, one of Barbour County's pioneer preachers

Married last night at the home of Mrs. W. H. Thornton, the bride's mother, Mr. Cliff A. Locke and Mrs. Retta Berry, by W. L. Pickard.

Thurs. Mar. 7, 1889
Married yesterday at the home of the bride's mother in Barbour County, by Rev. W. H. Patterson, Mr. W. E. Oldham, of Green Pond, to Miss Cora Sparks.

Thurs. Mar. 28, 1889
Mr. J. A. Roquemore, of Barbour County, and Miss Lucy M. Holmes, of Clay County, (Ga.) are to be married today.

Thurs. Apr. 18, 1889
Mr. Isaac Valentine and Miss Lulu McDonald, both of Ozark, Ala., were married in Georgetown, Ga., last Sunday.

Mr. W. P. Gary and Miss N. E. Reeves were married by Rev. T. H. Stout on Thursday last at Mt. Andrew, (Barbour County).

Thurs. Apr. 25, 1889
Dr. W. N. McNair, of Barbour County, and Miss Benton, daughter of Mr. Sam Benton, of Texasville, (Barbour County) were married in Georgetown, Ga., yesterday.

Married at the home of the bride's mother in Eufaula

yesterday, by Rev. H. W. Wade, Mr. F. S. Mills, of Clayton, and Miss Annie M. Seals.

Mr. T. Colbert Dawson, of Glennville, Ala., and Miss Ruth A. Howard were married at the home of the bride's mother, Mrs. Ann J. Howard, at Lynwood, on Thursday, by Rev. W. A. Carter. -Columbus (Ga.) Enquirer.

Miss Elizabeth Chase Pattillo and Mr. Jno. Shorter Cowles were married Saturday at the Trinity Church in Atlanta, Ga. -Constitution of Friday.

Married in Hoboken, near Eufaula, yesterday, by Rev. Father Shaw, Mr. Wm. H. Courtney and Miss Annie Mae Henry.

Mr. G. W. Blackman and Mrs. Hammock were married in Ozark (Ala.) on Thursday last.

Thurs. May 16, 1889
Married Sunday in Henry County at the home of the bride's parents, by Rev. I. F. Betts, Mr. R. W. Lisenby and Miss Dora Hill. -Abbeville (Ala.) Age.

Waldo S. Waterman, of near Diego, son of the Gov., and Miss E. Hazel Wood were married today at the home of Rev. Jesse Wood, of Butte County, by Rev. E. Graham. -Orreville (Cal.) Mercury. The parents of the bride were formerly of Eufaula.

Married in Columbia, Ala., at the Baptist Church, Mr. Geo. Cotton and Miss Ella Cody, daughter of Col. Cody, formerly of Barbour County.

Thurs. May 23, 1889
Mr. Jas. Rhodes, of Eufaula, and Miss Mamie Harwood, of Uniontown, Ala. were married yesterday at the home of her parents. (Note: This item was corrected in the next paper to read as above)

Thurs. May 30, 1889
Dr. J. G. Dean, of Dawson, Ga., and Miss Genie Brannon, of Georgetown, Ga., were married at the home of her grandfather, Col. T. L. Guerry, of Georgetown, on Wednesday.

Thurs. June 6, 1889
J. C. Cotton, Esq., lawyer of Cuthbert, (Ga.) and Miss Mamie E. Fellows, of near Cuthbert, were married Sunday.

Mr. Samuel Barnett and Miss Maye Thomas were married tonight at the home of the bride's father, Mr. W. H. Thomas, in Dallas, Tex., by Right Rev. A. C. Garrett. They will make their home in Birmingham, Ala. -Birmingham (Ala.) News of the 30th.

Thurs. June 13, 1889
Miss Moselle Walker was married recently at the home of her mother at Chunnenuggee Ridge, to Mr. Henry H. Hunter.

Rev. S. Addison McElroy and Miss Ellie Richter were married last night by Rev. Mr. McElroy, father of the groom, at the Presbyterian Church in Eufaula.

Thurs. June 20, 1889
Miss Alice Colby, formerly of Eufaula, was married in Birmingham a few days ago to Mr. Wm. Rosenstihl, Jr.

Thurs. Aug. 22, 1889
Mr. Jas. R. Newman and Miss Nancy Williams, both of Barbour County, were married in Clayton by Justice Jno. C. Williams, on Friday last.

81

Thurs. Sept. 12, 1889
    Mr. Hezekiah Williams and Miss Martha Critchen of Clayton
were married last Tuesday in Eufaula, by Rev. J. B. Cummings.

    Rev. J. I. Ayers, the Baptist pastor of Clayton, and Miss
Sallie Campbell were married in Clayton by Rev. Paul Winn.

Thurs. Sept. 19, 1889
    Mr. J. J. Parker and Miss Cora Windham, both of Ozark, (Ala.)
were married Tuesday last.

Thurs. Oct. 17, 1889*
    Mr. F. M. Flournoy and Miss Minnie Long, of Hurtsboro, (Ala.)
are to be married today in Hurtsboro.

    Mr. Meadows and Miss Lela Borders were married in Clayton
last night.

    Mr. Maximilian B. Wellborn, formerly of Eufaula, now of
North Alabama, and Miss Mary Graves, of Rome, Ga., are to be
married Oct. 17th.
(*Name of the paper changed to EUGAULA TIMES AND NEWS).

Thurs. Oct. 31, 1889
    Dr. A. S. Stegall, of Dale County, (Ala.) and Miss Daisy
Lightfoot, of Eufaula, were married in Abbeville today.

    Married at the M. E. Church in Clayton today, Mr. Lawrence
H. Lee and Miss Gussie, daughter of Judge A. H. Alston. Atten-
dants were: Mr. Perry Spencer, Jr., of Columbus, (Ga.) and Miss
Vela Lee; Mr. Geo. Peach and Miss Dellie Shorter, of Eufaula;
Mr. R. L. Petty and Miss Winn, both of Clayton; Mr. W. C. Petty
and Miss Williams, of Clayton; Mr. Ira Lampley, of Eufaula, and
Miss Marie Pickett, of Union Springs; Mr. J. C. Quillen and Miss
Foster, of Clayton. The ushers were Mr. Jeff Quillen and Mr.
Monroe Warren.

Thurs. Nov. 7, 1889
    Mr. Yancey Smith and Miss Anna Espy, daughter of Mr. Seaborn
Espy, were married yesterday at the home of the bride's parents
between Eufaula and Abbeville. -Abbeville (Ala.) Times.

Thurs. Nov. 14, 1889
    The marriage of Mr. Eugene C. Doughtie and Mrs. Emma I.
Wheatley, of Americus, (Ga.) will take place on next Thursday in
the Presbyterian Church in Americus.

    Married at Clanton, (Ala.) on the 6th of Nov., at the home
of Mr. Jno. Garner, by Rev. J. P. Sanders, Mr. Chas. S. Hamilton,
formerly of Eufaula, and Miss Piretta Acker, of Montevallo, (Ala.)
-Montgomery Journal of 7th inst.

    Mr. Peter Basil Clarke and Miss Susie Mudd, of Birmingham,
were married there Wednesday.

    Union Springs, (Ala.) Nov. 6. - Mr. K. T. Jones of this
place and Miss Viola Grace, of Ozark, (Ala.) were married in
Georgetown, Ga., yesterday.

Thurs. Nov. 21, 1889
    Married at Belcher (Barbour County) on Nov. 17th, at the
home of the bride's father, Mr. Jno. D. Glass, by Rev. R. B. Lee,
Miss Carrie Glass and Mr. Calab Golden.

    Married yesterday at the home of the bride's parents in
Midway, Ala., by Rev. T. H. Stout, Dr. R. P. Ivey and Miss Lillie
Jordan.

Mr. Bennett Bowden was married yesterday to Miss Lilly, daughter of Mr. Sam Houston, in the Rocky Mount neighborhood, by Rev. T. H. Stout.

Thurs. Dec. 5, 1889
Mr. Chas. R. McCall, of Union Springs, (Ala.) was married recently at Ocean Springs, Miss., to Miss Emily Foster.

Married in Birmingham yesterday, at the home of Capt. Jno. G. Smith, the step-father of the bride, by Rev. Pickard, Mr. Nick Shelly, of Eufaula, and Miss Nellie Hightower, formerly of Culloden, Ga.

Thurs. Dec. 12, 1889
Mr. Thos. A. Davis and Miss Annie Spann were married at the home of the bride's parents near Eufaula yesterday, by Rev. Dr. Hiden.

Married on the 5th at the home of the bride's father, Mr. J. H. Poston, (Barbour County) Mr. R. Dozier Powell and Miss M. Belle Poston, by Rev. T. H. Stout. Attendants were: Miss Irene Harwell; Mr. Jas. Hill, Miss Addie Dutton; Mr. Will Hudson, Miss Viccie Dutton; Mr. Walter Harwell, Miss Annie Swanson; Mr. Will Swanson, Miss Emmie Jordan; Mr. F. D. Bloodworth, Miss Eloise Andrews; Mr. B. F. Reid, Miss Sallie West; and Mr. Levy Foy, Miss Lou Poston.

Thurs. Dec. 19, 1889
The marriage of Miss Annie Freeman to Mr. Osborn R. Spurlock will take place Tuesday at Howe (Barbour County) at the home of the groom's mother, Mrs. J. M. Spurlock.

Mr. G. R. Anderson and Miss Ella Morgan, of Ozark, (Ala.) were married in Georgetown, Ga., yesterday at the home of Judge J. F. Mabrey.

Married near Cotton Hill, Ga., Mr. Robt. T. Boyett and Miss Kate J. McDuffie, at the home of the bride's mother in Randolph County, (Ga.) by Rev. T. H. Stout.

The marriage of Mr. G. S. Barnard, of Atlanta, (Ga.) to Miss Laura Dowling, of Daleville, Ala., is announced for the 22d inst. -Ozark (Ala.) Star.

Married last Thursday at the home of the bride's father, Mr. Ransom Byrd, by Rev. J. W. Parker, Mr. Jno. T. Bell and Miss Lela Byrd.

Thurs. Dec. 26, 1889
Mr. J. T. Dillard and Miss Anna Layton were married last Sunday by Rev. I. F. Betts. -Abbeville (Ala.) Times.

Mr. Jas. Jones and Miss N. B. Vining were married in Georgetown, (Ga.) on Wednesday.

Married at Glennville, (Ala.) Wednesday, Miss Roberta Bass, daughter of Capt. Jno. H. Bass, and Mr. Junius A. Flewellen, of Orange Lake, Fla., by Rev. Kerton. Attendants were: Mr. Earnest Flewellen, of Fla., and Miss Jennie Bass; Mr. Julius Mitchell and Miss Johnnie Bass; Mr. W. T. Berry, of Eufaula, and Miss Lucy Glenn; Col. Raiford Rivers, of Birmingham, and Miss Minnie Barnett; Mr. Croff Griffin, of Eufaula, and Miss Kate Persons; Mr. Flewellen Persons and Mamie McGough; Mr. Will Howard and Miss Susie McGough. Ushers: Messrs. W. W. Tarver, J. B. Garland, Percy Bass, Robt. Howard. Flower girls: Misses Mary Tarver and Lena Garland.

A double wedding near Lawrenceville, (Ala.) last Thursday united Mr. Press Anderson and Miss Mellie Hendley, also Mr. Jas. G. Holmes and Miss Laura Hendley, at the home of the father of the brides, Mr. R. D. Hendley.

Mr. T. D. McGough, of Eufaula, and Miss Annie Will Perry, daughter of Capt. E. C. Perry, were married in Glennville, Ala., last week.

EUFAULA DAILY TIMES
1889

Sat. July 20, 1889
Mr. Joe Jimmerson was married Thursday at Belcher, (Barbour County) to Miss Amanda West, by J. W. Gresham, Esq.

Sun. July 21, 1889
Mr. Mike Sally, of Abbeville, (Ala.) and Miss Hutchins of Howard's Landing, Ga., were married last Thursday. -Columbia (Ala.) Enterprise.

Sat. July 17, 1889
Married at Columbia, Ala., on the 24th, Mr. Jno. D. Ashton and Miss Addie Williams.

Sat. Aug. 31, 1889
Married, at the home of the bride's mother in Montgomery last Thursday, Mr. W. W. Coghill and Miss Loula F. Carter.

Wed. Sept. 4, 1889
Mr. W. G. Hunt, Jr., of Clio, (Ala.) and Miss Maud Coneedy, of Henry County, (Ala.) married yesterday, by Rev. J. B. Cummings.

Thurs. Sept. 5, 1889
Married at Belcher (Barbour County) on Tuesday last, by Rev. Thomas, Mr. Bradley, of Clayton, and Miss Mollie Bland, of Belcher.

Thurs. Sept. 12, 1889
Married at Union Springs, (Ala.) yesterday, Mr. Fred Pitts of Clayton, and Miss Viccie Walker, of Union Springs, Rev. Wade officiating.

Fri. Nov. 8, 1889
Haverhill, Mass., Nov. 1. - Miss Harriet Day, of Haverhill, and Jno. Tener, of the Chicago baseball club, married here today. They will live in Pittsburg.

Fri. Nov. 15, 1889
Married, Jang Landsig, a native of China, residing in Cleveland, and Miss Nellie H. Sparks, daughter of Mrs. G. W. Sparks, of Vernon, Conn., by Rev. Jos. H. Twitchell of Hartford. The groom came to this country in 1876.

Wed. Nov. 27, 1889
A. C. Lanier, of New York, married Mrs. Stella Sering in Indianapolis, Ind., on Friday last.

Thurs. Nov. 28, 1889
Married at Belcher (Barbour County) on Sunday, by S. H. Driggers, Esq., Mr. Anderson Bush to Miss Redman*. (*Marriage Records, Probate Office; Clayton, Ala.: Jas. A. Bush and Lizzie Redmond).

Wed. Dec. 4, 1889

Massillon, Ohio, Dec. 2. - Miss Anna W. Crane, daughter of Frank Crane, and Mr. Valentine Fries, of Erie County, were married Thursday.

1890

Sat. Jan. 4, 1890

Married at Newton, (Ala.) last Thursday, Mr. M. C. Oliver and Miss Mollie Bouie. -Ozark (Ala.) Star.

Married on Sunday near Ozark, by R. D. B. Griggs, Esq., Mr. M. B. Grace and Miss Nancy Buttoms. -Ozark (Ala.) Star.

Married in Troy (Ala.) Tuesday, by Rev. J. F. Purser, Mr. Jas. E. Henderson and Miss Mattie Hilliard, of Troy.

Married at the home of the bride's father, Mr. J. W. Johnson near Ozark last Thursday, by Judge Parker, Mr. Jas. R. Powell and Miss A. J. Johnson. -Ozark (Ala.) Star.

Mr. Geo. S. Banard, of Atlanta, Ga., and Miss Laura Dowling, of Daleville, (Ala.) were married at the home of her father on the 22nd ult. -Ozark (Ala.) Star.

Mr. S. J. Goff, of Decatur, Ala., and Miss Mattie Mathews, of Dale County, (Ala.) were married recently. -Ozark (Ala.) Star.

Married recently at the home of the bride's father, Mr. L. S. Martin, by Rev. A. L. Sellers, Mr. J. Yancy Crawford and Miss Julia Martin. -Ozark (Ala.) Star.

Married on the eve of Christmas at the M. E. Church, in Ozark, Mr. Chas. D. Carmichael and Miss Fannie Bowen, by Rev. C. L. McCartha. The groom is the son of Judge J. M. Carmichael. The bride is the second daughter of the late Dr. O. B. Bowen, formerly of Henry County. Attendants: Miss Wynona Bowen and A. T. Borders; Miss Pauline Carmichael and J. H. Adams; Miss Willie Dowling and A. G. Bowen; Mrs. Luta Bowen and F. B. Cullens; Mr. Jas. H. Davis best man, and Mr. Albert Bowen accompanied the bride. -Ozark (Ala.) Star.

Sun. Jan. 5, 1890

Married at the home of the bride's parents, by the Hon. J. C. Williams, Mr. C. R. Vinson and Miss Nora Nix. -Clayton Courier.

R. L. Hardwick and Miss Laura Boon were married at the home of Mr. R. S. Hardwick, who performed the ceremony during Christmas week. -Abbeville (Ala.) Times.

Mr. Jno. Jones and Miss Pelham, daughter of Rev. H. D. Pelham, were married at the home of the bride in Henry County, by Rev. Mr. Ward, during Christmas week. -Abbeville (Ala.) Times.

Mr. Jno. Elkins and Miss Millie Hunt were married in Henry County during Christmas week, by Mr. Charley Mobley, J.P. -Abbeville (Ala.) Times.

Mr. Jno. Spann and Miss Johnson, daughter of Mr. Alex Johnson, were married at the home of the bride's parents in Henry County during Christmas week. -Abbeville (Ala.) Times.

Mr. Andrew Davis and Miss Laura Grandbery were married at the bride's home in Henry County, by Rev. E. M. Knowles during Christmas week. -Abbeville (Ala.) Times.

Mr. Cody Grandbery and Miss Lizzie McClenny were married at the home of the bride's parents in Henry County by Alex Summerford, J.P., during Christmas week. -Abbeville (Ala.) Times.

Married in Henry County during Christmas week, by T. C. McClenny, at the home of the bride's parents, Mr. Jno. I. Monk and Miss Lizzie Shelly.

Tues. Jan. 7, 1890
    Mr. William Gilmer and Miss Minnie Brown, of Abbeville, were married in Georgetown, (Ga.) yesterday by Judge Lee.

Wed. Jan. 8, 1890
    Mr. M. J. Reeder, formerly of Barbour County, married at his home in Orangeburg County, S. C., on the 31st of Dec. last, to Miss Alice Fannin.

Fri. Jan. 10, 1890
    Mr. F. L. Merritt and Miss Emma Crymes, daughter of Dr. A. C. Crymes, were married at the home of the bride's father in Midway, (Ala.) last night, by Rev. Mr. Pilley.

Sat. Jan. 11, 1890
    Mr. Phil. Yarbrough, of Randolph County, and Miss Zella Hillman, of Quitman County, Ga., were married at the home of the bride's father on Wednesday, by Rev. Harris.

    Married Sunday in Georgetown, Ga., Mr. M. J. Garner and Miss Annie Blackman, both of this place. -Ozark (Ala.) Star.

Thurs. Jan. 23, 1890
    Married at the M. E. Church in Eufaula last evening, Mr. Walter Treutlen Berry and Miss Beal Herndon, by Rev. Dr. W. M. Motley. Attendants: Mr. J. B. Cummings and Miss Ellen Barnett; Mr. C. G. Barnett and Miss Laura Treutlen, of Washington, D. C.; Mr. Geo. W. Whitlock and Miss Lucy Glenn; Mr. E. L. Edmonson and Miss Lillie Barnett, of Athens, Ga.; Mr. Henry Crawford and Miss Sallie Caldwell; Mr. W. H. Foy and Miss Johnnie Bass; Mr. Geo. Beauchamp and Miss Leila Thornton; Mr. Ira Lampley and Miss Lula Walker; Mr. H. C. Holleman and Miss Mamie Harrison; Mr. Frank Crawford and Miss Pat Bass; Master P. E. Barnett and Miss Carrie Berry opened the gate to the Hymen's Alter, and Prof. Croley presided at the organ.

Thurs. Jan. 30, 1890
    Married yesterday at the home of the bride's parents, Mr. and Mrs. J. S. Wilson, near Eufaula, by Rev. Dr. Howard Key, of Cuthbert, Ga., Mr. Wm. F. Smith and Miss Adell Wilson.

Sat. Feb. 8, 1890
    Married at the home of Mr. Hart McCall, near Clio, Ala., last Thursday, by Rev. A. L. Sellers, Dr. C. M. McNair, of Ozark, and Miss Willie R. McCall of Barbour County.

Wed. Feb. 12, 1890
    Miss Rosser Flournoy, daughter of J. T. Flournoy, and Mr. A. S. Johnston, of Anniston, Ala., are to be married at the Episcopal Church in Eufaula, by Rev. Dr. Spaulding. (Note: Episcopal Church Records, Eufaula, Martha Rosser Flournoy married on Feb. 12th to Adam Saffold Johnston, by Dr. Erastus W. Spalding).

Thurs. Feb. 13, 1890
    At the home of the bride's father at Howe (Barbour County) yesterday, by Dr. Levy, of Selma, Miss Ellie Gaston was married to Mr. Abe Lehman, of Greenville, Ala.

Wed. Feb. 19, 1890

Married at the Episcopal Church yesterday, Mr. Frank D.
Bloodworth and Miss Sarah E. Ross, daughter of Mr. Jas. Ross.
Attendants were: Best man, Mr. W. H. Foy. Mr. W. J. Ross and
Miss Lucy Bloodworth; Mr. Frank Crawford and Miss Clara Bell
Kendall; Mr. Ed Edmonson and Miss Leila Thornton; Mr. S. H. Dent,
Jr., and Miss Lula Kendall. Ushers were Messrs. W. T. Stephens,
W. S. Goolsby, Johnnie Whitlock and E. H. Ross.

Fri. Feb. 21, 1890
Miss Catedonia Powell and Mr. Madison Metcalf were married
Tuesday. -Ozark (Ala.) Star.

Sat. Feb. 22, 1890
Mr. Chas. I. McLaughlin and Miss Leila Ricks were married at
Louisville, Ky., on the 18th. They will reside at Marshall,
Texas.

Thurs. Feb. 27, 1890
Married at the home of the bride's father, Dr. W. A. Mit-
chell, in Eufaula, yesterday, by Rev. H. W. Key, of Cuthbert,
Ga., Mr. Robt. M. Ormond, of Atlanta, Ga., and Miss Willia A.
Mitchell. Attendants were: W. T. Flournoy and Miss Lillie
Drewry; Mr. Chas. L. Bray and Miss Montine Thomas, of New York.
Miss Emma Brooks supplied the music.

Tues. Mar. 4, 1890
Married at the home of Mr. W. A. Jackson, by Rev. Mr. Mc-
Elory on Sunday last, Mr. Jas. Saunders to Miss Rachael Tisdale,
all of Eufaula.

Wed. Mar. 5, 1890
Married at the home of Mr. J. C. Guilford, by Rev. Mr.
DeBardelaben on Thursday last, Mr. Ed. Chestnut, of Sandy Point,
(Barbour County) to Miss Mary Warren, of Quitman County, Ga.

Thurs. Mar. 13, 1890
Mr. Chas. R. Keith and Miss Minnie Slaughter; and Mr. Gus.
McKinnon and Miss Callie Laney, all of Geneva, (Ala.) were
married recently. -Ozark (Ala.) Star.

Fri. Mar. 14, 1890
Married on the 12th at the home of the bride's father, Mr.
Thomas Weathers, by Rev. T. H. Stout, Mr. W. A. Hill, of Birming-
ham, Ala., and Miss Sallie L. Weathers, of Batesville, Ala.

Tues. Mar. 18, 1890
Married at Lodi (Barbour County) at the home of the bride's
father, Rev. W. E. Gilford (Guilford?), Mr. L. D. Smith and Miss
D. L. Gilford. Attendants were: Misses G. W. Barry, M. S.
Williams, Ella and Jennie Smith, Eveline Lee, Ida Smith, and G.
W. Williams.

Mr. Jeff Mooneyhan, of Crawford County, Ga., and Miss Laura
Wood, of Oak, (Barbour County) were married yesterday.

Mar. 23, 1890
Married at Headland, (Ala.) on the 16th inst., by Rev. S. J.
Knowles, Mr. J. Askew, of Dolthan, (Ala.) and Miss Tannie B. Sims,
of Headland. -Dolthan (Ala.) Light.

Tues. Mar. 25, 1890
Mr. Jas. Griffin and Mrs. M. N. Brannon were married Sunday
at the home of the latter in Eufaula.

87

Sun. Mar. 30, 1890
    Married on Tuesday evening, by Jno. C. Williams, Esq., Mr.
W. H. Williams and Miss Epsey Barron.

Tues. Apr. 1, 1890
    Married at Belcher (Barbour County) on Sunday, at the home
of Mr. J. W. Gresham, Mr. A. A. Richardson to Mrs. Winnie Miller,
J. W. Gresham officiating.

Sat. Apr. 5, 1890
    Mr. C. L. Solomon, of Cuthbert, (Ga.) and Miss Lillian
Lewis, daughter of Mr. and Mrs. Warren Lewis, of Quitman County,
(Ga.) were married at the home of Mr. T. J. Ellis in Quitman
County on Thursday last. -Cuthbert (Ga.) Liberal.

Wed. Apr. 9, 1890
    Miss Effie Williams, daughter of Hon. Jere N. Williams, was
married in Clayton yesterday to Mr. W. A. Leland of Charleston,
S. C., by Rev. Wade.

Fri. Apr. 11, 1890
    Married at the city court room yesterday, Mr. E. M. Glover
to Miss Ellie C. Crews, of Nance's Mill, (Barbour County) by
'Squire' Ben Nance.

    Mr. Wm. Dunaway and Miss Emma Tillsdale, of Eufaula, were
married in Georgetown, (Ga.) on Sunday.

    Mr. J. T. Faulk and Miss Carlisle, of Sylvan Grove, (Dale
County) were married in the court house last Thursday, by Judge
Parker. -Ozark (Ala.) Star.

    Married at Daleville (Ala.) last Sunday, by Rev. R. Deal,
Mr. Wm. Red and Miss Irene Lanier. -Ozark (Ala.) Star.

Sun. Apr. 20, 1890
    Mr. R. K. Bedell, of St. Louis, Mo., formerly of Eufaula,
was married in that city on the 18th inst., to Miss Lizzie Fears.

Fri. Apr. 25, 1890
    Married at the home of the bride's father, in Ozark last
Sunday, Mr. I. Ledbetter and Miss Ludie Skipper. -Ozark (Ala.)
Star.

    Miss Jennie T. Davis and Mr. Wm. W. Reed* will be married
in Atlanta on the 29th inst. Her brother, Mr. Geo. B. Davis, of
Eufaula will attend the marriage. (*From May 2nd paper the groom's
name: Wm. W. Reid).

Sat. Apr. 26, 1890
    Mr. Henry Ivey and Miss Henrietta O. Hayes, of Alabama, were
married in Georgetown, (Ga.) by Justice Cross on Wednesday last.
-Cuthbert (Ga.) Appeal.

Sun. Apr. 27, 1890
    Married at the home of the bride's sister, Mrs. C. E. Walker,
Mr. David Dawson Moore and Miss Sadie M. Grist, of Blakely, Ga.
-Columbia (Ala.) Enterprise.

Tues. Apr. 29, 1890
    Married on Sunday in Glennville, Ala., by Rev. Mr. Mills,
Mr. Jas. Staudte to Miss Mattie Whitmore.

Wed. May 7, 1890
    Married at the home of Mr. Jas. Orr on the 4th inst., Mr.

C. D. Bush to Miss Eugenia Woods, both of White Oak Springs,
Ala. (Barbour County).

Fri. May 16, 1890
       Married at Georgetown, (Ga.) on Wednesday, by Wm. M. Motley,
Mr. Z. A. Stallings, of Brundidge, Ala., to Miss Fannie Davidson,
of Georgetown.

       Mr. R. G. Humphrey and Miss Georgia Rowell, both of Eufaula,
were married in Georgetown, (Ga.) on Sunday.

Sat. May 31, 1890
       Tuskaloosa, Ala. May 29. - Married today at the Episcopal
Church, Miss Helen D. Clayton, daughter of the late Henry D.
Clayton, and Dr. Harry Rogers, of Memphis, Tenn., Rev. String-
fellow officiating.

Fri. June 6, 1890
       Married yesterday, Mr. W. Cary Thornton, of Columbus, Ga.,
and Miss Minnie A. Swanson, at Spring Hill, (Barbour County) at
the home of the bride.* (*Note Correction: Miss Neena Swanson
married Mr. Thornton, a sister to Miss Minnie Swanson who married
Mr. H. J. Long.)

Fri. June 13, 1890
       Married yesterday at the home of the bride's father in
Eufaula, Mr. Chas. Clinton Hanson and Miss Marie Adele Shorter,
daughter of Hon. Henry R. Shorter, by Rev. Dr. Spalding.

Tues. June 17, 1890
       Mr. P. O. O'Byrne and Miss Julia Wheeler were married at
the home of the bride's mother in Eufaula on Sunday, by Justice
Pruett.

Fri. June 20, 1890
       Rev. P. L. Thomas was married at Lodi on the 12th to Miss
M. E. Blanchett, both of Barbour County, by Justice T. D. Williams.

Sat. June 21, 1890
       Mr. Frank P. Crawford, of Anniston, Ala., and Miss Henrietta
Boone, of Hawkinsville, Ga., are to be married on June 25th.

Sat. June 22, 1890
       Dr. S. D. Gay, of Selma, (Ala.) and Miss Corrine Hunter, of
Mobile, were married Wednesday.

Thurs. July 3, 1890
       Married last Sunday at the Baptist Church in Newton, (Ala.)
by Rev. P. M. Calloway, Mr. W. E. Dunn and Miss Sallie Peters,
also, Mr. H. M. Hunter and Miss Georgia Peters. -Ozark (Ala.)
Star.

Fri. July 11, 1890
       Mr. T. E. Shadgett, of Dothan, (Ala.) and Miss Minnie Baker,
daughter of Mr. Joe Baker, were married at the home of the bride's
parents in Bakersville on the 3d ult. -Columbia (Ala.) Recorder.

Tues. July 15, 1890
       Marriages in Georgetown, (Ga.) yesterday were: Daniel
Phillips and Miss B. Dunlap; Buddy Tew and Miss Dunlap, and
Walter Atkinson and Miss Ida Thomas. Miss Thomas is from Henry
County, the others are from Barbour County.

Fri. July 18, 1890
     Mr. Jno. Creal and Miss Della Searcy, both of Barbour County, were married in Georgetown, Ga., by 'Squire' Lee on Tuesday.

Tues. July 22, 1890
     Mr. J. N. Bradley and Miss Grace Barbour, formerly of Baltimore, (Md.) were married by Rev. Motley, at the home of Mr. S. R. Foy, in Eufaula, on Sunday. Attendants were: Messrs. Chas. S. Bray and Beall Hart.

Thurs. July 24, 1890
     Last Saturday a week ago Miss Pauline Hardeman, daughter of State Treasurer, was secretly married to Mr. Jesse Thompson, Jr., of Augusta, (Ga.) in South Carolina. They will reside in Augusta.

Sat. July 26, 1890
     W. H. Hasty and Miss Lola Hall, from near Abbeville, (Ala.) were married Monday on the Ferry Boat crossing the Chattahoochee, by Rev. W. M. Burr. -Columbia, Ala. Recorder.

Thurs. Aug. 7, 1890
     Mr. Max Baldwin and Miss Carrie Guerry, second daughter of Rev. L. Guerry, were married in Georgetown, (Ga.) on yesterday. Both parties reside in Eufaula.

Fri. Aug. 8, 1890
     Married at the home of Col. H. L. Martin last Saturday, by Judge Parker, Mr. Henry Opp, of Andalusia, (Ala.) and Miss Addie Belle Gardner, of Troy, (Ala.). -Ozark (Ala.) Star.

     Married at the home of Mrs. F. M. Wood, Mr. W. A. Ham, of Opelika, Ala., and Miss Marie Wood, youngest daughter of the late Judge Fern M. Wood, by Rev. M. Everhart, of Decatur, Ga. -Montgomery (Ala.) Advertiser.

Wed. Aug. 13, 1890
     Miss Mattie Maughon was married in Ozark, (Ala.) Saturday to Mr. Mathews, of that place.

Thurs. Aug. 14, 1890
     Married yesterday in Troy, Ala., at the home of the bride's father, Rev. H. E. Brooks, by Rev. Jno. F. Purser, Miss Emma Brooks and Mr. O. Worthy. Ushers were Messrs. McBryde, of Troy, and Mr. Jno. Whitlock, of Eufaula.

Thurs. Aug. 21, 1890
     Mr. Edward Marcellus Butt, of Rome, Ga., and Miss Sallie Cunningham, daughter of Capt. Robt. Cunningham, of Newman, Ga., will be married at the M. E. Church in Newman on Sept. 3rd.

Sat. Aug. 23, 1890
     Mr. James McGee and Miss Estalena Stovall were married at the home of the bride's mother in Eufaula on Thursday, by Rev. W. M. Motley.

Fri. Aug. 29, 1890
     Married at the Baptist Church in Midway, (Ala.) yesterday, Miss Venie J. Feagin and Rev. J. M. Kelly, of Cochran, Ga., by Rev. J. O. Hixon.

Sat. Aug. 30, 1890
     Mr. Henry Roberts, of Clopton, and Mrs. Harrell, who lives near Haw Ridge, were married on Sunday last. -Ozark (Ala.) Star.

Tues. Sept. 9, 1890
    Married at Belcher (Barbour County) last Sunday, by 'Squire'
James, Mr. Ed Price to Miss Fletcher Williams, daughter of Mr.
Jno. Cochran Williams.

Thurs. Sept. 11, 1890
    Dr. W. B. Gibson, of Austin, (Tex.) and Mrs. Rosa Huey, of
Eufaula, Ala. were married yesterday at the Tenth Street M. E.
Church in Austin, by Dr. Edwin B. Chappell. Dr. Gibson was born
and reared in Travis County, and is a brother to Hon. A. J. Gibson. The bride is a daughter of Capt. Jno. C. McNab, of Eufaula,
and a sister of Mrs. W. L. Bryan, of Austin. -Austin (Tex.)
Statesman, 4th inst.

Sun. Sept. 14, 1890
    On the 7th inst., Mr. Levi Padgett and Miss Laura Russell
were married by C. H. McCall, Esq., all of Beat 8, (Barbour
County). -Clayton Courier.

Fri. Sept. 19, 1890
    Married in the court house last Friday by Judge Parker, Mr.
Jonas Lambert and Miss Laura Henderson, both of this county.
-Ozark Star, 17th.

Fri. Sept. 26, 1890
    Mr. E. R. Phillips, of Dean's Station, and Miss Cullie
Searcy, only daughter of Mr. T. R. Searcy, were married Wednesday
at Mt. Andrew, (Barbour County) by Rev. T. H. Stout.

Sun. Sept. 28, 1890
    Mr. Fred B. Cullens and Miss Annie Laura Davis were married
at Ozark last Wednesday, by Rev. A. L. Sellers.

    Mr. J. E. Scroggins and Miss Callie Dubose were married in
Beat 8, Barbour County, on the 20th inst.

Wed. Oct. 1, 1890
    Married at the home of Mrs. Henry Bradley, the bride's
mother, in Mt. Andrew, Ala., on Sept. 28th, Mr. W. A. Fortner, of
Dothan, Ala., and Miss Annie Bradley, of the former place.

Sun. Oct. 5, 1890
    Mr. Oscar Murphy and Miss Gertie Aman were married last
Sunday at the home of the bride's parents near Cureton's Bridge,
by Rev. C. C. Deal. -Abbeville (Ala.) Times.

    Mr. Jim Southerland and Miss Starling, daughter of Alfred
Starling, were married last Friday at the home of the bride's
parents, near Shorterville. -Abbeville (Ala.) Times.

Wed. Oct. 15, 1890
    Mr. Robt. Cunningham was married Oct. 9th at Decatur, Ala.,
to Miss Susie Everhart.

    Married last evening at the home of the bride's parents in
Eufaula, Mr. Frank Price and Miss Alice Gary, the daughter of
Capt. L. L. Gary.

    The marriage of Mr. A. P. Moye and Miss Lula Tumlin, both
of Cuthbert, Ga., is announced for 23rd inst., at Cuthbert.

Sun. Oct. 26, 1890
    Married in a balloon, at the State Fair Grounds, in Birming-
ham, on 24th, Mr. Thos. J. Mims and Miss Gertrude Pittman, both
of Brewton, Ala., by Rev. S. M. Adams, of Bibb County, Ala.

91

Wed. Oct. 29, 1890
     Mr. W. H. Holland and Miss Bettie Reeves were married on
the 21st, at the home of Mr. Wm. Dew, near Clayton, Elder B. F.
Newton, officiating.

Fri. Oct. 31, 1890
     Mr. Boling A. Blakely and Miss Emma Werner Forss were
married at Auburn on Wednesday last at the home of the bride's
aunt, Mrs. Riley.

Sat. Nov. 1, 1890
     Mr. Louis B. Farley and Miss Jette Means,* both of Montgo-
mery, Ala., were married Thursday last at the Court Street M. E.
Church. (*Oct. 22nd paper: Miss Annie Jette Means).

     Mr. Gaston A. Robbins, Esq., of Selma (Ala.) and Miss Ira
C. Alexander, of Faunsdale, Ala., were married Wednesday.

Wed. Nov. 5, 1890
     Married on 2nd inst., at the home of the bride's mother near
Mt. Andrew, Barbour County, Mr. Robert Bradley, of Hurtsboro,
(Ala.) and Miss Estelle Patterson.

     Married at the home of Mr. Jno. M. Edmonson, brother of the
bride, in Eufaula, on Nov. 4th inst., Miss Mattie Edmonson and
Mr. Chas. Duncan Barnes, of near Ozark, Ala., Rev. D. W. Barnes,
brother of the groom, officiating. Bridesmaids were: Misses
Mattie Walker, Mamie Harrison, Louise Shorter and Lula Walker.

Thurs. Nov. 6, 1890
     Mr. R. D. Gay, of Quitman County, (Ga.) was married yester-
day in Cuthbert, (Ga.) to Miss Annie Barfield of that city.

Sat. Nov. 8, 1890
     Mr. Thos. Slappey, of Americus, (Ga.) and Miss Lena McCar-
dell, of Macon, were married in Macon on Wednesday last.

     Mr. Geo. S. Jones and Miss Berta Hardeman, daughter of Col.
Isaac Hardeman, were married in Macon on Wednesday last.

     Announcement is made of the approaching marriage at Memphis,
(Tenn.) of Mr. Louis Woods, formerly of Eufaula, to Miss Norma
Goodman, at Calvary Church on Nov. 12th.

Tues. Nov. 11, 1890
     Abbeville, Ala., Nov. 8. - Mr. Jno. W. Seaborn and Miss
Annie J. McLean were married at the home of the bride's father
at Lodi, (Barbour County). Attendants: Mr. W. J. Seaborn and
Miss Emma Lewis; Jno. Snead, Jr., and Addie McLane; Jas. N. Zorn
and Annie Snead; Ed. Gillis and L. A. Morrison; H. D. McLane and
M. C. Morrison; L. J. Zorn and Clemmie Snead.

Fri. Nov. 14, 1890
     Capt. M. H. Amerine, of Montgomery, and Miss Effie Neely,
of Greenville, (Ala.) were married in Greenville on Wednesday
last.

Sat. Nov. 15, 1890
     Mr. Clarence P. Roberts, of Eufaula, and Miss Georgia C.
Archibald, of Oxford, Miss., were married on Tuesday in Oxford.
They will reside in Eufaula.

     At Clayton on Thursday, Mr. Geo. W. Peach was married to
Miss Vela Lee, daughter of Col. and Mrs. Alto V. Lee, by Rev.
Wade. Attendants were Mrs. Lawrence Lee, Miss Alma Peach, Miss

Weetie Warren, Miss Jennie Petty, Miss Mabel Clarke, Miss Agnes
Owens, Miss Norman Williams and Miss Pearl Foster. Ushers were:
Mr. L. H. Lee, Mr. Walter Petty, Mr. Arthur Peach, Mr. Monroe
Warren and Mr. Bates Warren.

Wed. Nov. 19, 1890
    Mr. Abner J. Teague and Miss Julia Amende were married at
the Court Street M. E. Church in Montgomery yesterday.

Thurs. Nov. 20, 1890
    Married yesterday, Mr. J. F. McTyer and Miss Lizzie C.
Thompson, of Columbia, (ALa.). They will reside near Eufaula.

    Mr. W. L. Madre, of Americus, Ga., and Miss Sarah L. Bivins,
of Auburn, (Ala.) were married Tuesday last.

Fri. Nov. 21, 1890
    Married in Glennville, Russell County, (Ala.) Mr. Will M.
Bray, of Eufaula, and Miss Mamie McGough, and also Mr. T. H.
Baarcke, of Mobile, and Miss Susie McGough, at the home of the
bride's mother.

    Mr. Jas. P. Hill and Miss Addie M. Dutton, both of Eufaula,
were married by Rev. Dr. J. C. Hiden yesterday at the home of
the bride's mother.

Wed. Nov. 26, 1890
    Mr. E. L. Smith, of Montgomery, and Miss Jodie Burnes, of
Fort Deposit were married by Rev. J. T. Howell on Monday at Fort
Deposit, (Ala.).

Thurs. Nov. 27, 1890
    New York, Nov. 25. - The wedding of Miss Annie Coudert,
daughter of Frederic R. Coudert, to Mackenzie Semple, formerly
of Alabama, was solemnized today at the home of the bride's
parents.

Sun. Nov. 30, 1890
    Mr. J. G. Jones and Miss Carrie Whiddon were married recent-
ly at the home of J. S. Kirkland, relative of the bride.
-Abbeville (Ala.) Times.

Wed. Dec. 3, 1890
    Mr. Jno. T. Vaughan and Miss Mollie Weathers were married
Nov. 30th at Malone's Chapel, near Eufaula, by Rev. T. A. Johnson.

Fri. Dec. 5, 1890
    Mr. C. C. Crow, of Hawkinsville, Barbour County, and Miss
Lula Price, of Eufaula, were married at the home of Mr. Jesse
Cobb, Eufaula, by Judge W. H. Pruett.

Sat. Dec. 6, 1890
    Mr. H. B. Fields and Miss Louise Foster, of Calera, (Ala.)
were married Wednesday in that place by Z. A. Dowling.

    Mr. C. D. Brown, of Cuthbert, (Ga.) and Miss Callie Grier,
of Milledgeville, (Ga.) were married last Tuesday.

    On Wednesday last, Mr. J. R. Powell and Miss Ida Oliver were
married in Shellman, Ga.

Sun. Dec. 7, 1890
    Martinsville, Ind., Dec. 5. - Miss Mary Hubbard, daughter of
the County Treasurer of this city, and Jas. Sedwick were married
at the home of the bride on Thanksgiving.

Tues. Dec. 9, 1890

Mr. Wm. J. Chambers, of Fla., and Miss Jennie Bass, of Eufaula, will be married at the M. E. Church in Eufaula, tomorrow.

Mr. Albert M. Owens, of Ozark, (Ala.) and Mrs. Lon F. Johnson, of Barbour County, were married on the 7th of Dec., in Eufaula, by Rev. T. A. Johnson.

Wed. Dec. 10, 1890

Mr. Phil Pearce, of Eufaula, and Miss Carrie Massey of Albany were married yesterday near Albany, Ga.

Rev. J. P. Margart and wife will celebrate the fiftieth anniversary of their marriage at their home near Batesville, Ala., on Dec. 23rd inst.

Fri. Dec. 12, 1890

Mr. Tolbert L. Dowling and Miss Polly Thomason were married at Abberfoil on Wednesday. -Ozark (Ala.) Star, 10th.

Mr. M. F. Pippin and Miss Ella C. Deal, both of Ozark, (Ala.) were married last Sunday at the home of Rev. R. Deal, by Rev. R. B. Arnold.

Mr. Chas. Abney, of Macon, Ga., and Miss Donie James, of Eufaula, were married the 10th inst., in Eufaula. Miss James is the daughter of Mr. J. B. James, and sister to Mrs. Geo. Sangree.

Mr. Wesley J. Galloway, of Abbeville, and Miss Minnie Speight, of Ft. Gaines, (Ga.) were married in Ft. Gaines last Thursday.

Sat. Dec. 13, 1890

Mr. L. M. Burrus and Miss Gena, daughter of Mr. and Mrs. Jas. H. Brown, were married recently at the home of the bride's parents in Columbus, Ga. -Enquirer (Ga.) Sun.

Wed. Dec. 17, 1890

Opelika, (Ala.), Dec. 17. - Mr. Daniel Bullard, of Chambers County, (Ala.) and Miss Sallie Cullom were married here today.

Announcement is made of the marriage of Miss Jennie, daughter of Dr. J. T. Jelks, of Hot Springs, Ark., to Mr. Gerald Ware, of Montgomery, (Ala.) on Dec. 30th.

Sat. Dec. 20, 1890

Mr. Abner H. Flewellen and Miss Emma Long* were married at Harris (Barbour County) on Thursday. (*Correction: The bride's name was Emma E. Long, married 18 Dec. 1890 at Spring Hill, (Barbour County) by A. H. Morse, Barbour County Marriage Records, Bk. 11, p. 593).

Sun. Dec. 21, 1890

Mr. J. L. Sanders, of Cuthbert, and Miss Bertie Gay, daughter of Mr. W. E. Gay, of Quitman County, Ga., were married recently by Rev. Mr. Baldy.

Mr. W. H. Samford, son of Col. W. J. Samford, of Opelika, (Ala.) and Miss Katie Park, of Troy, were married Thursday at the Baptist Church in Troy, (Ala.).

Tues. Dec. 23, 1890

Married in Lawrenceville, (Ala.) on Sunday last, Mr. Joseph Ward and Miss Elizabeth Clenny, by Rev. E. S. Ward.

Married near Louisville, Barbour County, by J. M. Danford, Esq., on Dec. 14, 1890, Mr. W. A. Hagler and Miss M. E. Norton.

Sun. Dec. 28, 1890
      Married at the home of the bride's father, near Hatcher's
Station, Ga., on the 24th inst., Mr. Early Craft and Miss Laura
Roberts, both of Quitman County, Ga., by Rev. J. G. Carley.

Tues. Dec. 30, 1890
      On Dec. 23, at Lumpkin, Ga., Dr. W. H. Potter and Mrs.
Georgie Bray were married. They will reside in Texas where Dr.
Potter is minister of a Methodist Church.

ADDENDA

THE EUFAULA DEMOCRAT, 1848

Wed. Jan. 19, 1848
      Married on 30th ult., in Montgomery County, by Rev. Mr.
Finley, Mr. Wm. H. Nichols, of Eufaula, to Miss E. Farley, of
Montgomery.

Wed. Feb. 2, 1848
      Married in Barbour County on 26th inst., by Rev. L. C.
Harrison, Mr. Edwin H. Cotton, of Randolph, Ga., to Miss Ardelier
Porter, of Barbour County, Ala.

THE HENRY COUNTY REGISTER

Sat. July 16, 1870
      Married on the 10th inst., at the home of the bride's father,
by Rev. L. R. Sims, Mr. R. C. Price, of Abbeville, to Miss Mary
E. Martin, of Henry County.

Fri. Feb. 12, 1875
      Dr. Z. J. Daniels, late of Eufaula, and recently appointed
an assistant surgeon in the Federal Army, and Miss Laura Keils,
daughter of E. M. Keils, ex-judge of Eufaula City Court, were
married at the St. Cloud Hotel in Washington city on 4th inst.

THE BLUFF CITY TIMES

Thurs. May 18, 1871
      Married in Pensacola, Fla., on May 4th, by Rev. J. Augustus
Pace, Pastor of the M. E. Church South, Mr. J. W. Gingles to
Miss Fannie Hutchinson.

THE HENRY COUNTY REGISTER

Fri. Oct. 13, 1876
      Mr. Elijah Kirkland and Miss Fanny Whitehead at Headland,
(Ala.) by J. J. Head, on Sept. 27, 1876.

THE EUFAULA WEEKLY TIMES

Thurs. July 26, 1877
      Capt. H. C. Cooke, of the U. S. Army, was recently married
to Miss Teresa Thom, of Alabama, and the bridal pair have left
for the Indian frontier.

THE TIMES AND NEWS

Tues. Jan. 14, 1879
      Married at the home of the bride's father, on the 7th inst.,
by Rev. W. H. Patterson, Mr. Jesse B. Davis and Miss Rebecca
Thornton, all of Barbour County.

Sat. Jan. 11, 1879
    The Rev. Mr. Glenn and Mrs. Cassady, relict of the late Rev. John Cassady, were married in Barbour County a few days since. (Court House Records: Jas. W. Glenn and Mary P. Cassady were married 1-9-1879).

Sat. June 7, 1879
    Mr. Chas. R. Chaires and Miss Mattie Wade, both of Tallahassee, (Fla.) married on the 29th ult.

THE EUFAULA WEEKLY BULLETIN

Wed. Mar. 14, 1883
    Married at the home of the bride's father, near Cotton Hill, (Barbour County) on Sunday last, Mr. C. E. Watson and Miss Mollie Wise, daughter of L. L. Wise.

THE EUFAULA DAILY TIMES

Wed. Jan. 20, 1886
    Mr. Seaborn Woodcock, of Randolph County, Ga., and Miss Willie Sanders, of Eufaula, were married last night at the home of the bride's mother.

Fri. Sept. 19, 1890
    Mr. E. B. Trammel, of Houston, Tex., and Miss Mary Mangham, of Daleville, Ala., were married Wednesday in Montgomery.

DEATHS

THE EUFAULA DEMOCRAT

E. C. Bullock, Editor and John Black, Proprietor & Publisher.

Wed. July 8, 1846
      Jas. R. Ranson, from Upson County, Ga., a volunteer attached
to the Georgia Light Infantry, died at Opelika, Ala., on the
29th ult.

      Died in Eufaula on the 5th of July, Edmund Jones, infant son
of Chas. and Mary Akin.

Wed. July 22, 1846
      Wm. B. Chandler, of Sumpter County Volunteers, died at the
city hospital in Columbus, (Ga.) on the 10th inst.

Wed. July 29, 1846
      Caleb J. McNulty, of Ohio, formerly Clerk of the House of
Representatives, died on a steamboat on the 10th inst., while on
his way to the seat of war. He was a private in one of the Ohio
Volunteer Companies. He was buried with military honors at
Helena, Ark.

Wed. Aug. 19, 1846
      Ex-Gov. Howard, of Maryland, died at his home in that state
a few days since.

      Col. Alexander McDonald died in Eufaula on Sunday last.

Wed. Sept. 9, 1846
      Wm. Saunders, aged 21, son of Col. E. W. Saunders, was
accidentally drowned in the Alabama River, near Cathawba,
(Cahaba?), recently. -Dallas County (Ala.) Gazette.

      Gen. Geo. W. Crabb, of Mobile, formerly a member of Congress
from the Tuscaloosa District in the state, and more recently
Judge of Criminal Court of the city of Mobile, died at Philadelphia, a short time since.

Wed. Sept. 16, 1846
      The death of A. V. Allen, of Russell County, (Ala.) occured
on the 4th inst.

Wed. Sept. 23, 1846
      Dr. Wm. A. Caruthers died recently in Savannah. He was
author of "Knights of the Horse Shoe", and other productions of
great merit.

Wed. Sept. 30, 1846
      Hon. Samuel A. Foot, formerly U. S. Senator, and afterwards,
Gov. of Connecticut, died at his home in that state on the 15th
inst.

      Thos. R. Dew, President of William & Mary College, Va.,
died lately in Paris, whither he had gone for a visit.

Wed. Oct. 14, 1846
      Hon. Samuel Bigger, former Gov. of Ind., died lately at his

97

residence in Fort Wayne.

1846-47

Wed. Dec. 2, 1846
    Hon. Wm. Findlay, aged 79, ex-Gov. of Pennsylvania, died at
the home of his son-in-law, Gov. Shunk, in Harrisburg recently.

Wed. Dec. 9, 1846
    Alfred Arnett, a young man living in Eufaula, was drowned
on Tuesday last, while attempting to swim across the river.

Wed. Dec. 25, 1846
    Hon. Francis X. Martin, age 84, late Chief of Justice of
the Supreme Court of Louisiana, died at New Orleans recently.
He was a Frenchman by birth, but emigrated to this country at an
early age.

    Thos. E., aged 12 years, son of the late Hon. C. E. Hays of
Georgia, and Sarah J., wife of Gen. Wm. Wellborn of this palce,
died on the 12th inst.

    Maj. Franklin C. Heard, aged 48, formerly of Augusta, Ga.,
died at Mobile on the 13th inst.

Wed. Dec. 30, 1846
    Mrs. Caroline Elizabeth, wife of Maj. Patrick B. Skipper,
died in Abbeville, (Ala.) on Dec. 11th.

Wed. Jan. 13, 1847
    Hon. Alexander Barrow, Senator from Louisiana, died at
Baltimore, recently, to which place he had accompanied a friend
as a second in a meditated duel.

    Capt. Isaac Holmes, of Macon, (Ga.) Guards, died in camp
near Monterey on the 6th ult. He left a numerous and dependent
family.

    Glennville, Ala., Jan. 2. - Hickson C. Owens died on the
22 ult., in New York where he had gone for a surgical operation.

Wed. Jan. 27, 1847
    Hon. Isaac S. Pennybacker, Senator from Virginia, died at
Washington on the 12th inst.

Wed. Mar. 10, 1847*
    Maj. Jno. M. Allen, U. S. Marshal for Texas, died suddenly
on the 10th inst. He was a native of Ky. He was the first
mayor of Galveston. -N. O. Delta of Mar. 1st. (*S. G. Cato,
Editor).

    John D. Miller, Esq., age 33, died in Eufaula on the 8th
inst.

Wed. Apr. 28, 1847
    Andrew T. Basset, aged 23, of Eufaula, died on the 21st.,
leaving a wife and two children.

Wed. May 12, 1847
    Col. Josiah Patterson died on the 13th ult., at Augusta,
Benton County, Fla. He was a native of Georgia.

Wed. Sept. 15, 1847
    Hon. Silas Wright, age 55, died at his residence in Canton,
St. Lawrence County, N. Y., on the 25th ult.

Chancellor Andrew Crenshaw died at his home in Butler County on 31st ult. He was one of the earliest settlers of Alabama. He was born in Laurens Dist., S. C. about 1784. In 1819 he moved to Butler County, Ala. -<u>Greenville Alabamian</u> and the <u>Flag & Advertiser</u>.

Wed. Sept. 22, 1847
Whitney Leroy, youngest son of Jesse W. and Ann Loe, died in Troy on the 4th inst.

Wed. Oct. 6, 1847
Samuel W. Langston, age 60, died at his home in Barbour County, (Ala.) on the 19th inst.

Wed. Nov. 24, 1847
William L., aged 21 months, son of Jno. W. and Louisa Johnston, died on the 20th inst.

Wed. Mar. 8, 1848
Jno. W. Moore, aged 34, died in Barbour County on the 27th ult.

Tues. June 6, 1848
Ada Amelia, infant daughter of B. R. and Matilda Caroline Lignoski, died in Glennville, Barbour County, on May 29th.

Tues. June 13, 1848
Elbridge G. Langston, age 23, died in Monroe County, Ga., on the 17th ult.

The infant daughter of R. Y. Langston died on 26th ult., and on 30th ult., Mary Ann Elizabeth, his wife, aged 18, died in Barbour County.

Tues. Sept. 12, 1848
Died in New York, 26th of July last, Mrs. Margaret Black, in the 49th year of her age.

Died in New York on the 29th of July last, Mary, the consort of Mr. Wm. Wallace, in the 28th year of her age.

Tues. Nov. 7, 1848
Hon. Dixon H. Lewis, age 57, U. S. Senator from Alabama, died today at the National Hotel in New York. Mrs. Lewis and his son were with him. -<u>New York Express</u>, 25th ult.

<u>Democrat</u> of Dec. 26, 1848: Hon. Lewis was born in Hancock County, Ga., and at an early age came with his father to Alabama.

Tues. Nov. 28, 1848
Hon. A. D. Sims, member of Congress from South Carolina, died recently.

Tues. Dec. 12, 1848*
J. M. Callaway, of Barbour County, died recently. (*Tennent Lomax, Editor).

Tues. Dec. 19, 1848
The death of Dr. Edward Skillman occurred at Baton Rouge, Louisiana, recently.

1848-49

Tues. Jan. 2, 1848
     The remains of the late Hon. Jas. A. Black, member of
Congress from S. C., reached Charleston on Sunday. They were
conveyed to Columbia yesterday.

     Mr. Jesse J. Jordan, resident of Macon County, Ala., died
of Cholera on board the Steamer Montgomery yesterday. He was
returning from a western trip.

Tues. Jan. 9, 1849
     Hon. Jas. Dellet died at his home in Clairborne, (Co.) on
the 21st ult. He was a native of S. C. and removed to Claiborne
in 1816, where he lived to the time of his death. -Flag and
Advertiser.

     John M. Moore died Dec. 8, 1848 at New Orleans. Burial in
Glennville, Ala., on 26th of Dec. 1848. He was born in Wilks
County, Ga., and came to Alabama as a young man, and for a long
time was a citizen of Eufaula. Survivors are his wife and
several children.

Tues. Jan. 16, 1849
     Hon. A. H. Sevier, late Senator from Arkansas, and Commis-
sioner to Mexico, died recently. -Picayune.

     Feb. 13, 1849: The funeral of Mr. Sevier took place at
Little Rock. -Arkansas Banner, of 9th inst.

Tues. Jan. 23, 1849
     Mrs. Louisa, age 48, wife of Green Malone, died near Eufaula
on Jan. 14th inst.

Tues. Feb. 27, 1849
     Died at her home in Eufaula on the 12th of Feb., Mrs. E. C.
King, aged 37.

Tues. June 5, 1849
     Geo. Porter, Esq., one of the editors of the N. O. Picayune,
died in that city last week. He was a brother to W. T. Porter,
Esq., editor of the N. Y. Spirit Of The Times.

     Walter Hickey, who was formerly editor of the Vicksburg
Sentinel, was recently killed in a duel near Brownsville, Tex.
He had just located in that region and was engaged in merchandis-
ing.

     Hon. Daniel Duncan, member of the House of Representatives
from Ohio, died in Washington Friday.

Tues. June 12, 1849
     Hon. Dutee J. Pearce, of Rhode Island, died on the 9th inst.

     Mrs. Albert Gallatin, age 83, died in New York on the 14th
inst.

Tues. June 26, 1849
     The deaths of Cassius M. Clay and Joseph Turner, Esq.,
occurred in Madison County, Kentucky, recently.

Tues. July 17, 1849
     Col. James Duncan, Inspector General of the Army, died in
Mobile on the 3d inst.

Tues. Sept. 4, 1849
     Mrs. Eliza, age 30, wife of L. J. Leaird, died on the 31st
ult. in Eufaula. Survivors are her husband and a family of small

children.

Tues. Oct. 2, 1849
     George Hargraves, Sr., of Columbus, (Ga.) died on the 23rd
ult.

Tues. Nov. 13, 1849
     Dr. Henry D. Cook, of Eufaula, died on the 11th inst.
Burial in the Odd Fellows burying ground. He leaves a wife and
child. Nov. 27th: Resolutions for Dr. Henry S. Cook.

Tues. Dec. 11, 1849
     Gen. Duncan L. Clinch died at Macon, Georgia on the 27th ult.

     G. W. Hardwick, one of the editors of the Columbus (Ga.)
Enquirer, died recently.

1850

Tues. Jan. 1, 1850*
     B. Franklin Spear, of Henry County Lodge No. 21, died
recently. (Henry Co., Ala.). (*Alpheus Baker, Jr., Editor).

Tues. Jan. 8, 1850
     Mr. Asahel Gaston, age 43 years and 6 months, died on the
1st inst., at his home near this place. (Columbus papers please
copy).

Jan. 22, 1850
     Mr. Daniel Hale, aged 119, of Franklin County, (Ga.) died
on Jan. 3d last. He leaves a son 76 years old and a grand-
daughter 22 years old. -Athens (Ga.) Banner.

Feb. 19, 1850
     Wm. S. Taylor, aged 62, formerly of Savannah, Ga., more
recently of Eufaula, died in this city on the 7th inst. He left
a wife and six children. -Commerical Advertiser.

Mar. 26, 1850
     Gen. Wm. Irvin, an old citizen of Henry County, lost his
life in the Steamboat disaster of the H. S. Smith when it took
fire on Sunday near Florence, on her passage from Columbus to
Apalachicola.

     Mrs. Sophia H., aged 19, consort of Capt. Tennent Lomax,
and daughter of Gen. R. C. Shorter, died on the 18th inst., in
Eufaula.

Apr. 30, 1850
     Susan Mariam Clayton, age 17, daughter of Nelson and Sarah
Clayton, Chambers County, Ala., died on 8th inst.

May 14, 1850
     The death of Wm. H. Lashly occurred near Decatur on the
21st inst. He was born in Virginia, but moved with his father
to Murfreeboro, N. C., from which place he emigrated to Miss.
He leaves a wife and three children.

May 28, 1850
     Dr. A. B. Clemens, physician of Columbus, Miss., died
recently. He was a brother of Senator Clemens.

June 11, 1850
     Rev. Jno. N. Maffit died suddenly at Mobile on the 28th ult.

101

He was born of humble parents in Ireland, and rose from obscurity
to the highest position in the Methodist demonation. He had been
in charge of the largest churches in New York and Boston, and
was once Chaplain of the U. S. Senate.

Mrs. Sarah E. Robinson, aged 31, wife of Thos. Robinson,
and daughter of Thos. C. and Eliza McDowell, of this place, died
on the 5th inst.

Mary Frances, age 24, wife of Wm. J. Lomax, Esq., of
Abbeville District, died on the 15th inst. -Augusta Constition-
alist.

Oct. 8, 1850
Miss Mary E. Hart, age 15, died in Eufaula on Sabbath morning.

Nov. 19, 1850
Mrs. Caroline Heron, consort of Dr. E. M. Heron, died near
Louisville, Ala., on 3d inst. She was a member of the Presby-
terian Church.

SPIRIT OF THE SOUTH
(Published in Eufaula, Ala.)

P. T. Sayre & E. C. Bullock, Editors; John Black, Publisher &
Proprietor.

1850-51

Dec. 3, 1850
The death of Milton J. Tarver, Esq., of near Auburn, in
Macon County, (Ala.) occurred on Wednesday last. He was the
Representative from Macon to the State Legislature in 1845.

Apr. 8, 1851
Rev. Jas. E. Glenn died at his home near Glennville on the
26th ult. (Ala.)

Mr. A. Treadwell, aged 55, died on the 4th ult., at the
home of Bird F. Robinson. -Montgomery Advertiser & Gazette.

May. 6, 1851
Commodore Jas. Barron, Sr., aged 83, Capt. of the U. S.
Navy, died at his home yesterday. -Norfolk Beacon, Thursday last.

Archibald Seals, aged 69, died at Enon, Ala., on the 26th
ult.

May 27, 1851
Hon. Jno. P. Booth died in Eufaula on last Friday. He was
formerly a Circuit Judge of this state.

Thurs. Sept. 18, 1851*
Mrs. Elizabeth Smith, residing in the northern part of
Logan County, died on the 8th inst. -Russellville (Ky.) Herald.
(*From: Southern Shield, published in Eufaula, Ala., by Benj.
Gardner.)

1855

Feb. 12, 1855
Mr. J. M. Field, manager of the Mobile Theater, died in
that city on Jan. 28th.

Mr. Stephen Keenan, Commission Merchant of Mobile, died on the 27th ult. in that city.

(Missing) 1855
Mrs. Caroline, consort of Gen. Thos. Flournoy, died in Eufaula on May 23rd. (1855).

Wm. Augustus Hays, age 12, son of Calvin and Mahala Hays, died at the home of his parents on May 16th (1855) in Abbeville, Henry County.

Nov. 6, 1855
Nathaniel W. Carmichael, age 22, died on the 25th ult., in Newton, Dale County, Ala.

Simpson R. Wilson, son of Levy R. and Margaret P. Wilson, died at the home of his parents on the 22nd in Barbour County.

Mr. Jas. N. Norrell, of Montgomery, died recently. -Montgomery (Ala.) Mail.

Nov. 13, 1855
Wm. M. Murphy, Esq., lawyer, died at his home in Selma, (Ala.) on Tuesday last.

Nancy Parmer, age 36, consort of Benj. Parmer, died in Barbour County on the 28th of Oct., 1855. She leaves an aged husband and eight children.

Dec. 4, 1855
Mr. G. A. Sengstak, of Mobile, died from accidental shooting last Sunday. -Mobile Register.

Mr. Wm. H. Trone, of Mobile, died there recently. -Mobile Register.

INDEPENDENT AMERICAN*
1855

E. B. Arms, Publisher & Proprietor; C. J. L. Cunningham & A. N. Worthy, Editors.

*(Published at Troy, Pike County, Ala.).

Wed. Aug. 15, 1855
Samuel J. Peters, citizen of New Orleans, died at his residence on last Saturday.

Wed. Sept. 3, 1855
Jas. A. Brooks, aged 38, died at his home in Monticello, Pike County, (Ala.) on the 30th of Aug. 1855.

Wed. Sept. 12, 1855
Died on the 5th inst., Marilda Ann, aged 2 years, daughter of Daniel H. and Kissiah Horn.

Wed. Sept. 19, 1855
The remains of Justus Wyman, Esq., were brought to this city for burial this morning. His death took place at Talladega Springs, where he had gone for his health. -Montgomery (Ala.) Mail.

Died on 10th of Sept., at the home of her father, Jno. Carroll, Sr., Miss Sarah Ann Rhody Carroll, age 18 years.

Wed. Sept. 26, 1855

Burrel Pugh, Esq., died at his home near Troy on the 20th inst.

Wed. Oct. 3, 1855
Nat. Harris, Esq., age about 43, citizen of Montgomery for 20 years, formerly of LaFayette in Chambers County, died last evening of yellow fever. He married a daughter of Jno. Duncan, Esq., of Autauga County. Survivors are his wife and several children. -Montgomery (Ala.) Mail.

Wed. Oct. 17, 1855
Died at the home of Geo. Thagard, in Butler County, on the 2nd of Oct. 1855, Jas. Abercrombie, son of Jas. L. and Sarah Thagard, aged 4 years.

Died in Troy on 10th inst., at the home of Benj. Gardner, Jno. Benj., infant son of Mrs. Mary E. Long.

Died on the 6th inst., Robt. B. Simpson, born 17th Feb. 1835, son of Arthur and Martha Simpson, of Pike County, Ala.

Wed. Oct. 24, 1855
Rev. Geo. H. Hancock, professor in Wesleyan Female College, died suddenly at his home near the college on Tuesday last. -Georgia Citizen. (Wesleyan Female College in Macon, Ga. established 1836).

Judge Thos. Clingman, of Carroll County, Missouri, was murdered on the 9th inst., by a field slave.

Wed. Nov. 14, 1855
Selma, (Ala.) Nov. 7. - The Hon. Wm. M. Murphy died at his home last night.

Judge Jas. J. Purdy, a resident of St. Louis for 39 years, died at Mt. Vernon, Ill., on the 12th inst.

Dr. W. Flake, an old resident of Eufaula, died on the 6th inst., at the home of his son-in-law, T. K. Appling.

Hon. Edward B. Dudley died last Thursday in Wilmington, North Carolina.

Wed. Nov. 21, 1855
Mr. Jehu Gentry, age 105, a soldier of the Revolution, died in Albemale County, Virginia a few days since.

Wed. Nov. 28, 1855
Chas. V. Doozenberry, aged about 50, late of China Grove, Pike County, Ala., died at the home of Ashfield Johnson, Esq., on the 20th inst. near Elba, Ala. -Elba (Ala.) Democrat.

Wed. Dec. 6, 1855
Rev. Thaddeus Fiske, D. D., aged 93, died at Charlestown, Mass., on the 14th of Nov.

1856

Wed. Jan. 9, 1856
Wm. Livingston, aged 78, died at the home of his son, Abraham Livingston, in Pike County, Ala., on 31st Dec. 1855.

Wed. Jan. 30, 1856
Mrs. Catherine Cook, consort of Jno. E. Cook, died on the 27th inst., in Monticello.

Wed. Apr. 30, 1856
     Rev. Jas. S. Belton, of the Alabama Conference of the M. E.
Church South, died in New York City on Mar. 24. He leaves a
wife, the daughter of James T. Burdine, Esq., of Pickens County,
Ala.

Wed. May 7, 1856
     Jas. Searcy, Esq., late Senator from Dale and Henry Counties,
(Ala.) died at his home on the 6th inst., at his home in Henry
County.

Wed. May 14, 1856
     Geo. M. Troup, aged 74, died at his home in Lawrens
(Laurens) County, Geo., on the 26th ult.

     Hon. Wm. Cosby Dawson, U. S. Senator, died at his home in
Greensboro. He represented Georgia several years in the National
Congress. -Savannah (Ga.) News.

Wed. May 21, 1856
     Mr. Isaac S. Folmar died at his residence in Troy, (Ala.)
the 8th inst.

                    SPIRIT OF THE SOUTH
                 (Published in Eufaula, Ala.)

Feb. 12, 1856
     Andrew J. Miller, Senator from Richmond, (Ga.) died at his
home in Augusta, (Ga.) on Feb. 3rd. -Times & Sentinel.

Feb. 26, 1856
     Mrs. Caroline Lee Hentz, formerly of Columbus, Ga., died at
Marianna, Fla., on the 11th inst. -Columbus (Ga.) Enquirer.

Mar. 11, 1856
     C. C. Lensbury, editor of the Kosciusho (Miss.) Chronicle,
died on the 19th inst. at that place. -Vicksburg (Miss.) Whig.

                    EUFAULA EXPRESS
                         1858
Joseph Butt, Editor and John A. Burton, Publisher.

Thurs. Dec. 9, 1858
     Mrs. Catherine T. McLelland, of Montgomery, died on the 2d
inst.

Thurs. Dec. 16, 1858
     Georgia Leonard, infant daughter of Wm. and Ann Guthrie,
died near Villula, Russell County, Ala., on the 13th inst.

Thurs. Dec. 23, 1858
     Col. Albert Pike, lawyer of Arkansas, died at New Orleans a
short time since.

     Hon. Jno. A. Tucker died at Dawson, Ga., on the 17th while
on his way home from his post in the State Senate. He was a
relative of Col. P. H. Colquit of Columbus. -Cuthbert (Ga.)
Reporter.

                         1859

Thurs. Jan. 6, 1859
     Gen. Jas. Gadsden died at his home near Charleston on the
26th inst. -Charleston (S.C.) Courier.

                         105

Thurs. Jan. 13, 1859
Dr. R. W. Williams, many years a citizen of this county, died at his home near Glennville, (Ala.) on Saturday. -Spirit Of The South.

Thurs. Jan. 20, 1859
Hon. James E. Belser died yesterday in Montgomery.

Thurs. Feb. 3, 1859
Gen. Thos. Flouroy, age 50, died in this city on the 20th ult. Burial from the M. E. Church to the Odd Fellows Cemetery.

Thurs. Feb. 10, 1859
Wm. H. Prescott, historian, died in Boston on the 28th ult. He was born in Salem, Mass., May 4, 1796, his father was Wm. Prescott, Boston jurist, and his grandfather was Col. Wm. Prescott, who fought at Bunker Hill. His mother was a daughter of Thos. Hickling.

Mr. Alfred Vail, proprietor of the Morse telegraph invention, died at Morristown, N. J. on the 18th.

Thurs. Mar. 17, 1859
Mr. Joseph Bonds of Macon, Ga., was killed in Baker County on the 12th inst. Burial in Macon at Rose Hill Cemetery. He leaves a family.

Thurs. Mar. 31, 1859
Mr. Winguit M. Turner died at Clayton, (Ala.) on the 28th inst. He was a native of Hancock County, Ga., but had been a resident of Barbour County for many years, during most of the time engaged in teaching.

Thurs. Apr. 28, 1859
Wm. Edgar, age 13 months and 23 days, infant son of G. C. and E. C. Beckham, died in Eufaula on the 18th inst.

Col. Thos. O. Elliott, lawyer of Charleston, (S.C.) died recently. -Charleston Courier.

Thurs. May 5, 1859
Dr. W. L. Cowan died at his home in Eufaula on the 2d inst. He leaves a large family.

Rev. D. B. Lyne died at Pensacola recently. -Wakulla Times. He was in the Volunteers in the Florida Campaign of 1857, and they remember him as "the Durm Head Revivalist."

Harriet S., age 5, youngest daughter of E. C. Bullock died on the 26th ult.

Mrs. Jno. Hardeman, of Eufaula, died yesterday.

Thurs. May 12, 1859
Mr. Jno. Burke was accidentally shot recently in Lebanon, Tenn., and was buried on the 30th ult., at his father's family burial ground. -Camden (Ala.) Republic.

Thurs. May 19, 1859
Daniel McRae, age 29, died in Eufaula on the 12th inst.

Jos. A., aged 6 years, son of Jos. C. and Elizabeth Barksdale, died on the 17th inst., near Ft. Browder in Barbour County.

Thurs. May 26, 1859
Hon. Francis H. Cone of Georgia died at his residence in

Greensboro, on the 18th inst.

Thurs. June 2, 1859
Hon. Geo. W. Thomas, age 52, died on the 30th of Apr. He
represented Stanislas County in the Legislature, (Calif.) He
was a native of Georgia, but emigrated to California from Texas
in 1849. (Stockton, Calif. papers).

Dr. Thomas (surgeon in the Army during the Mexican War) was
a native of Columbia County, Ga., and was a brother of Hon.
Thomas W. Thomas, of Elberton.

Thurs. June 16, 1859
Mrs. E. Q. Clark, age 36, consort of M. S. Clark, died in
Glennville, Ala., on the 11th ult.

Thurs. June 23, 1859
Walter McGinty, aged 8, son of Geo. W. and Elizabeth C.
McGinty, died in Eufaula on the 17th inst.

Jas. McRae, aged 5 months, 8 days, died in Eufaula on the
15th inst., and on the 19th inst., Stanton Slaughter, aged 5
months and 12 days, infant sons of Henry H. and Sarah C. Fields.

Thurs. June 30, 1859
Mrs. Mary Ann Broome, age 49, died at the home of her son
in Augusta, Ga., June 14, 1859. She was a member of the Baptist
Church in Burke County, Augusta and Savannah for thirty years.
She leaves a husband and three sons.

Thurs. July 21, 1859
Maj. Jno. N. Copeland, of Eufaula, died yesterday.

Thurs. Aug. 18, 1859
Ann Helen, aged 21, consort of Rev. Jas. S. Paullin, and
eldest daughter of Capt. Wm. B. Brannon, died in Eufaula on the
15th inst.

Wm. G. Lowman, aged 24, died in Eufaula on the 16th inst.

Thurs. Aug. 25, 1859
Died in Eufaula on 18th inst., Mrs. W. A. Shoftner, aged 35,
formerly of Columbus, Ga. She leaves a husband.

Thurs. Sept. 1, 1859
The death of Mrs. Bird Fitzpatrick, of Union Springs occurred recently. -Union Springs (Ala.) Gazette.

Thurs. Sept. 8, 1859
Benjamin Screws, resident of Barbour County for many years,
died at Shelby Springs on the 28th inst. He leaves a family.

Thurs. Sept. 15, 1859
Died in Eufaula on the 13th inst., Mr. Wm. A. Shoftner,
formerly of Columbus, Ga. He leaves four little children.

Thurs. Oct. 6, 1859
Georgia Virginia, aged 3 years, 6 months, only daughter of
Wm. and Eliza Brantley, died at Midway, Ala., on the 29th of
Sept.

Thurs. Oct. 20, 1859
Hilliard Ricks, a young man, died at the home of his father
in Clay County, Ga. on the 15th inst.

Moses Cox, Esq., native of Barbour County, died at White
Sulphur Springs, Ga., on 3d inst. Burial at Enon, Ala. -Clayton
(Ala.) Banner.

Thurs. Oct. 27, 1859
      T. J. Iverson, student of the South Alabama Institute, died
on the 14th inst., at his father's home in Henry County, (Ala.).

THE CLAYTON BANNER
(Published at Clayton, Alabama)

1860-61-62

Thurs. July 26, 1860
      Mr. Jno. Travis Fenn, a young man, died Saturday. He leaves
a wife, brothers, sisters and an aged father.

Thurs. Aug. 2, 1860
      Died in Atlanta, Ga., on the 15th of July, Julius Henry,
son of A. B. and Georgia Seals, aged 11 months and 11 days.

Thurs. Oct. 4, 1860
      The death of J. T. Kerbel, of Lowndes County, Ala., occurred
at Glennville Military Institute on Saturday.

      Opelika, Ala., Sept. 30. - The death of Jas. Taylor, Esq.,
occurred on the 29th ult., at LaFayette, Chambers County, Ala.
His son, David Taylor, was present at the time of death.

Jan. 10, 1861
      The death of Mr. Warren Jordan, of Midway in this county,
occurred on the 4th inst. He leaves a family. Interment at
Midway.

July 30, 1861
      Horace Bishop died in Adrian, Mich., recently, aged 100
years. He served four years in the Revolution, and stood sentry
over Maj. Andre at his execution.

Sept. 10, 1861
      Col. Egbert J. Jones, who laid down his life for his country,
died at Gordonville, Va., recently. Burial in Huntsville, Ala.
-Huntsville Democrat, 4th inst.

Thurs. Sept. 4, 1862
      Maj. Jefferson Buford died Thursday. Survivors are his
wife and children. (Tombstone inscription in Fairview Cemetery,
Eufaula, Ala.: Maj. Jefferson Buford / 17 Aug. 1807 / Union
Dist., S.C. / 22 Aug. 1862 / 1st wife Mary A. Rebecca White /
2nd wife Lizzie.)

THE HENRY COUNTY REGISTER
(Published at Abbeville, Ala.)

1867 & 1869

J. M. B. Kelly and E. R. Quillin.

Sat. June 22, 1867
      The funeral of Thos. J. Irwin will take place from his late
residence on the 23rd inst. (Henry County). The Masonic Lodge
members of Lawrenceville, Columbia, and Ft. Gaines are invited
to attend.

Sat. Aug. 17, 1867
Died on the 14th inst., at the home of J. M. B. Kelly, near
Abbeville, Launa Estelle, aged four years, youngest daughter of
Wiley C. and Lizzie Gordon, of Lee County, Ala.

Sat. Aug. 31, 1867
Rev. C. C. Calloway, of the M. E. Church and for the past
twelve or fifteen years a citizen of Greensboro, (Ala.), died
in that place on the 11th inst.

Sat. Sept. 7, 1867
Jno. Haeffler, a German, aged 52, residing at Lancaster,
Pa., buried his 33rd child last week. He has had three wives
and only four of his children are now living.

Mr. Pierce Butler died at his home in Georgia recently.

Mrs. Jesse Carter, of Mobile, Ala., died Friday in that city.

Sat. Sept. 14, 1867
Miss Mollie King was killed by lightning at the home of her
uncle, Col. Jno. W. Davis, in Selma, Ala., recently.

Sat. Sept. 28, 1867
An explosion of the boilers on the steamer Chipola, plying
between Eufaula and Columbus, Ga., caused the deaths of the
pilot, Mr. Geo. Couch and the clerk, Mr. A. F. Beery, on the
19th inst. -Eufaula News.

Sat. Nov. 2, 1867
Mr. J. T. Russell, Baptist minister, died at his home in
Tallapossa, (County, Ala.) last Tuesday.

Sat. Nov. 30, 1867
Mr. F. M. Galloway, age 24, formerly of Henry County, died
in Mobile on Oct. 30th of yellow fever.

Sat. Jan. 12, 1867
Rev. Geo. W. Malay, of the M. E. Church South, died last
Saturday at Urbana, Ohio.

Sat. Jan. 2, 1869
Dr. F. M. D. Hopkins, member of the present Legislature of
Georgia from Miller County, died recently.

Hon. Wm. L. Harris, age 61, of Georgia, died at Memphis,
Tenn., on the 26th ult.

The funeral of Mr. Luke Hurst will take place with Masonic
honors at Judson Church tomorrow. (Henry County).

Sat. June 9, 1869
Mr. Nelson Clayton, father of Maj. Gen. H. D. Clayton, died
on the 26th of last month at the home of his son-in-law, R. C.
Jeter, Esq.

Sat. Feb. 13, 1869
Wm. H. Ward, age 63, died at his home in Henry County on
the 6th inst. Member of the Baptist Church nearly 40 years.

Mr. Ellis Saddler, of Greensboro, N. C., was killed by the
falling of a tree on the 16th of last month.

Sat. Mar. 20, 1869
Mr. Chas. Wallace, editor of the Georgia Clipper, died on

2nd inst., at Warrenton, Ga.

Sat. Mar. 27, 1869
        Mr. Jas. Guthrie, of Louisville, (Ky.) died recently. He
was born in 1793, and has lived in Louisville since boyhood. He
began his political career in the Kentucky Legislature.

Sat. Apr. 24, 1869
        Savannah, Apr. 17. - Dr. Benj. Ayer died Friday near Louis-
ville, Ga. He was a member of the Georgia Legislature from
Jefferson County, (Ga.).

        Mr. Chas. Laney age 58, of Eufaula, died on the 11th inst.
-Eufaula Times.

Sat. May 8, 1869
        Thos. J. Crow, an old citizen of Florence, (Ala.) died on
the 20th inst.

        The funeral of J. N. Willis will be preached the 9th inst.,
at or near his late residence. Deceased having been a worthy
Master Mason, the usual burial ceremonies of the Fraternity will
be performed. (Henry County).

Sat. May 29, 1869
        Capt. R. H. Fletcher, citizen of Terrell County, (Ga.) died
on the 11th inst. -Dawson (Ga.) Journal.

Sat. July 3, 1869
        Maj. W. T. Gunter, formerly of Henry County, died on his
plantation in Dale County on Sunday.

Sat. Oct. 23, 1869
        Mrs. Susan M. Pearre, age 42, wife of E. E. Pearee, died on
the 14th inst., at her home in Henry County.

THE BLUFF CITY TIMES
(Published Eufaula, Ala.)

1869-70

J. M. Macon, Editor; John Post & J. M. Williams, Proprietors.

Thurs. Apr. 15, 1869
        Mrs. Dr. Cowan died recently at her home in Union Springs,
Ala., on Tuesday. She was one of the oldest citizens of Eufaula,
having removed since the war. Her remains are expected here for
burial.

Thurs. May 6, 1869
        Hon. Lewis L. Cato, lawyer of Eufaula, died recently. He
leaves a family.

        Mrs. Jno. McNab died at her home in Eufaula May 2d. She
came to Eufaula with her husband in 1836. In 1868, she with her
husband and children visited the place of her birth, the Island
of Islay, Scotland, and known as the Hebrides.

Thurs. June 24, 1869
        Mr. Hampton Ryan, an old citizen, died at his home in
Barbour County last week.

Thurs. July 8, 1869
        Dr. Bedell, of Henry County, (Ala.) died a few days since

from wounds received by a man in his employ.

Thurs. July 23, 1869
  Col. Chas. G. Armstead, of Mississippi, Commander of the 17th Confederate Cavalry, died at Jackson a few days ago.

Thurs. July 29, 1869
  Geo. H. Venable, one of the editors of the Petersburg (Va.) Index, died on the 18th inst.

Thurs. Sept. 2, 1869
  Mrs. L. L. Cato, wife of the late Hon. Cato, died last Monday in Eufaula. She leaves nine orphaned children.

Thurs. Sept. 16, 1869
  Yancey G. Freeman, an old citizen of Cherokee County, (Ala.) died recently.

Thurs. Sept. 23, 1869
  Col. J. B. Bibb, of Montgomery, (Ala.) died on the 14th inst.

Thurs. Oct. 14, 1869
  Col. J. C. B. Mitchell died at his home in Montgomery County (Ala.) on Monday.

  Mrs. Mary Pillow, wife of Gen. G. J. Pillow, died in Maury County, Tenn., on 3d of Oct.

  P. McLennan (of Louisville, Ala., Lodge No. 225) died in Barbour County recently.

  Mr. I. C. Browder, an old citizen of Eufaula, died on Tuesday.

Thurs. Nov. 4, 1869
  Mr. Jos. Pizzala, proprietor of the "European House" in Montgomery, (Ala.) died recently. He was a member of the Catholic Church.

Thurs. Dec. 2, 1869
  Dr. Jno. Marshall Wellborn, age 33, died at Millican, Tex., on Nov. 18, 1869. He was the son of Mrs. Roxanna Wellborn, of Eufaula. He married Miss Martha Peterson, the daughter of Dr. B. Peterson, formerly of Barbour County. Survivors are his wife, a son and a daughter.

  Mrs. Holliday H. Hodges, of Eufaula, wife of the late Dr. Hodges, and daughter of the late Jacob Lowman, of Barbour County, died on Thursday last.

Thurs. Dec. 9, 1869
  Chas. Petty, of Clayton, (Ala.) who died Apr. 27th, 1869, has now a monument erected over his grave by the Masonic Lodge members of that place.

Thurs. Feb. 3, 1870
  Mrs. Wm. Abney, one of the oldest citizens in Barbour County, died at her home near Eufaula last week.

Thurs. Feb. 17, 1870
  Mrs. Jabez McRae, daughter of Mrs. McKay, died last Friday at the late residence of her father in Henry County. (Ala.).

Thurs. Mar. 10, 1870

111

Mr. Lewis Coleman died in Eufaula last Sunday. He leaves a bride of but four weeks.

Thurs. Mar. 17, 1870
    Miss Betsey Thomas, aged 90, died at Portland, Maine, last week, leaving a brother, Elias, aged 98, and her sister, Happy, aged 100 years old on April next.

Thurs. Apr. 14, 1870
    Robt. Jennings, aged 2 years, son of Robt. J. and Cordelia Woods, died in Eufaula on Apr. 11th.

    Died in Eufaula on the 11th inst., Mrs. J. N. Robinson, at an advanced age.

Thurs. May 12, 1870
    Mrs. J. E. Price, wife of H. W. B. Price, died in Eufaula on the 9th inst.

    B. F. Petty, Jr., of Clayton, died recently. Burial from the M. E. Church.

Thurs. May 19, 1870
    Mr. A. H. Yarrington, age 64, died last Sunday. He had long been a resident of Barbour County, and several years immediately after the war he was Postmaster of Eufaula.

    Mr. L. M. Thweat, a young man, of Eufaula died recently.

    The death of Judge Merrill Ashurst is taken from the Santa Fe papers. He was born and raised in Alabama. Among his relatives are his sister, Mrs. M. N. Sheehan, of Eufaula, and Hon. R. T. Ashurst, of Tallapoosa County, (Ala.) is a brother. He was born in Putnam County, Ga., on 22nd of Nov. 1812. While he was still young, John and Francis A. Ashurst, his parents, moved to Montgomery, Ala.

Thurs. June 30, 1870
    W. D. Ethridge, Esq., merchant of Eufaula, died suddenly Tuesday last. Burial with Masonic honors.

    Died in Eufaula on the 26th inst., Mrs. Effie Williams, aged about 55 years.

Thurs. July 7, 1870
    F. A. Salisberry died in Barbour County on May 5th, 1870. He was born the 21st of Dec. 1843. Member of the M. E. Church.

Thurs. July 21, 1870
    Mr. Wm. Jones, aged about 60, died in Eufaula last week.

Thurs. Aug. 11, 1870
    Mr. L. Marburg, of Eufaula, died on 2nd of Aug. He was a member of the Phoenix Fire Company and the Hebrew Benevolent Society of Eufaula.

Thurs. Aug. 18, 1870
    D. H. Hamiter, of Fort Browder in Barbour County, died on Thursday.

    Mr. Jas. Cunningham, a resident of Eufaula for 25 years, died last week in Cuthbert where he was visiting. Burial in Eufaula.

Thurs. Sept. 8, 1870
    Mrs. Julia M. Brannon, wife of Mr. T. A. Brannon, an old

citizen of Eufaula, died at her home here on the 1st inst.

Mr. Nicholas Christian died in Eufaula last Saturday. Burial in Georgetown, Ga.

Mr. Nathaniel Pinkham died in Macon, (Ga.) last Sunday. He was President of the Macon Typographical Union.

Thurs. Oct. 6, 1870
Mr. Chas. K. Sparhawk, formerly one of the proprietors of the Tallahassee Floridian, died at St. Augustine, (Fla.) last week.

Thurs. Oct. 13, 1870
Mrs. Jno. Post died on Sept. 27th. -Troy (Ala.) Messenger.

Thurs. Oct. 20, 1870
Mrs. Charlotte Asher, wife of Mr. Simon Asher of Eufaula died on Oct. 11th. She leaves a husband and children.

Thurs. Oct. 27, 1870
Dr. Dabney Herndon, of Mobile, died there recently. Also, Col. L. T. Woodruff, of Mobile.

Thurs. Nov. 3, 1870
Dr. A. B. Brashear died at his home in Barbour County on the 19th inst. He was formerly of Miss., and came to Eufaula during the war. He leaves a wife and children.

Thurs. Nov. 17, 1870
Col. Jas. N. Ramsey died at his home in Columbus, Ga., recently. He was colonel of the First Georgia Regiment.

Thurs. Nov. 24, 1870
Mr. J. B. Jennings, formerly of Eufaula, but more recently of New Orleans, (La.) died in that city last Sunday of yellow fever. He was father-in-law to Mr. R. J. Woods, of Eufaula.

Col. Robt. C. Forsyth, brother to the editor of the Mobile Register, died in that city on the 16th of Nov.

Thurs. Dec. 23, 1870
Miss Mary Corbett, of Montgomery, Ala., was among the killed in the late Pacific Railroad accident.

1871

Published and edited by J. M. Macon.

Thurs. Jan. 26, 1871
The death of Mr. H. J. Maxey, of Dallas County, (Ala.) occurred last week.

Judge W. P. Chilton, of Montgomery, (Ala.) died on the 21st. from effects of a fall from a stairway.

Wm. Barrett, aged 84, retired tobacco merchant of Richmond, (Va.) died recently from burns received when his dressing gown caught fire.

Thurs. Feb. 16, 1871
Mr. Clayton R. Woods died at his home in Eufaula last Saturday. He came here from S. C. about 1836. He leaves a large family of children.

Mr. Jas. Herring died at his home in Eufaula last Thursday.

Thurs. Feb. 23, 1871
    Gen. J. B. Magruder died in Houston, Tex., on 19th inst.

Thurs. Mar. 9, 1871
    Mrs. Elizabeth McLean, wife of the late Dougald McLean,
age about 50, died in Eufaula on the 6th inst.

    Aaron Thomas died in Eufaula on 17th of Jan. last. He was
a member of Harmony Lodge of Eufaula.

Thurs. Mar. 30, 1871
    Mr. Isaac E. Young, a citizen of Tuscumbia, (Ala.) died
suddenly on the streets while talking to friends, a few days ago.

Thurs. Apr. 27, 1871
    Mr. Jas. R. Poston, living near Eufaula, died last Saturday.
He was in the prime of life. Burial at White Oak Church in
Barbour County.

    Col. M. B. Locke, age about 35, died on the 21st in Union
Springs, (Ala.). He was a brother Messers. Wm. H., and A. J.
Locke of Eufaula. He formerly lived in Pike County, Ala. He
married about three years ago to a daughter of Col. Henry Black-
mon, who survives him.

Thurs. May 4, 1871
    Geo. M. Ellis, aged 62, died recently in Chester County,
Penn.

Thurs. May 18, 1871
    Mrs. Joel Sims, an old citizen of Barbour County, wife of
Elder Sims, died on the 6th last.

    On the 3rd inst., Jno. Bullock died. (Barbour County).
-Clayton Courier.

Thurs. June 1, 1871
    Geo. E. Macon, Esq., died at his home in Barbour County on
the 21st. He was born at Penfield, Ga., on 13th May 1835. He
married in 1868 to Miss Jane, daughter of Dr. Jno. C. McNeil, of
Clayton. He leaves a wife and two children.

    Eugenia, youngest daughter of the late Jack Hardman, died
in Eufaula on the 28th. (Thurs. June 8, 1871 paper has Tribute
of Respect for Jack Hardman, died on 13th of May, 1871).

Thurs. June 8, 1871
    Died on the 4th inst., at her home, Mrs. Florida Wallace,
wife of W. C. Wallace, Esq., of Eufaula.

Thurs. June 15, 1871
    Died in Eufaula on June 13th, Henry Reynolds, a native of
England. He had been in Memphis several years previous to coming to Eufaula in 1865, where he had since lived.

Thurs. June 22, 1871
    Commodore Josiah Tattnall died in Savannah, (Ga.) last
night. He was born at Bonaventure, near Savannah, in 1796, and
will be buried at the same place.

Thurs. July 4, 1871
    Mary Belle, age about 7 years, youngest daughter of N. M.
Hyatt, Esq., died in Eufaula on the 30th of June.

    Died in Henry County, Ala., on 10th ult., Mrs. Mary M.

Jennings, wife of Dr. L. A. Jennings.

Thurs. July 20, 1871
Died at the residence of Judge F. M. Wood, near Eufaula, on the 18th inst., Mr. Olin Wood, aged about 70. Deceased was unmarried, having always made his home with the mother of Judge Wood till her death about three years ago, since which time he has lived with Judge Wood.

Thurs. July 27, 1871
Mr. H. H. Marschalk, editor of the Marengo Journal, died in Linden, (Ala.) last Sunday.

Willis Wingate, aged about 2 years, child of Willis L. Cox, Esq., of Henry County, (Ala.) died on 22nd inst.

Duncan Carmichael, Esq., died at his home in Clayton, (Ala.) on Tuesday last.

Thurs. Aug. 3, 1871
Died in New York City on the 24th of July, Mrs. Mary C. Harris, age about 40, wife of Judge Jno. M. Harris, of Vicksburg, Miss. Mrs. Harris and her husband were residents of Eufaula during the war.

Thurs. Aug. 10, 1871
Mrs. Mary Jane, wife of Harrison Purcell, Esq., of near Columbia, Ala., died on the 28th of June. She was the daughter of Jno. and Mary Ann Jones, and was born near Columbia, Ala., on 24 Aug. 1845. She married on 8th of Nov. 1866, joined the Presbyterian Church on 24th Nov. 1869. She leaves a family.

Thurs. Sept. 7, 1871
Richard Folsom, son of Mr. J. J. Folsom, died in Eufaula on Sept. 5th.

Thurs. Sept. 14, 1871
The death of Mr. Monroe Summerford occurred recently in Henry County, (Ala.).

Mr. B. F. Streater died at his home near Spring Hill (Barbour County) on last Sunday.

Mrs. Dolly Brown, for a long time a resident of Barbour County, died recently at the home of her daughter, Mrs. Hatch Cook, at Hamilton, Ga. Member of the M. E. Church.

Thurs. Sept. 21, 1871
Mr. J. R. Ware, an old citizen, died last Sunday. He was for several years a professor in the Union Female College of Eufaula.

Jno. G. McDuffie, of Eufaula, died on Aug. 11th, 1871. He was a member of the Odd Fellows of this place.

The death of Peter E. Morris, citizen of Tallapoosa County, (Ala.) occurred last week.

Thurs. Oct. 5, 1871
W. W. Castleberry died at his home yesterday in Clay County, Georgia.

Gen. Stand Watie, aged 65, prominent Cherochee, died at his farm on Honey Creek, Cherochee Nation, on Sunday last. He was an own brother of Elias Boudinot, a protage of Hon. Elias Boudinot of New Jersey and he adopted his name. The rest of the family bore the family name of Watie. -<u>Neosho Times</u>, 14th.

<u>Thurs. Oct. 7, 1871</u>
Dr. James Rumph, and old citizen of Union Springs, (Ala.)
died suddenly yesterday. -<u>Union Springs Times</u>.

Capt. B. W. Justice, formerly of Tuscaloosa, (Ala.) was
accidently killed in Raleigh, N. C. on the 23rd ult.

<u>Thurs. Oct. 26, 1871</u>
The death of Miller Force occurred at his place in Cherokee
County, (Ala.) on the 28th ult.

Col. J. E. Dennis, formerly a citizen of Selma, Ala., but
for the past two years a resident of Vicksburg, died recently.
-<u>Vicksburg Herald</u>.

Mrs. Ellen Flournoy, relict of the late Gen. Thos. Flournoy,
and sister of Gen. Alpheus Baker and Dr. P. DeL. Baker, died in
Euraula on Oct. 22nd.

Mr. J. M. Spidle, farmer of Green County, (Ala.) died from
a fall from the platform of the warehouse at Trussell's Ferry,
recently.

<u>Thurs. Nov. 9, 1871</u>
Died on 6th ult., Mrs. Jordan, wife of Rev. Junius Jordan
of Eufaula.

<u>Thurs. Nov. 23, 1871</u>
Mr. Luke Lott, of Ocheese, Fla., died at the Chewalls Hotel
in Eufaula on Monday. He was on his way to Miss., and was taken
sick enroute. He represented his county in the Legislature
before the war. He was buried in Eufaula.

Died in Macon, Ga., Nov. 17th from wounds received in the
army, Mr. Jno. F. Cargile, of Eufaula, Ala.

<u>Thurs. Nov. 30, 1871</u>
Ex-Mayor Wm. G. Mastin, age 36, of Huntsville, (Ala.) died
in that city on the 4th inst.

<u>Thurs. Dec. 21, 1871</u>
Mr. Thos. W. Lane died suddenly at the home of Dr. A. W.
Barnett, in Eufaula last Saturday. He formerly was editor of
the <u>Columbus Sun</u> and the <u>Savannah Republican</u>.

1872

Edited and Published by J. M. Macon.

<u>Thurs. Jan. 4, 1872</u>
Dr. Jno. W. Bledsoe, of Bullock County, (Ala.) died at
Midway on the 28th inst. He leaves a wife and seven children.

<u>Thurs. Jan. 11, 1872</u>
Col. A. A. F. Hill, of Barbour County, formerly of Athens,
Ga., died at his home near Eufaula on 6th inst. Burial at
Athens. He leaves a young wife and his mother.

Mr. Henry Dunn, aged 17 or 18 years, of Barbour County, was
killed last Friday when his mule threw him. He leaves a widowed
mother. -<u>Clayton Courier</u>.

<u>Thurs. Jan. 25, 1872</u>
Mr. Wm. Hardman, age about 24, third son of the late Jack

116

Hardman, died in Eufaula on Sunday.

Julia Langston, aged 16, daughter of R. Y. and M. E. Langston, died on the 10th inst.

Eliphalet Veal, of Barbour County, died recently. He was a member of the Harmony Lodge of Eufaula. He leaves a family.

Thurs. Mar. 21, 1872
The death of Col. Chas. Forsyth, son of the editor of the Mobile Register., occured recently in Mobile, (Ala.).

Thurs. Apr. 11, 1872
The death of Mr. Jno. Hartung occurred last Monday in Eufaula. He leaves a family.

THE HENRY COUNTY REGISTER
(Published in Abbeville, Henry County, Ala.)

1870

Jesse A. Corbitt, Proprietor & Editor.

Sat. Jan. 23, 1870
Rev. Justin Perkins died recently in Chicopee, Mass. He was for 36 years a missionary among the Nestorians.

Sat. Mar. 26, 1870
T. S. Floyd, of Columbia, Ala., Tax Assessor for Henry County, (Ala.) died on the 21st inst.

Sat. Apr. 30, 1870
Alexr. Boyd, Solicitor for Green County, (Ala.) died from gun wounds last Thursday. -Eutaw (Ala.) Whig, 7th inst.

Sat. May 7, 1870
Richmond, Va., Apr. 27. - At the Capital Building a gallery and wall fell today causing the deaths of Patrick H. Aylett, E. M. Schofield, City Assessor and brother to Gen. Schofield; Dr. J. D. Brock, editor of the Richmond Examiner; Julius A. Hobson, City Collector; S. Duggers, member of the house of Delegates; T. A. Grieves, Commission merchant of Alexandria; Samuel Eaton, of Boston, Mass.; Powhatan Roberts, of the Court of Common Pleas; Jas. A. Blamire, of Berlin, Prussia; S. E. Burnham, of Syracuse, N. Y.; N. P. Howard, lawyer of Arkansas; J. Watson, merchant of Danville; Thos. W. Wilcox, ex-Confederate; Gen. Saml. H. Hairston, Henry County; Chas. J. Grinnan, Washington, D. C.; Kobt. (Robt.?) H. Maury, Jr., land agent; Edward Ward, of England; Wm. H. Davis, coal merchant; T. P. Flag, Deputy U. S. Marshal; W. E. Randolph, of N. Y.; and R. E. Bradshaw, grocer.

Sat. June 11, 1870
Mrs. Jno. R. L. Grice, daughter of Rev. Geo. P. Kincey, died at her home in Abbeville on the 10th inst. Survivors are her husband and six children.

Sat. July 23, 1870
Mrs. Judith B., age 33, wife of Dr. I. Mendhiem, died near Abbeville this morning.

EUFAULA TRI-WEEKLY NEWS

1874

Jno. Black & Son, Proprietors.

Thurs. Mar. 19, 1874
    Jno. H. Lindle, editor of the Bangor Transcript, died in
Savannah, (Ga.) on Friday last.

Sat. Apr. 11, 1874
    Dr. C. J. Pope died at his home in Eufaula yesterday.
Burial from the Episcopal Church tomorrow.

Sat. Apr. 25, 1874
    Miss Eliza, age 18, daughter of Mr. and Mrs. William Court-
ney, died in Eufaula on the 22d inst.

Tues. Apr. 28, 1874
    Dr. Edmund Sheppard died in Eufaula on the 27th inst. He
was born in Cumberland County, N. J., Feb. 28, 1791, and moved
here in 1837, where he has since lived.

Thurs. May 21, 1874
    Mr. I. T. Hill, of Georgetown, Ga., died at his home last
night. He leaves a wife and several children.

Tues. May 26, 1874
    Mr. Wm. H. McNamee, Register in Chancery of Lee County,
(Ala.) died in Opelika on Friday.

Thurs. May 28, 1874
    Mr. R. H. Park, age 36, proprietor of the City Hotel at
Troy, Ala., died Monday. -Columbus (Ga.) Enquirer.

Sat. May 30, 1874
    Dr. Frank Lynch, of Montgomery, (Ala.) died there on
Wednesday last.

Tues. June 2, 1874
    Mr. Peter Cunningham, an old citizen of Barbour County,
died at his home near Clayton last week.

Mon. June 8, 1874
    Mr. Wm. H. Dismuke, age 75, died at his home near Weston,
(Ga.) on the 28th of May. He was one of the first settlers of
Southwest Ga., and had been a resident of Webster County about
45 years. -Dawson (Ga.) Journal.

Tues. June 16, 1874
    Hon. B. W. Walker died at Huntsville, (Ala.) yesterday.
(In the next issue of this paper: Judge Richard W. Walker.)

    Col. LaFayette Stow, of Eufaula, died Saturday at an ad-
vanced age.

Sat. June 27, 1874
    Mr. Rufus M. Johnson, age about 52, died in Eufaula on
Thursday.

Thurs. July 2, 1874
    Mrs. Sarah J. Garrett, age about 39, wife of James Garrett,
died in Eufaula Tuesday last. She leaves a husband and four
children.

Sat. July 4, 1874
    Gen. Jas. Cantey, age about 54, died at his home in Russell

County, (Ala.) on 30th ult. He was born in Camden, S. C., and
came to this section in 1845, where he married the daughter of
the late Col. Samuel Benton.

Sat. July 11, 1874
        Mr. Wm. N. Raney died at his home in Eufaula yesterday. He
was the son of Jas. H. and Sophie Raney, and was born in Barbour
County on 16th Mar. 1838. Burial from the Baptist Church.

Thurs. July 16, 1874
        Mr. Wesley Stone, age 60, died in Eufaula on Sunday. He
leaves a wife and four children.

Thurs. Aug. 6, 1874
        Mr. Marion McDuffie, engineer on the Montgomery and Eufaula
Railroad, died at his home near Ft. Deposit, (Ala.) last Monday.

Tues. Aug. 11, 1874
        Mr. Andrew W. McKenzie, age 34, died on the 9th inst. He
was born and raised in Eufaula.

Tues. Aug. 18, 1874
        Mr. Robt. Yarrington, age nearly 30, died at the home of
Mr. G. C. Beckham in Eufaula on the 17th inst.

Tues. Sept. 1, 1874
        Mr. E. C. Holleman, age 74, citizen of Eufaula, died at his
home on Friday.
        The death of Mr. M. M. Lipscomb, of Marengo County, (Ala.)
occurred on Monday.

Tues. Sept. 29, 1874
        Judge Wm. M. Byrd, of Selma, (Ala.) was killed recently in
a train accident. -Montgomery Advertiser.

Thurs. Oct. 1, 1874
        Leslie, age 6, youngest son of Mrs. Wm. N. Rainey, of near
Eufaula, died Saturday.

EUFAULA NEWS

1874

Tues. Oct. 27, 1874
        Mrs. Imogene F. Grace, wife of Thos. B. Grace, and daughter
of Mr. H. W. B. Price, died near Tallula, Miss., on the 14th
inst. (Dec. 31, 1874 paper: Burial at Columbia, Ala.).

Fri. Oct. 30, 1874
        Mr. W. L. Bowdon, age 28, died at the home of his mother in
Gordon, (Henry County, Ala.) on the 28th inst.

Tues. Nov. 3, 1874
        Mr. Ezekiel Wise, an old citizen of Barbour County, living
near Batesville, died last Saturday.

Sat. Nov. 7, 1874
        William Keils, son of E. M. Kiels, Judge of Eufaula City
Court, died in Eufaula on Thursday.

Tues. Nov. 17, 1874
        Michael E. Kehoe, age 50, died at the home of his brother,

119

Jno. F. Kehoe, in Birmingham, (Ala.) on Nov. 6th. The deceased was a native of County Wicklow, Ireland.

Tues. Nov. 24, 1874
     Geo. T. Mabry, age 24, died while on a visit to his uncle, Gen. Seth Mabry, in Clayton, Ala., on the 23rd inst. He was the son of Jno. R. Mabry, who preceded him to the grave at Shubuta, Miss.

Fri. Nov. 27, 1874
     Mr. W. H. Young, age 50, and Miss Minnie Morrow, both of the same house, were killed in a cyclone at Montevallo, (Ala.) on Monday.

     Mr. Laughlin McLean, over 70 years of age, the city bridge keeper, died in Eufaula on Wednesday. He was a Scotchman by birth, and had been a resident of Eufaula since 1836.

Sat. Nov. 28, 1874
     Col. P. B. Baldwin, age 47, of Union Springs, (Ala.) died on Wednesday. He leaves a wife and seven children.

Sat. Dec. 12, 1874
     Mrs. Nancy Dunn, an old citizen of Eufaula, died at the home of her son-in-law, Mr. Jas. Milton, on the 9th inst.

Thurs. Dec. 31, 1874
     Mr. M. W. Murphey, Marshal of Columbus, (Ga.) died on Sunday from gun wounds received by a desperado in that city.

1875

Sat. Jan. 9, 1875
     Mrs. Mary E. Comer, age about 36, wife of Mr. H. M. Comer, died in Savannah on the 4th inst. -Savannah Advertiser. Mrs. Comer was a daughter of Mr. Wilson M. Bates, formerly of Eufaula, but now of Griffin, Ga. She leaves three children.

Tues. Jan. 12, 1875
     Miss Lou Brannon, sister of Thos. Brannon, Sr., died in Eufaula on the 9th inst.

Sat. Jan. 16, 1875
     Mr. Jno. D. Hopkins, a citizen of Savannah, (Ga.) died in Florida on Saturday last. Burial in Savannah.

     Hon. R. H. Ervin, Senator in the State Legislature from Wilcox County, (Ala.) died recently at his home near Camden. -Montgomery Advertiser of Friday.

Tues. Jan. 26, 1875
     M. J. Jenkins, city Marshal of Lumpkin, (Ga.) died on Monday last.

Sat. Feb. 6, 1875
     Mr. Theodore Pruden died in Eufaula recently. He was connected with the Carriage Repository and Factory in Eufaula as master mechanic.

Sat. Feb. 13, 1875
     Mr. A. J. McIlvane died last Thursday at his home near Eufaula.

Sat. Mar. 6, 1875

Mrs. Jno. H. Dent, formerly of Barbour County, died in Rome, Georgia on the 20th ult.

Tues. Mar. 9, 1875
Mrs. Wm. A. McKenzie died at Opelika, (Ala.) on the 8th inst. Burial in Eufaula.

Tues. Mar. 23, 1875
Dr. L. F. W. Andrews died at his home in Americus, (Ga.) on the 16th inst.

Tues. Mar. 30, 1875
Mr. Thos. B. Craddock, a citizen of Henry County, (Ala.) died at his home near Lawrenceville on the 19th inst.

Thurs. Aug. 1, 1875
The death of Col. C. S. Holland, of Columbus, (Ga.) occurred in that city last Monday.

Thurs. Apr. 8, 1875
Mrs. Mary Lewis Hardee, widow of the late Gen. W. J. Hardee of Selma, Ala., died in St. Augustine, Fla., on the 6th inst.

Mrs. Ward, mother of Mr. Pat Ward, and Mrs. Annie Vaughn, died at her home in Macon, Ga. on Sunday last.

Sat. Apr. 10, 1875
Col. Geo. W. Gayle, age 68, of Selma, (Ala.) died recently in that city. -Selma Times.

The remains of Rev. J. Scaife, who died last Thursday in Camilla, Ga., will be interred in Eufaula Thursday.

Tues. Apr. 13, 1875
Mr. Wm. Rolf Wellborn, age 38, of Eufaula, died last Sunday.

Thurs. Apr. 15, 1875
The death of Col. J. R. Jones, living near Dawson, Terrell County, Ga., occurred recently.

Wed. Apr. 21, 1875
Mr. Turner D. Patterson, City Marshal of Eufaula, died last Monday. He was born in Caswell County, N. C. on 16th of Aug. 1810. He married 3 Dec. 1829, his wife died many years since. He came to Eufaula in 1855, and leaves a family of seven or eight grown sons and daughters. Burial in Eufaula.

THE HENRY COUNTY REGISTER
(Published in Abbeville, Henry County, Ala.)

1875

Merrill A. Sheehan, Publisher.

Fri. Jan 8, 1875
Judge Abram Martin, age 76, of Montgomery, (Ala.) died in that city on 1st inst. He was born in Edgefield Dist., S. C. and came to Alabama in 1832.

Fri. Jan. 15, 1875
Mrs. Catherine M. Barnes, age 29, wife of Jesse Barnes, late Circuit Clerk of Dale County, died in Clark, (Ala.) on Jan. 3d, 1875.

Fri. Feb. 5, 1875
     Mrs. Hattie Jackson, daughter of Judge E. W. Teague, former-
ly of Henry County, died on the 22nd ult. -Athens Post.

Fri. Feb. 19, 1875
     Mrs. Francis Wessels, wife of Col. Frank Wessels, and
sister of Maj. Calhoun, of the Columbus (Ga.) Enquirer.

     Col. Whitfield Clark, age about 50, of Clayton, (Ala.) died
last Sunday.

Fri. Feb. 26, 1875
     Mr. J. V. Dennard, citizen of Henry County, (Ala.) died at
his home near Shorterville on last Thursday.

     Mrs. Harriet M. Hudson, age 40, died on Feb. 13th near
Abbeville.

Fri. Mar. 5, 1875
     Mrs. Tempsey Cassady, age 70, died at Lawrenceville (Henry
County, Ala.) last Monday. Burial from the M. E. Church, of
which she was a member for fifty years.

Fri. Apr. 2, 1875
     G. F. Thompson, an old citizen of Dale County, (Ala.) died
at his home near Daleville on the 20th ult.

     Mr. Seaborn B. Bizzell, formerly of Abbeville, died in
Atlanta recently. He was a grandson of the late Jno. Whitehurst,
of Henry County.

Fri. Apr. 16, 1875
     David Dixon, Southern agriculturist, died at Oxford, Ga.,
on the 16th ult.

Fri. May 14, 1875
     David Cuchen, age about 60, a citizen of Henry County, died
last Friday.

     Cary P. Wolfe, an old citizen of Henry County, died at his
home a few days ago.

     Miss Mary Irwin Fluker, age 18, daughter of Col. B. M.
Fluker, died at the home of her father in Henry County on the
5th inst.

     Levi Creel, age about 35, died at his home in Henry County
on the 7th inst.

Fri. May 21, 1875
     Mrs. Sarah Forehan, age 85, died last Saturday at the home
of her daughter, Mrs. E. Blacklidge, in Abbeville. She has long
been a member of the Baptist Church. Burial in Abbeville.

     Mrs. Elizabeth Tally, age 55 or 60, died Wednesday at the
home of her son, Jack Tally. Burial in Abbeville. The deceased
had long been a resident of Henry County.

     Mr. Jno. Sheridan, age 75, died in Somerset, Perry County,
Ohio, on the 9th. He was the father of Gen. Phil. Sheridan, and
a native of the County Cavan, Ireland, he was of the Roman
Catholic faith.

Fri. June 11, 1875
     Maj. Wm. Allan, of Curl's Neck, on the James River, Virginia
died last week.

Mr. R. C. Clarke died at Wetumpka, (Ala.) last Saturday. He was the doorkeeper of the House of Representatives in Montgomery. -<u>Montgomery</u> (Ala.) <u>Advertiser</u>.

Fri. June 25, 1875

Mrs. Amelia Hubert, daughter of the late Geo. Culver, of Henry County, died at the home of her mother near Abbeville on last Sunday.

Col. Washington Toney of Barbour County, and who was a resident of Henry from 1845 to 1859, died at his home near Eufaula on Wednesday.

Fri. July 16, 1875

Mr. Jas. Wilcoxon, formerly of Henry County, was killed by lightning in Bullock County a few days ago.

Fri. July 23, 1875

Mr. Calab V. Kirkland, age about 80, and who had long been a resident of Henry County, died near Abbeville last Tuesday.

Mrs. Janie Goode, age 22, wife of Sam'l. W. Goode, Esq., and daughter of Mr. and Mrs. J. T. Kendall, of Eufaula, died last Saturday at the home of her parents.

Fri. Aug. 6, 1875

J. R. Smith, age about 35, City Clerk of Montgomery, Ala., died in that city recently. He was born in Columbus, his father being Mr. Jack Smith, who removed to Texas before the war. He is a brother of Capt. Jno. J. Smith. He married in Montgomery, and a wife and five children survive him. -<u>Columbus</u> (Ga.) <u>Enquirer</u>.

Fri. Sept. 10, 1875

The funeral of Westley Howerton will be preached on the third Sunday in this month at Ebernezer Church.

Fri. Oct. 22, 1875

Mr. Lige Lewis, of Chilton County, (Ala.) was killed by an unknown assassin on Wednesday. -<u>Montgomery</u> (Ala.) <u>Advertiser</u>.

Fri. Oct. 29, 1875

Mary A., age 23, wife of Jesse M. Kirkland, Esq., and daughter of the late Malcolm J. and Mary A. McRae, died on the 30th of Aug. 1875 at Tuxpan, Mexico.

Miss Sallie Appleyard, daughter of Mr. Jno. Appleyard, of Columbus, died yesterday. -<u>Columbus</u> (Ga.) <u>Enquirer</u>.

Mr. H. Hudgens, age about 72, a resident of Henry County for many years, died near Lawrenceville last Sunday.

Fri. Nov. 12, 1875

Col. Nich Davis, of Huntsville, Ala., died in that place last Tuesday.

Mr. Pickett Beggan, an old citizen, died at his home near Pine Apple, (Ala.) recently. -<u>Greenville</u> (Ala.) <u>Advocate</u>.

Fri. Nov. 26, 1875

Senator Oris S. Ferry died at his home at Norwalk, Conn., on Sunday last.

Fri. Dec. 24, 1875

The funeral of Rev. Z. Knowles was preached at Concord

Church in Henry County, by Rev. Dempsey Whiddon last Sunday.

1876

Fri. Jan. 21, 1876*
    Mrs. Rosannah Yon, a widow living near Newton, Dale County, (Ala.) was assassinated through the window at her home recently, while making a bed for a sick child. (*E. S. Sheehan, Publisher, J. A. Corbitt, Editor).

Fri. Jan. 28, 1876
    Mr. J. M. Mason, a planter living near Gordon in Henry County, was drowned Monday when he fell overboard a steamer near Ft. Gaines, (Ga.). -Eufaula Times.

Fri. Feb. 4, 1876
    Mr. Wm. Gamble, aged 68, of Henry County, died Wednesday.

Fri. Feb. 11, 1876**
    Mr. Geo. Lillie, aged about 45, died at Lawrenceville, Ala., on the 6th inst. Burial in Eufaula.(**E. B. Jordan, Editor).

Fri. Feb. 25, 1876
    Mr. Jonas Smith, of near Camak, Ga., died recently.

    Also, Mr. Cullen W. Wash, formerly of Clay County, Ga., died recently in Texas.

Fri. Mar. 3, 1876
    Mr. J. P. Lunsford, of Henry County, died on Jan. 12th, and his funeral will be preached by Rev. J. W. Parker at Old Salem Church on the 4th Sabbath in April.

Fri. Mar. 10, 1876
    Hon. T. J. Judge, of the Alabama Supreme Court, died in Greenville, (Ala.) recently.

Fri. Mar. 17, 1876
    Judge Wm. H. Walker died in Athens, (Ga.) on the 4th.

Fri. Apr. 7, 1876
    Mr. Wm. Blalock, aged about 26, died on Sunday. Burial at the family burying ground.

Fri. Apr. 21, 1876
    Mrs. Winny Ward, aged 85, died on the 13th at the home of Mr. Robt. Gamble. (Henry County).

Fri. May 12, 1876
    Henry K. Scott died at his home on the 7th of May in Henry County, Ala. He was born in Halifax County, N. C. on 7th of Mar. 1799, and was married to his present wife on Sept. 1819, and moved to Alabama Mar. 1831, where he resided to his death. He was the father of twelve children.

Fri. May 19, 1876
    S. S. Whitehurst, an old citizen, died at his home in Henry County on Sunday last.

Fri. June 2, 1876
    Mr. Robt. Knowles was killed by lightning in Henry County on the 24th of last month.

    Jno. Atkinson, aged about 75, died at his home in Henry

124

County on Saturday last.

Fri. June 23, 1876
Jno. Murphy, aged 15, died at the home of his grandfather, Stephen Hart, in Henry County, on the 17th inst.

Fri. June 30, 1876
Mrs. Addie Cassady, wife of A. A. Cassady, died at her home in Lawrenceville, (Ala.) on the 25th inst. She was the daughter of Rev. Jno. W. Norton, born in Barbour County, Ala., Aug. 1848, and joined the M. E. Church when quite a child. She was a sister to Rev. W. K. Norton. She leaves a husband and infant son. Burial at Lawrenceville.

Fri. July 7, 1876
Mrs. Sallie Kirkland, wife of Seymour Kirkland, of Abbeville, died on 4th inst., at the home of her father, Edmond Blacklidge. She leaves a husband, mother, father, several brothers and sisters and four small children.

Thos. Mathis, age about 75, died at his home near Abbeville, (Ala.) about three weeks ago.

Fri. July 21, 1876
Rollin A. Wellborn died in Eufaula on the 12th inst.

Fri. Sept. 1, 1876
Col. W. Garrett, age 69, of Coosa County, (Ala.) died on 22nd. He was Clerk of the House of Representatives in 1838, and Secretary of State from 1840 to 1852.

Fri. Sept. 8, 1876
Maj. Jno. W. L. Daniel, age 45, lawyer of Midway, in Bullock County, (Ala.) died on Thursday last.

Mr. B. F. Petty, an old citizen of Clayton, (Ala.) died on the 3rd inst. He was the father of Mrs. J. W. Foster.

Mr. Wm. C. Wilson, age 75, of near Columbia, (Ala.) died on the 30th ult.

Fri. Sept. 29, 1876
Capt. J. W. Sutlive, well known here, died of yellow fever at Savannah a few days ago.

Fri. Oct. 6, 1876
Mrs. Lemons Box, a very old lady, died at the home of her son-in-law, A. H. Hutto, in Abbeville on Saturday last.

Fri. Nov. 3, 1876*
The death of Francis P. Blair, age 87, father of Gen. Frank Blair and Hon. Montgomery Blair, is announced from Washington on the 18th ult. (*S. A. Fackler, Publisher).

Mortimer M. Cook, associate editor of the Montgomery Advertiser, died at Prattville, (Ala.) on the 16th ult.

Mrs. Elizabeth Raleigh, age 84, died in Eufaula on the 20th ult. She settled in Henry County with her husband in 1817. In 1837 she moved to Eufaula and has lived there since.

Fri. Dec. 15, 1876
The death of Capt. W. H. Dunlap, formerly of Pickens County, (Ala.) occurred in Mississippi on Nov. 13th.

1877

Published by M. A. Sheehan and J. T. Brown; R. D. Shrophire, Editor.

Thurs. May 10, 1877
   Samuel P. Russ, aged 81, died in New Orleans recently.

   The death of Jno. N. Gully occurred Sunday last at DeKalb, Kemper County, Miss. The culmination of a feud at this palce Sunday resulted in the deaths of J. F. Gilmer, A. McClellan, Jno. Chislom and David Rosser.

   Hon. Jno. Forsyth, age 66, editor of the Mobile Register, died at his home in Mobile on the 2nd inst.

   Jas. Foster, of Greenville, Ala., died on the 30th ult. He leaves a wife and four children.

   Jno. Lamar Edmonson, 15 months old son of Mr. and Mrs. R. Q. Edmonson, of Eufaula, died on Monday last.

Thurs. May 17, 1877
   Maj. Jas. E. Drake died at Yalaha, Sumpter County, Fla., on the 27th ult. He was formerly of Greensboro, Ala., and was a son-in-law of Ex-Gov. Polk, of Missouri.

   Dr. Jas. A. Kelley, aged 70, of Coosa County, Ala., died on the 2d inst.

   Mr. Oliver Hubbard, of Selma, Ala., died on the 7th inst.

   Mr. Daniel Jenkins, aged 87, of Scroggins Beat in Barbour County, and Mr. Wm. Beasley, aged 85, of Louisville Beat, both died on the 7th inst. -Clayton Courier.

Thurs. May 24, 1877
   Col. Jas. H. Dunklin, of Greenville, Ala., died at his home there on Monday last.

   Mr. Oliver Keeler, for many years a conductor on the Mobile and Montgomery R. R., died on the 18th inst.

   Mr. Wm. A. Reynolds, a druggist of Montgomery, died there on Saturday last.

   Thos. A. Malone's death occurred at Eight Miles Station on the Mobile & Ohio R. R. last Friday. His home was in Mobile.

Thurs. May 31, 1877
   The death of Mr. I. L. Holman, of near Tuscaloosa, (Ala.) occurred recently.

   Maj. C. A. Miller, Secretary of the State of Alabama in reconstruction days, died at his home in Maine a few days ago, aged 45 years.

   Dr. J. L. Cheney, of Columbus, Ga., died on Thursday last.

   Mrs. Thos. K. Wynne, wife of one of the proprietors of the Columbus (Ga.) Sun, died last Friday, aged 89 years.

   The death of Mrs. Columbus Chambliss, of near Antioch, Stewart County, Ga., occurred recently. She had been married about a year, and was Miss Amelia Wright, daughter of Y. F. Wright, of Stewart County, Ga.

Thurs. June 14, 1877

126

L. G. Calhoun, living near Hilliardsville, Henry County, (Ala.) died Sunday last, aged 56 years.

Thos. Marshall, age 78, died at the home of his son, D. M. Marshall, in Barbour County on May 26, 1877. He was born in S. C. Apr. 19th, 1799, and was a member of the Cowikee Baptist Church.

Judge Peebles, jurist of Georgia, died on the 3rd inst., in Atlanta, Ga.

Thurs. June 21, 1877
Mrs. Mary McElory, of Shelby County, accidentally shot and killed herself a few days ago.

Mr. Gidlen Sanders died at his home near Clayton on the 9th inst.

Mr. Silas R. Jones, age 55 or 60, living near Eufaula at White Church, died Sunday.

The death of Mrs. Amanda Hardner, of Pike County, (Ala.) occurred a few days ago.

Thurs. July 26, 1877
Hon. Thos. M. Williams, age about 70, father of Rev. Jere. Williams, died at Midway, Ala., about ten days ago. Interment at Lowndesboro, Lowndes County, Ala.

Ed. S. Jones, a young man of Selma, Ala., was drowned in the Alabama River on the 18th inst.

Died on the 21st, Oscar D., adopted son of Mr. and Mrs. T. J. Craddock, aged 2 months and 2 days.

Mrs. Sarah Jones, aged about 65, died at her home in Eufaula on Tuesday last. She was a member of the Baptist Church.

Thurs. Apr. 2, 1877
The death of Mrs. Richard Avery, of Perry County, Ala. occurred at her home on Saturday. She leaves a husband.

The deaths of Joel Osborn and Thos. Henderson resulted from a train accident recently. Both lived in Atlanta, Ga.

Mr. Wm. McLeod, of Eufaula, died recently. He had lived here nearly 40 years. He was born in Cumberland County, N. C., on Jan. 30th, 1810. When he was 18 he emigrated with his father to Washington County, Ga., thence to Stewart County, Ga., from whence he moved to Barbour County, Ala. He joined the M. E. Church in his 17th year. On Jan. 17, 1849 he married Miss F. E. Birdsong, who survives him.

Thurs. Aug. 9, 1877
Dr. J. R. Milton and Col. Jno. S. McMullan, both of Butler County, (Ala.) died a few days since.

Lillian Lulu, infant daughter of Mr. and Mrs. J. J. Creyon, aged six days, died in Eufaula on the 5th inst.

Thurs. Aug. 30, 1877
Mr. W. B. Norwood, aged 21, of Fort Deposit, drowned at Point Clear, off Mobile, (Ala.) in the presence of his invalid father and sister.

Edward E. McGehee, aged 17, son of Wm. A. and Cynthia A. McGehee, of Quitman County, Ga., died on the 25th inst.

Mrs. Ella Hartung, aged 24, wife of F. J. Hartung, died in

Eufaula last Thursday. Burial in the Masonic Cemetery. She
leaves a husband and an aged father.

Thurs. Sept. 20, 1877
        Prof. Jno. Darby, aged 73, died in New York on the 1st inst.
He was a teacher of eminence in the South, one time a resident
of Auburn, Ala.

        Anderson M. Hughes died near Newton, Dale County, (Ala.)
June 12, 1877. He was born in Virginia on Feb. 15, 1815, was
admitted to the bar in Ga. in 1836; served throughout the
Seminole War, was a member of the Georgia Legislature from
Randolph County in 1841, and has been residing in Dale County
since 1850.

        Judge L. B. Brown, of Dale County, (Ala.) died recently.

Thurs. Sept. 27, 1877
        Earnest, 14 year old son of H. L. Daughtry, of Opelika,
Ala., lost his life today by being run over by a train. -Opelkia
Times of 15th.

Thurs. Oct. 25, 1877
        Wm. J. Keyser, Esq., lumber dealer of Pensacola, Fla., died
suddenly in Liverpool on the 11th.

        Mrs. Emily H. Hailey died in Eufaula Oct. 17, 1877. She
was born in Monticello, Ga., Feb. 25th, 1825, and came to
Eufaula in 1839, joined the Baptist Church in 1853, married in
1845 to Wm. B. Hailey, who died many years ago.

Thurs. Dec. 20, 1877
        Joseph Nicholls died at Strassburg, Chilton County, Ala.,
yesterday. He was 58 years old, a native of Germany.

        Mr. Isaac Estill, of Talladega, (Ala.) died on Dec. 3rd.
He was born in Madison County, Ky., Nov. 1791, of Baptist
parentage. After the death of his father, his mother married
Rev. Reuben Mardis, a Methodist minister, and Hon. Samuel W.
Mardis and Dr. Jno. Mardis, who died some years ago in Shelby,
were children of the marriage. After leaving Ky. the family
settled near Winchester, Tenn.. Mr. Estill first married in
Tenn., but lost his wife a short time after his marriage. In
1839 he married Mrs. Cruikshank, mother of Hon. M. H. Cruikshank.
Mr. Estill had two sons killed in the war, Henry and William.
-Talladega Home.

THE EUFAULA TIMES AND NEWS

1878

Published by M. A. Sheehan & J. T. Brown; Richard Williams,
    Editor.

Thurs. Jan. 3, 1878
        The death of Col. Wm. Randolph Barleley, of Va. and Capt.
Wm. H. Kennedy, formerly of Petersburg, Va., occurred recently.

Thurs. Jan. 10, 1878
        J. B. Appling, Judge of Probate of Henry County, Ala., died
at his home in Abbeville a few days ago.

        Gabriel Mathis, aged 100 years, died recently in Dale County,
Ala.

        Capt. J. M. Macon died in Eufaula at the home of Mrs. C. J.

Pope, on 3d inst., aged about 40 years. Burial in Eufaula.

Mrs. Susie Dawson Mitchell, aged 25, died at her home in Glennville, Ala., on 6th inst. She was the wife of A. C. Mitchell, Jr.

Thurs. Jan. 31, 1878
Mr. Abner Flowers, formerly of Barbour County, died recently near Skipperville, Dale County, Ala.

Mrs. Nancy Ward, aged 105, died last Sunday. She was a native of N. C., but had lived most of her life in Alabama.

Capt. O. F. Riley, aged about 70, died last Saturday. He had long been a school teacher in the county.

Thurs. Mar. 7, 1878
Gen. John F. Beecher, aged 78 years, died in Pike County, (Ala.) Saturday.

Miss Willie Francis, sister to Maj. Francis, of Montgomery, died in Jacksonville, Fla., on the 25th ult.

Judge E. Richards, formerly of Barbour County, died at Ozark last Sunday. He was Probate Judge of Dale County.

Dexter, Me., Feb. 23. - The death of J. W. Barron, of Dexter Saving Bank, occurred this morning from wounds received from robbers at the bank.

Mr. Jno. A. Wood died at his residence in Henry County, on Saturday last. -Henry County (Ala.) Register.

Chas. E. Johnson, of Gordon, Ala., died at Raiford House (Columbus, Ga.) recently. He was about 23 years old, unmarried and a brother survives.

Thurs. Mar. 14, 1878
Mrs. Abscilla Peagler, aged 63, daughter of Grey Thigpen, who is now over 90 years of age, and relict of the late Capt. Geo. S. Peagler, died at the home of her son-in-law, Mr. Wm. M. Flowers, in Greenville on Sunday. -Greenville (Ala.) Advocate.

Miss Marie J. McIntosh, aged 75, died in New Jersey two weeks ago. She was a noted authoress, and a native of Georgia.

Dr. A. J. Powers died at Pineapple, Wilcox County, Ala., on the 26th of Feb.

Mr. Frank Fortner died at his home near Mt. Andrew (Barbour County, Ala.) on last Friday.

Thurs. Mar. 21, 1878
The wife of Col. T. M. Hogan, of Columbus, Ga., died Sunday of pneumonia.

Hon. J. E. Leonard, age 32, of New Orleans, La., died in Havana recently of yellow fever. He was to have been married in Cuba.

Thurs. Apr. 11, 1878
G. W. McRae died last Friday six miles west of Clayton. He had been a resident of Barbour County for thirty or more years. Burial at Pea River Church.

Thurs. June 6, 1878
Mrs. Jennie Schloss, of Macon, Ga., died in Eufaula on Monday last at the home of Mr. Schwed. She was a sister of Isaac Steuerman.

Thurs. June 13, 1878

Miss Lizzie Harper, age 23, died last Saturday at the home of her uncle in Henry County, (Ala.).

Died at his home in Eufaula on the 29th of May, 1878, Hon. Judge S. Williams. He was born in Hancock County, Ga., on Feb. 1804. He came to Barbour County when a youth. He served three terms as Judge of Probate, was a member of the Methodist Church.

Thurs. June 20, 1878

Mr. Andrew McKenzie died in Eufaula on 11th inst., aged 65 years. He was one of the earliest settlers of this place.

Annie Will, infant daughter of Mr. and Mrs. P. H. Morris, died in Eufaula on May 27th, born July 16, 1877.

Thurs. June 27, 1878

Jas. Kelly, of Lindwood, Pike County, (Ala.) was killed last week by the falling of a tree. He leaves a family. -Troy (Ala.) Messenger.

Thurs. July 4, 1878

Jno. W. Persons, of Auburn, Ala., died at his plantation in Macon County on the 21st of June.

Alderman A. G. Bedell died in Columbus, (Ga.) on Friday.

W. F. Patterson, aged about 30, formerly of Eufaula, died in Bainbridge, Ga., last Saturday.

Mr. Amos Cory died at his home in Eufaula on 22nd of May, 1878. He was born in Essex County, N. J. on Oct. 2, 1828. He came to Alabama about 1849 and settled in Tuskegee, then moved to this place in 1852, was a member of the M. E. Church. He leaves a wife and eight children.

Thurs. July 11, 1878

Mr. Asa Poole, of Charleston, S. C., died on the 28th ult. from hydrophobia.

Mr. N. O. Glover, of Bullock County, (Ala.) died at Union Springs on the 3rd of July. He was a former citizen of Barbour County.

Mrs. Jno. McKenzie died at her home in Meridian, Miss. last week. For many years she was a resident of Louisville, Alabama.

Mr. Samuel Heilbron, age about 45, died at his home in Eufaula last Sunday. He leaves a wife and two daughters.

Thurs. July 25, 1878

Mr. R. Burge, father of Mrs. Sterling B. Toney, of Eufaula, died at Grayson's Springs, Ky., last Saturday.

Thurs. Aug. 8, 1878

Frederick Hoadley, aged 12 years and 11 months, son of Mr. and Mrs. W. H. Bray, of Eufaula, died on 4th inst.

Mrs. Angelina P. Crane, wife of W. F. Crane, of Eufaula, died on the 24th of July. She leaves five small children.

Thurs. Aug. 15, 1878*

Gen. Thos. Rhett, who died in Baltimore Tuesday, was Chief of Staff of Gen. J. E. Johnston during the war. (*The Times And News, published Eufaula, by Jas. T. Goode, Editor).

Sat. Aug. 31, 1878

Near Shorterville, Henry County, Ala., last Monday, Master Richard, aged 11, son of Mrs. C. E. McAllister, was found dead, he had been kicked to death by a horse.

Judge W. J. Kincey, of near Eufaula, died on the 28th inst. He leaves a family.

Mr. E. E. Pearre, former resident of Eufaula, died on the 22nd at Gordon, Ala.

Thurs. Sept. 5, 1878
Brooklyn, N. Y. - Mr. M. J. Russell died here on Friday.

James Stapler, of Bladon Springs, died recently.

Stewart Washhart died near Huntsville, Ala., recently.

Rev. J. K. Armstrong, late of Alabama, died at Grenda, Mississippi, last Wednesday.

Mr. G. G. Greenwood, of Marshall County, Ala., father-in-law of Hon. R. K. Boyd, died recently.

The deaths of Mr. Elijah McCreary and L. A. Johnson, of near Evergreen, Alabama are announced.

Mrs. Alfred Johnson, Mr. E. C. Hardy and Mr. Geo. Beltzer, of Lowndes County, Alabama, died recently.

The deaths of S. K. Davis, Miss Martha, the daughter of Rev. W. Tucker, and Mrs. Julius Miller are announced in the Demopolis (Ala.) Journal.

Tues. Sept. 10, 1878
Princeton, Ky. - J. W. Riggs and J. M. Kuttrell, in attempting to escape from court on Aug. 26th, were instantly killed.

Thurs. Sept. 12, 1878
Jennie Carrie Belle, infant daughter of A. B. and C. E. A. Hooper, near Cochran's Station, (Ala.) died 6th inst.

Capt. A. J. Love, (Amos) of Thomasville died recently. He leaves a family. -Thomasville Times.

Thurs. Sept. 19, 1878
Mrs. Susan Pickens Calhoun, widow of the late Hon. Jas. M. Calhoun, of Dallas County, Ala., died on the 7th inst. She was a sister of Gov. Pickens of South Carolina.

Thurs. Sept. 14, 1878
John Stacks, of Walker County, Ala., died on 29th ult.

Thurs. Oct. 3, 1878
Mrs. Marshall Tarrant died on Tuesday last, in the 84th year of her age. -Talladega (Ala.) Reporter.

Sat. Oct. 5, 1878
Willie Jeshua Allen, eldest son of Dr. T. M. Allen, of Eufaula, died at Cotton Hill, Ga., Oct. 1st, 1878. He was born in Jonesboro, Ga., Dec. 1st, 1876.

Thurs. Oct. 10, 1878
The death of Mrs. Susan Norris, wife of Dr. Norris, occurred in Alexander City, Ala. She was a bride of three weeks, and the daughter of Dr. Parker.

Sat. Oct. 12, 1878
John McCarthy died in Bullock County, Ala., a few days ago.

He was a member of Gen. Clanton's Escort and a soldier.

The Bar of Montgomery met the 10th and held a meeting in honor of Col. W. D. Graham, deceased, and they attended his funeral in a body from the Presbyterian Church.

Mr. Joseph Holloway, aged 102, died in Monroe County, Ala., a few days ago.

The funeral of Mr. W. H. Foy will take place from his residence today. (Barbour County).

Mrs. Parilee Ricks Hart, aged 36, consort of Capt. Henry C. Hart, of Eufaula, died Aug. 28th, 1878.

Thurs. Oct. 17, 1878

Dr. James Pippin, of Mobile, Ala., died in New Orleans a few days ago of yellow fever.

Dr. J. W. Garrison, of Louisville, (Ala.) died recently.

Dr. Geo. Miors, formerly of Green County, Ala., died in Memphis a few days ago.

Mr. Reuben Sanders, of near Eufaula, died Tuesday. He leaves a wife.

Sat. Oct. 19, 1878

Dr. B. A. Bobo, of Thomasville, (Ga.) died in New Orleans of yellow fever. He leaves a wife and four children. His wife is from the Alston family.

Thurs. Oct. 24, 1878

Jefferson Davis, Jr., aged 21, died of yellow fever near Memphis last week. He was the last surviving son of ex-President Davis.

Sat. Oct. 26, 1878

Miss Mary Schoenburg, superintendent of the Jewish widows and orphans home at New Orleans, died on the 23rd inst., of yellow fever.

Rev. Chas. Smith, Pastor of the M. E. Church at Smith's Station, died three days ago.

Tues. Oct. 29, 1878

Mr. Wiley M. Camp, of Clopton, Dale County, Ala., died Saturday. He leaves a wife and several children. -Henry County Register.

Mr. Chas. Burrus, formerly of Eufaula, but for several years past, a resident of Columbus, Ga., died there Saturday.

Mr. Thos. Davis, of Chambers County, Ala., died recently.

Mrs. T. C. Doughtie died near Eufaula last Sunday.

Dr. Milton A. Roach, formerly of Barbour County, but for several years past a resident of Pattersonville, La., died of yellow fever at that place on 17th inst. Mrs. Roach is a sister of Mrs. Jno. C. Martin, of Eufaula.

Albert W. Plowman, of Henry County, (Ala.) died recently.

Thurs. Oct. 31, 1878

Col. Pen Yonge died at his residence in Spring Villa several days ago. (Alabama news).

Mr. Baer, father of Mr. Samuel Baer, of Eufaula, died Tuesday.

Sat. Nov. 2, 1878

Mr. Allen Chancey, of Tallahassee, Fla., died recently.

Mr. Geo. Garlington was thrown from a buggy near Lafayette, (Ala.) a few days ago and since died of injuries received.

Tues. Nov. 5, 1878

Mrs. Susan Vinson, of Georgiana, (Ala.) died recently.

Capt. Allen Brannon, of Henry County, (Ala.) died recently.

Thurs. Nov. 7, 1878

Mr. Chas. Helms, of Ball Play, near Gadsden, Ala., died recently.

Rev. David Lockheart, of near Daleville, (Ala.) died on the 3rd of Oct. He was 88 years of age.

Thurs. Nov. 26, 1878

Thos. H. Powers, of the drug house of Powers & Wightman, in Philadelphia, died three days ago.

Thurs. Nov. 28, 1878

Rev. Geo. Stewart, aged 65, Methodist minister of Summerville, Ala., died at his home on Saturday.

Samuel Pond died in Sumpter County, Ala., recently.

Dr. Jas. P. Peterson, of Greensboro, (Ala.) died on the 19th.

Dr. Carrington Spiers, of Montgomery, (Ala.) died on Friday last.

Tues. Dec. 3, 1878

Mr. Wm. Suttle, the aged father of Rev. Jno. A. Suttle, died at Rockford, Ala., on the 19th.

Chas. Harrison, of Edgefield, S. C. was accidently shot and instantly killed recently.

Sat. Dec. 7, 1878

Died in Clayton, (Ala.) on Sunday last, Mr. Friendly Grubbs, born Oct. 16th, 1817. He served in the Indian War and was engaged in the battle of Hobby's Bridge in 1836. He went to Texas from this country in 1841 and enlisted in Mier's expedition, he was captured and taken to the Castle of Perote, he escaped, and was recaptured and tested to determine if he would be shot by drawing a white or black bean. He was lucky, his life was saved by drawing a white bean. He returned to Barbour County in 1846, married in 1847 to a sister of Gen. Seth Mabry and Col. J. W. Mabry, who survives him. -Clayton (Ala.) Courier.

Mr. Wm. A. James was thrown from a horse and killed instantly, near Arlington, Ga., a few days ago.

Thurs. Dec. 12, 1878

Miss Louise King died in Augusta, Ga., last Saturday.

The death of Mr. B. McGaughey occurred at his home near Neal's Landing, Fla., on last Friday. His wife survives.

Thurs. Dec. 19, 1878

Col. Samuel Arrington, aged 72, of Montgomery, Ala., died on Sunday last. He was formerly from Nash County, North Carolina.

The death of Mr. J. N. Williams, of Greensboro, Ala., occurred on Saturday last.

Thurs. Jan. 2, 1879*
      Mrs. Jno. Robinson, nee Elizabeth Frances Bloomer, died
yesterday at her home. She was born in Madison, Ind., Mar. 5,
1821, married in Algiers, La., on Jan. 5, 1841. Survivors are
children: Jno. F. Jr., Gilbert N., Jas. H., Frank, Chas. Robinson,
and Mrs. Robt. T. Stickney. -Cincinnati Commerical. (*Eufaula
Publishing Co., Jas. T. Goode, Editor & Publisher).

Sat. Jan. 11, 1879
      A. H. Granger, of St. Louis, (Mo.) died at Cochran Station
(Barbour County, Ala.) recently. Burial in St. Louis.

Sat. Jan. 18, 1879
      John D. Snipes, formerly of Eufaula, died on the 16th inst.,
at Union Springs, Ala. Funeral services were from the Episcopal
Church in Eufaula. Interment in Eufaula.

Tues. Jan. 21, 1879
      The death of Col. R. W. Jemison, of Macon, Ga., occurred in
that place on Friday.
      Mrs. Mary Jane Shorter, age 54, relict of the late Gov. Jno.
Gill Shorter, died in Eufaula on the 20th inst.

Thurs. Jan. 23, 1879
      Miss Anna Crossman, daughter of W. H. Crossman of Eufaula,
died at Nashville on the 13th inst.
      Mr. M. McGuire, aged 85, died in Ruthmines (Dublin, Ireland).
He was the father of Mrs. M. A. Ryans, of Greenville, Ala., and
Mr. (Mrs.?) Wheelan and Mr. M. McGuire, of Hatchechubbee, Ala.

Tues. Jan. 28, 1879
      Died on 18th inst., Annie Laurie, infant daughter of Dr.
and Mrs. T. L. Appleby. -Troy (Ala.) Messenger.
      Jno. R. Robinson, aged 76, died at his home in Eufaula, Ala.,
last Friday.
      Mr. Gillespie, aged nearly 100, grandfather of Mrs. Samuel
Heibron, of Eufaula, died in Americus, Ga., last Saturday. Interment in Eufaula.

Thurs. Jan. 30, 1879
      John W. Johnson, aged 58, died at his home near Eufaula on
Wednesday. Burial in the Masonic Cemetery, Eufaula.

Thurs. Feb. 6, 1879
      Mrs. Wm. A. Clements died at the home of her husband on
Thursday last, seven miles east of Lumpkin, Ga.

Sat. Feb. 8, 1879
      J. E. Ellis, brother of J. M. Ellis, died in Union Springs,
(Ala.) last Thursday.
      Mr. Chas. Mathis, an old citizen of Dale County, (Ala.)
died recently.
      Mr. Alfred Hatch, age 80, of Hale County, (Ala.) died at
his home near Arcola on the 30th ult.

Tues. Feb. 11, 1879
      Dr. T. W. Mason, of Macon, Ga., died last Thursday. He
moved from Wetumpka, Ala., to Macon about 20 years ago.

Tues. Feb. 18, 1879
    Mrs. Emma Streater, wife of C. H. Streater, living at
Spring Hill, Barbour County, died Feb. 8th. She was born June
27, 1849, the daughter of Jas. M. Garrett, of Eufaula. She
married her second husband Apr. 23, 1878.

    Mr. J. E. Moore, formerly of Eufaula, died in Sherman, Tex.,
on 20th ult. He was a nephew of Col. D. M. Seals, of Eufaula.

Thurs. Feb. 20, 1879
    The infant child, age 3 months, of Mr. Thad Doughtie, died
Monday, and was buried from the residence of Wm. Doughtie, near
Eufaula. Mrs. Thad Doughtie died shortly after the birth of
this child.

Sat. Feb. 22, 1879
    Mr. B. F. Hood, brother of the editor of the Monroe (Ala.)
Journal died recently in Bibb County, (Ala.).

Thurs. Mar. 6, 1879
    Mrs. Cory, relict of the late Amos Cory, died Tuesday. (Sat.
Mar. 22 paper: Mrs. Mary A. Cory was born in Merriwether County,
Ga., on Jan. 10, 1834, but lived in Alabama the greater portion
of her life.).

    Judge Wade Keys died at his home in Montgomery last Sunday.
He leaves a wife and several children. -Montgomery (Ala.)
Advertiser.

Sat. Mar. 9, 1879
    Mrs. Jane Nobles, age 91, died at her home in Henry County,
Ala., on day last week. She was a war pensioner.

Sat. Mar. 15, 1879
    John Reese, age 85, of Clayton, (Ala.) died suddenly at his
home recently.

    Mr. Irwin Waller, age 70, a citizen of Hancock County, died
in Sparta, Ga., recently.

    Hector P. Blue, aged 75 years, died at his home near Union
Springs, Ala., on the 3d.

    Mr. Belair L. Wymau, of Montgomery, died recently. He
leaves a wife and three children.

    Col. W. H. Houghton died at his home in Union Springs, Ala.,
on Tuesday last. He was born in Green County, Ga., in 1809.

    William Brooks, age 74, the founder, or the first settler
in Brooksville, Coosa County, Ala., died at his home on the 1st
inst.

    J. H. Lewis, aged about 50, died in Eufaula Thursday. He
leaves a wife and several children.

    Dr. Wm. Kelsoe, age 72, and one of the first settlers of
the county, died near Troy recently. (Pike Co., Ala.).

Tues. Mar. 25, 1879*
    The death of J. E. O'Bryne occurred at Apalachicola, Fla.,
last Sunday. Burial in Eufaula. Survivors are his mother,
brother and sisters. (*A. A. Walker, President, Robt. F. Nance,
Secretary of The Times and News.

Wed. Apr. 23, 1879
    Capt. Edward L. Young, age 97, of Norfolk, Va., died recent-

ly. He commanded a privateer in the War of 1812. He had been a member of the Masons for 66 years.

Thurs. Apr. 24, 1879
Mrs. A. B. Davis, of Columbus, Ga., died Monday last. She had lived there since 1828, and was the daughter of Gov. Wm. Schley.

Mrs. Jno. L. Jackson, of Columbus, Ga., died on Sunday last.

Sat. Apr. 26, 1879
Alexander Lewis, aged 99, died recently near Tuskagee, Ala. In that county, (Macon) in the last four years died Isaac Runyan, aged 117; Sam'l. Glover, aged 110; and Mrs. Brittain Stamps, aged 93 years.

Col. Jno. H. Lovelace, aged 55, died in Hamilton, Ga., last Tuesday.

Mr. C. S. Bears, Jr., of Mobile, Ala., died recently.

Mrs. M. M. Patton, of Lowndes County, (Ala.) died recently.

Tues. Apr. 29, 1879
Rev. J. D. Porter, Presbyterian minister, died recently near Alto, Texas.

Sat. May 3, 1879
Capt. Thos. Mehin, formerly a captain on the Chattshoochee River, died on the 21st inst., in Indiana County, Penn., aged 79 years. He came to this river in 1836, and left in 1861.

Mr. Russell Jones was killed last week while running timber on Pigeon Creek. He lived in the lower part of the county. (Butler County, Ala.) Survivors are his wife and two children. -Greenville (Ala.) Advocate.

Col. Jas. T. Donald an old citizen of Mobile, Ala., died on the 21st in Mississippi.

Tues. May 6, 1879
Eugene Jordan, aged 21, son of Dr. Jordan of Springvale, Ga., died on the 4th inst. Burial at Cuthbert, Ga.

Col. Thos. Evans, lawyer of Sandersville, Ga., died on the 30th ult.

Mrs. Passmore, aged 94 years, of Louisville, Ala., died on the 27th ult.

Wed. May 7, 1879
Hon. Eli S. Shorter, aged 56, died in Eufaula yesterday. He was born in Monticello, Jasper County, Ga., on Mar. 15, 1823. Survivors are his wife and children.

Ignatius Terrell, of Pike County, (Ga.) died on Wednesday last.

Mobile, (Ala.) 27th. - A. H. Shelden, M. D. died yesterday.

The death of Mitchell Eisner, aged about 60, occurred Monday last at Macon, Ga. He was a Bavarian by birth, but for many years a citizen of Macon.

Thurs. May 8, 1879
Mrs. Walter T. Johnson, nee Madge Snider, of Macon, Ga., died on Sunday last.

Jno. T. Cox was killed by lightning last Thursday near

Albany, Ga. He was a brother of Maj. W. B. Cox, of Atlanta.

Mrs. Lucretia Ann Stevens, consort of J. C. Stevens, died in Eufaula last Tuesday. She leaves a son, Charley.

Hon. Jno. L. Harris, Judge of Brunswick, (Ga.) Circuit Court, died on the 5th inst.

Tues. May 13, 1879

Mrs. Peter F. Thomas, of Lawrenceville, Ala., died last Friday. (Henry County).

Mrs. Henry E. Hughes of near Ozark, Ala., died last week.

Sat. May 17, 1879

Nathaniel Hicks Barden, Esq., aged 72, died Wednesday last at his home in Hamilton, Ga.

Mrs. Charlotte Colby, aged about 55, died in Eufaula on Thursday last. Survivors are three daughters.

Tues. May 20, 1879

Samuel W. Fields, son of B. B. Fields, Esq., aged about 24 years, died near Eufaula on Saturday last.

Col. W. D. Haralson, age 80, died in Selma, (Ala.) on the 12th inst.

Rev. H. T. Bussey, age 63, of Brookfield, (Ga.) died on the 12th inst.

Mr. Jno. A. McIntosh, of Thomas County, Ga., died on Friday last.

Thurs. May 22, 1879

Maggie, aged three years, daughter of Mr. D. D. and Mrs. S. E. Reeder, (Barbour County) was killed on the 11th inst., by having a wash trough to fall on her.

Sat. May 24, 1879

Edward B. Young died at his home in Eufaula on Thursday last. He was born in New York City on Aug. 24, 1802. When he was 21 years old, he came South to Macon, Ga. He married June 11, 1832 to Miss Ann Fendall Beall, and came to Eufaula in 1837.

Mrs. Hattie E. Raleigh, of Troy, (Ala.) died on Saturday night.

Thurs. May 29, 1879

Seaborn O'Neal died Sunday last in Muscogee County, Ga.

Dr. Wm. T. Peay, age 75, teacher of Savannah, Ga., died last Wednesday.

Mr. William McIntyre, an old citizen of Savannah, Ga., died last week.

Sat. May 31, 1879

Mr. E. J. Johnson, of Macon, Ga., died Thursday last.

Capt. Geo. A. Nicoll, of Savannah, Ga., died on Monday last. Also, Herman A. Crane, Esq., an aged citizen.

Rev. Mr. Samuel Knight, age 86, died recently at his home at Hickery Bluff, Hillsborough County, (Fla.). He was a soldier of the War of 1812 and was a native of Georgia, he went to Fla. not long after the cession of that state to the United States.

Tues. June 3, 1879

Mr. Joseph Graham, of Henry County, (Ala.) died last Thursday.

Thurs. June 5, 1879
Mr. Wood Worthington, age about 50 years, a wheelright and wagon maker by trade, died yesterday in Eufaula.

Mr. Emanuel Kern, of Columbus, Ga., died suddenly on Sunday.

Dr. Jno. S. Merriwether died recently in Greene County, Alabama.

Mrs. E. J. Eldrige, of Americus, Ga., died Thursday.

Dr. Cullen Battle, age 94, died Wednesday at the home of Gov. Jno. Gill Shorter near Eufaula. He was born in Edgecombe County, N. C. on Mar. 11, 1785. He came to Eufaula in 1836, (then known as Irwinton) from Powelton, Ga. In 1838, he with others, organized the Baptist Church. He is survived by his wife, Mrs. Jane L. Battle, nee Miss Lamon, Dr. Archibald J. Battle, Maj. Gen. Cullen A. Battle, of Tuskagee, and granddaughter, Mrs. Mollie S. Perkins. Burial in the Shorter burial grounds in Eufaula.

Tues. June 10, 1879
Mr. D. J. Shipp, of Green Hill, Stewart County, (Ga.) died recently.

Mr. Hugh W. Caffey, of Montgomery died Wednesday.

Died in Opelika, (Ala.) last Friday, Miss Mollie Stephens, also, Mrs. Hugh Echols died in the same city recently.

Mrs. L. J. Wells, relict of the late Stephen Garrard Wells, died at the home of her son, Mr. H. P. Wells, near Crawford, Ala.

Mr. Wm. Lyles, age 70 odd years, living on Cowpen Creek, died Friday. -Florence (Ala.) Gazette.

Thurs. June 12, 1879
Mr. Alsey Fuller, age 75 years, died near LeGrange, (Ga.) on Monday last.

Hon. Peter Fair, Judge of Baldwin County, (Ga.) died on Sunday last.

Mrs. Susan L. Bragg, wife of Walter L. Bragg, of Montgomery, died on Sunday last.

Tues. June 17, 1879
Capt. Thos. Godwin, aged 90 years, and Mr. C. A. Mallory, aged 50 years, of Jackson County, (Fla.) died recently.

Mrs. Nancy J. Maudlin, of Newton, (Ala.) died on the 8th inst.

Thurs. June 19, 1879
Samuel Shoenfeld, of Georgetown, Ga., died yesterday. He leaves a brother, Louis Shoenfeld. Interment in Eufaula in the Hebrew Cemetery.

Sat. June 21, 1879
Mrs. Gazie Raisler, daughter of Mr. Gaz. Williams of Barbour County, died recently near Athens, Ga. Burial in Eufaula on Wednesday last. Her first husband was the late A. A. Hill, of Barbour County.

Mrs. Acrail Byrd, of Dale County, (Ala.) died on the 15th.

The son of Mr. E. A. DeBoss, of Quitman County, (Ga.) was accidentally killed recently.

Master Tommie Kent, age 13 years, son of Mr. G. C. Kent, was drowned in the river at Columbus on Sunday.

Mr. David Newton, Sr., of Geneva County, (Ala.), aged 106 years, died at his home near Big Creek recently.

Tues. June 24, 1879
Mrs. Hattie Wells died Sunday last. She leaves a husband. Burial in Smithville, Ga.

Mr. Jno. Treanor, an old citizen of Milledgeville, (Ga.) and who had lived there forty years, died last Thursday.

Rev. Aminius Wright, minister of the M. E. Church, died in Columbus, (Ga.) last week.

Wed. June 25, 1879
Col. Jno. W. Davis, of Selma, (Ala.) died on the 18th inst.

Thurs. June 26, 1879
Mr. A. J. Bassett, of Bullock County, Ala., died near Mount Hilliard on the 15th inst.

The funeral of Mr. Jas. L. Daniel, age about 80, will take place from the home of his son-in-law, W. T. Simpson today. He leaves a large family of grown children.

The death of Mr. Thos. Richards, Esq., occurred near Henry County line on the 23rd inst. He was born in Pendleton District, S. C. on the 14th of Sept. 1798. He had lived in Barbour County for 45 years.

Sat. July 1, 1879
Capt. P. C. Conley, of Mobile, (Ala.) died on the 24th at Louisville, Ky.

William Ball died Tuesday last in Blakely, Georgia.

William M. Abney died in Eufaula recently. He was born in Edgefield District, S. C. on Nov. 21st, 1802. He joined the M. E. Church in Eufaula in 1845. Survivors are several children.

Wed. July 2, 1879
Maj. L. B. Sanders, of Lee County, (Ala.) died at his plantation near Auburn on Sunday.

Mr. Jno. Wier, Teller of the Mobile Saving Bank, died in Mobile recently. -Mobile (Ala.) Register.

Thurs. July 3, 1879
Mrs. Lucy Lanier, aged 63, died Tuesday last. The funeral will take place from the First Baptist Church.

Mr. D. G. Fitzpatrick died at his home near Thompson Station in Bullock County, (Ala.) on Sunday last.

Sat. July 5, 1879
Mr. T. J. McBain, age 74, an old citizen of Thomasville, (Ga.) died last week.

Wed. July 9, 1879
Dr. J. R. Simmons, of Americus, (Ga.) died on Thursday last.

Mr. S. M. Potts, former Representative of Jackson County in the General Assembly (Ga.) died recently at the home of his son.

Mrs. M. A. Oattis, nearly 80 years old, died in Greenville, (Ala.) on the 28th ult.

Mrs. Bryant Reeves, of Eufaula, died on Tuesday last.

Thurs. July 10, 1879
Eddie (Eddeline) age about 12 years, daughter of Moses Alexander, of near Eufaula, was thrown from a buggy yesterday and killed.

Dr. Jno. Fisher, citizen of Charleston, S. C. died recently.

Kennard H. Jones, Chief of Police in Philadelphia, Pa., died on the 5th inst.

Milton J. Saffold, well known in Alabama, died in a hospital in San Francisco, on Saturday last.

Rev. L. M. Smith, D. D., age about 53, President of the Southern College at Greensboro, (Ala.) died in Birmingham on the 4th inst. Burial at Greensboro.

Capt. Chas. A. Hamilton, of Macon, (Ga.) died suddenly on Monday last.

Sat. July 12, 1879
Mrs. Bamer Dunwoody, age 86, of McIntosh County, (Ga.) died recently.

Tues. July 15, 1879
R. B. Dickson, aged 65, living near Steep Creek in Lowndes County, (Ala.) died suddenly on the 15th inst.

P. H. Perry, aged 63, of Russell County, (Ala.) died at his home near Seale on the 7th inst.

Jno. B. Garrett, for many years a street overseer in Montgomery, Ala., died on the 10th inst.

Mrs. J. E. Thompson, of Chattahoochee County, (Ga.) died on Thursday last.

Mrs. Hubbard Van Horn, of Chattahoochee County, (Ga.) died on Thursday last.

Mr. Isaiah Johnson, who was born Aug. 1790, died in Leon County, (Fla.) on the 2nd inst., where he had been living since 1828.

Mrs. Sarah B. Dorsey, of Miss., who died recently, bequeathed two large plantations and a sea coast villa to ex-President Jeff. Davis.

E. W. Bostick, aged 49 years, died in Eufaula yesterday. Survivors are his wife and several children.

Sat. July 19, 1879
Mrs. Gentry, wife of Mr. Butler Gentry, of Clay County, (Ga.) died on Saturday last.

Mrs. Kate Butler, aged 104, died last Thursday. From Lumpkin (Ga.) Independent.

Miss Emma Walker, of Fort Gaines, (Ga.) died on Saturday last.

Mr. A. B. Luce, hotel man of Savannah, (Ga.) died in that city Saturday.

Tues. July 22, 1879
Mr. Fabyan Thomas, an old citizen of Dougherty County, (Ga.)

140

died last week.

Jno. Berrien Whitehead, of Baker County, (Ga.) died at his home near Newton on the 13th.

Wed. July 23, 1879
Mrs. Sarah Nance died in Selma, (Ala.) on the 12th.

Mrs. Mary A. May died at Forkland (Ala.) on the 14th.

Mrs. Alice Bates, wife of Mr. Walter Bates, died at her home in Batesville, Ala., on Monday last. Burial in Eufaula. She was the daughter of J. P. Margart, of this county. Survivors are one child and her husband. (Tues. Oct. 28th: Alice R. L. Margart was the daughter of Rev. Jno. P. and Mrs. A. C. Margart was born in Newberry County, S. C. on Apr. 2, 1857; removed to Barbour County, Ala., Oct. 1861; married Mr. Bates on Nov. 1, 1877; died of typhoid fever on July 15, 1879).

Mr. Hugh McAree died recently in Mobile, (Ala.) from injuries received in being thrown from a buggy.

Mr. Thos. Cunningham, foreman of the Mobile (Ala.) Register, died recently.

Mrs. Mary Cobb, age 82 years, died at Girard, (Ala.) recently.

Mr. Jeff Darby, editor of the Troy (Ala.) Messenger, and Mrs. Woodard Griffin, died recently in Troy. -Union Springs (Ala.) Herald, 14th.

Mr. Stuart W. Cayce, of Mobile, (Ala.) died on the 15th.

Mrs. Laura Bishop, wife of Mr. C. H. Bishop, of Spring Hill, (Barbour County) died on the 11th inst. She had been married seven months.

Sat. July 23, 1879
Mr. Council B. Wright, of Macon, (Ga.) died at Ashville, North Carolina, on the 22nd inst.

Mr. M. L. Binswanger, of Macon, (Ga.) died on Thursday last.

Tues. July 29, 1879
Mrs. Davis, wife of Macy Davis, died on Saturday last at her residence about seven miles from Clayton.

Mr. Jno. Stoddart, of Savannah, (Ga.) died on Friday last.

Mrs. Wm. Grubbs, age 73 years, living near Cotton Hill, (Barbour County) died on the 7th inst.

Wed. July 30, 1879
Mrs. Elizabeth Sims, age 110 years, died in Lee County, (Ala.) on Saturday last.

Thurs. July 31, 1879
Mrs. Jane Reid, aged 80 years, mother of Mr. Wyatt Reid, of White Oak Station, (Barbour County) died on Tuesday last.

Hon. Wm. Gray Little, Jr., Senator from Sumpter County, (Ala.) died on Thursday last at Fairfield, in Pickens County, Alabama.

Hon. J. M. Brennan, Representative to Georgia Legislature from Bryan County, (Ga.) died on Saturday last.

Maj. Henry Bryan, age 43 years, of Savannah, Ga., died recently.

Sat. Aug. 2, 1879

Dr. Alford J. Ravenscroft, age 54 years, railroad agent at Troy, (Ala.) died last Monday. He leaves a family.

Mr. Michael Levy, of Tallahassee, (Fla.) died on Tuesday last.

Tues. Aug. 5, 1879

Dr. W. W. Noland died on the 27th ult., in Clayton, Ala.

Mr. Phillip Palmer, age 87, died recently in Colbert County, (Ala.).

Thurs. Aug. 7, 1879

Mrs. Ellen W. Callaway, aged 63, wife of Rev. P. M. Callaway, of Newton, Dale County, (Ala.) died on the 27th ult.

Charlie Robinson, son of Prof. Allen Robinson, died near Wetumpka, (Ala.) last week.

Mr. Victoria Barie, age 90 years, died in Savannah, (Ga.) on the 1st inst.

Mr. Geo. W. Gafford, a painter by profession, living at Columbus, (Ga.) died Saturday last.

The death of Mrs. Geo. C. Chafin, wife of Dr. T. P. Chafin, is announced in the Columbus, Ga., paper of 5th.

Sat. Aug. 9, 1879

Mrs. Sturgeon, wife of Rev. J. C. Sturgeon, died in Orion, Pike County, (Ala.) on Wednesday last.

The Advocate announces the deaths in Greenville, Ala., of Mrs. Mary Dunkin on the 30th ult., and Mrs. Ellen Payne on the 5th inst.

Mrs. Lou Alexander, wife of Moses Alexander, died at her home near Eufaula recently. Burial in White Oak Cemetery.

J. C. Duff, deputy U. S. Marshall, was shot and killed by illicit distillers on Thursday last in the mountains of Poke County, Tenn.

Mr. F. J. Cowart, editor of the Troy (Ala.) Messenger lost by death his only child, Ethel, on Monday last.

Tues. Aug. 12, 1879

Hon. Johnathan Bliss, age 80, of Gainesville, Sumter County, (Ala.) died on 27th ult., at Cleveland, Ohio.

Thurs. Aug. 14, 1879

Jno. M. Saunderson, aged 70, died recently in Limestone County, Ala.

Mr. Jno. Nestor, an aged citizen of Virginia, living near Hillsville, died on the 12th inst.

Mr. S. T. Walker, merchant of Macon, (Ga.) died Monday last.

Sat. Aug. 16, 1879

Franklin L. Owens, Sr., one of Mobile's oldest citizens, died there last week. He was a native of Virginia, and has lived in Alabama for 46 years.

Mr. Asa Lynch, of Muscogee County, (Ga.) died on Monday last.

Judge W. L. Mozley, of Franklin, Heard County, (Ga.) died one day last week.

Sat. Aug. 23, 1879
    The death of Mr. Chris B. Streater, of Spring Hill, (Barbour County) occurred Thursday last.

Wed. Aug. 27, 1879
    Mrs. Wesley Bishop, age 40, died at her home in Barbour County, on the 4th of July, 1879.

Thurs. Aug. 28, 1879
    Mr. Wm. Snell, age 91, died in Dale County, Ala., on the 11th inst.

    Maj. Jas. H. Felder, of Union Springs, (Ala.) died on Sunday last.

Wed. Sept. 3, 1879
    Wm. Spivey, of Stewart County, (Ga.) died last Friday. He leaves a wife and five children.

    Gen. Jno. B. Hood died of yellow fever in New Orleans on Saturday. He left eleven children. His wife died a short time ago. His daughter, Lydia, age about 10, died in the afternoon following her father's death. (From Thurs. Sept. 25: The surviving children were Annabel and Ethel Genevieve, twins, age about 9; Jno. Bell, Jr., age about 8; Duncan Nirbert, age about 7; Marion Maud and Lillian Marie, twins, age about 6; Odile Musson and Ida Richardson, twins, age about 3; Anna Gertrude, age on Sept. 15th, seven weeks old. Col. Sam'l. Flower is Admr. of the Estate. The children at present are under the care of their maternal grandmother.)

    Dr. J. H. Watts, an old resident of Clay County, (Ala.) died on the 22nd ult.

Wed. Sept. 10, 1879
    Mrs. Wm. Beach died in Columbus, (Ga.) on the 2nd inst. She leaves a husband and one child.

    H. B. Beecher, of Columbus, (Ga.) died on Friday last.

    Mr. C. P. Stewart, aged 75, of Pike County, (Ala.) died at his home near Goshen Hill on the 31st ult. He had been a resident of the county for more than fifty years. He reared a large family, most of whom survive him. -Troy (Ala.) Messenger.

    Fannie Marian, aged 19 months and 16 days, the little daughter of Mr. and Mrs. F. P. Tennille, died on the 31st of Aug. last, at the home of her parents in Georgetown, Ga.

    Mrs. Virginia Clark, wife of Prof. Clark of Berryville, died recently from an accident at Eureke Springs, Carroll County, Ark. Survivors are her husband and child.

Thurs. Sept. 18, 1879
    Chas. Brady, an old policeman of Columbus, Ga., died on the 11th.

    D. T. Driggers, Jr., of Bibb County, (Ga.) died on the 9th inst.

    Mrs. Fannie Williams, of Columbus, (Ga.) died on Thursday last. She leaves a husband and eight children.

    Mr. Phil. D. Savre, of Montgomery, (Ala.) and Gilbert Long, of Montgomery County, died on Monday last.

Sat. Sept. 20, 1879
    Mr. Elisha Calhoun, age about 80 years, of Russell County,

died at his home near Seale, Ala., on the 15th.

Hon. J. L. Williams, Judge of Probate of Clay County, (Ala.) died on the 5th inst.

Col. T. B. Bethea, for many years a prominent citizen of Alabama, died in Montgomery on Saturday.

Mr. Robt. S. L. Shackleford and Judge Wm. A. Rawson, both of Stewart County, Ga., died last week.

Col. C. A. Cloud, of Chatham County, (Ga.) died on the 14th inst.

Thurs. Oct. 9, 1879
Mr. Bird G. Terry, of Montgomery County, (Ala.) died suddenly last Monday at his home near Pine Level.

Judge E. A. McMahon died near Tallahassee (Fla.) on the 26th ult.

Miss Lock Ina Weems, who was adopted as the daughter of the 15th Alabama Regiment at the Blue Springs Reunion, died on the 6th inst. -Union Springs Herald.

Mr. Daniel T. Sheehan died at the residence of his son-in-law, S. W. Giddon. Funeral will take place from the Catholic Church. (Oct. 14th, 1879: He was born in Ireland, County of Cork, province of Muster, on the 1st of Oct. 1812, died the 3rd of Oct. 1879 in Eufaula, Ala. At the age of 14, after having spent seven years at school, he was apprenticed to a linen merchant in the city of Cork, to learn the science of book-keeping and served the full term of his apprenticeship. He left Ireland in 1836, sailed from New York, after a stay in the north - landed in Savannah and proceeded to Montgomery. In 1842 he married Mrs. Martha Naomi Creyon, daughter of Col. Jno. Ashurst, of Autauga County, Ala., and reared a family of six children.)

Sat. Oct. 11, 1879
Samuel P. Bell, Esq., age 62, of Savannah, died on the 4th inst.

Rev. Jas. Wilson, an aged Presiding Elder in the M. E. Conference for 50 years, died last Wednesday in Athens, Ga.

Tues. Oct. 14, 1879
Mr. Fred. Glover, age 43, of Americus, (Ga.) died on the 7th inst.

Thurs. Oct. 16, 1879
Mr. W. S. Cole, age 60 years, of Bullock County, Ala., died on Sunday last.

Sat. Oct. 18, 1879
Chas. H. Sporman, aged 13, son of Geo. H. Sporman, died on Thursday last in Eufaula.

David Gawley Lewis, nineteen months old son of Mr. and Mrs. Andrew Lewis, died on Thursday last in Eufaula.

Sat. Oct. 25, 1879
Hon. H. A. Woolf, of Linden, (Ala.) died on the 23rd.

Wed. Oct. 29, 1879
Mr. Hiram Edmunds, age 66 years, an old resident of Montgomery, Ala., died on Thursday last.

Sat. Nov. 1, 1879
    Dr. Chas. B. Berry, of Mobile, (Ala.) died on Saturday last.

Tues. Nov. 4, 1879
    Mrs. Samuel W. Oliver, of Dallas County, Ala. died recently.

    Jno. R. Wilder, merchant of Savannah, died at his home in
Marietta, Ga., on Saturday last.

    Mrs. Fannie Rowe, wife of Dr. A. T. Rowe, of Auburn, (Ala.)
died last week.

Wed. Nov. 5, 1879
    Mr. Ed. Worsham, age 24, well know among railroad men at
Montgomery, died in Atlanta recently.

Thurs. Nov. 6, 1879
    Mrs. Dr. Woodruff, of Columbus, (Ga.) died on Saturday last
in Forsyth, (Ga.).

Tues. Nov. 11, 1879
    Maj. W. T. Stubberfield died in Montgomery on Friday last.
He was an old citizen and was connected with the early history
of this state, having served in the Indian Wars and the War with
Mexico.

    Mr. Henry Kindred, age 60 years, a resident of Russell Coun-
ty, Ala., died on Friday last. Survivors are his wife and six
children.

    Mr. Wm. Massey, of Chattahoochee, (Ga.) died on Thursday.

    Miss Nannie Chapman, of Schley County, (Ga.) age 16, died
recently.

Thurs. Nov. 13, 1879
    The death of Geo. P. Crymes occurred recently at the home
of his brother, Dr. Albert C. Crymes, near Batesville, Ala.

    Mrs. Lou Pullen died in Abbeville, (Ala.) on the 1st of Nov.

Sat. Nov. 14, 1879
    Mrs. C. Chaffin, wife of Mr. T. W. Chaffin, and the daughter
of Dr. M. N. Barron, of Troy, (Ala.) died in that city on Wednesday last.

    Rev. Elisha Williams, age nearly four score, died at his
home near Brundidge, (Ala.) on the 1st inst. -Troy (Ala.)
Messenger.

    Mr. Jas. Knight, an old citizen of Pike County, (Ala.) died
last Wednesday.

Tues. Nov. 18, 1879
    Thos. H. Watts died at his home in Eufaula yesterday.
Burial in Georgetown, Ga. Survivors are his wife and several
children.

Thurs. Nov. 20, 1879
    Mr. Phillip Holt, of Elmore County, (Ala.) died on typhoid
on the 10th inst.

    Rev. Joel Sims died in Barbour County on the 18th inst.
He had been in the employ of the Eufaula Baptist Association as
an Evangelist for the last fifteen or twenty years.

Tues. Nov. 25, 1879

Mrs. Ella V., aged 24, wife of J. M. Morris of Eufaula, died on Monday last. Mrs. E. R. Hathaway, of Montezuma, Ga., and Mrs. W. R. Greene, of Opelika, are her sisters.

Mr. Irwin Aycock, of Randolph County, Ga., died last week.

Mr. Moultrie Moses died at his home in Savannah, Ga., last Wednesday.

Wed. Nov. 26, 1879
Seaborn Solly, age 82, of Marengo County, (Ala.) died on the 2nd inst.

Thurs. Nov. 27, 1879
Mrs. Jno. W. Hobbie was buried in Montgomery, Ala., last week.

Col. Jno. M. F. Ewvin, of Jackson County, Fla., died at his home in Greenwood last week.

Tues. Dec. 2, 1879
F. M. Dunnaway, of Stewart County, Ga., was killed by an accident in his sugar mill last Friday. He leaves a wife and several children.

Mr. Jno. T. Curry died at his home at Orion in Pike County, (Ala.) on the 22nd.

Mr. Jefferson Darby died at his home in Troy, (Ala.) last Monday.

Tues. Dec. 3, 1879
Mr. Geo. W. Brown, of Columbus, (Ga.) died last Tuesday.

Hon. Albert Martin, who served several terms in the General Assembly from Jefferson (County), died last Monday in Birmingham, (Ala.).

Judge Edward S. Dargan, of Mobile, (Ala.) died last Monday.

Rev. Isaac Childress, Methodist minister for thirty years in Gadsden, (Ala.) died on the 9th inst.

Tues. Dec. 9, 1879
Mr. Ezekiel Alexander died at his home near Eufaula on the 6th inst. He was born in Hancock County, Ga., on Mar. 3rd, 1803. He moved with his father when quite young to Jones County, Ga., and when eighteen years old he removed to Ft. Gaines on the Chattahoochee River. A year or two later, he with his father's family, his mother having died, crossed the river into Alabama, whence after a stay of a few years, moved back to Jones County and married his first wife, Miss Edna Dawson, who was the mother of all of his children, notwithstanding he was afterwards married twice. He changed his residence to Dale County, Ala., afterwards to Pike County, Ala., and in 1834 to the home in Barbour County in which he died.

Mr. D. G. Duncan, aged 49, who formerly held a position with the New Orleans Bee, and the Picayune, died in the Crescent City on the 5th inst.

The remains of Oscar L. Ricks were brought to the home of his father, Col. R. G. Ricks, in Clay County, Ga., on the 5th inst. He had been a resident of Jackson County, Florida.

Tues. Dec. 16, 1879
Robert, youngest son of Col. J. L. Pugh, was accidentally shot and killed in Eufaula yesterday.

Sat. Dec. 20, 1879
   Mrs. Doughtie, nee Miss Sallie Farley, died on Sunday in
Montgomery, Ala.

   Mr. E. B. Browne, age 53, a compositor on the Advertiser
in Montgomery, (Ala.) died recently.

   The death of Rev. W. P. Pledger occurred at Marham House,
in Atlanta, on Saturday last. He was a Methodist minister sent
to serve at Decatur, (Ga.). Burial in Atlanta.

   Wm. W. Webb, formerly a resident of Eufaula, was killed at
Deertone, Mo., by the accidental bursting of a gun. He was a
nephew of Capt. Jno. N. Webb, of Eufaula.

1880

Thurs. Jan. 1, 1880
   J. H. Hicks, formerly of Decatur, (Ala.) died recently in
Russell, Kansas.

   Capt. W. R. Knox, of Birmingham, (Ala.) died recently.

   Judge Peter S. Strozier, of Albany, (Ga.) died recently.

Sat. Jan. 3, 1880
   Hon. Geo. Smith Houston died at his home in Athens, Ala.,
last Wednesday. He was born in Williamson County, Tenn., in
1809. When he was twelve years old he came with his parents to
Lauderdale County, Ala., and in 1834 he moved to Limestone County,
where he lived until his death.

   Mr. Thos. Malcomson, of Savannah, (Ga.) died recently.

   Mr. Jno. K. Roddenberry, of Cario, (Ga.) died on the 23rd
ult.

   Mr. Jas. Campbell, age 24, son of Col. W. L. Campbell,
living near Gainesville, (Fla.) died last Thursday. -Gainesville
(Fla.) Bee.

Tues. Jan. 6, 1880
   Miss Annie M. Fannin, age about 28, died at the home of her
aunt, Mrs. Eli S. Shorter, in Eufaula, on the 3d inst.

Sat. Jan. 10, 1880
   Mr. B. P. Hall, of Cherokee County, (Ala.) died two days
ago.

Sat. Jan. 17, 1880
   Mr. F. N. Gilbert, of New York, died at the Central Hotel
in Eufaula last Thursday. He was enroute to Quincy, Florida.
Burial in Eufaula. He leaves a wife.

Sat. Jan. 24, 1880
   Mrs. Mary Ann Sylvester died at the home of her son-in-law
Mr. Jonathan Thornton, near Eufaula on the 22nd inst. She was
Miss Rembert, born at Sumter, S. C. on Dec. 29, 1798, married
Demarcus Sylvester, who died in 1870, at her native home of Feb.
1818. Burial in the Presbyterian Cemetery from the Baptist
Church in Eufaula.

   Mr. W. P. Shultz, of Selma, (Ala.) died on Wednesday.

Tues. Jan. 27, 1880
   Mr. W. F. Hurst, of Victoria, Coffee County, (Ala.) died
recently.

Thurs. Jan. 29, 1880
    Mr. Owen McGarrigle, age about 40, died at Talbotton, Ga.,
recently. Survivors are his wife and two children.

Tues. Feb. 10, 1880
    Mr. Jas. Fitzgerald, of Stewart County, Ga., father of Mr.
J. E. Fitzgerald, formerly of Eufaula, died last Saturday.

    The funeral of Mr. T. H. Watts, formerly of Eufaula, will
be preached in Georgetown, Ga., on the 15th inst.

    Dr. Jas. T. Robinson, age about 45, died at his home in
Quitman County, Ga., on the 7th inst. He was born in Warren
County, Ga., in 1835. His first dental office was established
in 1858 in Eufaula.

Thurs. Feb. 19, 1880
    Mr. Jno. McEnery, age about 29, of Nashville, Tenn., died
at the boarding house of Mr. M. O'Byrne in Eufaula, last Thursday. Burial in Nashville.

Sat. Feb. 23, 1880
    Mrs. W. H. King, daughter of B. B. Fields, Esq., of Barbour
County, died at her home in Clayton last Tuesday. She leaves a
husband and children.

    Dr. S. P. Barnett died in Quitman County, Ga., on the 10th
of Feb. 1880. He was a native of Ashville, N. C., he moved to
Habersham County, Ga., soon after he was grown. After two years
he moved to Cassville, Cass County, Ga., thence to Randolph
County. He leaves a wife and four boys and one girl.

Thurs. Feb. 26, 1880
    Augusta, Ga., Feb. 23. - H. L. Wright, age 29, son of the
editors of the Chronicle and Constitution, died yesterday in
Jefferson County, (Ga.). He was the son of the late Gen. A. R.
Wright.

Tues. Mar. 6, 1880
    The Rev. Samuel Anthony, of Americus, Ga., died on the 3rd
inst. He was 73 years old.

Sat. Mar. 27, 1880
    The death of Jno. H. Mosely, of Charlotte County, Virginia,
occurred Monday night.

    Mr. Robt. McGough, age about 22, died at the home of his
father at Glennville, (Ala.) on last Sunday.

Thurs. Apr. 1, 1880
    Mrs. Sarah Tye, living near Georgetown, Ga., died on Sunday
last.

Thurs. Apr. 10, 1880
    Mr. Jno. E. Andrews died a few days ago in Dale County,
(Ala.).

    Elder Charles Steward, one of the oldest Primitive Baptist
ministers in Dale County, (Ala.) died at his home near Crittenden's Mill last Thursday.

    Mr. Bethune McDonald died in Coffee County, (Ala.) recently.
He lived in Bullock County, (Ala.).

    Mr. S. Hartz, more than 60 years of age, died at the home
*NOTE: Quitman County, Ga. made from Randolph & Stewart, 1858.

148

of Mrs. Heibron in Eufaula. Burial in the Jewish Cemetery in
Eufaula.

Sat. Apr. 24, 1880
        Mrs. M. Fannie Smith, age 27, daughter of Mrs. Mary Wyly,
of Louisiana, and consort of Mr. R. E. Smith, died at her home
near Toccoa City, Ga., on the 10th inst. Deceased was a native
of Barbour County. She leaves a husband and three children.

Tues. May 4, 1880
        Mr. Madison Stubblefield, son of Mr. M. Stubblefield,
Eufaula, died on the 28th ult., in Franklin County, Tenn.

        Mr. Larkin Newman, citizen of Coosa County, Ala., died on
the 26th ult. -Montgomery Advertiser.

Tues. May 11, 1880
        Mrs. Rebecca Baer, age about 31, wife of Mr. Samuel Baer,
died at her home in Eufaula last Wednesday. Burial in the
Jewish Cemetery.

Tues. May 18, 1880
        Albion, N.Y., May 14. - Hon. Samford E. Church, Chief
Justice of the New York Court of Appeals, died at his home this
afternoon.
        Mrs. Augusta Slaughter, mother of Mr. A. Slaughter of
Eufaula, died at her home in Braunsbach, Kingdom of Wuetemberg,
Germany, on the 14th of last April.

Sat. May 22, 1880
        Mrs. Caroline Morris died at the home of her daughter, Mrs.
R. A. Wellborn in Eufaula on the 20th inst. She was born in
New York City in July 1792, was a member of the Presbyterian
Church for many years.

Tues. June 1, 1880
        Mr. E. J. H. Dunn, age about 45, died at the home of Mr.
M. O'Byrne in Eufaula last Saturday. He formerly taught school
near Bainbridge, Ga.

        Mr. Ira Hobby, an old citizen of Troy, (Ala.) died on the
22nd.

Thurs. June 3, 1880
        Dr. J. W. Pitts, of Columbus, Ga., died Monday. Burial at
Perote, Ala.

        Col. Wm. Thos. Avery, who was lately drowned in Arkansas by
the upsetting of a boat, and who resided near Memphis, was well
known to many Alabamians as a gallant Confederate officer. He
was Lt. Col. of a regiment commanded by Gen. Alpheus Baker.

Thurs. June 10, 1880
        Mrs. M. A. Harrison, age about 34, wife of Mr. W. H. Harri-
son, died in Eufaula on the 7th inst. Survivors are her husband
and one child. Burial in Cuthbert, Ga.

Thurs. June 17, 1880
        Mr. Alonzo M. Thweatt, age about 35, died at the home of
his brother, Mr. J. M. Thweatt, on the 15th inst.

Thurs. June 24, 1880
        Washington, June 19. - Gen. Jno. A. Sutter, the first
discoverer of gold in California, died here today.

Sat. June 26, 1880

Mrs. Fannie Taylor, age about 20, wife of Mr. A. D. Taylor, died at the home of her father in Eufaula on the 24th inst. She leaves a husband and an infant.

Mr. Ed. J. Stephens, age about 25, died last Thursday in Eufaula.

Tues. June 29, 1880

Miss Mary M. Jones, age 35, died in Eufaula on the 28th inst.

Sat. July 3, 1880

Allen V. Robinson died on the 26th inst., at Leachapoke, Elmore County, (Ala.). He was born at Barnwell Court House, S. C., in 1810, came to Alabama early in life, and was one of the pioneers of Eastern Ala. In 1838 he began his profession as a teacher of dancing, which he followed until his death.

Tues. July 13, 1880

Mr. Jno. T. Estes, age about 25, brother of G. H. Estes of Eufaula, died at his home in Marianna, Fla. last Friday. He leaves a wife.

Thurs. July 15, 1880

Mrs. Emma Taylor, age about 25, died in Eufaula yesterday.

Thurs. Aug. 19, 1880

Augusta, (Ga.) Aug. 17. - Ex-Gov. Herschel V. Johnson, age 68, died at his home in Jefferson County, Georgia last night.

Sat. Aug. 21, 1880

Hon. Jas. A. Selden died at his home in Virginia on the 19th inst.

Sat. Aug. 31, 1880

Mr. C. E. Dozier, who formerly resided in Eufaula for a short time, died in Talbotton, Ga. last Wednesday.

Sat. Sept. 4, 1880

Hon. Walter F. Shropshire, brother of Maj. R. D. Shropshire of Eufaula, and Superintendent of Public Instruction in Tenn., died on the 17th of August.

Thurs. Sept. 9, 1880

Mrs. Martha E. Vaughan, age about 60, the mother of Mr. N. H. Vaughan, died in Eufaula yesterday.

Fri. Sept. 17, 1880

Capt. W. J. Henry died at his home in Seale (Russell County, Ala.) on the 7th inst.

Sun. Sept. 26, 1880

Mr. Robt. L. Bass, an old citizen of Columbus, Ga., died in that city on the 16th inst.

Fri. Oct. 1, 1880

John Reid, Jr., citizen of Mobile, (Ala.) died on Thursday last.

Fri. Oct. 15, 1880

D. R. Mills, age 76, of Buncombe District, Washington County, Ga., died Saturday. His niece and a daughter died the same day, all with typhoid fever.

Mr. W. C. Curington, age about 63, living near Jernigan, (Russell County, Ala.) died Wednesday. He leaves a wife and seven children.

Wed. Nov. 3, 1880*
Mr. Stephen Thomas, an old citizen of Quitman County, (Ga.) died at his home near Morris Station on the 20th of Oct. He leaves a wife and four children.

*(Name of paper changed to Eufalula Times and News, W. D. Jelks, Proprietor.)

Geo. Henry Sporman, age 36, died in Eufaula on the 31st ult. He leaves a wife and three children.

Mrs. Salina Watson, age about 80, widow of Mr. Ned Watson, died at the home of M. Jno. Watson, near Eufaula on last Monday.

Fri. Nov. 12, 1880
Mr. Geo. Robt. Holloway, age between 65 and 70, died at his home in Clay County, Ga., on the 9th inst.

Wed. Nov. 24, 1880
Mrs. Esther Shoenfeldt, widow of S. Shoenfeldt, formerly of Eufaula, died at Grand Rapids, Miss., on the 12th inst. Her husband died in Georgetown, Ga., a few years since. Survivors are a son and a daughter.

Thurs. Nov. 18, 1880
Manning Ray, age 70 years, died at the home of his brother in Coosa County. He was born in Tenn. in 1810, and his parents moved to Alabama in 1814. He married a daughter of Jas. Benson, of St. Clair County, and they settled in Tallaedga County. His wife and eight children survives. Burial in Barbour County at Mt. Pleasant Church. *(From Eufaula Times and News, Weekly.)

Thurs. Dec. 2, 1880
Mr. A. J. Surles died at his home in Quitman County, Georgia last Monday.

Thurs. Dec. 9, 1880
Mr. Alexander Stewart, age about 84, died at his home near White Oak in Barbour County recently.

Thurs. Dec. 23, 1880
Alice Jane Calhoun died last Sunday at Wynton, near Columbus, Ga. She was a sister of Jno. D. Miller of Eufaula.

THE CLAYTON COURIER

1880

Published at Clayton, Ala., by Edgar R. Quillin.

Sat. Aug. 14, 1880
Mr. C. (Creed) A. Ingram of Clayton died suddenly last Saturday. Burial with Masonic honors.

Mrs. Martha Beasley, wife of Mr. Jno. Beasley, died on the 11th inst. in Barbour County. She was born in Washington County, Ga., Mar. 4, 1802. When very young she moved with her parents to Baldwin County, Ga., where she married on Mar. 7, 1819, and moved to Barbour County on Jan. 1821.

Sat. Aug. 21, 1880

Gen. Wm. Orlando Butler died yesterday at Carrolton, Ky. He was a native Kentuckian, born in 1793, his father being Gen. Percival Butler. He practiced law for twenty-five years in Kentucky, was a member of Congress (1839-1843). Served in the War of 1812, commanded American Army in Mexico.

Mr. D. D. Guerry, formerly of Clayton, died in Eufaula on Saturday last.

Mrs. West Norton and her little child, of near Mt. Andrew, (Barbour County) died from burns on Tuesday.

Sat. Sept. 4, 1880

Mr. Wm. E. Davis, better known as Euchee Bill Davis, age 93, died in Pike County, (Ala.) on the 14th ult. He emigrated from North Carolina to Alabama in 1833 and soon afterwards settled in Pike, where he has since resided. He served in the War of 1812. He leaves a large number of children. Troy (Ala.) Enquirer.

Sat. Sept. 11, 1880

The deaths of the following known to be lost in the disaster of the steamer City of Vera Cruz near St. Augustine, Fla., on Sunday, Gen. Alfred T. A. Torbert; Edward Van Sice, Capt.; Frank M. Haines, first mate; J. E. Whitney, second mate; and passengers: Mrs. R. Ames, E. Burns, Miss A. Clark, Miss Sadie Fay, Mrs. A. Garcia and child.

Sat. Sept. 18, 1880

Rev. J. A. Wallace, Presbyterian minister, died at Aberfoil in Bullock County, (Ala.) on Wednesday last.

Mrs. Elizabeth Carter, aged 58, died at her home in Clayton last Monday. She was born in Jasper County, Ga., in 1822. She was a member of the M. E. Church for 35 years. She leaves a husband.

Sat. Oct. 9, 1880

Mrs. J. P. Price, of Barbour County, died on the 31st of Sept. She leaves a husband.

Sat. Oct. 30, 1880

Mrs. Betsy Blair, age 68, wife of Mr. Wm. Blair, died at her home near White Oak (Barbour County) on Monday.

Sat. Nov. 6, 1880

Bishop Daniel S. Doggett died at his home in Richmond, Va., on Wednesday. He was born in Lancaster County, Va., in 1810. -Atlanta (Ga.) Constitution.

Sat. Nov. 13, 1880

Mr. Mathew Laseter, age nearly 94, died at the home of his daughter-in-law near Clayton on Thursday.

Sat. Nov. 20, 1880

Mr. R. A. Osmer, Supreme Treasurer of the Knights of Honor, died in Atlanta on Tuesday last. Burial at Jamestown, N. Y., his home.

Thurs. Nov. 20, 1880

Rev. Herbert Tiller, aged 79, minister of the M. E. Church, died at his home near Clayton on Sunday of last week.

Sat. Nov. 27, 1880
    Mr. Pharoh Carroll, living at Elamville (Barbour County) died on Monday last. He leaves a wife and several children.

    Gov. Jas. D. Williams, age 72, of Indiana, died at Indiapapolis on Saturday. He was taken ill on 2nd inst.

Sat. Dec. 11, 1880
    The death of Wm. Mattox, an old citizen of Abbeville, S. C. occurred Thursday. He leaves a wife.

Sat. Dec. 18, 1880
    Mr. Thos. Stringer, who moved to Texas from this section a few months since, died last week in that state.

THE EUFAULA WEEKLY BULLETIN

1881

J. D. Hoyl, Proprietor.

Sat. Mar. 19, 1881
    Capt. R. W. Goldthwaite died Friday in Dallas, Tex. Burial in Montgomery.

    Samuel Gales died in Memphis, Tenn., Saturday last. He had been a citizen of that city 38 years.

    Col. G. Hodges, age 79, died in Louisville, Ky., on the 16th.

    Dr. Alexander L. Hamilton, late President of Andrew Female College in Cuthbert, (Ga.) died in that city recently.

Sat. Mar. 26, 1881
    Dr. A. C. Simmons, age about 40, of Drayton, Dooly County, Ga., died Friday. He was a brother of Mr. J. M. Simmons of Americus and of Judge T. J. Simmons, of Macon, Ga. Survivors are his wife and six or seven children. -Americus (Ga.) Republican.

    Mr. Nat. Powell, son of Col. R. H. Powell, of Union Springs, (Ala.) died at his home in Esperance, Fla., on Monday last.

    Mr. J. T. Crow, age 60, the managing editor of the Baltimore Sun, died Wednesday last.

    A. Kenne Richards, turfman, died at his home in Scott County, Ky., on the 19th.

    Mr. J. H. Young, of Tallapossa County, (Ala.) died on the 19th inst.

Sat. Apr. 9, 1881
    Mr. Jewett G. DeVotie, age 40, died Sunday in Columbus, Ga. He had been connected with the Georgia Press since 1860. He was the son of the Baptist divine, Rev. J. H. DeVotie, D. D.

    Mrs. U. L. Weston, wife of one of the editors of the Dawson (Ga.) Journal, died recently.

    Mr. Jonathan Thomas, age about 70, died near Eufaula on Sunday. Burial at New Hope Church.

    The funeral of Capt. W. B. Blackmon took place from the First Baptist Church Sunday. Burial in the new Masonic grave yard.

    Mr. Lewis Scranton, business man of Mobile, died on Saturday last.

Sat. Apr. 16, 1881

Mrs. Catherine Alexander, age 60, consort of the late Ezekiel Alexander, who died a little over a year ago, died Saturday last at her home on the Abbeville road.

Mr. B. Frank Cargile, age 34, died at his home in Eufaula Sunday last. He leaves a wife and a step son and daughter.

Mr. Samuel G. Reid died at his home near Montgomery on Friday last.

Rev. Robt. Irvine, for many years pastor of the First Presbyterian Church of Augusta, Ga., died in that city on Friday last.

Sat. Apr. 23, 1881

The death of W. J. Stanley, of Whiteville, Columbus County, N. C., occurred recently. Survivors are his wife and six children.

Sat. Apr. 30, 1881

Hon. M. P. O'Conner, Congressman from the Charleston, S. C. District, died Tuesday last.

Col. Malachi W. Davis, age 72, and unmarried, a citizen of near Glennville, died Friday. Burial at Glennville, Ala.

Mr. David Collins, age about 78, father of Mrs. Jno. M. Bowden, of Eufaula, died Saturday at his home in Jackson County, Florida.

Mr. Elisha M. King, age about 53, died at his home near Louisville on the 26th inst. He leaves no family of his own, his wife died some time since.

Sat. May 7, 1881

The death of Patrick Reagan occurred at Savannah, Ga., last Sunday. He leaves a wife and several children. -Morning News (Savannah, Monday last.).

Col. J. J. Jolly died at his home in Gainesville, Ala., on last Thursday.

Dr. Chas. McGill, age 75, physician of Richmond, Va., died last Thursday.

Sat. May 14, 1881

Miss Lela Martin, age 12 years, youngest daughter of Capt. and Mrs. Jno. O. Martin, died at her parent's home in Eufaula on Thursday.

Sat. May 21, 1881

Mrs. Reeves, age 76, mother of Rev. W. N. Reeves and J. H. Reeves, died in Eufaula on Monday. She was a member of the Baptist Church.

Sat. May 28, 1881

Dr. J. Glasgow, citizen of Greenville, Ala., died recently.

Col. Jno. L. Mustain, age 76, died Monday at Warm Springs, Merriwether County, Ga.

Mr. Pleasant T. Tullis, age about 75, the father of Mr. J. W. and E. B. Tullis, of Eufaula, died last Saturday at his home in Troy, Ala.

Mr. Rufus L. Fannin, age 34, of Montgomery, died on Thursday last.

154

Sat. June 4, 1881
The death of Maj. W. J. Bethea, of Early County, Ga.,
occurred on Wednesday. Survivors are his wife and four children.
-Ft. Gaines (Ga.) Tribune.

Mr. Ed. C. McGruder, age about 46, died at his home in Clay
County, Ga., yesterday.

Mrs. Julius C. B. Mitchell died Thursday at her home in
Mount Reigs, (Ala.). -Montgomery (Ala.) Advertiser.

Jno. Duncan McCormick, age 41, died at his home in Eufaula
Sunday. He was born in Louisville, Barbour County, on 22nd Dec.
1840, and in 1866 he moved to Eufaula where he has resided since
that time. He leaves a wife and four children.

Dr. McD. Grant, citizen of Russell County, died at his home
near Seale, (Ala.) on last Friday.

Mr. Lewis Deal, age 80, of Dale County, (Ala.) died on the
23rd inst.

Sat. June 11, 1881
The death of Rev. W. P. R. Newberry occurred in Elks Valley,
Tenn., on the 6th inst.

Mrs. Frances Bullard, nee Hicks, died at her home in Eufaula
yesterday. She had been a member of the First Baptist Church in
Eufaula since 1837.

Dr. Wm. Bethune, age about 40, of Abbeville, Ala., died at
his home Saturday. Survivors are his wife and four children.

Sat. June 18, 1881
Mr. Jesse Thomas, age about 28, merchant of Clayton, died
last Thursday.

Sat. June 25, 1881
Jas. R. Wooten, citizen of Cuthbert, Ga., died last Thursday.

The death of Tyree Garrett, of Pulaski County, Ga., occurred
on the 20th.

Mrs. Mattie L. Whitaker, age about 20, wife of Mr. Elam
Whitaker, died at the home of her mother, Mrs. McRee, in Quitman
County, Ga., on Tuesday last.

Mrs. Mary Hatfield died at the home of her son-in-law, J. A.
Watson, in Barbour County, on the 15th inst.

Sat. July 2, 1881
Mrs. Jane Peters, of Columbus, Ga., died on Monday last.

Chief Justice Hiram Warner, of Ga., died in Atlanta on
Thursday last.

Sat. July 9, 1881
Mrs. Saran English, age about 70, died Wednesday in Eufaula,
at the home of her daughter, Mrs. Jas. Ross.

Judge W. P. Jordan died at his home in Georgetown, Ga., last
Thursday.

Sat. July 10, 1881
Mrs. Margaret Dowd, living in Galveston, Tex., died recently.
She was the only sister of Senator Jones of Florida.

Mr. W. A. Gaston, age nearly 40, of Lampsaes, Western
Texas, died on the 27th of Jan. He was a brother of Mr. A. L.

Gaston, of Eufaula.

Mr. Britton Searcy, age 65, died at his home at Skipperville Dale County, (Ala.) on Thursday. He was the father of Mr. Jesse Searcy, of Eufaula.

Mr. Wm. Foy, age 30, died at his home in Clayton on last Saturday. He leaves a wife and several children.

Rt. Rev. J. B. Kerfoot, Episcopal Bishop of Pittsburg, Pa., died on Sunday last.

Sat. July 23, 1881
Mr. Otis J. Gresham, a young merchant of Montgomery, died on Tuesday.

The death of Thos. L. Boyton occurred in Pickens County, S. C. on the 20th inst.

Mr. Jno. A. Appleton, age 65, eldest of the brothers composing the publishing house of D. Appleton & Co., N. Y., died recently.

Dr. J. H. Thomas, age 50, died at his home at Crawford, Russell County, Ala., on Monday.

Mr. Isham Carroll, age about 70, died at his home in Barbour County, on Friday.

Col. R. L. Mott, of Columbus, (Ga.) died in Atlanta recently.

Mr. Richard Frazer, formerly of Montgomery, but recently a resident of Jemison, Ala., was killed by a train last Saturday in the presence of his wife and daughter.

Sat. July 30, 1881
Mr. Leonard Page, age 69, planter of Sumter County, Ga., died on Thursday last.

The death of Mr. A. B. King, city Marshal, occurred at Uniontown, (Ala.) last night. -Selma (Ala.) Mail, 23rd.

Rev. Morgan C. Turrentine, age about 80, of the Ala. Conference, died on the 15th inst., in N.C. where he had gone to visit relatives. He was a pioneer minister to this section of the country. He preached to the Indians in 1824 near Columbus, (Ga.).

Sat. Aug. 6, 1881
Rev. W. G. Campbell, an aged and widely known Presbyterian minister, died at Harrisonburg, Va., on last Wednesday.

Mrs. A. C. Gordon, of Abbeville, wife of Gen. Gordon, died at her home last Monday.

Mr. Robt. Parker, age 84, and a resident of Montgomery since 1828, died Friday last.

Mr. Geo. Keipp, Jr., of Selma, died Friday.

Sat. Aug. 13, 1881
Hon. Jno. M. Townsend, a citizen of Limestone County, (Ala.) died at Athens, on the 8th inst.

Mr. Jas. W. Jordan, age about 50, living in Henry County, (Ala.) died on Sunday last.

Dr. W. A. Andrews, age about 65, died at his home near Spring Hill (Barbour County) on Monday last. Burial at Spring Hill.

Sat. Aug. 20, 1881
    Prof. Thos. C. Worrill, age 50, of Newton, Dale County,
(Ala.) died Friday. He leaves a wife and two children. Burial
in Clayton.

    Col. D. H. Burts, lawyer of Columbus, Ga., died in that
city last Thursday.

Sat. Aug. 27, 1881
    Dr. Daniel Sneed, age 60 or 65, living at White Pond in
Barbour County, died on Friday last.

    Mr. A. F. Turner, age 70, who lived for the last thirty
years near Enon Church in Henry County, died on the 19th inst.

    Mr. Jas. Smith, age about 28, of Stewart County, Ga., died
at his home on the Eufaula and Lumpkin road on last Monday. He
leaves a wife and one child. Burial at Wesley Chapel, Stewart
County.

Sat. Sept. 10, 1881
    Jas. Harvey Joiner died at Talladega, (Ala.) on Thursday
last.

    Mr. Alfred McGee died at his home near Eufaula on Wednesday.
Burial at the Primitive Baptist Church near his residence. He
came to Barbour County in 1843.

    Mr. Jno. Hendrix, an aged citizen of Barbour, died last
Saturday at the home of his son, Mr. W. B. Hendrix, near Eufaula.
He was the father of Mr. B. N. Hendrix.

Sat. Sept. 17, 1881
    The funeral of Capt. Henry Otis took place in Georgetown,
(Ga.) last Tuesday.

Sat. Oct. 1, 1881
    Mr. Jno. Jones, age about 80 years, died at his home near
Troy on last Monday. He had been a citizen of Pike County,
(Ala.) for many years.

    The death of Jas. D. Turner occurred in the Waverly Hotel
at Charleston, (S.C.) on Tuesday.

    The death of Capt. Henry McCormick, of Columbus, (Ga.)
commander of the steamer Caddo Belle, occurred Monday at Wolfolk's
bend in the Chattahoochee River. He leaves a wife and three
children in Columbus.

    Mr. Huson Odom, aged about 45, merchant of Franklin, Henry
County, (Ala.) died on the 27th ult. He had no family of his
own.

Sat. Oct. 8, 1881
    Dr. J. R. Janes, citizen of Dawson, Ga., died on Sunday
last. Oct. 15, 1881, Mrs. Janes, wife of Dr. J. R. Janes, died
suddenly on Tuesday.

    Maj. W. H. C. Price, editor of the American Grocer, died at
his home in New York last Saturday. He was born in Alabama in
1832, was a major in the Confederate Army.

    Mr. Thos. R. Grace, age about 55, died Friday in Rome, Ga.
Burial in Ozark, Ala.

    Mr. Wiley J. Williams, age about 21, son of Wm. J. Williams,
of Henry County, Ala., died Oct. 1st in Macon, Ga. Burial in
Henry County.

Sat. Oct. 15, 1881

Hon. Mark H. Cruikshank, of Talladega, Ala., was thrown from a horse Monday which caused his death. He was elder in the Presbyterian Church.

Ex-Justice Jas. S. Clark, of Decatur, Ala., died on the 8th inst.

Sat. Nov. 12, 1881

Mr. Thos. Broach, age 75, of Stewart County, (Ga.) died recently.

Mr. Jno. D. Grant, aged about 50, planter in the neighborhood of Spring Hill, (Barbour County) died a few days since.

Sat. Nov. 19, 1881

Mrs. H. H. Epping, of Columbus, Ga., died at her home on Monday last.

Jas. L. Ridgely, age about 75, died in Baltimore, (Md.) on Wednesday.

Sat. Nov. 26, 1881

Oliver C. Waddell, who recently removed to Arkansas from Texas, settling on the White River in Stone County, died recently from a bite of a tarantula.

Mr. Farquay McKay, living near Louisville, in Barbour County, died last Sunday.

The death of A. B. Thornton, editor of the Boonville (Mo.) News, occurred Monday.

Sat. Dec. 3, 1881

Mr. Zodock J. Daniel, Esq., of Eufaula, died Nov. 26th. He was born in Granville, N. C., 25th Sept. 1810. On the 15th of Nov. 1832, he married in Baldwin County, Ga. to Miss Anna H. West, daughter of Joseph West, of Lenoir County, N. C. By this wife he had seven children, only two of whom are now living, Mrs. M. F. Van Hoose, of Senoia, Ga., and Dr. Z. J. Daniel, of Washington, D. C. She died while on a visit to her daughter in Griffin, Ga., on the 11th of Sept. 1865, Mr. Daniel was again married in Midway, Bullock County, Ala., to Miss Sarah E. Griffin, daughter of Mr. Jas. Griffin, of Griffin, Ga. By this wife he had three daughters, two of whom survive him. He became a resident of Eufaula in 1837, and this place has been his home ever since. About 1833, while living in Milledgeville, Ga., he united with the Baptist Church. He is the last of a family of eleven children, having six brothers and four sisters.

Sat. Dec. 10, 1881

Mrs. Anna Jameson, a widow living at Lake Butler, in Bradford County, Fla., died last Sunday.

Mr. Jno. Tyler Howard, age 48, of Quitman County, Ga., died last Sunday. He married a daughter of Col. Dawson, of Glennville, Ala.

Mr. Geo. W. Harrison, age 53, merchant of Louisville, (Ala.) died Monday. He leaves a wife and three children.

Capt. Dan. Jones, merchant of Mobile, (Ala.) died on Friday.

Sat. Dec. 17, 1881

Dr. Thos. W. Grimes, age 60, of Columbus, Ga., died on Monday last.

Mrs. Mary Mabry, of Clayton, mother of Gen. Seth Mabry and Hon. Jas. W. Mabry, died yesterday at the home of her son, Gen. Mabry. Had she lived until the 23rd inst., she would have been 100 years old.

Miss Rebecca Bates, age 88 years, died in Mass. on Wednesday. She was a heroine of the Revolutionary War.

Sat. Dec. 24, 1881
    Mr. V. R. Tommey, age about 70, formerly a merchant of Eufaula, and President of the Eufaula Bridge & Banking Co., died in Atlanta last Saturday. He was a member of the Methodist Church.

THE CLAYTON COURIER

1881

Edgar R. Quillin, Publisher.

Sat. Sept. 3, 1881
    Jno. King Walker was instantly killed by a horse running away on Wednesday, near Augusta, Ga.

Sat. Sept. 24, 1881
    Hon. Forney Renfroe, mayor of Opelika, died on the 16th inst.

    Mr. Geo. Passmore, living near Louisville, (Ala.) died on Saturday last.

    Mr. Aaron Kent, of Barbour County, died suddenly Thursday of last week.

Sat. Oct. 1, 1881
    Mr. T. P. Howard was killed by the running away of his horse in Blount County, (Ala.) on Sunday.

    Hon. Jno. A. Cuthbert, lawyer, age 94, died at Mobile, on Saturday last.

    Died on Sunday last, Mrs. Julia Williams, wife of A. T. Williams, of Shorter's Station. She was the only daughter of Maj. Lovard Lee, of Clayton, and sister of Capt. A. V. Lee.

Sat. Oct. 22, 1881
    Mr. Joe Whigham, living at Blue Springs, (Barbour County), an old citizen, died Thursday last.

    Prof. J. W. Wright, of Troy, (Ala.) died there on Sunday last.

    Mr. Richard Bearden, of Madison County, Ala., died last Sunday.

Sat. Oct. 29, 1881
    Mr. Isham Guttery, of Walker County, Ala., was killed by a tree falling on him last week.

Sat. Nov. 5, 1881
    Mrs. Celeste Darby and Mrs. Oglethrope Worthy died in Troy, Ala., on Monday of last week. They were sisters-in-law.

Sat. Nov. 26, 1881
    Mrs. F. McKay died at her home near Louisville, Ala., on Sunday.

Mrs. Halsted died near Clayton on Wednesday. She was the daughter of Mr. Norman Bowden.

Mr. Wm. Chapman Shields died recently from injuries received in an accident. -Athens (Ala.) Courier.

Sat. Dec. 3, 1881
Mr. Frank Johns, an aged citizen of near Elamville, (Barbour County) died on the 3rd ult.

Sat. Dec. 10, 1881
Alexander James, brother to M. P. James, at Carpenter, (Ala.) died near Shellmound, Tenn., on Thursday last.

Sat. Dec. 31, 1881
Rev. S. Patterson, of the Alabama Conference, died at his home at Mt. Carmel, Ala., on the 23rd inst.

EUFAULA TIMES AND NEWS

1881

W. J. Jelks, Proprietor.

Thurs. Jan. 13, 1881
Mr. Isaac Loebe, merchant of Ft. Gaines, Ga., died last Thursday. Burial in the Jewish Cemetery in Eufaula.

Thurs. Jan. 20, 1881
Mr. Joel Lowery, age 90, of Bibb County, (Ala.) died recently.

Thurs. Jan. 27, 1881
Capt. Jno. McMahon, citizen of Savannah, Ga., died on Thursday. He was an officer of the Mexican War.

Mrs. J. S. Cade, living near Batesville, (Ala.) died last Sunday.

Mr. Levi Edge, living near Spring Hill in Barbour County, died last Tuesday of typhoid fever. Two weeks ago his oldest son died.

Thurs. Feb. 3, 1881
Dr. W. H. Bond, citizen of Salem County, Ark., died on the 27th ult.

Mr. Wm. Horatio Thornton died at his home in Eufaula on the 27th. He was born near Washington in Wilks County, Ga., on May 8, 1816. On Apr. 10, 1845 he married Miss Mary Butler Shorter. He is survived by four children. (Correction: Dr. Wm. Horatio Thornton. Source: Backtracking In Barbour County, by Annie Kendrick Walker.)

Thurs. Feb. 10, 1881
Mrs. A. J. Daniels, age 72, died at the home of her son-in-law, Mr. T. J. Craddock, in Eufaula. She was a member of the Baptist Church for 40 years.

Mrs. H. E. Graves, formerly of Eufaula, died in Montgomery, Ala., on the 29th ult. She was born in Abbeville, S. C., and was the only daughter of Judge Lomax and Eliza Tennent. She was the mother of Mr. T. P. Graves, of Eufaula.

Thurs. Feb. 24, 1881

Mrs. M. A. Freeman, of Fort Gaines, (Ga.) died recently.

Dr. A. L. Hamilton, President of Andrew Female College, died last Tuesday at Cuthbert, Ga.

Thurs. Mar. 17, 1881
Mr. W. D. Howe, age about 60, died at his home near Eufaula last Monday.

Thurs. Apr. 28, 1881
David Collins, infant son of Mr. and Mrs. Jno. M. Bowdon, aged 3 months, died at the home of his parents in Eufaula last Monday.

The grandfather of this child, Mr. David Collins, and for whom he was named, died at his home in Jackson, Fla., on the 23rd inst., aged about 76 years.

Thurs. May 5, 1881
Mr. Robt. S. Stephens, of Albany, Ga., drowned last week in the Flint River.

Mr. Jno. A. Caffey died at his home near Montgomery on the 28th.

Thurs. May 12, 1881
Mrs. Ella Owens died at Abbeville, (Ala.) on the 7th inst. Burial at Sardis, near Abbeville.

Thurs. May 28, 1881
Zachariah Renfroe, an old citizen of Henry County, (Ala.) died at his home near Headland on the 20th inst.

Thurs. June 16, 1881
Wm. A. Clements, of Stewart County, Ga., died recently.

Thurs. June 23, 1881
Mr. Jesse N. Thomas, of Clayton, died recently. He leaves a wife and two children.

Thurs. July 7, 1881
Mrs. C. S. Cutts, of Americus, Ga., died last week.

Col. Wm. H. Chambers, of Auburn, (Ala.) who one time represented Barbour County in the State Legislature, died recently.

Thurs. July 14, 1881
Mr. P. D. Stephens, age about 30, of Clayton, died recently. He leaves a wife and two children.

Miss Clara V. Givens, age 19, of Tampa, Fla., died yesterday while on a visit to her brother, Mr. T. W. Givens, in Eufaula. Burial in Eufaula.

Thurs. July 21, 1881
Mrs. Elizabeth Simpson, of Russell County, (Ala.) died recently.

Thurs. July 28, 1881
Maj. A. D. Banks, a resident of Hampton County, Va., died at Fortress Monroe recently. Burial at Hampton on Friday.

Mr. Geo. W. Doswell, living near Abbeville, (Ala.) died last week.

Mr. Jno. Caldwell Graddy, age 18, died in Georgetown, (Ga.)

on Wednesday of last week.

Thurs. Aug. 11, 1881
O. C. Lowe, living near Green Hill, Stewart County, Ga., died from injuries received when thrown from a mule.

Thurs. Aug. 18, 1881
Mr. B. D. Gullett, the manufacturer of the famous Gullett gin, died recently at his home in Amita, La. He commenced his long and useful life's work in Eutaw, Ala.

Mr. J. C. Poole died at the residence of his brother-in-law, B. F. Lokey, in Clay County, Ga., on the 11th inst.

Died on Friday last, the infant daughter of Capt. and Mrs. J. W. Tullis. On Monday last, the infant child of Mr. and Mrs. Warren Dent.

Mr. Geo. Stokes, age 23, living near Clio, (Ala.) died on the 9th inst.

Thurs. Aug. 25, 1881
Mrs. Binion, wife of Rev. M. L. Binion, of Webster County, Ga., formerly pastor of the Baptist Church in Dawson, died today.

Thurs. Sept. 1, 1881
Mr. J. R. Thames, aged 38 years, died at Greenville, Ala.

Mrs. Ann S. Yarrington, sister of Maj. Wallace Screws and Mrs. J. N. Williams, of Barbour County, died at Seale, (Ala.) on last Monday.

Thurs. Sept. 15, 1881
Cincinnati Gazette. - Col. Wm. M. Shannon, of Camden, S. C. died at DeBois' bridge, Darlington County, South Carolina, on July 5th, from effects of a duel.

Mr. Marion P. Ezell was killed near Pulaski, Tenn., Tuesday. He leaves a wife and several children.

Mrs. Jane A. Hill, aged 65, formerly a resident of Clayton, but more recently of Talbotton, Ga., died at the latter place. (From The Clayton Courier, Sept. 10th: Mrs. Hill died 24th of August.)

Col. Erasmus T. Beall, aged 68, for a long time a citizen of Stewart County, Ga., died at Milledgeville on Monday. Burial in Lumpkin, Ga.

On the 30th of last month, Mrs. Sarah A. Lee, an old resident of Barbour County, died at Lake City, Fla. She was the mother of Rev. C. C. Lee, of Louisville, (Ala.) and Mrs. J. W. Stokes and Mrs. Newman, of Henry County, Ala.

Thurs. Sept. 22, 1881
Mrs. Peter Thomas, of Henry County, (Ala.) died recently. She was a wife of less than a year.

Mr. Salathiel Forham, one of the oldest citizens of Henry County, (Ala.) died near Abbeville a few days ago.

Thurs. Oct. 13, 1881
Rev. Dr. Stuart Robinson, well known Presbyterian minister, died recently in Louisville, Ky. (From The Eufaula Weekly Bulletin, Oct. 15th: Rev. Robinson died on the 6th inst.)

Jno. McDale, ex-Chief of Police, of Wilmington, N. C., died from gun wounds received from a gambler.

The wife of Mr. Judge A. Rollins, of White Oak, (Barbour County) died last Thursday.

Rev. Wade H. Weatherby, one of the oldest men of the county (Henry County, Ala.) died last Saturday.

Thurs. Oct. 27, 1881
Died recently at Norfolk, Va., Mr. S. S. Sanford.

Mr. Wm. Mount, late of Ft. Gaines, Ga., but for many years a citizen of Henry County, (Ala.) died recently.

Thurs. Nov. 3, 1881
Mrs. J. W. Sheffield, aged nearly 44 years, died in Americus, Ga., on the 22nd inst. Her maiden name was Davis, and her native home was Davisboro, Washington County, Ga.

Mr. Jesse Harrell, of Stewart County, Ga., was thrown from a colt last week and died from injuries received.

Mr. Edward Dowling, Jr., died at Ozark, (Ala.) a few days since.

Thurs. Nov. 10, 1881
Miss Foy Johnson, daughter of Prof. P. W. Johnson, formerly of Clayton, died in Perry, Ga., on Oct. 26th.

Died in Dale County, (Ala.) lately: Mrs. M. L. DeShazo; Mr. A. E. Payne, Esq.; Mr. Thos. P. Kennedy; Mr. Smith Haimans; and Mrs. Ellen E. Bagwell.

Judge W. O. Fleming died at his home in Bainbridge, Ga., on Thursday last.

Mrs. Corbitt, mother of our townsman, J. A. Corbitt, Esq., aged over 80, died at Clopton, (Ala.) on the 5th inst. Burial took place at Lawrenceville, Henry County, Ala.

Mr. W. W. Hays (Henry County, Ala.) living near Columbia died last week and was buried at Columbia on the 4th inst.

Near Dothan, (Ala.) last week, Thos. J. G. Clark, Esq., one of our oldest citizens, breathed his last.

Rev. James Best died on the 2nd inst. (Henry County, Ala.).

Thurs. Nov. 24, 1881
Mrs. M. A. McCoy died at her home near Abbeville, (Ala.) on last Friday. (Thurs. Dec. 1, 1881 paper: Mrs. McCoy, wife of Farqhuar McCoy, was buried at Pea River Church. (Barbour County).

Thurs. Dec. 1, 1881
Near Aberdeen, Miss., three sons of Mr. Phil Walker were murdered. Mr. Walker was a former resident of Russell County, Ala. The family were moving to Arkansas from Mississippi. The bodies were interred recently at their father's old home in Russell County.

Thurs. Dec. 8, 1881
Mrs. Jas. W. Roberts died in Henry County, (Ala.) recently. It was only a few days since Mr. Roberts lost a daughter.

Walter R. Williford died at his home in Columbia, (Ala.) last Thursday. It was only last spring that his young wife was buried.

Mr. Jno. Tyler Howard, of Quitman County, (Ga.) died last Sunday.

J. D. Hoyl, Proprietor.

Wed. Jan. 4, 1882
Mr. Jno. Sisk, a painter, of Eufaula, died last Monday.
Burial from the Catholic Church.

Wed. Jan. 11, 1882
Rev. Jas. Cameron, pastor of the Second Presbyterian Church
of Oakland, Calif., died last Thursday.

Mrs. Minerva C. Stacey, aged 41 years, 11 months, formerly
of Clayton, died in Eufaula on Jan. 8th, 1882. She was born in
North Carolina in 1840, married in N. C. in 1855. Mr. Stacey
died in N. C. in 1860, and she came to Eufaula that year to her
father. She leaves two sons, Jno. and Jas. Stacey, of Eufaula,
and six sisters and four brothers.

Wed. Jan. 18, 1882
Col. Wm. H. Sparks died suddenly at his home in Marietta,
Ga., on last Saturday.

Wed. Jan. 25, 1882
Dr. Edwin A. Burfoot, a young physician of Mobile, was
drowned yesterday. He leaves a widowed mother and a young wife.
-Mobile (Ala.) Register.

Wed. Feb. 1, 1882
Dr. Wm. Butler, age 92, a staff officer of Gen. Jackson in
the War of 1812, died at Jackson, Tenn., recently.

Mrs. Sarah F. Williamson, wife of Mr. Henry E. Williamson,
Sr., died at her home in Eufaula on Saturday. She was born in
Greene County, Ga., Apr. 1, 1826. Before her marriage she was a
Miss Collier. In 1844 she married Mr. Williamson in Talbotton,
Ga., from which point her husband and family removed to Eufaula
some twelve or fifteen years since, and where they have since
resided. She leaves a husband and five children.

Mrs. Elizabeth Jane, aged 61, consort of Col. Wm. Doughtie,
died at her home near Eufaula on the 25th. She was the mother
of thirteen children, ten of whom are living. Burial from the
M. E. Church.

Wed. Feb. 8, 1882
Dr. N. S. Angier, once State Treasurer of Georgia, died in
Atlanta on last Friday.

Wed. Feb. 15, 1882
Mrs. Lee Teague died Saturday at her home in Columbia,
Henry County, (Ala.).

Gen. Wm. McCrea, Superintendent of the Western & Atlantic
R. R., died in Augusta, Ga., on Sunday.

Mr. Chas. J. Tucker, aged about 33, lawyer, died in Lumpkin,
Ga., on Thursday last. His father, Jno. A. Tucker, lawyer of
Lumpkin, died before the war.

Capt. Jno. L. Hayes, age about 56, of Henry County, (Ala.)
died at his home in Gordan on the 11th inst. He represented
Henry County in the Legislature before the war.

NOTES

NOTES

Wed. Feb. 22, 1882
Charleston, S. C., Feb. 15. - Bishop Wm. May Wightman, of M. E. Church, aged 74, died at his home in this city this morning. He was licensed to preach in 1827.

Wed. Mar. 1, 1882
Mrs. Belle Solomon, wife of Capt. R. A. Solomon, died at her home in Clayton on the 27th inst. She was a sister of Mr. Ben. Chitty, of Eufaula. She leaves a husband and six children.

Mrs. Ann M. Estes, age 94, wife of Maj. W. C. Estes, died at Cotton Hill, Ga., on Friday.

Mr. Jas. A. Davis, age about 50, lawyer of Orlando, Fla., died at his home there on Thursday last. He was a brother to Mr. E. Frank Davis, of Eufaula.

Wed. Mar. 15, 1882
Mr. W. F. Acee, merchant of Columbus, Ga., for thirty years, died at his home in that city on Friday last.

Mrs. Levi Wilkinson died at her home in Clopton, Dale County, (Ala.) on Monday.

Mr. W. Wooley, aged 65, of Quitman County, Ga., died on the 6th inst.

Mr. Colson Guilford, an old citizen of Quitman County, Ga., died last Tuesday. He was the father of Mr. Jno. Guilford, of Eufaula.

Mr. P. W. Curry, late of Eufaula, died in Columbus, (Ga.) last Sunday. Burial in Savannah.

Wed. Mar. 22, 1882
Capt. Phillip H. Alston, age 52, citizen of Columbus, (Ga.) died in that city on Sunday last.

Wed. Mar. 29, 1882
L. T. Dowing, lawyer and U. S. Commissioner, died suddenly in Columbus, Ga., last Friday.

Col. Wm. Thompson, age 70, journalist and author, who for the last 32 years has been managing editor of the Savannah Morning News, died at his home in Savannah on Friday.

Mr. Wm. P. Cox, age 63, of Eufaula, died at his home yesterday. He removed from Madison County, Ga., to Barbour County on the 10th of Dec. 1859. He had been married twice, his first wife being Miss N. M. Bridges, who died on the 8 Sept. 1856, and his second wife was Miss Elizabeth Moore, who with two grown children survive him. Funeral from the M. E. Church, of which he was a member.

Wed. Apr. 5, 1882
Mr. Wm. B. Dixon, age 38, merchant of Cuthbert, Ga., drowned last Saturday. He leaves a wife and four children. He was a brother-in-law of Messrs. Ralph and Young Johnston, of Eufaula.

Wed. Apr. 12, 1882
Mr. Samuel Wilkerson, Jr., aged about 34, of near Clopton, (Ala.) died Tuesday. He leaves a wife and children.

Mrs. E. B. Johnston, of Eufaula, died at her home here last Friday. Burial in Columbus, (Ga.).

Wed. Apr. 19, 1882

Mr. C. N. Sheats, age about 50, died at his home in Eufaula last Wednesday. He leaves a wife and several children.

Wed. Apr. 26, 1882
Mr. Geo. M. Allen, age 33, died at his home in Eufaula on the 18th inst. He leaves a wife. Funeral took place from the Presbyterian Church.

Wed. May 3, 1882
Mrs. Malinda J. Craddock, age 33, wife of T. J. Craddock, of Eufaula, died on Friday. She was a member of the First Baptist Church.

Wed. May 10, 1882
Mrs. Cynthia O'Hara, aged over 86, of Eufaula, died yesterday. She was born in Edgefield District, S. C., her maiden name being Cobb. She was a relative of Gov. Bibb, Alabama's first Governor, also Governor Cobb, of Alabama, and Gov. Howell Cobb, of Ga. She came to Eufaula in Dec. 1858, and was the mother of ten children, only five of whom are living. Mrs. Jno. F. Kehoe, of Eufaula being the youngest child. She was a member of the Methodist Church.

Mrs. G. Gunby Jordan, of Columbus, (Ga.) died on Tuesday last.

Hon. Horace Maynard, of Tenn., died suddenly on Wednesday last at his home in Knoxville.

Wed. May 17, 1882
Dr. H. H. Hubbard, age 55, late Surgeon General of the Confederate Army, died last Monday in San Francisco.

Judge J. Q. Smith, of Alabama, died in Washington city last week. Burial in Montgomery, (Ala.) on Tuesday last.

Mr. Reuben J. Thornton, age 42, oldest son of Mr. J. M. Thornton, of Barbour County, and brother to Dozier and Jno. Thornton, of Eufaula, died last Sunday at his home at Pine Grove, near Eufaula. He had been living in Texas for some years and recently returned to Barbour County. He leaves a wife and six children. Member of the Baptist Church. Burial at Cowikee Church.

Mrs. C. A. Nutting, of Macon, Ga., died on Tuesday last.

Judge S. B. Jones, an old citizen of Sandersville, Ga., was killed by lightning on Wednesday last.

Wed. May 31, 1882
Col. Wm. H. Tucker, merchant of N. C., died at Raliegh on Friday last.

W. J. A. Bethune, aged 29, son of Mr. and Mrs. Jno. G. Bethune, died in Eufaula on the 24th of May. He leaves a wife, father, mother and a sister.

W. C. Bond, about 30 years of age, of Wynnton, (Ga.) near Columbus, died Tuesday. He leaves a wife and two children.

Wed. June 7, 1882
Mr. Geo. Hutto, aged 84, died Thursday last at Roeville, Henry County, (Ala.).

Wed. June 14, 1882
Dr. Wm. Wimberly, aged 65, died at his home in Stewart County, Ga., on last Saturday week.

Hon. Sidney Ed. Bowdon, age about 37, a member of the State Legislature from Henry County, died on the 9th inst., in Troy where he had gone for medical treatment. He leaves a wife and three children. He was brother-in-law to Mr. A. H. Thomas, of Clayton. He married the youngest daughter of Mr. Elias Thomas, of Henry County. Burial in Clayton, where he had been living.

Mrs. Jno. D. Roquemore died at her home near Eufaula on the 13th inst. She leaves a husband and five children. She was Miss Mary Hunter.

Mr. A. R. Hatfield age about 50, died at his home near Eufaula on Monday. He leaves a wife and seven children. Burial at Bascom Church, near Eufaula.

Mr. Sanders C. Echols, aged about 50, formerly of Ft. Browder in Barbour County, died at Bryan, Texas on the 9th inst. He moved to Texas in 1865. He was a half brother to Mr. R. Cherry, of Eufaula.

Wed. June 21, 1882

Mrs. Isaac Winship, aged 81, died at Macon, Ga., on the 12th inst.

Rev. Robt. T. Jackson, Rector of the Episcopal Church of Richmond, died at Petersburg, Va., on Friday. He was formerly Rector at Macon, Ga., and a native of Petersburg.

Mr. Beverly Creyon Walker, aged 23, died on the 17th inst., at the home of his parents, Mr. and Mrs. A. A. Walker, in Atlanta, Ga. Burial in Eufaula.

Wed. July 5, 1882

Col. C. B. Talaferro, an old citizen of Columbus, (Ga.) died on Wednesday.

Wed. July 12, 1882

Mrs. Jane Atwood, age 45, died at her home near Union Church in Quitman County, Ga., on 3rd inst. She leaves a husband and seven children.

The death of Maj. L. W. R. Blair, candidate for Governor of South Carolina, occurred at Camden, S. C. on the 4th inst.

Wed. July 19, 1882

Col. Ed. Woods, age 55, a citizen of Selma, (Ala.) died at his home there on Thursday last.

Mrs. F. M. Irby, wife of Col. H. J. Irby died near Eufaula on May 4th, 1882. She was born in Monroe County, Ga., June 13, 1824. Member of the Baptist Church.

Wed. Aug. 9, 1882

Mr. Chas. Linn, aged 68, died at his home in Birmingham on last Monday.

Mr. Peyton D. Saunders, aged 85, died on the 6th inst., in Abbeville, (Ala.). For many years he was a member of the Missionary Baptist Church. He leaves a large family of children.

Mr. Jesse B. Wright, aged about 50, of Columbus, Ga., died last Sunday. He leaves a wife and seven children.

The death of Col. J. R. Proctor, of New Orleans occurred last Tuesday. He was brother-in-law to Gen. Beauregard.

The death of Mr. Robt. G. Mullens occurred at Clanton, Ala., on Tuesday last.

Wed. Aug. 16, 1882
     The funeral of Col. Wm. M. Wadley, age 68, President of the
Central R. R., took place this afternoon at his home in Broling-
ton, near Macon, Ga. He was born in Brentwood, N. H. and moved
to Georgia when a young man. He married Miss Rebecca Everingham,
who survives him, also a son.

     Mrs. W. D. Henderson, of Troy, (Ala.) died on Tuesday.

     Hon. Edward Hillsbury, aged 58, ex-mayor of New Orleans,
died in that city on Thursday last.

Wed. Aug. 23, 1882
     Mr. Jno. McLendon, aged 85, died at the home of his son,
Mr. Jack McLendon, at Jernigan, (Ala.) on last Friday.

     Dr. Jas. Gillespie, age about 60, died at his home in
Abbeville, (Ala.) last Tuesday.

     Senator Benj. Harvey Hill, of Atlanta, Ga., died on the 16th
inst. He was born in Jasper County, Ga., Sept. 14, 1823. Survivors are his wife and several children.

Wed. Aug. 30, 1882
     Mrs. Leila H. Owens, age 29, wife of E. H. Owens, died on
the 16th inst., at Orange Hill, Washington County, Fla. She was
a sister of Mr. J. H. Simonton, of Eufaula. She was reared in
Abbeville, Ala. She leaves a husband, widowed mother, and four
children.

     W. G. Patterson, of Montgomery, (Ala.) died last Sunday.
He leaves a wife and three children.

Wed. Sept. 6, 1882
     Mr. Andrew J. Carmichael died in Dale County, (Ala.) recent-
ly.

     Mrs. Silas Jones, aged 58, died on Monday last. Burial near
White Church, (Barbour County). Mr. Jones died some three years
ago. Survivors are three or four grown boys.

Wed. Sept. 13, 1882
     Mrs. Thos. Kennedy, of Quitman County, Ga., died on the
31st, leaving a husband and an infant only a week old.

Wed. Sept. 20, 1882
     Mr. Willie A. McNeil, formerly a citizen of Barbour County,
died recently in Texas.

     Mr. Lyman Wells, aged about 38, died in Chattanooga, Tenn.,
last Tuesday. He leaves a wife and three children.

     Col. Sam G. Grasty, well known in Eufaula, died of yellow
fever recently in Brownsville, Texas.

     Rev. Henry P. Pitchford, who had been in the Methodist
ministry near a half century, died at his home in Harris County,
Ga., on the 11th inst.

Wed. Sept. 27, 1882
     Mr. A. G. James, an old citizen of Dale County, (Ala.) died
recently.

     Mrs. F. Tiller, of near White Oak (Barbour County) died on
Sunday last.

Wed. Oct. 4, 1882
     Mrs. Julia Sapp, wife of Capt. Phillip A. Sapp, died at her

home in Eufaula on the 3rd inst. She was born in Abbeville
District, S. C., and was married to Capt. Sapp in Lumpkin, Ga.,
in 1850. In 1856 they removed to Eufaula where they have resided
since. She was a sister to Gen. Alpheus Baker, of Louisville,
Ky., and Dr. P. DeL. Baker of Eufaula. Burial from the Catholic
Church.

Wed. Oct. 11, 1882

Rev. J. W. Christian, editor of the Alabama Christian
Advocate, died in Birmingham on last Saturday.

Rev. Z. A. Owens, Baptist minister died of yellow fever
last week, in Pensacola, (Fla.).

Mrs. Elizabeth A. Sanders, aged 77, died in Eufaula at the
home of her son, Mr. Thos. Sanders, on Thursday. Burial in
Columbus, (Ga.).

Wed. Oct. 18, 1882

Gen. O. C. Horne died at his home in Hawkinsville, Ga., on
last Wednesday.

Miss Fannie J. Rudd, aged 16, daughter of Mr. S. J. Rudd,
of Henry County, (Ala.) died Thursday.

Wed. Oct. 25, 1882

Mr. Jas. Carr died suddenly at his home at Cox's Mill in
Barbour County on Wednesday. -Clayton (Ala.) Courier.

Wed. Nov. 1, 1882

Mr. Geo. Lowman, formerly of Eufaula, died recently in
Pensacola, (Fla.) of yellow fever. He was a brother of Mr.
Thornton Lowman, of Barbour County, and his mother, Mrs. Sterns
lives in Eufaula.

Mr. Thos. J. Craddock, aged 47, died in Eufaula last Sunday.
His wife died about a year ago. He leaves no children.

Mr. Mike B. Koonce, of Columbia, Henry County, (Ala.) died
last Saturday.

Dr. W. L. Milligan, of Ozark, (Ala.) died on last Sunday.

Mrs. Orustus Bell, of Eufaula, died on Wednesday. She
leaves a husband and children.

Wed. Nov. 8, 1882

Rev. T. J. Rutledge, of the Alabama Christian Advocate,
died in Birmingham on last Tuesday.

Dr. Wm. L. Mitchell, died in Athens, Ga., on Tuesday last.

Wed. Nov. 15, 1882

Rev. Dr. A. T. Twing, Episcopal clergyman of New York city,
died Saturday.

Mr. Tom H. Offutt, U. S. Marshal for Montgomery, (Ala.)
District, died at Troy, (Ala.) on Friday last. Burial in
Montgomery.

Mr. Stephens Miller, aged 85, resident of Tuscaloosa, (Ala.)
died at his home in that city on Friday.

Mr. Wm. Grubbs, aged 80, died near Sandy Point in Barbour
County, on the 10th inst. He raised a large family.

Mrs. Abbe Phillips, aged 29, died Friday last at her home
in Quitman County, Ga. Burial at Sharon Church in that county.

Dr. J. D. Stearns died near Geneva, Ala., on Monday last.

Mr. Alfred Bethea died at his residence at Verbena, Ala., on Monday last.

Wed. Nov. 22, 1882
Mrs. Sarah Parish died at her home in Dale County on the 7th inst., leaving several little orphaned children, as their father died several years ago in Texas.

Mr. Ephraim Wise, aged 84, living fourteen miles south of Eufaula, died yesterday.

Mr. F. J. Springer, proprietor of the Springer Opera House in Columbus, Ga., died on Friday last.

Mrs. D. L. Southwick died in Eufaula on last Saturday. She leaves a husband and five little children. Burial from the Episcopal Church.

Mrs. Charlotte Bowdon, wife of Sam Bowdon, merchant of Gordon in Henry County, (Ala.) died at her home Thursday. She leaves several children. She was sister-in-law of Mr. Jno. M. Bowdon, of Eufaula.

Wed. Nov. 29, 1882
The death of Mr. Manning L. Drew, age about 50, occurred near White Oak (Barbour County) on Sunday last.

Jas. Cowardine, age 72, founder of the Richmond, Va., Dispatch, died Tuesday last.

Dr. Jno. E. Bacon, an old citizen of Columbus, Ga., died on the 19th inst.

Wed. Dec. 5, 1882
Gen. Dan. Tyler, aged 83, a resident of Montgomery, (Ala.) from 1873-1878, and of late a resident of Anniston, Ala., died in New York on last Thursday.

Mrs. W. H. Birdsong, of Dangerfield, Texas, formerly a resident of Eufaula, died last Wednesday at her home in Texas.

Wed. Dec. 13, 1882
Mr. Burrell Rachels, aged about 35, died Saturday at the home of his mother at White Oak in Barbour County. He was born and raised in Barbour, but for the last eleven years had been living in Texas and the Indian Territory, and married an Indian half breed. His wife died a while back and his health becoming bad, he returned to his old home.

Mrs. Rebecca Hollis, aged about 65, of near Georgetown, Quitman County, Ga., died on Tuesday last.

Dr. Geo. F. Cooper, Baptist preacher of Georgia, but of late years physician of Americus, (Ga.) died on Sunday last.

Maj. Gus Henry, son of Hon. Gustavus A. Henry, of Tenn., died at his home in Tuscumbia, Ala., on the 4th inst.

Wed. Dec. 20, 1882
Hon. Jas. S. Lyon, lawyer of Richmond, Va., died on Monday last. In 1824 he went to New York with the Virginia committee to escort the Marquis de LaFayette to Richmond.

Maj. Geo. M. Bates, aged 76, died at his home near Eufaula on Dec. 15th.

Mr. Eben Curry, of Dale County, (Ala.) died on Sunday last.

THE CLAYTON COURIER

1882

A. H. Thomas, Editor.

Sat. Jan. 21, 1882
Mr. Wallace Drewry, a young man, of Louisville, (Ala.) died Monday last.

The remains of Mrs. G. W. Pappot, nee Marie Campbell, of Savannah, Ga., who died in that city about five years since, were brought to this place Tuesday and interred in the Clayton Cemetery.

Sat. Feb. 4, 1882
Died at the home of her parents near Mt. Andrew (Barbour County) on the 25th ult., Miss Jennie Smith.

The death of Jacob Santapher, aged 20 years, of Eufaula occurred on Tuesday last.

Sat. Feb. 25, 1882
W. D. Durham, of near Hood, Harris County, Ga., died Thursday.

Michael Crenshaw, age 93, died at his home near Hurtsboro, (Ala.) on Monday of last week.

Mr. Alfred West, aged about 72, died Sunday last at his home at White Pond. (Barbour County).

Sat. Apr. 8, 1882
Mr. Chas. A. McDonald, lawyer of Dawson, Ga., died on Friday.

Mr. Jas. Carruthers, age 77, died at the residence of his daughter, Mrs. J. S. Paullin, in Clayton, on Friday last. He was a member of the Baptist Church. Burial in the Masonic Cemetery in Clayton. (Notice in the Eufaula paper: Jas. L. Carruthers.).

Sat. May 27, 1882
Mrs. Thos. M. Coker, age 42, died near Cotton Hill on Friday. She leaves a husband and seven children.

Sat. June 3, 1882
Rev. J. Stratton Paullin died on Thursday last in Clayton. Survivors are his wife and children. (From The Eufaula Weekly Bulletin, Nov. 8, 1882: Rev. Paullin was born June 7, 1837 in Eufaula. His parents were Wm. S. and Eliza Paullin.).

Sat. June 17, 1882
Mr. Green B. Carlisle, age 73, died at Brundidge, Pike County, (Ala.) on the 4th of June.

Geo. N. Stewart, lawyer, died at Mobile last week. He was admitted to law practice in 1821.

Sat. July 29, 1882
Mr. Levin Duncan, age 72, died on the 15th inst., at his home in Jackson County, Fla. He was the father of Mr. C. F. Duncan, of near Clayton.

EUFAULA TIMES AND NEWS

Thurs. Jan. 12, 1882
    Mr. W. H. H. Jackson, a former resident of Eufaula, died at Brannon's Stand, (Henry County) Christmas week.

    Hon. C. C. Clay died near Huntsville, Ala., last week. He was born in 1817, admitted to the bar in 1839, was a legislator and judge until 1848, was U. S. Senator from Alabama in 1853, and Confederate States Senator in 1861.

Tues. Jan. 31, 1882
    Col. I. A. Wilson, late Senator from Bullock County, (Ala.) died a few days since.

    Mr. Jno. E. Martin, Clerk of the Circuit Court of Geneva County, (Ala.) died recently.

    Prof. S. M. Ainsworth, of the Athens (Ala.) Courier, died recently.

    Mrs. J. T. Robertson died at her new home in Texas recently. She had been living there for about a year, being a former resident of Eufaula for over twenty years. Her youngest son, Gilbert, preceded her in death only three days.

Tues. Feb. 7, 1882
    Mr. J. D. Dudley, postmaster at Fort Gaines, (Ga.) died on the 26th inst.

    Died at Cotton Hill, in Barbour County, on the 1st inst., Mrs. Lucy Houston, aged 30 years, wife of Sam Houston.

    Gen. Seth Mabry died at his home in Clayton on the 1st inst. He had lived in Barbour County for forty years, and was sheriff in 1849-50.

Tues. Feb. 28, 1882
    D. Webster Davis, post master at Darion, (Ga.) died in that city recently.

    Harvey Hitching, of Barnesville, (Ga.) died recently.

    Mrs. Isaac Steel, of Big Shanty, (Ga.) died at her home on Wednesday.

    Mr. Bradley Boswell died recently near Farriorville, Ala.

Tues. Mar. 14, 1882
    Gen. Zach. Deas died in New York on the 6th. He removed from his native state, South Carolina, to Mobile, Ala., at an early age. He organized and equipped the 23rd Alabama regiment. At the close of the war he went to N. Y. where he was engaged in the cotton business.

Tues. Mar. 21, 1882
    Mrs. Martha Bailey died at her home in Eufaula on last Thursday.

Tues. Apr. 4, 1882
    Judge D. H. Hunt, of Harris County, Ga., died recently, age 75 years.

Tues. Apr. 11, 1882
    Mr. J. Henry Mann, sheriff of Irwin County, Ga., died on the 21st inst.

    Mr. Wm. Knight died near Louisville (Barbour County) at the

age of 90 years.

The death of Mr. Wm. H. Locke occurred at his home in
Eufaula, Ala., on the 15th of Jan. 1882. He was born in Pike
County, Ala., Oct. 9, 1832, married Miss Ann Judson Sylvester,
the daughter of Demarcus Sylvester. Survivors are his wife and
ten children.

Tues. Apr. 18, 1882
     Rev. Absalom Stephens died at his home in Polk County, (Ga.)
last Monday, age 75 years.

     Mr. Robt. J. Richards died on the 27th Mar. 1882, age 34
years, 8 months and 8 days. He leaves a wife and five children.
(White Pond, Barbour County).

Tues. Apr. 25, 1882
     Mr. Antone Basler, of Savannah died recently.

     Mr. C. M. Powell, of Perry County, (Ala.) died recently.
He was seventy odd years of age.

Tues. May 2, 1882
     Dr. M. G. Haygood died in Lowndes County, (Ala.) last week.

Tues. May 9, 1882
     Rev. T. O. Summers, D. D., the distinguished Methodist
divine, died in Nashville last week.

Tues. May 16, 1882
     Mr. H. N. Walker died last Saturday at his residence in
Eufaula.

Tues. May 30, 1882
     Mr. Abram Pierce, of Washington County, Ga., died last
Saturday.

     Mr. R. P. Tucker, of Royston, (Ga.) died last Monday.

     Mr. W. M. Moore died in Eufaula on the 22nd inst. He leaves
a family.

     Mr. H. R. Tarwater, of Nashville, died there recently. He
was a brother to Mrs. F. B. Moodie, of Eufaula.

Tues. June 6, 1882
     Mrs. Jno. R. Robertson, aged about 60 years, died at her
residence in Eufaula on Thursday.

Tues. June 20, 1882
     Mr. B. J. Rutherford, of Berrien County, (Ga.) died recently.

     Mr. Jas. Aiken, of Jackson, Butts County, (Ga.) died last
Thursday.

Tues. July 11, 1882
     William H. Sears, of Jasper County, (Ga.) died last week.

     Mrs. Ann Angell Young, first wife of the late Brigham Young,
died recently in Salt Lake City, aged 79 years. She was a
native of Ontario County, N. Y.

     Mrs. S. A. Whigham died at her home near Eufaula on last
Friday.

     Capt. Anthony Stow died in Brooklyn, N. Y., last Friday, age
71. He was a former resident of Eufaula and the father of Mr.
Ed. Stow, of this city.

Mrs. Zulika Reed died at the home of her sister, Mrs.
Georgia Mitchell, on Saturday, age 37 years. Her home was at
Fernandina, Fla., she was the daughter of Mr. Russell Flewellen.
Burial in Columbus, (Ga.). (July 18th issue of *Times*: Mrs. Reed
died at Glennville, Ala.).

Tues. July 18, 1882
    Mrs. Eliza McLendon, of near Morris Station, Quitman County,
Ga., died on the 13th inst. She leaves nine children, all
married.

Tues. July 25, 1882
    Mr. Geo. H. Elliott, aged 82 years, of Sapelo Island, near
Savannah, died on Friday last.

Tues. Aug. 1, 1882
    Col. Alfred Shorter died in Rome, Ga., July 18th. He was
born Nov. 23, 1803.

    Mr. Henry Martin, age 85, of Dallas County, Ala., died at
his home near Summerfield on the 16th. He was born in Stewart
County, Ga., in 1797.

Tues. Aug. 29, 1882
    The death of J. R. Cunningham, of near Thomasville, Ga.,
occurred last Thursday.

    Mrs. Catherine Owen, aged 75, relict of Wm. Owen, of Girard,
Ala., died last week at her home in Russell County, (Ala.).

Tues. Sept. 5, 1882
    Died in Eufaula last Saturday, Miss Cullie B. Black,
daughter of the late Mr. Jno. Black, Esq. The funeral took place
from the Baptist Church.

Tues. Sept. 12, 1882
    Miss Leila Sims died recently in Greenville, Ga.

    Miss Kate Russell died in LaFayette, Ga., recently.

    Mrs. Betsy Titcomb died at Smithville, Ga., on the 31 ult.
Burial in Dawson, Ga.

Tues. Sept. 19, 1882
    Judge A. F. Allgood died near Rome, Ba., a few days ago.

    Col. Wm. M. Nicholls died Wednesday last at the home of his
brother-in-law, W. T. Akers, at McIver's Station, (Ga.).

    Mr. H. C. Bibbs, formerly of Macon, Ga., died in Eufaula
on Thursday.

Tues. Sept. 26, 1882
    Miss Florence Battle, daughter of Gen. C. A. Battle, died
in Tuskegee, (Ala.) a few days ago.

    The death of Maj. B. H. Lewis occurred in Pike County, Ala.,
a few days ago.

Tues. Oct. 17, 1882
    Hon. Wm. Manning Lowe, of Huntsville, Ala., died recently.
He was born in Huntsville, Madison County, Ala., on Jan. 12, 1842.

    The death of Mr. Ansel McAllister occurred near Spring Hill
(Barbour County) on the 7th inst.

Tues. Oct. 24, 1882

Royal Woodward died recently in Albany, (Ga.). He was the owner of one of the largest private libraries in the country.

Bishop Robt. Paine, age 85, of the M. E. Church, South, died at Aberdeen, Miss., on Friday.

The deaths of Gen. Jos. A. Mabry and his son, J. A. Mabry, Jr., occurred recently at Knoxville, Tenn.

Mr. Daniel Stewart, of White Oak, (Barbour County) died on the 20th inst.

Tues. Dec. 12, 1882
Hon. Benj. H. Hill died at his home in Atlanta on the 6th of August last.

Tues. Dec. 19, 1882
Mrs. Richard K. Bedell, of Hilliardsville, (Ala.) died in Columbus, (Ga.) recently.

1883

Tues. Jan. 9, 1883
Mrs. T. E. J. Home died near Clopton, (Ala.) on the 31st last.

Tues. Jan. 23, 1883
Dr. Samuel A. Mudd died Wednesday at his home near Bryanston, Charles County, S. C.

Mrs. Margaret Methvin, aged 75, of Quitman County, Ga., died Sunday.

Tues. Jan. 30, 1883
S. Warren Mays, aged about 30, of Augusta, Ga., died in Eufaula at the home of Maj. Geo. C. Ball on Monday. He was the step-son of Hon. Henry W. Hilliard. Burial in Augusta, Georgia.

Tues. Feb. 6, 1883
Mr. Chas. T. Williams, architect, age about 30, died today in Clayton. He leaves a wife and several children.

Tues. Feb. 13, 1883
Col. Anderson G. Jones, of Crawford, Russell County, (Ala.) died yesterday.

Tues. Feb. 20, 1883
Dr. J. A. Hayes died in Union Springs, (Ala.) last week.

Col. Richard Jones, the father of the wife of Gen. Jos. Wheeler, died at Wheeler, Ala., last week.

E. H. Grouby, aged 49, founder of the Early County News, died at Jackson on the 9th inst. He was born in Montgomery, Ala., and has a brother in that city, and a son at Abbeville, Ala.

Tues. Feb. 27, 1883
Mrs. Chas. Laney, of Abbeville, Ala., died recently. She was a wife of only about a year.

The infant child of F. J. Dehoney, and grand-child of Mr. Wm. Doughtie, died Friday.

Died in Corsicana, Texas, Mrs. Mary Antoinett Goodson Bush, wife of Wm. (Billy) Bush, the son of Council Bush. Mr. and Mrs. Wm. Bush were formerly of Barbour County.

Tues. Mar. 6, 1883

Mr. Jno. D. Stewart, aged about 75, died at his home in Quitman County, (Ga.) last Monday.

Tues. Mar. 20, 1883

Mr. Jno. M. Bowdon, aged 50, died at his home in Eufaula last Wednesday. Burial in the Masonic Cemetery. (The Eufaula Bulletin of Mar. 21st: Survivors are a wife and three children.)

Col. Wyatt W. Smith, aged 69, died at his home in Eufaula Saturday. Burial in Midway.

Tues. Apr. 2, 1883

Hon. Thos. H. Herndon died in Mobile Wednesday. He was born in Greene County in 1828 (that part of Greene County later formed part of Hale County.) His father was from Virginia, his mother was a daughter of Judge Harry Toulmin, of Washington County.

Thos. L. Pittman died on his way home from Ark. He was reared in Quitman County, (Ga.) and emigrated to Ark. several years ago.

Tues. Apr. 17, 1883

Mr. W. J. Rivers, son of Rev. R. H. Rivers, D. D., formerly of Eufaula, now of Greenville, Ala., lost his life in the steamer Wylly last night. He leaves a wife and six children.

Also, H. L. Palmer, of Columbus, purser of the Wylly, lost his life in the steamer disaster.

Homer B. Powell, son of Col. R. H. Powell, of Union Springs, (Ala.) died at Ft. Worth, Texas last week.

Mr. Jas. Cooper died near Columbus, (Ga.) Tuesday last.

The death of Mr. Ivey Doles occurred in Seale, Russell County, (Ala.) on last Tuesday.

Tues. Apr. 24, 1883

Capt. Benj. E. Mitchell, aged 48, died at his home in Eufaula Monday. Before the war he was book-keeper for the St. Charles Hotel in New Orleans. During the war he served in La., and was present at the fall of Vicksburg. He afterwards lived in Mobile, where he married. He had been a resident of Eufaula for about twelve years. (Eufaula Bulletin, Apr. 18th: Survivors are his wife and three children).

Tues. May 8, 1883

Mr. Stephen Williams died on the 24th ult., at the residence of his son-in-law, Capt. Thos. Hardwick, near Hatchechubbee, (Ala.). Burial at the Williams family burying ground near Seale, (Ala.).

Died yesterday at the residence of H. L. McGehee in Columbus, (Ga.). Mr. W. G. Woolridge, aged 75, of Chattahoochee County, (Ga.). He was the father of Ab Woolridge, and grandfather of Wm. H. Vigal, of Eufaula.

Tues. May 15, 1883

Hon. Rufus K. Boyd, aged about 45, died at his home in Guntersville, (Ala.) on the 10th inst. He was born in Wilkinson County, Tenn. At an early age he went with his parents to Missouri, where he lived until the close of the war. He came to Marshall County, Ala., in 1865, where he married and lived until his death.

Tues. May 22, 1883
     Mr. W. D. Grace, of near Seale, Ala., died at his home
Friday. His wife died nine days ago. Burial at Uchee Chapel.

     Mr. Jas. Brock died at Clio, (Ala.) on Wednesday, at an
advanced age.

Tues. May 29, 1883
     Dr. G. R. Mendenhall, formerly of Russell County, (Ala.)
but late of Clopton, Ala., died recently.

     The death of Mr. Amasa Stone, of Cleveland, Ohio, occurred
today. (Cleveland, May 11th). Survivors are his wife and
daughters, Mrs. Jno. Hay and Mrs. Samuel Mather.

Tues. June 12, 1883
     Chas. C. Fulton, aged 67, died Thursday in Baltimore, Md.
He was born in Philadelphia. He was owner of the Baltimore
American newspaper.

     Mr. Green Goodson, an aged man, died at his home near Ozark,
Ala., a few days ago.

Tues. June 19, 1883
     Mrs. Harriett Billings died Friday at the home of her
daughter, Mrs. M. J. Black. She had lived in Eufaula since 1839.
She was the mother of Jno. D. Billings, and mother-in-law of the
late Jno. B. Black.

     Died at Ft. Gaines, Ga., on the 15th inst., the infant
daughter of Mr. and Mrs. A. S. Brown and grand-daughter of Capt.
J. N. Webb, of Eufaula.

Tues. July 3, 1883
     Capt. Henry C. Hart died at his home in Eufaula Wednesday.
He was born at Providence, R. I., Feb. 12, 1829. He moved with
his parents to Eufaula about 1834. Burial from the Episcopal
Church.

     Maj. J. N. Kelley, of Barbour County, died near Bush post-
office last Saturday.

Tues. July 7, 1883
     Col. Daniel Morgan Seals, aged about 70 years, died at his
home in Eufaula Thursday. He was born in Warren County, Ga.,
and came to this section when quite young, being a resident of
Barbour County during the Indian War of 1836.

     Mr. Sam. Pollak, age 40, of Montgomery, drowned at Long
Beach, N. J. on Sunday. He leaves a wife and four children.

     Mr. Buckner Peacock, of Skipperville, (Dale County) died
last Saturday.

Tues. July 10, 1883
     Bessie, nine year old daughter of Jno. C. Abney, of near
Eufaula, died Wednesday. Burial in Eufaula.

     Dr. Paul DeLacy Baker, aged about 54, died at his home in
Eufaula yesterday. He was a brother to Gen. Alpheus Baker.

     Mr. Daniel McRaney, age 65, died at his home near Clayton
on July 1st. He was an old citizen of Barbour County, having
taught school in the county in 1840.

     The funeral of Mrs. Lurenna Caruthers, aged 84, took place
from the residence of her son-in-law, Capt. G. A. Roberts, in
Eufaula on last Friday.

Tues. July 17, 1883

Mrs. Frank Bowdon, nee Miss Bessie Jeffries, of Uniontown, (Ala.) died at Talladega recently.

Mrs. Wesley V. Nobles, formerly of Henry County, died in Texas recently. Survivors are her husband and child.

Tues. July 24, 1883

Mrs. Jane A. Battle, age nearly 84, widow of the late Dr. Cullen Battle, of Eufaula, died in Tuskegee, (Ala.) on Friday. Burial in Eufaula. She was the mother of Dr. Archibald J. Battle, of Macon, Ga., Gen. Cullen A. Battle, of Tuskegee, and the late Mrs. Jno. Gill Shorter.

Tues. July 31, 1883

Mr. Jno. H. Butts, formerly of Columbus, Ga., died in Montgomery, Ala., July 15th. He was married to Miss John Geline M. Winter, daughter of the late Jno. G. Winter, who survives him.

Col. Wm. B. Bowen, who represented Barbour County in the Legislature before the war, died at his home in Tuskegee last Saturday. He leaves a wife and four daughters.

Rev. Aaron Helms, age 67, of the Primitive Baptist Church, died at Blue Springs (Barbour County) on July 20th.

Mr. Wm. Doughtie, age 70, died at his home in Eufaula on Sunday.

Tues. Aug. 21, 1883

Mrs. Henry Jernigan died in Dale County, (Ala.) recently. -Ozark (Ala.) Star.

Tues. Aug. 23, 1883

Mr. Hiram Jay, aged 73, and father of Thos. and Lemuel Jay, died yesterday near Ward's Station. -Cuthbert (Ga.) Enterprise.

Rev. M. F. Sumner, D. D., Baptist minister, died at Verbena on the 22d. His daughter, Mrs. Ashley and his son accompanied his remains to Marion, Ala., for burial. -Montgomery (Ala.) Advertiser.

Hon. Jeremiah S. Black, aged 73, died at his home in York, Pa., last Sunday. He was born in Somerset County, Pa., on Jan. 10, 1810.

Tues. Sept. 4, 1883

Mr. Marks Asher, age about 50, drowned recently when he fell overboard the steamer City of Augusta, about 25 miles south of Frying Pan Shoals. He was on the return to Eufaula from New York, where he had gone to purchase merchandise for his firm. He moved to Eufaula in 1866 and lived here about eight or ten years, when he moved away and afterwards returned in 1876 and has lived here since that time. He married Miss Harrison, of New York in 1877. He leaves a wife and three children.

Tues. Sept. 11, 1883

Mr. James M. Dixon died at Skipperville, Dale County, (Ala.) recently. -Ozark (Ala.) Star.

Tues. Sept. 18, 1883

Mr. Ryan Bennett, of Barbour County, died Tuesday, aged 75 years.

Died at Lawrenceville (Henry County) on the 15th inst., Mrs. Martha J. Holly, relict of the late Green B. Holly.

Maj. Thos. Peters, of Birmingham, died recently in Louis-ville, Ky.

Mr. W. A. Malley, age 40, of Spring Hill (Barbour County) died Monday. He leaves a wife and three children.

Mrs. Margaret Grantham, daughter of G. Walker Williams, died on the 13th at Cotton Hill, (Barbour County). She was a sister to C. M. Williams.

Hon. Farish C. Furman, age 37, of middle Georgia, died recently.

Tues. Sept. 25, 1883
Gen. D. C. Turrentine, of Gadsden, Ala., died at his home on the 1st inst. He was a member of the Methodist Church, and the father of Mr. Dick Turrentine.

S. S. Murdock, Esq., a citizen of Columbus, (Ga.) died recently.

Tues. Oct. 1, 1883
Mrs. Henry D. Clayton, Jr., died in Eufaula Thursday. She was Jennie Allen, daughter of Gen. W. W. Allen. Her remains were taken to Montgomery for burial. Survivors are her husband, father and mother.

Tues. Oct. 16, 1883
Dr. S. W. Dent died at his home in Charles County, Maryland last Sunday, aged 78. He was born in that county in 1806. He is survived by his wife, three sons and five daughters. He was the father of Capt. S. H. Dent, Mr. Geo. Dent, and Mr. Warren F. Dent, of Eufaula.

Edward S. McCurdy, planter of Lowndes County, Ala., died recently.

Jno. McFadden, a teamster of Omaha, was killed by lightning recently.

Mrs. Mary Satawhite, (Satterwhite?) of Winfred, Ga., was killed by lightning recently.

Tues. Oct. 23, 1883
Mr. H. G. Peterman, of Shorterville, and Robt. Gamble, of near Abbeville, (Ala.) died last week. Mr. Gamble was the first white male born in Henry County.

Dr. Lee A. Jennings, of Hawridge, died recently. -Ozark (Ala.) Star.

Gen. Jas. B. Stedman died in Toledo, Ohio, on Thursday. He was Chief of Police of Toledo.

Hon. J. K. Edwards, probate Judge of Lee County, (Ala.) died in Opelika Saturday, aged 40 years. He leaves a wife and two children.

Tues. Oct. 30, 1883
Mr. J. S. Frazer, age about 50 years, died at his home near Hurtsboro, Ala., Thursday. Survivors are his wife and two children. He was a member of the Methodist Church.

Mrs. R. C. Jeter died at her home in Opelika Monday. She was a sister of Gen. H. D. Clayton, of Clayton, and Mrs. J. C. Pope, of Eufaula. Burial in Opelika.

The funeral of Mr. Thos. Cargile took place yesterday. (Euafaula). He was eighty odd years of age.

Tues. Nov. 6, 1883
Hon. Taul Bradford, age 43, died at his home in Talladega, (Ala.) last Sunday.

Mr. Lindsey J. Sims, of Stewart County, (Ga.) died last week. He leaves a wife and two children.

Tues. Nov. 13, 1883
Mrs. Betsy Williams died near Otho, (Henry County, Ala.) on Wednesday, aged 65.

Mr. P. W. Willims, of Dale County, (Ala.) died at his home on Saturday last. -Ozark (Ala.) Star.

Mr. R. A. Tarver died in Macon, (Ga.) on Tuesday. He was one time agent of the Montgomery & Eufaula Railroad.

Tues. Nov. 20, 1883
Dr. J. Marion Sims, age 70, died in New York on Tuesday. He graduated in 1835 at Jefferson Medical College in Philadelphia and located at Lancaster, S. C. for a year, thence to Mt. Meigs, in Montgomery County, (Ala.) in 1836, returned to South Carolina and married Miss Theresa Jones, sister of Dr. B. R. Jones, of this city. He located in Montgomery in 1840. In 1851 he went to New York and was the founder of the "Womans Hospital". -Montgomery (Ala.) Advertiser.

Miss Mary Sanders, formerly of Eufaula, died on Wednesday in Columbua, (Ga.).

Mr. Thos. Joseph, business man of Montgomery, died recently.

The death of W. L. Graham occurred near Macon, (Ga.) recently in a train accident. A book found on his person had "W. L. Graham, Elmore County, Ala." His wife lives in Eufaula.

The funeral of Mrs. Beall Guerry took place in Georgetown, (Ga.) Sunday. She was a sister to Mr. S. W. Goode and Mrs. Mercer.

Tues. Nov. 27, 1883
Mrs. Holtzclaw, wife of Gen. Jas. T. Holtzclaw, of Montgomery, and sister of Mr. Thos. Cowles, of Eufaula, died in Montgomery yesterday.

Rev. Dr. M. B. Harden, of LaGrange, Ga., will be buried there tomorrow. He was pastor of the Baptist Church in Union Springs, (Ala.) during the sixties.

The funeral of Mrs. W. E. Price took place from the family residence in Eufaula yesterday.

Tues. Dec. 11, 1883
Selma, Ala., Nov. 30. - E. K. Marshall, from New York died here today. He leaves a wife and family.

Mr. A. Stow, of Brooklyn, N. Y. died there recently. Burial in Eufaula.

Tues. Dec. 18, 1883
Prof. D. Hughes, of Greenville, Ala., died recently.

Mr. Green Beauchamp, aged 81, died at his home in White Oak, (Barbour County) yesterday. Interment at White Oak Cemetery. He came to Eufaula in 1818.

Tues. Dec. 25, 1883
Jackson, Fla., Dec. 19. - The death of Maj. Wm. Page Couper

occurred last night at Leesburg, (Fla.). He was a civil engineer on the M. & E. Railroad, and formerly lived at Union Springs, Ala., where he married.

Mr. Jose Wilkerson, of Uchee, Russell County, (Ala.) died recently. -Russell Register.

Mrs. W. B. McLendon, of Quitman County, Ga., died recently. -Cuthbert (Ga.) Appeal.

THE CLAYTON COURIER

1883

Sat. Sept. 15, 1883
Rev. Moses W. Helms, age 72, died on the 4th inst., at his home in Vernon, Fla. He was a preacher of the Primitive Baptist Church. He was the father of Mrs. E. R. Quillin, of Clayton, Mr. T. C. and A. C. Helms, of this county, he also left a wife and four other children.

Sat. Sept. 22, 1883
Mr. Jere Smith, age about 63, of Mt. Andrew, (Barbour County) died last Sunday. Survivors are his wife and children.

Sat. Oct. 6, 1883
Mrs. Nancy Johns, age 78, widow of Frank Johns, died at her home near Elamville, (Barbour County) on Tuesday.

Mrs. Turner, wife of Dr. A. Turner, living near Williams Station, died on Tuesday last.

Mr. L. G. Hightower, formerly of Barbour County, and father of Mr. Jesse C. Hightower, of Clayton, died recently at his home in Henry County. Burial in Clayton.

Sat. Oct. 13, 1883
Mr. Green Stephens, an old citizen, died at his home near Spring Hill (Barbour County) on Saturday. He was the father of Mrs. M. R. Hill, Mrs. Dr. W. B. Stewart, and Mrs. R. E. Brown, of our town.

Sat. Nov. 24, 1883
Judge R. D. Thornton, of Collins Station, Ark., died last Thursday. He emigrated from this city about a year previously to his new home. -Union Springs (Ala.) Herald.

Sat. Dec. 1, 1883
W. O. Baldwin, Mayor of Union Springs, (Ala.) died on Tuesday last.

THE EUFAULA WEEKLY BULLETIN

1883

J. D. Hoyl, Proprietor.

Wed. Jan. 3, 1883
Hon. Peter M. Rowland, Probate Judge of Chambers County, (Ala.) died at his home in LaFayette on Friday.

Mrs. Vassie L. Sporman, wife of Alderman Chas. F. Sporman, died at her home in Eufaula on Sunday.

Also, Miss Mary R. Malone, died at the home of her mother in Eufaula on Monday.

Wed. Jan. 10, 1883

Col. P. J. Quattlebaum, age 46, U. S. Engineer in charge of the work on the Chattahoochee and Flint Rivers for the past seven years, died in Columbus, Ga., on Thursday last. Member of the Episcopal Church. Burial at Covington, Ky.

Hon. Frank W. Sykes, of Lawrence County, (Ala.) died last Saturday.

Mrs. Martha M. Robinson, age 61, wife of Mr. Thos. Robinson, formerly of Eufaula, died on last Saturday at her home near Smithville in Henry County, (Ala.). She was the step-mother of Capt. W. F. and Charlie Robinson, of Eufaula. She was a Mrs. Standiford when she married her now surviving husband. Burial in Eufaula.

Henry Brigham, aged 71, merchant and Pres. of the Merchant's National Bank, in Savannah, died on Monday.

Died in Savannah, Ga., on last Saturday, Col. E. C. Anderson, aged 68, ex-mayor and Pres. of the Ocean Steam Ship Company, also, Dr. Wm. Charters, aged 78.

Mrs. Sarah Brown, age 25, wife of J. T. Brown, of near Cotton Hill (Barbour County) died on Thursday. Burial at Hepworth, near Eufaula.

Hon. F. S. Lyon, age nearly 82, died at his home at Demopolis, (Ala.) on Thursday. He had been a citizen of Alabama since 1817.

Dr. Acee Pond, aged 85, a citizen of Columbus, Ga., since 1825-26, died at his home there on Sunday last.

Mr. Harry W. Bell, associate editor of the Selma (Ala. Times, died in that city recently.

Wed. Jan. 18, 1883

Mrs. Mary A. Moore, sister of Col. D. M. Seals, died on Sunday last at her home in Eureka Springs, Ark.

Mr. J. R. Billips, of Russell County, (Ala.) died on Saturday last at Pensacola. Burial in Columbus, (Ga.).

Capt. W. M. Eanes, age 60, for many years a steamboat man on the Alabama River, died in Clarke County, (Ala.) recently.

Wed. Jan. 24, 1883

Mr. Jno. W. McAllister, age 57, died at home at Spring Hill (Barbour County) last Sunday. Burial at Spring Hill.

Mr. Henry W. Baker, age 67, died at his home in Eufaula on Saturday. He was a northern man by birth, but came to Eufaula in 1838-39. Member of the Baptist Church. He leaves a family.

Representative J. S. Shackleford, of N. C., died in Washington on Thursday last.

Gen. Oden G. Clay, aged 82, citizen of Lynchburg, Va., died last Wednesday.

Wed. Jan. 31, 1883

Mrs. Wm. L. Yancey died in Athens, Ga., on Saturday last. Burial in Montgomery, (Ala.) beside her husband.

Mr. Irvine Railey, age 55, of Pike County, (Ala.) died last Sunday.

Wed. Feb. 14, 1883

Mrs. Catherine B. McKay, age 72, wife of the late Archibald

McKay, died Thursday last at the home of her son-in-law, Mr. Chas. McDowell, in Eufaula. Deceased was born and reared in N. C. She was a member of the Presbyterian Church.

Fri. Feb. 23, 1883*
                          Deaths in Alabama
At. Ft. Payne, G. Souther; In Uniontown, Frank Dureen; On Lookout, Henry Alfred; in Dale Co., Wm. E. Barnes; in Prattville, Mrs. Isabell Davis; near Prattville, Miss Octavia Rucker; in Prattville, Charlie Edwards; near Havana, W. B. Hayden; at Belleville, Simon K. Norred; in Calhoun Co., Mrs. Melissa Ann Martin; near Castleberry, Mrs. Eliza Ingraham; at Hartselle, Benj. Sandlin; at Decatur, Dr. J. T. Cantwell; in LaFayette, Abner Webb; near Scottsboro, Mrs. J. W. Finney; in Tallapoosa Co., Mrs. Martha Weston Wagner. *(Advertiser and Mail, published Montgomery, Ala., bound with The Eufaula Weekly Bulletin as a supplement.)

Sun. Feb. 25, 1883*
                          Deaths in Alabama
In Livingston, Judge P. G. Nash; in Autauga Co., A. J. Hall; in Huntsville, Mary E. Stegall; in Athens, Jno. Hammerly; near La Place, Mrs. Mary Lamar; in Greene Co., Dr. Baltzell; in Eutaw, Mrs. H. W. Moody; in Limestone Co., Albert Harvey; in Greene Co., Henry Sanford; in Tallapoosa Co., W. J. Coley and Mrs. Mary F. Speer. *(Advertiser and Mail, published Montgomery, Ala., bound with The Eufaula Weekly Bulletin as a supplement.)

Wed. Mar. 7, 1883
     Rev. S. R. Williams, of Lentzville Circuit, near Athens, Ala., died recently.

     E. Samuels, merchant of Parish, Texas, died last Saturday.

     Mr. Wm. H. Pratt, age 72, a citizen of Mobile sine 1836, was killed in an accident at Birmingham, (Ala.).

     The death of Mr. Moses T. Ray occurred in Montgomery last Saturday. His wife died about two years since, survivors are two little children.

     Mrs. M. Elizabeth Andrews, divorced wife of J. D. Andrews, of Eufaula, died in Macon, Ga., Feb. 21st.

     The death of W. A. Key, young conductor on the Savannah, Florida & Western R. R., occurred last Wednesday. He leaves a wife and two children in Macon, Ga.

Sun. Mar. 11, 1883*
     Danville, Va., Mar. 10. - C. R. Evans, editor of the Milton North Carolina Chronicle, died this morning at Milton. *(Advertiser and Mail, published Montgomery, Ala., bound with The Eufaula Weekly Bulletin as a supplement.)

Wed. Mar. 14, 1883
     Hon. J. M. Floyd, of Covington, Ga., died on last Monday.

Wed. Mar. 21, 1883
     The death of Mr. J. T. Tucker, aged about 60, of Seale, Russell County, (Ala.) occurred on Tuesday. He leaves a large family, among them are Justice W. A. L. Tucker, of Seale.

     Frederick Lunger, aged 75, the oldest locomotive engineer in this county, died last week at Davenport, Iowa. In 1835, in England, he ran the first locomotive built by Geo. Setphenson.

Mrs. Nancy Oakley, an old citizen of Columbis, (Ala.) died on Monday.

Mr. Frank Howard was killed last week at the steam saw mill near Lawtonville, Ga., in Burke County.

Mrs. Leola McSwain, wife of Eli McSwain, of Clopton, (Ala.) died on the 13th inst.

Dr. H. G. Henderson, young physician of Opelika, (Ala.) died on Sunday last.

Hon. Thos. S. Flournoy, politician in Virginia for the last forty years, died at his home in Halifax County on last Tuesday.

Wed. Mar. 28, 1883
Mr. Neil Gillis, an old citizen of Barbour County, died Sunday. -Clayton Courier.

T. O. Howe, Postmaster General, died at his home in Wisconsin on Sunday.

Chas. O. Lamotte, of the Savannah Morning News staff was drowned in that city on Sunday last.

Miss Saphie, age about 17, daughter of Dr. and Mrs. S. A. Holt, died at her home in Eufaula last Saturday.

Mr. Simpson Moore, aged nearly 72, of Quitman County, Ga., died yesterday.

Mrs. Ann B. Dense died in Macon, Ga., on Tuesday last. She was the mother of conductor Jim Dense.

Wed. Apr. 11, 1883
Mrs. Mary A. Tullis, aged 70, died in Troy, Ala., on Apr. 1st, 1883. She was born in South Carolina and moved with her relatives to the vicinity of Macon, Ga., and with her husband came to Pike County shortly after the war. She leaves a large family. Several of her children are in Texas. -Troy (Ala.) Messenger.

Mrs. Susan McRee, age 24, of Florence, Stewart County, Ga., died Monday. She was the daughter of Mr. Francis and Mrs. W. A. Waller, of Stewart County.

Hon. C. B. Lawrence, ex-Chief Justice of Illinois, died suddenly in Decatur, Ala., on Sunday last. He had just arrived with his wife and was enroute to Florida. He taught school for fifty years near Montgomery.

Mr. A. J. Carver, Sr., formerly of Eufaula, died at Dawson, Ga., on Tuesday last. -Dawson (Ga.) Journal.

Mr. A. P. Pryor, aged 72, for fifty years a citizen of Columbus, Ga., died at his home in that city on Thursday last.

Wed. Apr. 18, 1883
Mr. Chas. M. Williams, age 29, died at his home in Eufaula on Saturday. He was married in Macon, Ga., in the fall of 1880 to Miss Clifford Spain, who survives him.

Mrs. Sarah Ann Farrior, aged about 50, died at her home near Clayton on Tuesday. She was the wife of Wm. M. Farrior. She was the mother of 16 children, twelve of whom are living.

Wed. May 2, 1883
Rev. E. Wadsworth, D. D., over 50 years of age, minister of the M. E. Church, died at his home in Greensboro, Ala. on Tuesday.

May 16, 1883
    The Selma (Ala.) paper announce the deaths of Dr. J. Hendree and Mrs. Hardy, widow of the late Jno. Hardy, of that city.

    Dr. W. K. Chambliss, aged near 50, died Friday at his home in lower Montgomery County, (Ala.). -Montgomery Advertiser, of Sunday last.

    Col. T. N. Macartney, aged about 45, lawyer of Mobile, died suddenly in Montgomery recently. He leaves a wife, nee Miss Emanuel, of Mobile, and four children. (From same issue of The Bulletin: Thos. J. Macartney was brother-in-law to Capt. Benj. E. Mitchell, of Eufaula.)

Wed. May 23, 1883
    Mrs. R. B. Ridley, daughter of Senator Hill, died Monday in Atlanta, from injuries received from jumping from a buggy while the horse was running away.

Wed. May 30, 1883
    Mrs. Margaret Williams, age 74, of Quitman County, Ga., died Sunday last. Burial at Rocky Mount Cemetery.

    Also, Mrs. Edne Pittman, aged 73, died at her home near Georgetown, Quitman County, Ga., on Friday last.

    Mr. Gilbert McRae, aged about 65, citizen of Barbour County, died last Wednesday at his home near Clayton.

    Mr. Jno. A. Davis, an old citizen of Henry County, died on the 20th inst., near Abbeville. -Abbeville (Ala.) Times.

Wed. June 6, 1883
    Capt. Hosea Ballou, aged 90, of Washington City, the oldest Free-Mason in the U. S. died on the 29th inst. He was a Mason in 1818, and Master of his Lodge in 1821.

    Mrs. Mary Pinkston, aged about 60, living in Quitman County, Ga., died on Sunday last.

    Mrs. Martha Parmer, aged 86, of Cotton Hill in Barbour County, died on Monday last.

Wed. June 13, 1883
    Mr. H. G. Glover, age 68, a citizen of Barbour County, died Saturday last at the home of his son-in-law, Mr. Prudden, at Suspension in Bullock County, (Ala.). Burial at Batesville, (Ala.).

    Mr. Alpheus L. Gaston died at his home in Eufaula on the 6th inst. He was born Jan. 5, 1828. Survivors are his wife and four children. Member of the Baptist Church and a citizen of Eufaula for about 35 years.

    Dr. Alexr. Mears, aged 85, died at his home in Oxford, Ga., on Wednesday.

    The death is announced on May 21st at Nashville, Tenn., of Col. Buckner H. Payne, aged 84 years.

Wed. June 27, 1883
    Mrs. J. W. Daniel, of Calhoun County, near Jacksonville, Ala., died recently.

Wed. July 4, 1883
    Mrs. Gooden P. Morris, aged 80, died near Columbia, in Henry County, (Ala.) on the 25th ult.

The burial of Mrs. Ella Craddock took place at Raliegh, N. C. yesterday. She was a sister of Mr. Chas. Haley of Ft. Gaines, (Ga.).

Wed. July 11, 1883
Mr. Henry C. Bell, living near Neal's Landing, Fla., died on the 1st inst. He had been living there since 1837.

Miss Ermine Laney, age 16, of Russell County, (Ala.) died on Saturday at the home of her parents near Columbus.

Wed. July 18, 1883
Mrs. Charity Kaigler, age 77, relict of the late Jno. J. Kaigler, and mother of Rev. F. L. and Capt. Geo. W. Cherry and also the late Mrs. E. S. Cole, died at the home of her son, Capt. Cherry, near Gold Hill, (Ala.) on the 7th inst. Burial at Opelika from the M. E. Church, of which she was a member for nearly fifty years. -Opelika (Ala.) Times, 13th.

Dr. Jas. L. Ware, age about 50, of Montgomery, died at the home of his father-in-law, in Russell County, (Ala.) on Sunday last.

Wed. July 25, 1883
Judge Martin J. Crawford, of Columbus, Ga., died Sunday at the home of Mr. A. G. Redd. He was Associate Justice of the Georgia Supreme Court. He was born in Jasper County, Ga., Mar. 17, 1820.

Wed. Aug. 1, 1883
Mrs. Polly Ellis, aged 75, died at the home of her son, T. J. Ellis, in Quitman County, Ga., on Monday. Burial at Union Church.

Mrs. Maggie Copeland, wife of Maj. M. M. Copeland of Montgomery, died recently.

Wed. Aug. 8, 1883
Mrs. Josephine M. Singer, wife of Mr. Joe E. Singer, late of Eufaula, died at her home in Atlanta on Sunday. She leaves a husband and four children, the oldest about twelve years of age.

Wed. Aug. 16, 1883
The funeral of Miss Teresa McTyer, who died at the home of Mr. A. H. Merrill, took place from the Presbyterian Church on Thursday.

THE CLAYTON COURIER

1884

Sat. Jan. 12, 1884
Mrs. Jas. Coleman was burned to death at her home near Notasulga, (Ala.) on Sunday, by her dress accidentally catching fire.

Sat. Jan. 19, 1884
Mrs. J. M. Keshey, of Skipperville, (Henry County, Ala.) died recently. -Ozark (Ala.) Star.

Mr. J. M. Garner, for many years a merchant at Ozark, (Ala.) died on the 8th inst. -Ozark Star.

Mr. B. W. Stone, age 86, died Monday. He had lived near Montgomery all his life. -Montgomery (Ala.) Advertiser.

Sat. Jan. 26, 1884

Mrs. Jas. C. Flournoy died on Monday last. Burial in Clayton. Survivors are her husband and children.

Sat. Feb. 16, 1884

Dr. A. A. Jones, of Florence, (Ala.) died on the 8th.

Col. R. D. Boykin, of Wilcox County, (Ala.) was murdered at his residence last week.

Sat. Mar. 15, 1884

Col. A. H. Johnson, a citizen of Montgomery, died in that city on Sunday.

Col. Wm. H. Wood, age 66, died at his home in Columbia, Ala., on Saturday. He was at one time Senator from Henry County, and at the time of his death was proprietor and editor of the Columbia Observer.

Deacon Benajah Wilkes Wood died Jan. 27th. He was born Aug. 26th, 1850, was a deacon of the Shiloh Church, Pike County, Ala., married on Jan. 27, 1874 to Miss Clara, daughter of Deacon F. A. Boykin, of Union Springs, Ala., by whom he had six children.

Sat. May 10, 1884

Mr. Mike (M. W.) Blair, of Louisville, (Ala.) died at his home on May 2nd.

Sat. June 21, 1884

Mr. Brassy Holly, age 97, of White Pond, (Barbour County) died Sunday. He had a number of children. -Eufaula Times.

Mrs. Posey Clark died at her home in Pollard, Ala., on the 14th inst. She was the daughter of Mr. Jno. C. Williams, of Clayton, and a bride of a few months.

Sat. June 28, 1884

Mr. W. C. Bostick died at his home in Louisville, (Ala.) on last Friday night.

Mr. Bob Jackson died at his home in Louisville, (Ala.) on Thursday of last week.

Sat. Aug. 2, 1884

Mrs. Dicey Young, age 65, died at her home near Mt. Andrew on Monday. (Barbour County).

EUFAULA WEEKLY TIMES AND NEWS

1884

W. D. Jelks & Company.

Tues. Jan. 8, 1884

Patrick H. Pepper died in Mobile yesterday. During the war he was prominently identified in blockade running.

Mr. M. E. Jones, age about 50, of Eufaula, formerly of Seale, died Saturday. He leaves a wife and nine children.

Tues. Jan. 8, 1884

Mrs. Lucretia Patterson, wife of Jno. L. Patterson, died Tuesday in Washington.

The death of Dr. D. T. Morrow, of Gadsden, (Ala.) occurred on the 29th.

Mrs. Caroline Hampton Preston, aged 89, died last week in Columbia, S. C. She was the youngest daughter of Gen. Hampton, of the Revolution.

Col. Richard Knight, age 73, died at his home in Henry County, Ala., on Oct. 7th last. He emigrated from South Carolina to Henry County when a youth. He reared his seven orphaned grandchildren, whose father was the late Dr. C. W. Bedell.

Tues. Jan. 29, 1884
Col. Esau Brooks, aged about 80, formerly of this county, but for the past 18 years of Daleville, Dale County, died on the 18th inst.

Mr. Thos. Sapp, aged 29, died at his home in Eufaula on Wednesday. He was the adopted son of Capt. and the late Mrs. P. A. Sapp.

Tues. Feb. 5, 1884
Jno. Butler, son of C. P. Butler, Agricultural Commissioner of South Carolina, was accidently killed last Tuesday.

Mr. Jno. Napper, an old citizen of the county, died at his home near Smithville last week. -Abbeville (Ala.) Times.

Mr. Ridley Barron died at his residence in Eufaula on Thursday.

Mr. J. F. Daniel, merchant and a resident of Columbus for 52 years, died Tuesday.

Tues. Feb. 12, 1884
Mr. F. J. C. Henson, age 76, of Union Springs, formerly Eufaula, died Friday. He left a large family, among whom is Mrs. Keller, of Eufaula.

Mr. Edward Tabor died on the train between Smithville and Eufaula recently. He was editor of the Evansville (Ind.) Journal. Survivors are his wife and sister. Burial at Evansville.

Mrs. Daniel Partridge, of Selma, (Ala.) died recently.

Walter D. Carter, of Montgomery, died recently.

Tues. Feb. 19, 1884
Mrs. Wm. T. Hurston, of near Clopton, Ala. died last Saturday. -Ozark (Ala.) Star.

Tues. Feb. 26, 1884
Mrs. J. H. Burdishaw died recently at her home in Skipperville, at an advanced age. -Ozark (Ala.) Star.

Mr. Aris Mison, aged 82 years, died recently. -Ozark Star.

Mr. J. G. Talley, for many years a resident of Abbeville, died recently at Hot Springs. He went to Longview, Tex., in 1872 where he has resided since. -Abbeville (Ala.) Age.

Dr. G. M. Mendenhall, age 66, long a resident of Russell County, died in Henry County, (Ala.) on 3d ult. -Russell Register.

Mr. Jno. G. Bethune, formerly of Columbus, Ga., died in Wilmington, Delaware.

T. F. Sheldon, business man of Mobile, died recently.

Tues. Mar. 4, 1884
Mrs. Boddie, widow of Abijah Boddie, died last week. Inter-

ment in Pleasant Hill Cemetery on Friday. -Ozark (Ala.) Star.

Mr. Jas. M. Spurlock died at his home in Eufaula yesterday. He was born in Twiggs County, Ga., on the 14th of June, 1822, and came to Barbour County in 1848. Survivors are a wife, two sons and two daughters.

Mrs. Sarah C. Reese, aged about 82 years, died at the home of her son, Prof. King. She was born in New York. Interment at Clayton.

Mr. W. D. Carver, formerly of Eufaula, died in Dawson, Ga., yesterday. -Dawson (Ga.) Dispatch.

Miss Fannie Lou Scaife, daughter of Prof. J. F. Scaife, died in Camilla, Ga., Sunday. Burial in the Masonic Cemetery in Eufaula. She was a member of the Methodist Church.

Rev. T. C. Hurston and daughter, Alice, aged 16, were drowned in the Catawba, North Carolina River, Saturday.

Tues. Mar. 11, 1884

Mrs. Mary Brown, widow of Jno. Brown, of Harper's Ferry fame, died Friday in San Francisco. She met her husband at New Elba, N. Y., married him in 1832, his first wife, Dianthe Lusk, having been dead about two years. He was 32 and she 17. He was born at New Elba. Four years after his death, she settled with son, Solomon, in Calif.

Mrs. Wright Merritt, of Morgan, Ga., died on the 5th inst.

Mr. Davis Gilder, age about 21, died near Morgan, Ga., recently.

Mr. Jas. M. Spurlock, Jr., age about 24, died last Sunday. Funeral from the M. E. Church.

The remains of Mrs. Nancy Cowles, of Opelika, were taken to Georgetown, (Ga.) the home of her daughter, Mrs. Jno. Lee, for interment. She was the mother of Mr. Jas. L. Roquemore, of Opelika.

Tues. Mar. 18, 1884

Mrs. J. J. Brown died at her home in Eufaula recently. She leaves a husband and infant twin daughters five months old, and two or three other children.

Chas. N. Romain, a retired lawyer of Petersburg, Va., died in New York on Monday.

The funeral of the late Solicitor of the Treasury, Hon. Kenneth Raynor, was held at Raleigh, N. C. on Tuesday.

Mr. B. F. Burnett, of Ft. Gaines, Ga., (Clay County) died recently.

Tues. Mar. 25, 1884

Mrs. Henry Hutto, wife of A. H. Hutto, of Abbeville, died last Sunday. -Abbeville (Ala.) Times.

Mrs. Jas. Fussell, who removed several months ago from Chattahoochee County, Ga., to Eufaula, died Wednesday.

Bishop H. H. Kavanaugh died in Columbus, Miss., on the 16th inst. He was born in Scott County, Ky., in 1801, and had been a minister for 62 years. He was chosen a Bishop in 1854 at Columbus, Ga. He was on his way to his home in Louisville from New Orleans, when forced to stop in Miss.

Mr. Wesley Bishop died at his home near White Oak (Barbour

County) yesterday, aged 65. He was born in Twiggs County, Ga.,
Oct. 20th, 1819. He leaves a family of four sons and two daughters.

Tues. Apr. 1, 1884
Mr. Jno. W. Buttons, (Dale County) died recently. -Ozark
(Ala.) Star.

Frank Myers was accidently killed in Mobile on Tuesday by
lumber falling on him.

Mr. Wm. Sauls, mate on the steamer Thronateeska, accidently
fell overboard which caused his death, on last Monday. His home
was in Columbus, (Ga.). He leaves a wife and five children.

Tues. Apr. 8, 1884
On Thursday the steamer Rebecca Everingham burned near
Florence, Ga. Thirteen perished, among the white passengers:
J. C. Hightower, Barbour County. (formerly of Talbot Co., Ga.);
Misses Avant and Simpson, Cuthbert and Ft. Gaines; J. B. Yates,
Bainbridge; and E. D. Williams, LaGrange, Ga.

Tues. Apr. 15, 1884
Mrs. Eliza Goldthwaite, widow of the late Judge Henry Goldthwaite, died in Mobile on Sunday.

Mr. Thos. Hart, pioneer citizen of Chambers and later Lee
County, (Ala.) and who moved to Texas about a year ago, died
there recently. His wife died soon afterwards. -Brownville
(Tex.) Free Press.

The remains of Mr. Ben E. Mitchell who died several months
ago and was buried here, were disinterred and sent to Mobile,
the home of his family.

Tues. Apr. 22, 1884
Mr. W. Easley, of York Station, Sumpter County, (Ala.) was
accidently killed at Meridian, Miss., a few days ago.

The death of Geo. I. Lunsford, aged 80, occurred in Macon,
(Ga.) on Wednesday. He was for a number of years conductor on
the Southwestern R. R.

Mr. Samuel Dunlap, of Eutaw, Greene County, (Ala.) died
there on Friday.

Mr. Jno. N. Kelly, formerly of Eufaula, died on the 11th
inst., in Jacksonville, Fla. He leaves a wife in Eufaula and
three children.

Tues. Apr. 29, 1884
W. H. Lent, secretary of Bodie Mining Co., was found dead
on Jefferson Square in San Francisco.

Joshua Hansman, *merchant of Birmingham, was killed when
thrown from his buggy on Saturday. *(Eufaula Bulletin, Apr. 30th:
Joshua Hausman, of Tuscaloosa.)

Mr. Jno. Fearn, of Abbeville, (Ala.) died recently. He
leaves a wife and two children.

One of the infant twins of Mr. J. J. Brown, whose wife died
a short time since, died Sunday.

Tallulah, Ga., Apr. 21. - Henry Ellard, farmer of Habersham
(County, Ga.) died recently. His wife died a few months ago,
and his daughter, age 17, also died recently. Father and
daughter were buried in the same grave.

Died at the residence of Dr. P. R. Holt, Joseph Grey Blount, infant son of H. P. and Loula F. Blount, age one year, one month and ten days. Apr. 24th, '84.

Tues. May 13, 1884

Mrs. Jas. C. Johnson, of Covington County, (Ala.) died at her home in Andalusia on the 1st inst. Interment at Ozark. -Ozark (Ala.) Star.

Mrs. D. H. Bishop, of Spring Hill, Barbour County, died there today. Survivors are her husband and three children.

Mr. Gabe Stern died in New Orleans. Interment in Eufaula today. Survivors are his wife and Mr. Ben Stern.

Tues. May 20, 1884

Mr. Wm. Faust, of Skipperville, in Dale County, Ala., died last week.

Tues. May 27, 1884

Mrs. Eli Welch, *of Quitman County, (Ga.) died last Wednesday. She leaves five children. *(Eufaula Bulletin, May 28th: Mrs. Mollie Welch, age about 35. Burial at the Grady graveyard).

Tues. June 3, 1884

Mr. Wm. McKenna, Philadelphia journalist, died on Sunday from injuries received by a falling scaffold. He was a soldier of the late war.

Mrs. Nelson Trawick, died in Dale County, (Ala.) and was brought to Abbeville, the home of her son, T. A. Trawick, for the last rites.

Died in Henry County on Monday, Mrs. Jno. J. Ward, the mother of Jno. B., and Jas. Ward.

Tues. June 10, 1884

Mr. A. W. Barnes, living near Eufaula, died Friday.

The death of Mr. Joseph B. Dykes occurred at his home at Cochran, Barbour County, on June 1st. Survivors are his wife and father.

Died last Sunday, Mr. Geo. Barrett, the oldest man in Quitman County, (Ga.). He moved into what is now Quitman County shortly after the war of 1812. He has lived the last few years with his son-in-law, Jas. Wright.

Tues. June 17, 1884

Rev. Dr. J. L. Dagg died at Hayneville on the 11th inst. He was born in Middleburg, Va., in 1794, ordained in the Baptist ministry in 1817, served in Va., and Pa. In 1836 he came to Tuskaloosa, Ala., and took charge of the Alabama Female Athenaeum until 1844 to become the President of Mercer University, in Ga., resigned in 1857 to engage in religious writing.

Tues. July 1, 1884

Mr. Jas. M. Matthews, one of the oldest citizens of Dale County, died at his home in Echo yesterday. -Ozark Star.

Tues. July 8, 1884

Mrs. C. A. Sheally, daughter of Mr. Hart Collins of Clayton, died at Hawkinsville, in this county, on Thursday. She leaves a husband and two small children.

Ex-Gov. David P. Lewis, age about 60, died at his home in

Huntsville, (Ala.) on Thursday.

Mrs. Ben Bernstein, formerly of Eufaula, died in Louisville, Ky., on Thursday.

Mrs. J. R. Harwell died Monday. Burial took place from her home in Eufaula. (Eufaula Bulletin, July 2: Mrs. J. H. Harwell.)

Tues. July 14, 1884

Mr. Jno. M. Bludworth died at his home on Eufaula Street on Wednesday, aged 75. His wife and two daughters survive him. He was born in New Hanover County, N. C., Sept. 12th, 1808. In 1818 he moved to Jasper County, Ga., and resided near Monticello, where he engaged in gold mining, afterwards he lived in Columbus, Ga., in 1833-34 he removed to Eufaula. He married Harriett Woods, and was the brother-in-law to Wm. H. Woods, of N. Y., Sam and Chas. Woods, of Savannah, and R. J. Woods, of Eufaula. He was also brother-in-law to Hon. Jno. M. McKleroy, Capt. Jno. W. Tullis and Mrs. Julia Sylvester, of Eufaula.

Mrs. Jno. Tucker and her eighteen months babe were instantly killed by lightning at Salem, Ala., recently.

Tues. July 22, 1884

Columbia, S. C., July 15. - The death of Rev. Jno. G. Sessions, Baptist minister living at Sand Hill, occurred recently. He leaves a wife.

Tues. July 29, 1884

Mrs. Mary Russell, an aged lady of Spring Hill Beat, (Barbour County) died Wednesday.

Mr. N. N. Thornton, of Harris, (Barbour County) died in Montgomery on Thursday. He leaves a wife. Burial in Montgomery.

Tues. Aug. 5, 1884

Capt. Elmore Fitzpatrick, of Montgomery, died recently.

Tues. Aug. 12, 1884

G. L. McEachern, age 29, of Leesburg, Fla., formerly of Barbour County, died a week ago. He leaves an aged father.

Mr. Eugene Byars, the proprietor of the Georgetown (Ga.) Echo, died in Cuthbert last Thursday.

Henry Eugene Ross, aged about 16, died at his home in Eufaula on Wednesday. All of his immediate family were present, except a sister in Wisconsin, and a brother, Charlie, in Lynchburg.

Tues. Aug. 19, 1884

Mr. Jacob Arnold, of near Abbeville, (Ala.) died on Thursday, aged about 75 years.

Mr. M. K. Wood, of King's (Barbour County) died on Tuesday, aged 70. He leaves a wife.

Tues. Aug. 26, 1884

Miss Susan Dunn, sister to Mr. Wm. Dunn, living near Clayton, died Sunday. Burial in Clayton.

Mrs. Sarah McEachern, wife of Mr. Daniel McEachern, died at her residence in Leesburg, Fla., on the 6th inst. Her son, Gilbert, died on the 2d.

Maj. J. G. Bethune, of Clopton, Dale County, (Ala.) died on Monday last.

Mr. Chas. W. Jackson, aged 32, son of the late J. F. Jackson, Esq., of Montgomery, died there yesterday. His wife was an Eufaulian. -Montgomery (Ala.) Advertiser, of Saturday.

Tues. Sept. 2, 1884
Gen. Wm. J. Greene died on the 19th inst., at Six Mile, Bibb County, (Ala.). He was born in North Carolina in 1817.

Mr. C. C. Watkins, of Mobile, died in Montgomery last Thursday. He leaves a son.

Frank, the five year old son of Mr. S. A. Day, formerly from New England, died recently.

Mr. Hiram Hall, aged 80, died at his home near Eufaula on Thursday.

Clayton, Ala., Aug. 29. - Mr. N. Allen Petty drowned at Wynns mill pond this morning. (Sept. 9th issue of Times: Mr. Petty's father was drowned at sea many years ago.)

Mr. D. H. Bishop lost by death his 13 year old daughter yesterday. He buried his wife a few months ago. (Barbour County)

Tues. Sept. 9, 1884
Mrs. Washington Keller, of Reading, Pa., died last week.

Senator Henry B. Anthony, of Rhode Island, died at his home in Providence last Tuesday.

Judge Wm. S. Mudd died in Birmingham on Tuesday last, in the 70th year of his age.

Bishop Geo. F. Pierce died at his home near Sparta on Wednesday last. He was born in Greene County, Ga., on the 3rd of Feb., 1811. He leaves a wife, one son and three daughters.

Died on Saturday at her residence at Louisville, (Ala.) Mrs. Nancy McLennan, aged about 90.

Mrs. J. B. Vinson, nee Miss R. U. Gregory, living on Washington Street, (Eufaula) died Tuesday last. Interment at Clayton. She leaves a husband and two children.

Mr. C. M. Lowe, of Lumpkin, Ga., died on Saturday last in Atlanta.

Mrs. R. A. Alston, widow of the late Col. Bob Alston, and sister-in-law of Judge Alston, of Clayton, died Friday last at her home in Atlanta.

Mr. Thos. A. Brannon, formerly of Eufaula, died in Macon, Ga., aged about 75. His sons, Thos. and William accompanied his remains for burial in Eufaula.

Mrs. Margaret Turner, of White Oak, (Barbour County) died on the 29th ult. Burial in Clayton.

Capt. Edward R. Flewellen, of Spring Hill, (Barbour County) died at the residence of his daughter, Mrs. Georgia Mitchell, in Russell County, aged about 75 years. His wife died in 1877. Survivors are five children. Burial in Columbus.

Mrs. Hattie Murray, wife of Jno. C. Murray, and baby, and Frankie Horton, all of Brierfield, Ala., were victims of a cyclone near Evansville, Ind., last week. They were passengers on the steamer which overturned in the Ohio River, and were drowned.

Tues. Sept. 16, 1884
Mahlon Runyon, of New Brunswick, N. J., died last Monday.

Survivors are his wife and two daughters.

Miss Lula Richards, of Richard's Beat, died last Sunday.

Mr. Jas. Martin, recently of Ft. Gaines, but previously of Abbeville, died at the former place on Friday. Burial in Abbeville, (Ala.). He was the son of Dr. A. L. Martin, and leaves besides his father, a large family of sisters and brothers, a wife and three children.

Mrs. Emma Bateman, aged about 65, died recently at White Pond, (Barbour County).

Atlanta (Ga.) Constitution, 12th. - Dr. Wm. Green Drake, formerly of Midway, Bullock County, Ala., died at his home on Peachtree Street yesterday. He leaves a wife and four children.

Tues. Sept. 23, 1884
Mrs. Betsy Peacock, aged about one hundred years, died Sunday last at Hilliardsville, Henry County. (Ala.).

Mr. Mike B. Pickett was killed in Eufaula in a cotton compress fire yesterday. Burial in Americus, Ga.

Tues. Sept. 30, 1884
Mrs. Sarah Boler Baker, relict of the late Dr. Paul DeLacy Baker, died on the 25th inst. The funeral took place from the First Baptist Church, burial in the Shorter Cemetery, Eufaula, Ala.

Mrs. Cynthia Redmon, wife of Peter Redmon, died on the 21st inst., at her home near Eufaula. She was an old resident.

Tues. Oct. 7, 1884
Hon. U. L. Jones, former Probate Judge of Pike County, (Ala.) died recently.

Mr. A. Lewis died at his home yesterday, aged 67 years. He was a native of New York City and came south when young. He lived at Lumpkin, Ga., Fort Gaines, Ga., Eufaula and Columbus. He was the father of Mr. Jas. A. Lewis, of Eufaula, and Mrs. Seals, of Atlanta, and leaves five young children of his second marriage. -Columbus (Ga.) Enquirer.

Mr. Ben Cody died Monday at the residence of his brother, Mr. M. Cody, Sr., of Eufaula. Many years a member of the Baptist Church. -Columbia (Ala.) Enterprise.

Maj. M. M. Copeland, about 60 years of age, uncle to Dr. W. P. Copeland, of Eufaula, died at his home in Montgomery yesterday.

Mrs. Isaiah Taylor, age about 70, of Quitman County, Ga., died last Sunday. On last Saturday was the 50th anniversary of her marriage to the husband who survives her.

Maj. Gaz. D. Williams, aged 67 years, a resident of Barbour County for forty years or more, died at his home sixteen miles north of Eufaula on the river road.

Mr. Allen Bass, aged 73 years, died Sunday last at the home of his sister, Mrs. W. Tonty, near Eufaula. Interment in Seale, Russell County. For a number of years he lived in Columbus, Ga.

Tues. Oct. 14, 1884
Mr. Jas. W. Hardie died in Montgomery, Ala., on Sunday last.

Carver McCrary, six year old son of Mr. and Mrs. E. B.

McCrary, died Thursday last at the family residence in Eufaula. Interment in Georgetown, (Ga.).

Miss Emma Ingram died last Saturday at the home of her brother, Mr. Jno. Ingram, near Eufaula. Burial at White Church.

Tues. Oct. 21, 1884

Mr. R. Huggins died suddenly at his home in Batesville, Ala., yesterday.

Dr. J. K. Barnum, of Lumpkin, Stewart County, Ga., died on the 16th inst.

Mrs. Geo. M. Bates, age 72, living near Eufaula, died yesterday. She was the relict of the late Maj. Geo. M. Bates. Burial at White Church, four miles north of the city.

Col. Richard H. Powell died in Union Springs, (Ala.) on Wednesday last.

Mrs. Eva McTyer, daughter of B. B. Fields, Esq., of Barbour County, died at her home in Bainbridge, Ga., on the 14th.

Tues. Oct. 28, 1884

Augusta, Ga., Oct. 19. - Dr. L. A. Dugas died here today, aged 79 years of age.

Mrs. Joel White, aged 70, and for the last fifty years of her life a resident of Montgomery, Ala., died there on Saturday.

Rev. H. H. Davis, living near Eufaula, died yesterday. He was a Methodist minister and a farmer, and served at White Church, (Barbour County).

Col. T. H. Pickett, of Dawson, (Ga.) died Saturday. He leaves a wife and eight of nine children.

Mrs. F. Strauss died yesterday at her home in Eufaula. She was the sister of Messrs. Maurice and Abe Beringer. She leaves a husband and four children.

Tues. Nov. 18, 1884

Mr. Jno. A. Eddins, of Pineapple, Wilcox County, (Ala.) was killed by a train in Montgomery on Wednesday.

Mr. Price Williams, aged 73, died Monday last in Mobile. On the dame day and place, Col. Gabriel Jordan died.

Mrs. W. G. Hepburn, of Clayton, died Tuesday. She leaves a husband and two children. -Clayton Courier.

Mrs. Mercilla Walker, aged about 90 years, living near Eufaula, died on the 14th inst. Burial at Epworth Church.

Mr. Jas. Phillips died Saturday at Lawrenceville, (Ala.) aged 36 years. He leaves a wife and four or five children.

Mrs. Fannie T. Watts, relict of the late Thos. H. Watts, died in Eufaula on Saturday. Burial in Georgetown, (Ga.). She was a sister of Mrs. E. B. McCrary, of Eufaula, and Mrs. R. G. Morris, of Georgetown. She leaves three children, Mrs. Whitaker (a daughter by her first husband, Mr. Pittman), Miss Katie Watts, aged 15, and Tommie Watts, aged five or six years old.

Mr. Richard J. Yarrington, associate editor of the Advertiser died in Montgomery, (Ala.) on Wednesday, aged 53. He was a brother of Mrs. Green C. Beckham, of Eufaula.

Tues. Nov. 25, 1884

Miss Roxie Guilford, sister to Mr. Jno. Guilford, died

yesterday at the home of her brother in Quitman County, (Ga.).

Tues. Dec. 2, 1884

Mobile, Nov. 28. - Mrs. Ann T. Hunter, age 81, died here tonight. She was the daughter of Judge Harry Toulmin, of the old Mississippi territory.

Mr. W. W. Smart, age 45, living near Eufaula, died last Saturday. Survivors are a wife and several children.

Mr. Sidney Blair, of White Oak, (Barbour County) aged about 38, died on the 23rd last. He leaves a wife and four children.

Mr. Ralph Johnston, age 31, died at the home of his sister-in-law, Mrs. W. Y. Johnston, in Eufaula on last Sunday.

Mr. J. L. Barnes, of Americus, Ga., died here on the 28th inst., while visiting his son, Mr. Z. A. Barnes. He was born in North Georgia, Dec. 8, 1807. He leaves four sons and a daughter.

Mr. H. F. Russell, of Augusta, Ga., died there on the 12th inst. He leaves a large family.

Mrs. S. W. Anthony, *nee Marion Snipes, formerly of Eufaula, died on the 30th of Oct. last, at her home in Davilla, Milan County, Texas, of typhoid pneumonia. She was a sister of Mrs. Hattie Barkley and Mrs. S. A. Danforth, ** and an aunt to Mr. E. C. Bullock and Mrs. Maria Catteville, of Eufaula. *(Wife of Dr. Samuel Wesley Anthony, who was the son of Rev. Sam'l. Anthony, of Ga. Data given by Mrs. N. V. Grimsley, Stillwater, Okla., the granddaughter of Marion S. Anthony.) **(Correction: From 1860 Barbour Co., Ala. Census, Joshua H. Danforth).

Tues. Dec. 9, 1884

Mr. Jno. Gillis, aged 74, died at his home near Louisville, (Ala.) last Monday. He leaves a family. -Clayton Courier.

Mr. Henry, father of Jas. Henry, died at his son's home near Eufaula yesterday.

Miss Maggie Clark, many years a resident of Eufaula, died Sunday at the home of her sister, Mrs. Sellers, near Troy, (Ala.). She was a sister of Mrs. A. J. Carver, Sr. Burial in Troy.

The funeral of Miss Helena Cohen, whose death occurred in Americus, Ga., took place in Eufaula last Sunday.

Mr. Jas. D. Williford died recently and his remains were taken to Columbus, Ga., for burial, where he formerly lived and where two of his daughters now reside.

Mr. T. C. Johnson, aged 47, of Fla., formerly of this city, and brother to W. A. Johnson, died Sunday last.

Mr. J. J. Folsom died in Eufaula Wednesday. He leaves a wife and several children.

Tues. Dec. 16, 1884

Mrs. Elizabeth Smith, 106 years old, died near Abbeville, (Ala.) last Sunday. She was the mother of ten children.

Dr. W. W. Flewellen, of Columbus, Ga., died there on Monday, aged 75 years. Burial in Columbus.

Mr. Jos. Catchings, of Quitman County, Ga., aged 86, died on the 10th inst., at the home of his son, F. E. Catchings. He was born in Greene County, Ga., in 1798, but since 1854 he had been a resident of Quitman County.

Tues. Dec. 23, 1884
Greensboro, Ala., Dec. 15. - Mrs. Theresa, wife of Sam G. Briggs, aged 66, was buried here today.

Mr. Mathew P. Blue, aged 60 years, and born and raised in Montgomery, died Saturday last.

Tues. Dec. 30, 1884
Rev. W. S. Ellison, D. D., minister of the M. E. Church, died on the 26th at his home in Clayton, aged about 80 years.

Dr. W. A. Walker, of Hatchchubbee, Russell County, (Ala.) died on Tuesday last, aged about 56 years.

THE EUFAULA WEEKLY BULLETIN

1884

Wed. Jan. 2, 1884
Mr. W. B. Langdon, a resident of Columbus, (Ga.) for fifty years, died in that city recently.

Mr. H. T. Long, formerly of Auburn, Ala., died recently in Greenville, Texas.

The death of Capt. Frank Webb, coal merchant of near Tuscaloosa, (Ala.) occurred on Monday.

Wed. Jan. 9, 1884
Mr. Jas. Davidson, aged 73, of Montgomery, died on Sunday last.

Mr. Jno. C. Moore, aged 71, died yesterday at Hawkinsville in Barbour County. He was from Madison, Ga., and had been living in this county since 1865-66. He was the father-in-law of Mr. Croff. Cox, of Eufaula, and of Dr. J. T. Battle, of this county. Burial in Eufaula.

Mr. Alexr. Ross, carriage and wagon manufacturer of Opelika, died on the 29th. He was a younger brother of Mr. Jas. Ross, of Eufaula. -Opelika (Ala.) Times.

Wed. Jan. 16, 1884
Hon. Phillip Phillips died at his home in Washington on Monday. He represented Mobile in Congress from 1853-55. He had resided in Washington for a number of years. Burial in Savannah, Ga., at Laurel Hill Cemetery.

Mr. Jas. H. Garner, merchant of Ozark, (Ala.) died on the 9th inst.

Also, Mr. Wm. Judah, an old citizen of Dale, died recently.

Mrs. W. J. Stanley died near Newton, (Ala.) on the 7th inst. -Ozark (Ala.) Star.

Mrs. Charlotte Welch, aged about 68, died at her home in Quitman County, Ga., on Thursday.

Wed. Jan. 23, 1884
Mrs. Herschel V. Jackson, wife of Ex-Gov. Jackson, of Georgia, died at her home in Louisville, Ga., on last Monday.

The death of Geo. W. Heath, of Americus, Ga., occurred last Friday.

Hon. W. R. Spear, lawyer of Mississippi, and editor of the Vicksburg Herald, died last Saturday.

The death of S. A. Rogers, a young citizen of Norfolk, Va., occurred last Sunday.

Mr. Urban L. Weston, until recently one of the proprietors of the Dawson (Ga.) Journal, died at that place last Monday.

Wed. Feb. 6, 1884
Mr. Wm. Young Johnston, age about 39, died in Eufaula yesterday. Survivors are his wife and four children. Burial in Eufaula.

Wed. Feb. 20, 1884
Judge Benijah Smith Bibb, of Montgomery, died there on Sunday. He was born in Elbert County, Ga., Sept. 30th, 1796. In 1819 he married Miss Sophia Gilmer, sister of Gov. Gilmer, of Georgia, who survives him. Member of the M. E. Church. -Montgomery (Ala.) Advertiser.

Mr. Alec. Reddick, an old citizen of Pike County, (Ala.) died on the 8th inst.

Wed. Feb. 27, 1884
Miss Ella Methvin, age 22, died Monday at the home of her father, Mr. W. T. Methvin, in Clay County, Ga.

Wed. Mar. 19, 1884
Mr. Jno. G. Abercrombie, age 63, died at his home in Russell County, (Ala.) on last Monday.

Wed. Mar. 26, 1884
Jno. Jay Cisco, age 79, banker of New York City, died on Monday.

Wed. Apr. 2, 1884
Mrs. Mary Lawson Smith, wife of Col. Milton A. Smith, died in Henry County, Ala., on Mar. 22nd. She was born in Houston County, Ga., Sept. 28, 1834; joined the M. E. Church in 1858. Burial at White Oak Church in Barbour County.

Mrs. Eliza Pierce, age 60, widow living in the western part of Randolph County, Ga., died Sunday. Burial at Sharon Church.

Mr. Wm. Taylor, livery stable man of Eufaula, died yesterday at the home of his mother in Cuthbert, Ga.

Wed. Apr. 9, 1884
Mr. Neal D. McNeill, who lived in Pike County, (Ala.) near Perote for many years, died on Mar. 14th last at the home of his son-in-law, Mr. Wm. F. Haywood, Montgomery County, N. C. Burial at Sharon Church in that county.

Wed. Apr. 16, 1884
Jno. B. Patron, once speaker of the Mexican House of Delegates, one of the richest men in the territory, was assassinated on Saturday by a cowboy.

The death of Mr. Wm. Landsberg, of Macon, Ga., occurred on Monday.

Ex-Gov. Jno. M. Gregory, aged 80, of Virginia, died at Charles City on Wednesday last. He was the Governor of Va. in 1842.

Wed. Apr. 23, 1884
Hon. J. H. McDonald, Judge of Probate for Lawrence County, (Ala.) died Thursday.

Wed. Apr. 30, 1884
The death of Mr. Armstead Gove, living in the Red Hill
District of Stewart County, Ga., occurred on Apr. 22. The
survivors are his wife and several children.

Rev. J. Ellis, Episcopal minister, died suddenly in Atlanta
last Tuesday.

Maj. W. P. Vanderveer, an old citizen of Montgomery, and
for many years a member of the First Baptist Church, died Sunday.
He leaves a family.

Mr. Albertus Johnson, age about 34, son of Mrs. A. J. Gaston,
by her first husband, died Tuesday at his mother's home near
Eufaula. He leaves a wife, but no children.

Wed. May 7, 1884
Capt. Willis O'Brannon, master of the steamer, "Mary",
plying the Alabama River, died at Selma on board the boat on
Saturday last.

J. H. Nettles, Esq., of Montgomery, died in that city on
last Sunday.

Mrs. Z. A. Crumbley, age 86, died at her home in Quitman
County, Ga., on Tuesday last. She was the mother of Hon. J. J.
Crumbley.

Mr. W. H. McCrany, of Dale County, (Ala.) accidently shot
and killed himself a few days since. He leaves a wife and three
children.

Wed. May 14, 1884
Mr. Jos. Carter, living near Madison, Fla., died on last
Sunday.

Col. Jno. A. Tyson, an old citizen of Fort Deposit, in
Lowndes County, Ala., died last Sunday.

Wed. May 21, 1884
Chas. O'Conor, retired lawyer of Nantucket, Mass., died
about May 12th. He was a native of New York City, born in 1804,
the son of an Irishman, a member of the Catholic faith.

Miss Willie Russell, aged about 18, daughter of Dr. W. A.
Russell, of Batesville, (Barbour County) died on Friday of
typhoid pneumonia. On Wednesday her younger sister, aged about
16, died of the same disease.

Mr. Chas. Anderson, an aged citizen of Dale County, (Ala.)
died recently at his home in Skipperville. Burial at Salem
Church. A few days after Mr. Anderson's death, his aged widow
was buried by his side.

Wed. June 4, 1884
Edwin A. Cameron, a young man of Baldwin County, Ala. was
assassinated on last Saturday. -Mobile (Ala.) Register.

Rt. Rev. Benj. Bosworth Smith, the oldest Episcopal Bishop
in the country, died in New York City on Saturday last. He was
born at Bristol, R. I., June 13, 1794.

Mrs. Caroline Reese, age about 60, widow of the late J. W.
Reese, died Monday at the home of her brother, Mr. J. F. Martin,
living near Spring Hill in Barbour County. Burial at Anderson-
ville, Ga.

Wed. June 11, 1884

Jas. Watson Webb, a veteran editor of New York, died on
last Saturday.

Wed. June 18, 1884

The death of Wm. Houck, farmer of Newcomerstown, Ohio,
occurred on Monday last.

Rev. Alexr. J. Baird, D. D., age 60, minister of Cumberland
Presbyterian Church, died suddenly at a New York hotel on Sunday
last. He was on his way to attend the Presbyterian Alliance at
Belfast, Ireland. Burial at Nashville, Tenn.

Wed. June 25, 1884

Mr. Jas. M. Gay, a young man living near Blakely, Ga., died
yesterday. He had been married only a few months. Survivors are
his wife, mother, sister, and two brothers. -Early County (Ga.)
News.

Mr. J. W. T. Catchings, aged 60, of Clay County, Ga., died
yesterday.

Geo. W. Hamans, of Irwin County, Ga., died on the 7th inst.

Wed. July 2, 1884

Mrs. Garlington Lucas, aged 65, of near Hilliardsville, in
Henry County, (Ala.) died on the 30 ult. Burial at Liberty
Church.

Wed. July 23, 1884

Mrs. Caroline E. Brown, mother of Artemus Ward, died in
Waterford on July 12th. She was born in the same town in Sept.
1806, the daughter of Calvin Farrar. She married the late Maj.
Levi Brown, and had two sons, Cyrus W. Brown, well known writer,
and Chas. F. Brown, better known as Artemus Ward. -Portland (Me.)
Argus.

Mr. Jos. D. Adams, age about 24, of Quitman County, Ga.,
died on Monday last. He leaves a wife and infant son.

Mr. M. C. Bell, of Barbour County, died on Wednesday. He
had lived at White Oak, but had recently moved to a point between
Clayton and Louisville, (Ala.). (The Clayton Courier Sat. July
18, 1884: Mr. M. C. Bell buried in Clayton.)

Wed. July 30, 1884

Mr. Moses Lemle, merchant of Opelika, (Ala.) died on last
Wednesday.

Mrs. A. A. Janney, of Montgomery, died at her home in that
city on Monday last.

Mrs. A. M. Patterson, aged about 60, died on the 25th inst.,
at the home of her son-in-law, Mr. Walter Bates, near Batesville,
(Ala.) Burial in Americus, Ga., her old home.

Wed. Aug. 13, 1884

Mrs. G. S. Cox, aged about 60, mother of Mrs. Wm. Smitha,
of Eufaula, died Saturday.

EUFAULA WEEKLY TIMES AND NEWS

1885

W. D. Jelks, Proprietor.

Tues. Jan. 6, 1885

J. W. Martin, railroad agent at Decatur, (Ala.) the oldest
agent on the road, died Monday.

Mrs. Sion L. Hill, an aged widow, died at the home of her
son-in-law, Mr. Q. C. Hunter, of this place on the 25th inst.
-Ozark Star, of 31st.

Mrs. Rosa Wood, aged 80, died Sunday last at Lawrenceville,
Henry County, (Ala.).   She was the mother of Mr. Green Wood, Mrs.
Geo. Searcy, and Mr. W. H. Wood, of Troy.

Capt. B. A. Berry, of Columbus, Ga., died in that city on
Monday last.

Tues. Jan. 13, 1885
Mr. Ananias Averett died at his home in Daleville, (Ala.)
on the 28th of Dec. last. -Ozark (Ala.) Star, 7th.

Mrs. Ramsey Sims died at her home in Newton on Sunday last,
leaving a husband and two daughters. -Ozark (Ala.) Star.

M. Alleck Goolsby was killed in a cyclone in Macon County,
Ala., on Sunday. He was a brother of Mrs. John Sheally, of
Eufaula.

Mr. S. Lee Terrell, an old citizen of Stewart County, Ga.,
died Sunday last.

Tues. Jan. 20, 1885
Miss Lizzie W. Thomas, of Atlanta, Ga., who was attending
school at Orange Courthouse, Va., died on Tuesday from burns she
received when her clothing caught fire.

Mr. J. Harrison Faulk, age about 34, and unmarried, of near
Clayton, was accidentally killed on the 15th inst.

Tues. Jan. 27, 1885
Mr. Thos. W. Perry, age about 38, and unmarried, died at
his home near Seale, Russell County, last Monday.

Tues. Feb. 10, 1885
Mrs. J. B. Warren died at her home Friday. Survivors are
her husband and children. -Clayton Courier.

Mr. Jno. Fondren, an aged citizen of Henry County, died
near Abbeville, (Ala.) last Tuesday.

Dr. C. B. Lampley, brother of the lamented Col. Harris D.
Lampley of Barbour County, died at his home in Greenville.
-Ozark (Ala.) Star, 4th inst.

Rev. Jno. Foster, son of Rev. Gordon Foster, of Tuskegee,
died at his father's home in that place on the 5th inst.

Mrs. F. M. Blackwell, age about 60, died near Eufaula last
Sunday.

Col. Robt. G. Ricks died in Eufaula yesterday. He was born
in Halifax, N. C. on the 24th of July 1808, and had lived in
Clay County, Ga. about 40 years, until his recent removal to
Eufaula. Burial at the Ricks burying ground on the old Ricks
plantation in Clay County, Ga. Survivors are his wife and
several children.

Tues. Feb. 17, 1885
Mrs. T. C. Helms, aged 95, died at Louisville, Ala., on the
14th inst.

Miss Eugenia Haygood, daughter of Mr. and Mrs. A. W. Haygood, of Fort Gaines, Ga., died on the 8th inst.

Tues. Feb. 24, 1885
Mr. Cicero A. Sanders died Feb. 11th, 1885 at Cochran Station in Barbour County, Ala. He was born Aug. 30th, 1860. Survivors are his wife, one child, his parents, a brother and three sisters.

Mr. W. J. Howard, aged 58, of Russell County, died on Tuesday last at his home near Seale. His wife survives him.

Tues. Mar. 3, 1885
Mr. Ollie Root, late of Prattville, Ala., died in Birmingham on Tuesday last.

Mrs. Archey McEachern died Wednesday, leaving a husband and three children. -Clayton Courier.

Mr. U. W. Wilkes, an aged citizen of Barbour Countu, died at the home of his son-in-law, Mr. J. P. Price, at Star Hill, on Sunday last. -Clayton Courier.

Ex-Gov. R. M. Patton, age 77, died at his home in Florence, Ala., on Saturday last. Burial in Huntsville.

Mrs. Elizabeth Broffhy, age 45, a sister of Mr. Sandy McCarroll, of Barbour County, died on Friday last. Burial at White Oak.

Col. Jos. Clisby, age 67, died Thursday at his home at Vineville, near Macon, Ga. He was a brother of Jno. Clisby, of Verbena, Ala., and an uncle of Mr. L. Clisby, of Eufaula.

Tues. Mar. 10, 1885
Mrs. Alex McCoy, living near Abbeville, died on the 3rd inst. -Abbeville (Ala.) Times.

Mr. E. D. Thomas, age 51, of Jernigan, Russell County, (Ala.) died on Tuesday last.

Tues. Mar. 17, 1885
Mrs. P. A. Butts, of Cox's Mill Beat, Barbour County, died in Atlanta where she had gone for treatment. Burial near her home on Friday. -Clayton Courier.

Mr. Elijah Kirkland, age 35, who had just moved from Holmes County, Fla., to Henry County, (Ala.) died near Abbeville last Tuesday. Survivors are his wife and three children.

Mrs. W. A. Lewis, of Barnes's Cross Roads died a few days ago. -Ozark (Ala.) Star, 11th inst.

Hon. F. A. Nisbet, age 70, died last Saturday at his home in Oswichee, Russell County, (Ala.).

Gen. Pat. McIntyre died at his home in Eufaula yesterday.

Mrs. Lou Thomas, age 48, relice of the late Elliot Thomas, died at her home in Eufaula on Tuesday last.

Tues. Apr. 7, 1885
Mr. Jos. Whatley died last Monday. Burial at Judson Church. -Abbeville (Ala.) Times, 3rd.

Mr. Mart Hutto, farmer, living near Abbeville, died last Monday. Burial at Sardis Church. -Abbeville (Ala.) Times.

Mrs. Geo. P. Raney, nee Fannie Heath, formerly of Tuskegee, died in Texas recently, a bride of about a year. The mother of Geo. P. Raney, of near Cliett's Station, (Ala.) died last

Thursday. -<u>Montgomery Advertiser</u>, 3rd.

Col. Ed. S. Ott, age 70, died Thursday at his home near Batesville, Barbour County. Burial in Eufaula.

Mrs. Chas. Redmon, age about 45, died near Eufaula on Tuesday last. Survivors are her husband and children.

Mrs. Annie S., wife of Mr. Bridges Smith, of the <u>Macon Telegraph and Messenger</u>, died at her home in Macon, Ga., last Tuesday. Survivors are her husband and three children.

Mr. Jas. J. Henry, age about 30, unmarried, living at Hoboken (near Eufaula) died Friday.

Tues. Apr. 14, 1885
    Col. H. M. Tompkins, age 81, died recently. -<u>Clayton Courier</u>, Apr. 11th.

Ex-Judge Wyatt G. M. Gholson died Monday at his home in Prattville, Autauga County. (Ala.).

Mrs. Jno. S. Faulk, of Dale County, died at her home in Skipperville a few days ago. -<u>Ozark</u> (Ala.) <u>Star</u>, 15th inst.

Mr. Jas. P. Hamrick, an old citizen of Dale County, died at his home on the 5th inst. -<u>Ozark Star</u>, 15th inst.

Mr. Jas. T. Brown, age about 50, a grocery merchant of Eufaula, died at his home here yesterday. He was born in S. C. and came to Eufaula from Macon, Ga. about 1868-69. He was a printer by profession and was connected with the <u>Bluff City Times</u> and the <u>Eufaula Daily Times</u>. He married Miss Lizzie McLeod four or five years ago, who survives him.

Tues. Apr. 28, 1885
    Mr. Wm. H. Telfair, yard-master of the L. & N. Railroad at Pensacola, was accidently killed on Monday last. He was married to the second daughter of R. M. Williamson, Esq., of Montgomery. -<u>Montgomery Advertiser</u>, 21st.

Mrs. F. M. Summerlin died at Batesville, Barbour County, on the 25th inst. Survivors are her husband and daughter.

Dr. Jno. F. Shepherd, of Daleville, Ala., died at his home on Sunday.

Mr. Reuben Atwell, age about 54, of near Enon Church in Quitman County, Ga., died Tuesday last. Burial at Enon M. E. Church. His wife died several years ago. Survivors are his six children.

Mr. Rowland Kettleman, age 22, from New York, died in Eufaula on Wednesday. His sister, Mrs. Katie Bradt, of New York, reached here a few days before his death. Burial in New York.

Mr. Chris. Cooper, age about 35, of Quitman County, Ga., died Saturday. Survivors are his wife and three or four children.

Tues. May 5, 1885
    Mrs. E. P. Petty, formerly of Barbour County, died in Arkansas recently.

Tues. May 19, 1885
    Mrs. S. J. Norton, wife of Mr. Thos. Norton, died at the home of her parents, Mr. and Mrs. Norman McCraney, on Sunday last. -<u>Clayton Courier</u>.

Col. Macimillian Bethune Wellborn, age 60, died Friday in

Eufaula. He came to Eufaula in 1835 with his father, Col. M. B. Wellborn. In 1857 he married Miss Emma J. Dent, the daughter of Maj. J. H. Dent, of Barbour County. Survivors are his wife, six sons and one daughter, Mrs. Warren F. Dent.

Mr. Andrew Jackson Ramsey, age about 52, died at the Hughuley boarding house in Eufaula yesterday, a citizen of the city for about 30 years, a brick mason by profession.

Tues. May 26, 1885
Mrs. Matilda Grissett, age 65, wife of Dan'l. M. Grissett, living near Clayton, died Wednesday. She was a member of the Primitive Baptist Church at Antioch. She leaves a husband and three children. -Clayton Courier.

Mrs. Green Rabon, of Clopton, Dale County, died Thursday. -Ozark (Ala.) Star, 20th inst.

The death of Rev. J. R. Reasoner, pastor of the First Presbyterian Church in Collinsville, (Ala.) occurred on the 21st.

Mrs. Annie Dawson Mitchell, wife of A. C. Mitchell, Jr., died in Eufaula on the 22d inst. She was Annie Dawson Snider, of Macon, Ga., married Apr. 30, 1884. Burial in Macon in Rose Hill Cemetery.

Tues. June 2, 1885
Mrs. Council Bush, of Barbour County, died Thursday. -Clayton Courier.

Mr. Jos. L. Perkins, ex-mayor of Selma, died Friday last.

The death of Ernest Louis Catteville, city clerk of Eufaula, occurred Wednesday. He was born in Pensacola, Fla., Dec. 28th, 1836. He moved with his parents to Eufaula in 1837. His father was a lace merchant from France. His mother died in Paris, France, when Louis was ten or twelve years old. Survivors are his wife, four daughters and two sons.

Tues. June 9, 1885
Maj. Henry Stokes, aged about 78, died at his home near Louisville, (Ala.) on Monday last. He leaves a wife and a number of children. -Clayton Courier.

Mrs. Sarah Rachels, aged 70, died Tuesday last at her home near White Oak, in Barbour County.

Tues. June 16, 1885
Mrs. Emily H. Tubman, age 91, of Augusta, Ga., died on the 9th inst. She was a native of Virginia, but moved to Augusta in 1818 from Ky.

Mrs. Anna Gorman, of Opelika, (Ala.) died Thursday.

Mr. Jno. Gibson, an old citizen of Dale County, died at his home in Newton on Tuesday. -Ozark (Ala.) Star, 11th.

Mr. Noah H. Paramore died at his home near Ozark last Wednesday. -Ozark (Ala.) Star, 11th.

Mr. J. C. Morrison, age 73, died at his home in Huntsville, Ala., on Sunday last. He was the father of Mr. Morrison of Clayton. -Clayton Courier.

Mr. H. C. Robinson, a former resident of Eufaula, died in northern Arkansas recently.

Prof. M. A. McNulty, Pres. of the South-west Georgia Male & Female College, in Dawson, Ga., died in that city Friday.

Mr. Frank Ashurst, age 26, and unmarried, died Sunday in Eufaula at his family residence. He was a native of Tallapoosa County, Ala., but came to Eufaula from Columbia, Henry County, two years ago. Survivors are his mother, sister and brother.

Tues. June 23, 1885
Lynchburg, Va., June 16. - Col. Jesse S. Burke, farmer, died at his home near Charlemond, Bedford County, last night.

Mrs. Elizabeth Howell, age 91, died at her home in Oak Level, Cleburne County, (Ala.) on the 8th inst. She was the mother of nine sons and five daughters, was a member of the M. E. Church for 75 years.

Mr. W. H. Barrow, age about 66, died in Eufaula on Wednesday.

Mrs. Geo. M. Allan died at Griffin, Ga., while visiting her sister, Mrs. Malcom McCoy. She was a sister of Mr. Chas. McDowell, of Eufaula. Burial in Eufaula.

Tues. June 30, 1885
Mr. Geo. McGee died at his home near Seale, Russell County, (Ala.) on the 17th inst.

Mr. A. J. Jones, railroad agent at Union Springs, (Ala.) died Saturday. Survivors are his wife and a large family of children.

Tues. July 7, 1885
Miss Donnie Clark, age about 25, daughter of Mr. Jonas Clark, died Wednesday at her father's home in Eufaula.

Mrs. W. W. McDaniel died at her home in Texasville, Barbour County, on the 28th. Survivors are her husband and five or six children.

Tues. July 14, 1885
Geo. Hardeman, farmer, died at his place in Oconee County, Ga., on last Friday.

Dr. Cicero Stovall, age about 43, of Glennville, in Russell County, Ala., died on the 12th inst. He was a brother of Mr. Geo. W. Stovall and a half brother of Mr. Jno. W. Roquemore. Survivors are his wife, a son, and a daughter.

Mrs. Fannie M. McDaniel, age 42, wife of Maj. W. W. McDaniel, of Henry County, (Ala.) died at her home on June 25th.

Tues. July 21, 1885
Mr. Wm. Norris, age 75, died on Sunday last at Selma, (Ala.) where he had been living for 59 years.

Mr. Jno. T. Barbour, an old merchant of Pine Level in Montgomery County, (Ala.) died on Friday of last week.

Mr. R. C. Keeble, wholesale grocery merchant of Selma, (Ala.) died on Tuesday.

Tues. July 28, 1855
Mr. Cyrus W. Phillips, an old citizen of Montgomery, died last Tuesday. Burial in Montgomery, (Ala.).

The funeral of Mr. W. H. Barrow, age 48, took place in Eufaula on the 22nd. He leaves five children, Mrs. Malone of Otho is a daughter.

Jas. H. Braswell, Treasurer of Choctaw County, (Ala.) died on the 18th inst.

Thurs. Aug. 4, 1885

Mr. Geo. Ross, age about 55, planter of Lowndes County, (Ala.) died at his home near Calhoun on Tuesday. Survivors are his wife and two or three daughters.

Dr. M. D. Cannon, age 83, of Perry County, Ala., died at his home in Marion on last Wednesday.

The funeral of Capt. P. A. Sapp, age nearly 52, took place yesterday. He was a native of Burke County, Ga. He married Miss Julia Baker, a sister of Gen. Alpheus Baker, and the late Dr. Paul DeLacy Baker. Survivors are his son, Wm. Everitt Sapp, of Eufaula.

Thos. A. Terry, of Henry County, (Ala.) died on the 25th ult. -Abbeville (Ala.) Times, 31st inst.

Mrs. Louis Miller, age over 87, died at her home near Rocky Mount in Barbour County, recently. Survivors are her husband and several daughters.

Mrs. W. C. Brooks, of Rutledge, formerly of Abbeville, (Ala.) died last Saturday. Interment in Georgia.

Tues. Aug. 11, 1885

Atlanta, Ga., Aug. 6. - Geo. P. Humphries, architect, died today from an accident near his home.

Dr. J. C. Mosely, of Geneva County, (Ala.) died last week. -Ozark (Ala.) Star, 5th inst.

Dr. Geo. M. Bobbitt, age about 35, dentist of Eufaula, died on Saturday. Survivors are his wife and one child.

Mrs. Mary A. Lang, an aged citizen of Barbour County, died at the home of her son, Hon. Jas. Lang, of Louisville, on Friday. Burial at Louisville.

Mr. W. H. Johns, planter of Ward's Station, Ga., died last Sunday. He formerly lived in Clayton.

Mr. T. M. Johns, age about 70, merchant and planter of Bullock County, (Ala.) died near his home at Pine Grove on Friday last.

Col. Jos. A. Woodward, age 80, of Talladega, (Ala.) died recently. For many years he was prominent in South Carolina politics, and was a member of Congress from the Abbeville District.

Tues. Aug. 18, 1885

Col. Thos. Dodamead, age 68, R. R. Superintendent of Richmond, Va., died there on Friday.

Mr. Wm. E. Pond, deputy clerk of Muscogee Superior Court, died at his home at Columbus, Ga., on Sunday. -Columbus (Ga.) Enquirer Sun, 11th.

Mrs. Mary Ward, age 54, died Wednesday at the home of her nephew, Chas. L. Perry, in Eufaula.

Tues. Aug. 25, 1885

Mrs. Jno. Whiddon, of near Abbeville, died on the 15th inst. -Abbeville (Ala.) Times.

Tues. Sept. 1, 1885

Mrs. Scynthia Bobbitt, relict of the late Dr. G. M. Bobbitt, of Eufaula, died Sunday at the home of her parents, Mr. and Mrs. A. A. Crews, of near Clayton. She leaves a small daughter.

Burial in Eufaula.

Tues. Sept. 8, 1885
     Mr. R. M. Gunby, formerly of Columbus, Ga., died at his
home on last Thursday at Atlanta, Ga.

     Dr. J. P. Holmes, dentist of Macon, Ga., died last Wednesday
at Vineville, (Ga.).

Tues. Sept. 15, 1885
     Mr. J. W. Bickley, age 60, of near Columbus, Ga., died
recently.

     Mr. Mathew Fenn, age 88, died at his home near Clayton on
last Monday.

     Mrs. Julius Malone, wife of Rev. Malone, of Judson in Henry
County, (Ala.) died recently. She leaves a large family of
children.

     Mrs. Dudley Sheppard, of Union Springs, (Ala.) died on
Monday last.

     Mr. Edward M. Holloway, of Dallas County, (Ala.) died last
Tuesday.

     Mrs. Jno. A. Davidson, of Stewart County, Ga., died last
Tuesday.

Fri. Sept. 25, 1885
     Col. Jas. N. Lightfoot, age about 47, died at his home in
Eufaula on Thursday. Survivors are his wife, a son, Lawrence, a
daughter, and a step-daughter, Mollie McAllister. Burial in
Abbeville, Ga.

     Mr. Henry Benton, age about 33, died at his mother's home
in Eufaula yesterday.

     Hon. J. L. F. Cottrell, formerly of Lowndes County, Ala.,
died recently at his home at Cedar Keys, Fla.

     Mrs. Elizabeth J. Patton, wife of Dr. J. O. Patton, died in
Montgomery on last Tuesday.

Fri. Oct. 2, 1885
     Mr. Christopher Tompkins, age 74, of Hector, Bullock County,
died on the 24th inst. He had been a citizen of Alabama for
over fifty years.

     Mr. J. T. Smith, Jr., age 29, living near Eufaula, died
Wednesday. Burial at Midway Church, in Russell County.

     Judge G. T. Yelverton and Capt. M. Kimmey died within the
last few days in Coffee County, (Ala.).

     Mrs. Willie Price, living near Clayton, died on Tuesday.

     Mrs. Mollie Faulk, wife of F. M. Faulk, of Elamville,
(Barbour County) died Tuesday last. She had been married about
a year.

Fri. Oct. 9, 1885
     Mrs. Mary Sherry, age about 58, wife of Mr. Jas. Sherry,
died at her home in Hoboken, near Eufaula, last Wednesday.
Survivors are her husband and son. Burial from the Catholic
Church.

     Mr. B. F. Morris, age about 30, died on Saturday at his
home in Georgetown, Ga. He was the son of Col. R. G. Morris.

Mrs. D. Dabney, age 90, died at her home in Montgomery on the 1st inst.

Fri. Oct. 16, 1885

Mrs. E. B. Thompson, of Marion, (Ala.) died on the 13th.

Mr. Emory Ketchens, age about 40, living in Quitman County, Ga., died Wednesday.

Mrs. Laura Holt, age about 40, died in Eufaula Friday. She was a sister of Sheriff G. T. Long. Survivors are her husband and three children.

Mr. Elijah Payne, for many years a citizen of Dale County, (Ala.) died last Saturday. -Ozark (Ala.) Star, 7th.

Mr. Henry Blackwood died in Geneva, (Ala.) last Saturday. -Ozark (Ala.) Star, 7th inst.

Fri. Oct. 23, 1885

Mr. A. T. Grady, an old citizen of Bullock County, died in Union Springs, (Ala.) last Wednesday at the home of his son, Mr. R. J. Grady.

Col. Geo. W. Davenport died at his home near Preston, Ga., on Saturday. He one time filled the office of Ordinary of Webster County. -Americus (Ga.) Recorder, 18th.

Dr. W. J. Stanford, who moved from Henry County, (Ala.) with his family to Texas last winter, died recently. His wife and two children preceded him in death only a few months. Just before the doctor left for the West he lost two of his children by death, and now there are only three surviving members of what was a little over a year ago, a family of nine.

The death of Jno. W. Raborn occurred near Columbia, Ala., last Friday.

Mrs. Mart Hutto, age about 45, widow of M. V. Hutto, died at her home near Pleasant Grove Church Wednesday. She leaves three boys and one girl. -Abbeville (Ala.) Times.

Rev. Dr. J. W. Jones, age 80, of Shelby County, Ala., died recently.

Jr. Jas. Perry, age 60, of Butler County, (Ala.) died on Thursday.

Fri. Oct. 30, 1885

Mr. Eli Bolton, age 85, died at his home near Clio, Ala., on Friday last. -Clayton Courier.

Mr. Jno. McGehee, an aged citizen of Rutlege, Butler County, (Ala.) died Wednesday.

Fri. Nov. 6, 1885

Dr. Jno. Purifoy, of Mt. Meigs, Montgomery County, (Ala.) died on Tuesday last.

Mr. Mark Rigell died at his home in South Fla. about the 14th inst. -Ozark (Ala.) Star.

Mr. B. W. Barnett, an old citizen of Union Springs, (Ala.) died Wednesday last.

Fri. Nov. 13, 1885

Greensboro, (Ala.) Nov. 5. - Mr. Alex. H. Williams, aged about 46, died today. He was editor and proprietor of the Greensboro Watchman.

Mr. Alex. Frazer, age about 70, of Auburn, (Ala.) died on
Tuesday.

Mr. Sampson Darden, of Tuscaloosa County, (Ala.) died last
Saturday.

Fri. Nov. 20, 1885
Rev. Thos. Tabb, of Marion, (Ala.) died on Saturday last.

Mrs. Lucy A. Johnson, of Montgomery, died in that city on
Monday.

Mr. Henry E. Williamson, Sr., died last Friday at the home
of his son-in-law, Mr. E. J. Black, in Eufaula. He was born in
Sampson County, N. C., Mar. 12, 1818. He moved with his parents
while young to Jones County, Ga., where he was raised, and in
early manhood he removed to Talbotton and conducted a large
carriage repository. He came to Eufaula in 1872. Survivors
are four sons and one daughter.

Mr. Wm. A. Grantham, of Greenwood, Fla., formerly of Henry
County, Ala., died on the 7th inst.

Mrs. Fannie Evarts, age 45, died Friday in Eufaula at the
home of her father, Mr. Jonas Clark. She leaves two children.

Thurs. Nov. 26, 1885
Col. Marcus A. Bell, of Atlanta, died at his home in that
city on Tuesday last.

Mrs. Joseph Dill died at her home in Talladega, (Ala.) on
Monday last.

Mrs. Elizabeth Stephens, age 65, died Saturday last at
Milton, Fla., at the home of her daughter, whither she had gone
to visit. She was the mother of Messrs. Calvin J. and Henry R.
Stephens, of Eufaula.

Thurs. Dec. 3, 1885
Mr. R. W. DeBardleben died at his home in Montgomery on
Monday.

Mr. F. E. Reese, of Demopolis, (Ala.) died on Sunday.

Rev. Julius Phillips, an aged Methodist preacher, died at
his home in Seale (Russell County, Ala.) last Sunday.

Mrs. Eliza D. Walker, widow of LeRoy Pope Walker, died at
her home in Huntsville, (Ala.) last Thursday.

Thurs. Dec. 10, 1885
Mr. H. C. A. Smith, age 75, died at his home in Lee County,
(Ala.) on Monday last.

Hon. Joshua Prout Coman, an old citizen of Athens, (Ala.)
died last Thursday.

The death of Mr. M. Gusdorf, cotton and commission merchant
of Selma, (Ala.) occurred on Friday.

Thurs. Dec. 24, 1885
Mr. Archibald Campbell Wise, coroner of Barbour County,
died at the home of his sister-in-law, Mrs. Mary A. Barnett, in
Eufaula. He was born in Edgefield Dist., S. C. on Mar. 13th,
1804. He came to Barbour County in 1836, to Clayton, where he
had a drug store for a number of years. He married on Oct. 6th,
1853 to Mrs. Elmira D. Martin, who survives him.

Mr. and Mrs. David Fuller, of near Camp Hill in Tallapoosa

County, (Ala.) died in a few days of each other. They were
married Jan. 14th, 1817, and had lived together sixty-nine years.
-Opelika (Ala.) Times.

Thurs. Dec. 31, 1885
The death of Rev. Jno. R. Elmore occurred near Clayton,
Indiana, on Christmas Day.

Mrs. Willie C. Jelks, age 28, died at her home in Atlanta,
Ga., on Dec. 25th. She was Miss Willie Cowan, of Eufaula, and
married Mr. R. C. Jelks, of Atlanta on Jan. 18, 1883. She leaves
three sisters, Mrs. R. A. Fleming, Union Springs; Mrs. W. H.
Denson, of Gadsden; and Mrs. J. M. Buford, of Atlanta, and her
brother, Mr. J. G. Cowan, of Abbeville, Ala.

Mrs. A. A. Madden, widow living in Lee County, (Ala.) died
on Monday. She leaves five children.

Mrs. Hannah Pierce, age about 35, wife of Mr. Jno. Pierce,
of Stewart County, Ga., died Christmas night last.

Mrs. Stallings, nee Miss Ella McAllister, daughter of A. M.
McAllister, of Barbour County, died at her home in Greenville,
Ala., on Thursday last.

Mrs. Joe N. Haley died at Saffold, Early County, Ga., on
Thursday last. Survivors are husband and baby girl.

EUFAULA DAILY TIMES

1886

Fri. Jan. 1, 1886
Rev. Dr. Robt. Nall, aged 80, Presbyterian minister, died
last Tuesday in Jackson, Tenn. He was for fifty years Clerk of
the Synod of Alabama, and for over twenty years pastor at Mobile.

Sat. Jan. 2, 1886
Mr. Jas. Byrd, of Lee County died at his home in Browneville
on Thursday last. His wife died about three months ago. Four
little orphan children are left.

Tues. Jan. 5, 1886
Mrs. Emma Sholes, aged 35, daughter of Mr. Delaware Morris,
and widow living with Mr. Milton Smith, near Eufaula, died last
Sunday.

The death of Robt. T. Hoyt, merchant of Rome, Ga., occurred
last Sunday.

Mrs. Kate Beebe, wife of Mr. Eugene Beebe, of Montgomery,
died suddenly Saturday.

Wed. Jan. 6, 1886
Mrs. Epsey S. Lewis, aged 67, died at her home near White
Pond, in Barbour County, on last Monday. She leaves ten children.
Burial at White Pond.

Thurs. Jan. 7, 1886
Col. A. J. Lane died at his home in Sparta, Ga., on Saturday last.

Mrs. Kate Williamson, of Hayneville, (Ala.) died on Monday
last.

Mr. Jas. F. Wood, farmer of Autauga County, (Ala.) who
lived near Benton, died suddenly in Selma on Monday.

Hon. Wm. J. Smith died at his home near Batesville, Autauga County, (Ala.) on Monday last.

Mrs. Harriet M. Bennett, widow of the late Col. Jas. Bennett, died at her home near Shorterville, (Henry County) a few days ago. She leaves several sons and daughters.

Sat. Jan. 9, 1886
Mr. Jason G. Jones, of Oak Grove, Montgomery County, died Thursday last.

Mr. Wm. McClenny, an aged citizen living near Headland, Ala., died on Friday last.

Mr. D. A. Day, aged about 65 years, was accidentally killed on Wednesday in Atlanta near Whitehall Street crossing by a train.

Tues. Jan. 12, 1886
W. B. Williams, age 72, died in Charleston, S. C. on Saturday. He was for many years a prominent cotton factor in that city.

Wed. Jan. 13, 1886
Hon. Benj. Conley died at his home in Atlanta on Sunday.

Thurs. Jan. 14, 1886
Mr. Ang. Lewis, of White Pond, (Barbour County) died at his home yesterday. Survivors are several children, and brothers, Geo. and Jas. Lewis.

The death of Mrs. Janet Allen occurred yesterday in Eufaula at the home of Geo. C. McCormick. The deceased was in her 79th year of age, and was the wife of the late Dr. G. L. Allen, of Eufaula. She was born May 1810 in Kilbarchan, Scotland, and was married to Dr. Geo. L. Allen of the same city, on Feb. 29, 1835. The couple took passage for America in 1840, and came direct to Eufaula, where she has resided since. She raised four children, Mr. Geo. M. Allen, deceased, Mrs. Beauchamp, Mrs. Geo. C. McCormick and Mrs. W. D. Danforth. She has been a life long member of the Presbyterian Church.

Fri. Jan. 15, 1886
Dr. M. P. Inge, of Tuscaloosa, (Ala.) died Wednesday.

Mr. Jno. Treutlen Berry died on the 14th inst., at the home of his brother, T. G. Berry, in Eufaula. He was born in Russell County, Ala., Mar. 21, 1861.

Col. Edmund Richardson, of New Orleans, died suddenly in Jackson, Miss., on the 11th inst., aged 73 years.

Sun. Jan. 17, 1886
Mr. M. C. Stokes, an old citizen of Montgomery, died Thursday.

Mr. Jas. Collins, son of Col. Hart Collins, died on the 12th in Texas. -Texarkana.

Tues. Jan. 19, 1886
Mrs. C. F. Fountain, wife of Rev. Fountain, pastor of the Baptist Church at Greenville, (Ala.) died on Saturday last.

Maj. Marion Banks, aged 72, of Tuscaloosa, (Ala.) died on Saturday.

Dr. Thos. A. Keene, of Danville, member of the House in the

Virginia Legislature, died last Saturday.

Wed. Jan. 20, 1886
 J. H. McKenna and Jonas Goodman were shot and killed at
Vicksburg, Miss., on Monday last.

Thurs. Jan. 21, 1886
 Mr. Daniel McKenzie, an old citizen of Barbour County, died
at his home in Louisville on Monday.

Fri. Jan. 22, 1886
 Mr. Jonathan M. Jones, living near Brewton, (Ala.) was
killed by a train last Wednesday.

 Maj. J. Butler Vaiden, of Marion, (Ala.) died on the 20th.

 Alice, the two year old daughter of Mr. and Mrs. A. L.
Raleigh, of Eufaula, died yesterday.

Tues. Jan. 26, 1886
 Mr. Sidney Abernathy, of near LaFayette, (Ala.) was killed
accidentally one day last week.

 T. T. Tyree, an old citizen of Mobile, died there last
Saturday. He leaves a wife, but no children.

Wed. Jan. 27, 1886
 Mrs. J. R. Horn, aged 45, of Clopton, Ala., died last
Sunday. She leaves quite a family of children.

Thurs. Jan. 28, 1886
 Mrs. O'Neal, wife of Judge Simon O'Neal, died at her home
in Seale, Russell County, Ala., on Tuesday last.

Fri. Jan. 29, 1886
 Rev. Dr. Evander McNair, pastor of the Presbyterian Church
in Eufaula during and just after the war of the States, died a
few days since in North Carolina.

 Hon. David R. Atchinson, of St. Joseph, Mo., died on the
27th inst., age 79.

Sun. Jan. 31, 1886
 Mr. H. H. Bush died at his home near Oateston, (Barbour
County) on Thursday last.

 Col. Vance Lamar, citizen of DeKalb County, (Ala.) was
killed at Valley Head on Thursday by a falling of a tree.

Tues. Feb. 2, 1886
 Mr. J. Wesley Thomas, age 72, who came to Eufaula in 1834,
and has resided here ever since, died Sunday at the home of his
son-in-law, in Macon, Ga. Burial in Eufaula. Survivors are
Mrs. Thomas and son, Green, and Mrs. Wynn, son-in-law and
daughter of the deceased.

 Hon. Neil S. Brown, aged 76, ex-Gov. of Tenn., died at his
home in Nashville last Saturday.

 Dr. I. N. Gorman, age 62, of Nashville, died on Friday.

Wed. Feb. 3, 1886
 Mr. Wash Harris, aged 72, of near Opelika, Ala., and who
was on his way from Texas to visit relatives, fell from the cars
in Louisiana last Monday and was killed.

 Ex-Chancellor Neil S. Graham, age 68, died at his home in

Tuskegee on Monday last.

Fri. Feb. 5, 1886
   Robt. Rauchenstein died in Mobile on Wednesday. He was the
surveyor of the Mobile & Ohio R. R.

Tues. Feb. 9, 1886
   Mrs. Marie A. Heidt, age about 50, wife of David Heidt, of
White Pond in Barbour County, died Sunday last. She was a
sister of Mr. Austin Cargill, of Eufaula, and the mother of four
children.

Wed. Feb. 10, 1886
   Mr. A. Roemer, an old citizen of Montgomery, Ala., died on
Sunday last.

   Mrs. W. P. Gary died at Harris (Barbour County) on Monday.
Survivors are her husband and children. Burial in Midway, Ala.

Thurs. Feb. 11, 1886
   Mrs. Rebecca Voluntine, aged 85, mother of Mr. Jas. Volun-
tine (Clayton, Ala.) and mother-in-law of Mr. Jno. Smithwich, of
Barbour County, died a day or two ago, aged 85 years.

   Eddie Culp died near Oak Grove Church on the 5th inst.
-Abbeville (Ala.) Age, 8th.

Fri. Feb. 12, 1886
   Antonio Baudine, the famous restaurant man of Troy, (Ala.)
died recently. He was a native of Rome, Italy.

   Mrs. L. S. Chitwood, aged about 40, of Oswichee, in Russell
County, Ala., died Monday. Survivors are her husband and six
children.

   Mr. Jno. C. Hickey, aged 49, died on the 10th inst., at his
home at Hoboken, (near Eufaula). Burial from the Catholic
Church. He is the fifth person of his family to have died within the last twelve or fifteen months, his surviving widow lost
her mother, father, brother, sister, and now her husband.

Sat. Feb. 13, 1886
   Mr. Jonathan Trimmel died near Hudspeth in Henry County,
(Ala.) where he had lived for 60 years. Had he lived until the
28th of Aug. next, he would have been 103 years old. (Wed. Feb.
17, 1886: Times: Mr. Trimmell, of Beat 13, died on Feb. 8th.)

   Mr. T. T. Smith, of Smithville, Henry County, Ala., died on
the 10th inst.

Sun. Feb. 14, 1886
   Mrs. Ellen Stone, an aged woman, and mother of Mr. Marshall
Stone, living near Otho, Henry County, (Ala.) died at the home
of her son on Friday last.

Wed. Feb. 17, 1886
   Mrs. Joseph Pippin died Tuesday near Hardwicksburg, (Henry
County, Ala.) leaving a husband and an infant.

Thurs. Feb. 18, 1886
   Mrs. Susan O. Smith, wife of Capt. Jno. G. Smith, died in
Birmingham yesterday. Capt. Smith was recently mayor of Eufaula.
Burial from the First Baptist Church in Eufaula. Survivors are
her husband and son, Albert, and a daughter, Miss Ollie Smith.

Fri. Feb. 19, 1886

Jno. Leveridge, lawyer, died at his home on Wednesday in New York City.

The funeral of Ex-Gov. Horatio Seymoor took place in Utica, N. Y. on Tuesday.

Sat. Feb. 20, 1886

The funeral of Mrs. Emma Bounds, wife of Rev. E. M. Bounds, of St. Louis, took place from the M. E. Church in Eufaula yesterday. She died at the home of her father, Dr. A. W. Barnett, of Eufaula on the 18th inst. Survivors are her husband and three children, two girls and a boy.

Sun. Feb. 21, 1886

Col. L. N. Whittle, lawyer of Macon, Ga., died in that city on Thursday last.

Mr. Geo. Troublefield, aged about 40, of near Eufaula, died on Friday last. He leaves a family.

Wed. Feb. 24, 1886

Mrs. John Tye, of Quitman County, Ga., sister of Mrs. W. J. Brown, of Eufaula, died on Thursday.

Mr. R. H. Wynn, aged about 65, died at his home near Louisville, Ala., on Sunday.

Dr. J. W. Hall, of Geneva, (Ala.) died suddenly on the 16th inst.

Thurs. Feb. 25, 1886

Dr. Monroe J. Warren, of Clopton, (Ala.) died recently.

Fri. Feb. 26, 1886

M. F. M. Rushton, aged about 60 years, and known as the "King of Merchants" in Rutledge, Crenshaw County, (Ala.) died on Thursday last.

Mr. Joshua Underwood, aged between 35 and 40 years, of Girard, Ala., died on Tuesday. He leaves a family.

Mr. B. A. Nance, of near Richmond, Va., died a few days ago. Survivors are his wife and seven grown children. One of his sons is a physician, and another is a lawyer. Mr. L. F. Nance of Midway, (Ala.) is a brother of the deceased.

Sat. Feb. 27, 1886

Mr. Jas. Lynch was drowned in the Tallapoosa River near Louina on Thursday.

Mr. W. C. Gimmer, Esq., of Dale County, Ala., died on Feb. 14th.

Sun. Feb. 28, 1886

Maj. Henry St. Paul, age 87, at one time the editor of the Mobile Times, died in New Orleans last Friday.

Mrs. J. H. Mathews, of Mobile, was burned to death while fighting fire near her home at Grand Bay, (Ala.). Her husband was a merchant and steamboat man of Mobile.

Thurs. Mar. 4, 1886

Dr. Egbert B. Johnston, Sr., aged about 60, died at his home in Eufaula yesterday. He leaves two children, Dr. E. B. Johnston, Jr., and Jno. Johnston. Interment at Tuskegee, Ala.

Fri. Mar. 5, 1886
    Rev. Dr. Samuel Ramsey Wilson, aged 68, Presbyterian minis-
ter, died in Louisville, Ky., on Wednesday.

    Richmond, Va., Mar. 3. - Mrs. J. P. Sampson was fatally
burned today at her home at Manchester. Her daughter, Miss
Bertha, is in a critical condition from burns.

Sat. Mar. 6, 1886
    Mrs. Abner Jones, an old citizen, died at Jones' Switch, in
Autauga County, Alabama, on last Monday.

    H. S. Park, aged 50, cotton dealer of Columbus, Ga., died
on Thursday last.

    Lieut. Josiah Chance, of the 17th Inf. U. S., died recently
at Trenton, Ohio. He was a brother to the Hon. Mahlon Chance,
of Ohio; Capt. Jesse Chance, and Mrs. Stanley Huntley. -N. O.
Times Democrat, Dec. 13.

Sun. Mar. 7, 1886
    Dr. Henry Mitchell Hunter, aged 78 years, died at his home
near Eufaula on Friday last. Interment in Eufaula. Survivors
are his wife of his second marriage, and his children and step-
children.

Tues. Mar. 9, 1886
    Mr. Albert Walden, 70 years of age, and a resident of
Barbour County for more than fifty years, died last Saturday.
Burial at Mount Pleasant Church. He was the father-in-law of
Commissioner Sam McCarroll.

Wed. Mar. 10, 1886
    Miss Pherrie Baker, age 17, oldest daughter of Gen. A. Baker,
late of Eufaula, died on the 9th inst., at Louisville, Ky.

Tues. Mar. 11, 1886
    Mrs. Clarke Christian died yesterday in Quitman County,
Georgia.

    Senator J. F. Miller, of Calif., died in Washington on
Monday from the effects of a wound received in the war.

Fri. Mar. 12, 1886
    Mrs. E. H. Locke, wife of Dr. E. H. Locke, of Troy, Ala.,
died yesterday at her home in that city.

    Mrs. Browne, wife of Hon. N. H. Browne, Judge of Probate
in Tuscaloosa County, (Ala.) died last Monday. She leaves six
little children.

    Capt. Chas. Blain, aged about 75, well known river man,
died in Columbus, (Ga.) on Wednesday.

Sat. Mar. 13, 1886
    Mrs. Caroline A. Smith, age 78, mother of "Bill Arp", the
Georgia humorist, died on Wednesday last.

    Mr. Jas. Field, of Girard, (Ala.) died on Thursday last.

Tues. Mar. 16, 1886
    Mrs. Florida Roper, of Red Level, (Ala.) died from burns
on Monday.

    Mr. Wm. Gugel, engineer on the train running between Macon
and Montgomery, the son of Mr. D. M. Gugel, of Macon, (Ga.) and
Mr. Jas. Lewis, of Montgomery were both killed Sunday in a train

accident.

Wed. Mar. 17, 1886
Mr. E. L. James, tax assessor of Lowndes County, died last Sunday.

Mrs. Geo. Bancroft, wife of the historian, died at her home in Washington on Monday last.

Mr. Hugh Dover, an old resident of Columbus, Ga., died on Monday last.

Fri. Mar. 19, 1886
Col. C. J. Cooper, an old merchant of Oxford, (Ala.) died on the 17th inst.

Mr. W. J. Herring, of Crawford, Russell County, Ala., died on Wednesday.

Mr. Patrick Whalan, aged 56, died at his home near Hatche-chubbee, Russell County, Ala., on the 17th. He leaves a wife, but no children.

Sat. Mar. 20, 1886
Miss Donie Wolf, daughter of Mr. R. W. Wolf, living near Shorterville, Henry County, (Ala.) died from burns received on the 16th inst.

Sun. Mar. 21, 1886
Ex-Gov. E. H. Moren, aged about 61, died at his home in Centerville, Bibb County, Ga., on the 19th inst.

Fri. Mar. 26, 1886
Mrs. M. L. LaCount, of Clayton, Ga., died recently. Survivors are her husband and two children.

Sat. Mar. 27, 1886
Nathaniel Hawkins, aged 91, of St. Clair County, (Ala.) fell dead at his stable door while feeding his stock.

A two year old child of Mr. Ed. Martin, near Eufaula, died Thursday in Union Springs, (Ala.). Burial at Bascom Church. Mr. Martin's wife died last year.

Thurs. Apr. 1, 1886
Mr. Nimrod Long, son of Mrs. Long, of Old Spring Hill, (Barbour County) died Tuesday last, in the 19th year of his age.

Mr. Jas. Mobly, of Henry County, (Ala.) died at his home near Smithville, on the 28th ult.

Rev. Abner H. Borders, aged 74, died in Atlanta, Ga., on Tuesday last. Interment in Clayton, Ala. He leaves two daughters, one of whom is now the wife of Chancellor Foster, and the other was the second wife of the late Rev. Stratton H. Paullin.

Fri. Apr. 2, 1886
Mrs. Elizabeth Miller, aged about 70, the widow of the late Lewis Miller, died at her home near Seale last Saturday.

Sun. Apr. 4, 1886
Dr. P. H. Mitchell, aged about 54, of Talbot County, Ga., died on Saturday last.

Wed. Apr. 7, 1886
Mr. Jno. Miller, an old citizen of Apalachicola, Fla., was

drowned near that place on Saturday last.

Fri. Apr. 9, 1886
    Mr. Jas. W. Johnston, a citizen of Union Academy Beat, Montgomery County, Ala., died on Monday last. He was in the prime of life.

Sat. Apr. 10, 1886
    Mrs. Howard, wife of Dr. T. C. Howard, of Girard, Ala., died on the 8th inst.

Tues. Apr. 13, 1886
    Hon. Arthur Hood, aged 62, died at his home in Cuthbert, Ga., on last Saturday.

Thurs. Apr. 15, 1886
    Mrs. Elizabeth Dubose, of Columbus, Ga., died Tuesday last. She was a sister of Mrs. E. S. Ott and an aunt to Mrs. A. H. Alston of Barbour County.

Fri. Apr. 16, 1886
    S. F. Moore, of Brownville, Lee County, (Ala.) died last Tuesday.

Sat. Apr. 17, 1886
    Mr. Daniel Fuller, of Montgomery County, Ala., died on the 15th inst.

Sun. Apr. 18, 1886
    Died on Monday last, Mr. J. R. McCraney, of Barbour County. Burial at Clayton.

Wed. Apr. 21, 1886
    Mr. Neil Munn, a citizen of Dale County, Ala., died on Friday last.

Sun. Apr. 25, 1886
    Mr. Isaac Hill died at his home in Notasulga, (Ala.) on Friday.

    Mr. W. Z. Pruitt died Wednesday last at Columbia, Henry County, (Ala.) leaving a wife and several small children. Burial in Harris County, Ga., the deceased's old home.

Tues. Apr. 27, 1886
    Mrs. Alexander Lamb died at her home in Russell County, (Ala.) on last Friday.

    Mr. W. J. Hodges, a farmer living near Atlanta, died on Sunday last.

Wed. Apr. 28, 1886
    Mr. John T. Cunningham died suddenly at his plantation in Macon County, (Ala.) on Sunday.

    Mr. Green B. Johnson, aged about 60, of Beat 14, and ex-deputy sheriff of Henry County, (Ala.) died at his home last Thursday. -Abbeville (Ala.) Age, of 27th.

    Mrs. Morris Nobles died near New Hope Church, near Abbeville, on the 20th inst. -Abbeville (Ala.) Age, of 27th.

Fri. Apr. 30, 1886
    Col. T. H. B. Rivers, age 75, of Glennville, (Ala.) died on the 28th.

Tues. May 4, 1886
    Mrs. M. E. Brown died on the 27th ult., at the home of her son-in-law, Mr. Jas. E. McCormick, at Louiville in Barbour County.

Wed. May 5, 1886
    Mrs. Rebecca Cole, aged about 55 years, died on the 3d inst. at the home of her son-in-law, Mr. Jas. Wash of Quitman Co., Ga. Deceased was a sister of the late Mrs. Wm. Doughtie, of Eufaula.

Fri. May 7, 1886
    Mr. David G. Judge, aged about 25, a lawyer of Greenville, Ala., died in that city on Tuesday. He was the son of the late Thos. J. Judge, of Montgomery.

Wed. May 12, 1886
    Dr. C. D. Parke, physician of Selma, (Ala.) died on last Saturday.
    Rev. Isaac U. Wilkes, of Brierfield, dropped dead in Montgomery on last Wednesday.

Thurs. May 13, 1886
    Mr. Robt. Thompson, aged about 50, living in Beat 13, died on Saturday last. (Barbour County).

Sat. May 15, 1886
    Mrs. Dr. N. J. Bussey, of Columbus, Ga., died last Thursday morning.

Sun. May 16, 1886
    Mrs. Alexander Smith, aged about 50, of Browneville, Lee County, Ala., died Friday last.
    Miss Kate Johnston, daughter of the late Maj. Leroy F. Johnston, died at the home of N. N. Curtis, in Columbus. The funeral took place from the Episcopal Church in Eufaula yesterday. Deceased was a sister to Mr. Young Johnston, of Eufaula, Principal of the public school.
    Robt. Gibson, of Macon, Mo., died recently. He was born in Randolph County, N. C., 1766, and was 121 years old. His first wife died in 1849, and his second wife in 1876. By the first wife he had sixteen children, thirteen of whom are still living, the eldest is 84 years old.

Wed. May 19, 1886
    Mr. A. D. Bayne, an aged citizen of LaFayette, (Ala.) died on Sunday last.

Sat. May 22, 1886
    Mr. M. W. Oliver, the oldest citizen of Perry County, (Ala.) died on Thursday.

Sun. May 23, 1886
    Dr. Dio Lewis, author, died at Yonker, N. Y. on Friday.
    A little daughter of Rev. J. O. Keener died in Selma on Friday.

Wed. May 26, 1886
    Mrs. J. B. Stanley, wife of Col. Stanley, editor of the Greenville Advocate, died at her home in Greenville, (Ala.) on Sunday last.

Fri. May 28, 1886

Mrs. Caroline Thompson, aged 61, widow of Col. W. T. Thompson, founder of the Savannah Morning News, died on Wednesday. She was Miss Corrie, of Augusta, and leaves a daughter and three sons.

Sun. May 30, 1886
Mr. Wm. Butler, of Greenwood, Fla., died last Friday at the home of his son-in-law, Capt. T. H. Moore, in Columbus, Ga. Interment in the family burying lot in Greenwood, where rest the remains of his wife and several children, three of whom lost their lives in the War of the States. Mr. Butler was the father of our townsman, Mr. A. C. Butler, now of Quitman County, Ga., and had he lived 'till next August, he would have been 83 years old, having been born in that month of 1803, in N. C. He removed to Harris County, Ga., to Greenwood, Fla., in 1854, where he has since resided. Nearly 60 years ago he united with the Baptist Church.

Mrs. Martha B. Roberts, the mother of Mrs. V. D. Tharp, of Eufaula, died in Girard, Russell County, (Ala.) on Friday last.

Wed. June 2, 1886
Mr. Jas. Fuller, aged 82 years, died on Sunday last in Girard, Russell County, (Ala.).

Dr. Wm. O. Baldwin, of Montgomery, Ala., died Sunday last. Had he lived 'till the 9th of August next he would have been 68 years old. He was born in Montgomery County, and within three miles of the spot where he died.

Thurs. June 3, 1886
Mr. C. T. Floyd, of Opelika, (Ala.) died Sunday last.

Mr. Jno. Coleman, aged about 45, a farmer of Bullock County, (Ala.) living near Three Notch, died yesterday.

Sat. June 5, 1886
Mr. E. T. Fowlkes, assistant secretary of the Central City Insurance Company, also, Mrs. W. M. Weaver, died in Selma on Thursday last.

Capt. P. E. Barnett, aged about 50, died Thursday. He was a native of Wilkes County, Ga., but moved to Russell County, Ala., some thirty years ago, where he lived until 1872, when he removed to Opelika. He lived there until August of last year, when he removed to Eufaula. He leaves a wife, four sons and three daughters.

Sun. June 6, 1886
Mrs. Chas. Phelham, *wife of ex-Congressman Phelham, of Alabama, died Thursday last at her home in Washington. *(Phelham was also spelled Pelham in the same article.)

Tues. June 8, 1886
Miss Hattie Buck, of Mobile, died Saturday, and Mr. Jas. Carr, cotton broker, also died in Mobile on the same day.

Mr. Calvin B. Seymour, father of Mrs. P. H. Morris, of Eufaula, died at his home in Atlanta, Ga., on Saturday.

Mrs. Jno. W. Roquemore died Saturday last. She was buried at the family burying ground above Eufaula.

Mrs. Wm. Shirley, aged 67, died last Sunday at the home of her husband near Lawrenceville, in Henry County, (Ala.). She leaves a husband and nine grown children.

The funeral of Jno. Kelly took place at St. Patrick's
Cathedral, New York. He was born Apr. 20, 1821, died June 1,
1886.

Wed. June 9, 1886
    Mr. Jim Holtzclaw, a well known barber of Montgomery for
the last thirty years, died Monday.

Fri. June 11, 1886
    Mrs. James, mother of Mr. J. James, died at her home near
Eufaula yesterday. She had been an invalid for the past five
years.

Sat. June 12, 1886
    Mrs. W. A. Huguley, aged about 52, died last afternoon at
the home of her husband on Broad Street, (Eufaula). Burial will
take place in Barnesville, Georgia.

    Mr. Jno. Daniels died at his home in the northern part of
the county on Thursday last, aged 72 years. (Dale County, Ala.).

Tues. June 15, 1886
    Mr. Jno. R. Hayes, age about 50, died at his home north of
Eufaula yesterday. He leaves a wife and four children.

Thurs. June 17, 1886
    Mr. Calvin Whitehead, of Geneva County, (Ala.) died Thursday.

Sun. June 20, 1886
    Mrs. M. C. Quick died on Friday last. She leaves a husband
and children.

    Mrs. Taylor Bradly, sister-in-law to Mr. Henry Bradly of
Clayton and daughter of J. L. Hightower, of Texas, died suddenly
last Sunday. She leaves a husband and four children. Burial in
Clayton. -Clayton Courier.

Thurs. June 24, 1886
    Mr. Jas. Cooper, aged about 30 years, died suddenly last
Tuesday while on a visit to his father-in-law, Mr. Hatcher
Vickers. He leaves a wife and two children.

Sun. June 27, 1886
    Mrs. Mary E. Beauchamp died Friday at her home in Eufaula.
She was born in Kilbarchan, Scotland, on July 16, 1836, and came
to America with her parents, Dr. and Mrs. G. L. Allen, in 1840
and settled in Eufaula in the early part of 1841. She was
married to Mr. A. H. Beauchamp on Feb. 21, 1854. She was the
mother of Mr. Geo. H. Beauchamp, Miss Florence Beauchamp, and
Mrs. W. E. McCormick, and sister of Mrs. Geo. C. McCormick, and
Mrs. W. D. Danforth. Burial in Eufaula.

Thurs. July 1, 1886
    Two daughters of Wm. Miller, ages 12 and 10 years, were
burned to death Sunday in a house near Sherman, Texas.

Sat. July 3, 1886
    Thos. G. Berry died Thursday last. He was the second
child of Mr. T. C. and Caroline Treutlen Berry, born in Russell
County, Ala., on Nov. 6, 1857. He was orphaned of both father
and mother, and became the guardian of his three sisters and
three brothers. One brother and two sisters preceded him in
death. He was married July 1883 to Miss Retta Thornton, of
Eufaula. He is survived by his wife and baby. Burial in Eufaula.

Wed. July 7, 1886
Abbeville, Ala., July 4. - Henry Brainard Reynolds, aged
19, son of Mrs. Laura Reynolds, died recently near Clopton, (Ala.)
Mrs. Reynolds is the widow of the late Henry Reynolds.

Sun. July 11, 1886
Mr. S. B. Adams, aged about 25, died at the home of Mr. M.
Vaughn, near Howe, (Barbour County) on Friday. Burial at
Pleasant Hill.

Sat. July 17, 1886
M. W. A. Cliatt, aged about 42, a brother to M. L. Cliatt,
died at his home near Jernigan yesterday. He left a wife and
two children.

Mr. David Davis died recently. He was President of the
Senate. -Wilson (N.C.) Advance.

Mrs. Richard Pearce, of Quitman County, Ga., died at her
home on Thursday.

Thurs. July 22, 1886
Mr. J. A. Hutto, of Lawrenceville, Henry County, (Ala.)
died recently.

Sun. July 25, 1886
Mrs. Richard Stratford died at her home near Howe, Barbour
County, on Friday. She left an infant and two other children.

Wed. July 28, 1886
Mr. S. D. Parker, age 35, of Ozark, (Ala.) died at his home
on Monday. He leaves a wife and several children.

Fri. July 30, 1886
Mrs. Cox, aged 77, wife of Col. W. B. Cox, of Bullock
County, (Ala.) died yesterday at the home of her daughter, Mrs.
D. M. Seals, in Eufaula. She was also the mother of Mrs. Z. F.
Nance, of Midway, (Ala.); Capt. T. J. Cox, of Bullock County;
T. N. Cox, Esq., of Bullock County; Jas. N. and W. H. Cox.
Burial at Enon.

Sun. Aug. 1, 1886
Mr. Wm. Blair, an old citizen, died at his home near Clayton
on Saturday last. He was a member of the Primitive Baptist
Church. -Clayton Courier.

Tues. Aug. 3, 1886
Mr. J. P. Hughey, Jr., died at the residence of his father-
in-law, Capt. Jno. C. McNab this morning.

Thurs. Aug. 5, 1886
Mr. T. J. Florence, aged about 70, of Spring Hill, in Barbour County, died Tuesday. Survivors are his wife and children.

Sun. Aug. 8, 1886
Mr. Tommie Reynolds, eldest son of Dr. J. C. Reynolds, died
Sunday. -Clayton Courier.

Jimmie Holeman, aged 15, son of S. J. Holeman, of near
Star Hill, (Barbour County) died last Monday. -Clayton Courier.

Wed. Aug. 11, 1886
Miss Nettie Whigham, aged 19, daughter of T. G. Whigham, of
Batesville, (Ala.) died yesterday.

Mrs. Cleckley, daughter of Mrs. Roxana Wellborn died at Norcross, Ga., the latter part of last month.

Mr. H. B. Bush, age 23, son of Mr. Eason Bush, died near Oakston on Saturday.

Sun. Aug. 15, 1886
Dr. Stephen D. Parker, of Ozark, (Ala.) died recently. -Ozark Star.

Tues. Aug. 17, 1886
Mr. Ernest K. Brannon died at his home in Eufaula on Sunday. He left a wife and one child.

Thurs. Aug. 19, 1886
Mrs. J. J. Harrell, living on the Dale Road in Eufaula, died yesterday.

Nettie Louise, age one year, daughter of Mr. and Mrs. R. W. Williamson, died at Geneva, Ga., on Tuesday and was buried from the residence of Mr. E. J. Black, in Eufaula.

Sat. Aug. 21, 1886
Henry O'Reilly, the first editor of the first daily newspaper in Rochester, N. Y., died on the 17th inst.

Tues. Aug. 24, 1886
Mrs. Harris, age about 80, of Glennville, (Ala.) died there Sunday. She was the mother of Mr. Burrell Harris, a former resident of Eufaula.

Sat. Aug. 28, 1886
Died one day last week near Cottonwood, Rev. Joseph Messer, aged 70 years. Burial in the Messer burial ground in Beat Six. -Abbeville (Ala.) Times.

Sun. Aug. 29, 1886
Mrs. Harriet Raleigh, aged 54, died at her home in Eufaula yesterday. She leaves a husband and one son, Mr. A. L. Raleigh. Deceased was born in Bullock County, Ga., in 1832, moved to Henry County in 1834, came to Eufaula in 1836.

Tues. Aug. 31, 1886
Mrs. Hester Van Houten, aged 81, of Patterson, N. J., died recently. She was the mother of Prof. J. C. Van Houten, of Eufaula.

Tues. Sept. 7, 1886
Woodstock, Ill., Sept. 5. - Capt. Jno. Axey, of Carol, died suddenly at Marengo, Ill., yesterday. He was born in England in 1821 and came to this country in 1838.

Wed. Sept. 8, 1886
Mr. Ambrose J. Wellborn, age 35, died at his home in Tubb (Barbour County) on Monday. He was unmarried, the son of S. N. Wellborn, of Eufaula. Survivors are his father, step-mother, and three brothers, Mr. Wm. Wellborn, of Tubb; C. B. Wellborn, of Howe, (Barbour County); S. N. Wellborn, of Montgomery. Burial took place yesterday at Antioch Church.

Tues. Sept. 14, 1886
Wm. S. Preston, Esq., one of Dale's oldest citizens, died at his home in Echo Beat last Friday. -Ozark (Ala.) Star.

Fri. Sept. 17, 1886
    Mr. J. B. L. Allen, age about 26, died at Gainsville, Ga.,
yesterday. Burial in Eufaula. Survivors are his father, mother
and Messrs. T. M., Sam, William, and Sanford Allen. (Survivors
given in Sept. 18th issue of Times)

Tues. Sept. 21, 1886
    Mrs. Mary Ann Jackson died Sept. 19th, at the home of her
son, Rev. H. E. Brooks, in Eufaula. She was born Feb. 1st, 1808.
Besides her only son, she leaves two daughters, Mrs. Emily Moore,
of Mobile and Mrs. Josephine Woody, of LaGrange, Tex.

    Col. Mike Holmes died at his home near Otho, Henry County,
(Ala.) yesterday.

Wed. Sept. 22, 1886
    Mr. Thos. J. Lavin, formerly a tailor of Eufaula, died in
Trenton, N. J. recently.

Sun. Sept. 25, 1886
    Mr. Geo. M. Fabler, city marshal of Longview, Tex., died
recently.

    A. D. Owens, merchant of Creswell, Martin County, N. C.,
died there recently.

    Mr. Jas. Norton, an old citizen, died at his home near
Clayton on Friday. He was the father-in-law of Mr. J. L.
Steward, of White Oak, (Barbour County).

Wed. Oct. 6, 1886
    Mrs. Margaret Sapp, of Montgomery, died recently. She was
the sister of Mr. J. W. Reid, of White Oak, (Barbour County).

Tues. Oct. 12, 1886
    Mr. Ben C. Hendrix, age about 55, of near Malone's Chapel,
died Saturday. Survivors are his wife and four or five children.

    Col. Angus McAllister, of Henry County, (Ala.) died suddenly
at his home in Shorterville, on last Saturday. He served in the
State Senate of Alabama from Henry County in 1840-42, and was
elected in 1847.

Wed. Oct. 14, 1886
    Mr. Jno. McLeod, aged about 70, died at his home at White
Oak, (Barbour County). He leaves one child, Mrs. Chas. F.
Stewart, of White Oak.

Sat. Oct. 16, 1886
    Chas. A. Hailey, age 25, died in Columbus, Ga., on yesterday.
He was born and reared in Eufaula. Burial will take place from
the home of his cousin, Mr. M. J. Black, in Eufaula.

Sun. Oct. 17, 1886
    Died at his residence near Louisville, (Ala.) on Saturday
last, Mr. Jas. Capel, aged 86 years and six months.

Tues. Oct. 19, 1886
    Mr. Thos. Ventress, aged 60, died at his home in Clayton on
the 17th. He leaves a family of several children.

    Dr. J. E. Carter, age about 55 or 60, of Lumpkin, in
Stewart County, Ga., died at his home Sunday. He leaves a wife
and five or six children.

    Mrs. Bessie Wathall, wife of Richard B. Wathall, and daughter of Mr. Parker Hatch, died in Newbern, Hale County, last week.

Thurs. Oct. 21, 1886
      Mr. J. T. Goode, brother of Col. Sam'l. Goode, died in
Cochran. He was a former resident of Eufaula and was connected
with the press. He was born and reared in Stewart County, Ga.

      Mr. R. E. Skipper, aged about 30, died at Bainbridge, Ga.,
on Tuesday. He was a brother to Sheriff Skipper of Henry County,
Ala., and was reared in Abbeville. Burial in Abbeville.

      Mrs. Flora McNeill, an aged lady, living near White Oak,
died Tuesday. She was a sister-in-law to Mr. Jno. McLeod.

Thurs. Oct. 28, 1886
      Mrs. N. H. McAllister, of Shorterville, died recently.
-Abbeville (Ala.) Age.

Fri. Oct. 29, 1886
      Mr. J. C. Christian, aged about 74, died at his home in
Georgetown, (Ga.) yesterday. He had been Treasurer of Quitman
County for about fifteen years.

Sun. Oct. 31, 1886
      Mr. T. H. Hogan, living at Cuthbert, (Ga.) died Friday. He
was for a number of years in the employ of the South-Western
Railroad.

      Died at Hawkinsville, Oct. 22, 1886, Mrs. Salina L. Jones,
age 76 years. She was the mother of Messrs. C. J. and Robt.
Jones, and Mrs. W. S. English. Member of the Baptist Church.

Fri. Nov. 5, 1886
      Mrs. Lawrence Austin, 50 years old, was burned to death
near Decatur, (Ala.) one night last week.

      J. W. Jordan, age 75, died at Greenville, (Ala.) last week.

Wed. Nov. 10, 1886
      Mr. S. J. Belcher, age 70, died Sunday. Burial took place
at the County Line Church. (Barbour and Henry Counties).

Tues. Nov. 16, 1886
      Mrs. Florence, mother of Sam, Chas., and Pete Florence,
died Saturday at her home in New Colridge, at an advanced age.
(Barbour County death).

Sat. Nov. 20, 1886
      Mr. Nelson Trawick, aged about 70, died at his home near
Newton, Dale County, (Ala.) on Tuesday last. Burial at Newton.
He was the father of T. A. Trawick. -Abbeville (Ala.) Times.

Tues. Nov. 23, 1886
      Wayles Wynton, a newspaper man, died in Birmingham on
Saturday.

Wed. Nov. 24, 1886
      Miss Rhetta Holly, aged 19, died at the residence of Mrs.
Jane Hutto, in Henry County, (Ala.) on Sunday last.

Fri. Nov. 26, 1886
      Mrs. Thos. W. Cowles, aged 50, died at her home in Atlanta.
(Dec. 24th issue of Times: Mrs. Laura Shorter Cowles was born
July 9, 1836 in Monticello, Ga. She married Capt. Thos. W.
Cowles on May 9, 1854. She was the daughter of Gen. Reuben C.

Shorter, and sister of Gov. Jno. Gill, Eli S., and Maj. R. Shorter.).

Sun. Nov. 28, 1886
       Mr. Jno. A. Scott, age 65, of Bush in Barbour County, died on Friday.

Tues. Nov. 30, 1886
       Mr. Monroe Hendricks died at Apopka City, Fla., recently. He spent most of his life in Barbour County, Ala., and several years ago he moved to Florida.

Sun. Dec. 5, 1886
       Mr. J. H. Turner, aged about 34, died at his father's home near Eufaula on Thursday. Burial at Pleasant Hill Cemetery. Deceased was a member of the Baptist Church.

       Mrs. S. A. Sims, age 33, died at her home (Barbour County) recently. -Clayton Courier.

Wed. Dec. 8, 1886
       Mr. Sam Pinny, of Greenville, (Ala.) was killed accidentally while logging on last Friday week.

       Mr. J. V. Kersey died in Birmingham, Ala., recently.

       Mrs. Margaret Jerome, widow of Gen. Jerome, died recently in New York City.

Fri. Dec. 10, 1886
       Jno. Crossman, age 96, died at China, Maine, recently. He leaves six sons and one daughter.

       Justus Rose, age 95, of Granville, Mass., died recently. Also, Geo. Boss, age 93, of Baltimore died Saturday. Both heroes of the War of 1812.

Sat. Dec. 11, 1886
       Mr. R. L. Watt, of the Windsor Hotel in Montgomery, died recently.

       Mr. Bob Peterson, a former Eufaula tailor, died recently in Montgomery.

Sun. Dec. 12, 1886
       Walter G. Ryals, age 26, of Birmingham, Ala., died on the 10th. He was reared in Cartersville, Ga., and was editor of the Anniston Hot Blast for about a year. His father is President of Mercer University, at Macon, Ga.

Tues. Dec. 14, 1886
       Mrs. Eugenia Woodward, of St. Louis, died there last Sunday. Burial at Carrollton, Ill. She was the daughter of the late Gov. Carroll, of Illinois.

Wed. Dec. 15, 1886
       Mrs. Mary Beall, wife of E. H. Beall, Esq., of Lumpkin, Ga., died recently. -Lumpkin (Ga.) Independent.

Sat. Dec. 18, 1866
       Mr. Pomp Saunders, age about 50, died at his home near Dunwoody's Mill on Thursday. Burial at Liberty, Ga., the home of his childhood. Survivors are his wife and four children.

Sun. Dec. 19, 1886

Mrs. Jas. Baxter, of Louisville, Barbour County, died on last Friday.

Mr. Ben Brazell died last Sunday near Abbeville, Ala. -Abbeville (Ala.) Times.

Mr. Mitchell Blankenship, aged about 45, died in Henry County on last Wednesday. -Abbeville (Ala.) Times.

EUFAULA DAILY TIMES AND NEWS

1887

W. D. Jelks, Proprietor.

Tues. Jan. 11, 1887
Mr. M. Marburg, a former Eufaula merchant, died in New York recently.

Capt. N. R. Halliday, age 79, died last Friday at home in Stewart County, (Ga.).

Tues. Jan. 18, 1887
Mr. Asher Reaves, aged 86 years, died Thursday. He was a citizen of the county. -Clayton Courier.

Mrs. H. Dowling, of near Clayton, died on the 7th inst. She leaves a husband and grown children. -Clayton Courier.

Master Carlson Guilford, of Georgetown, (Ga.) 16 years old, died yesterday.

Mr. A. P. Crawford, age about 41, son of Dr. and Mrs. Alex F. (Penn) Crawford, of Batesville, (Barbour County) died at the home of his parents recently.

Wed. Jan. 19, 1887
Mrs. N. E. Hardman, wife of Thos. L. Hardman, once city clerk, but now deceased, died at her home in Eufaula yesterday. She leaves three sons. Burial from the Catholic Church.

Little Eva West, four year old daughter of Mr. E. R. West, of Eufaula, died on Monday.

Fri. Jan. 21, 1887
Mr. Wm. Lacey, an old citizen was killed last night north of the city on the L. & N. Railroad by a train. -Birmingham (Ala.) Age, of the 20th.

Mrs. Theresa Brady, who resided here a number of years and kept a store opposite the court house, died recently in a Catholic home for the aged in Mobile, where she had been for two or three years.

Tues. Jan. 24, 1887
Mr. Jacob Smith, aged 82 years, and the father of Col. Milton Smith, died at his son's home below Eufaula. Burial at White Oak, (Barbour County).

Mr. Thos. Warr, an old citizen living near Prospect Church, (Barbour County) died on Tuesday last. -Clayton Courier.

Mr. John Hurst, living between Clayton and Louisville, died last Saturday. -Clayton Courier.

Alice, age three years, daughter of Mr. and Mrs. W. H. Nix, died on last Saturday. -Clayton Courier.

Tues. Feb. 1, 1887
Col. Ben Morris died recently near Ft. Worth, Texas. He
was formerly a resident of Clayton and was a son-in-law of Mr.
Wm. Blair, who died recently in this county. He moved about
eight or nine years ago to Texas. He leaves a large family in
Texas. -Clayton Courier.

Thurs. Feb. 10, 1887
Mr. Jos. A. Adams, of the Ozark (Ala.) Star, died on the
4th inst., leaving a wife and six children.

Sat. Feb. 12, 1887
Miss Gatra Brown, age 20 years, died in Birmingham last
Tuesday. Burial at Hurtsboro, Ala., the former home of her
parents.

Mr. Jno. N. Webb, aged 75, formerly of Eufaula, died at his
home in Ft. Gaines, (Ga.) on the 7th.

Sun. Feb. 13, 1887
Mrs. Ellen Bowdon, age about 28 years, died Monday last.
She leaves two little children, Eddie and Lucille, motherless
and fatherless. -Clayton Courier.

Wed. Feb. 16, 1887
Mr. L. G. Wilson, of Perote, Ala., died on the 13th at his
home. He leaves a wife, formerly Miss Carrie Irby, and three
children.

Sat. Feb. 26, 1887
W. P. Floyd fell dead while working in a new ground cutting
in Pike County, (Ala.) a few days since.

Mr. Needham Lee, an old citizen of Barbour County, died at
his home near Clayton on Thursday. He was the father of Mr.
Robt. Lee.

Tues. Mar. 1, 1887
Mr. Henry Bradley died at his home in Clayton Sunday. He
was buried in that place with Masonic honors.

Thurs. Mar. 3, 1887
Mobile, Ala., Mar. 1. - S. C. Blackman, Jules Rembert and
his two children, of Demopolis, Mrs. W. F. Rembert and three
children, of Demopolis, and Theo L. Graham, of Grutes, perished
in the fire aboard the steamer W. A. Gardner on the Tombigbee
River this afternoon three miles below Gainesville, Sumter
County, Ala.

Fri. Mar. 11, 1887
Z. M. Moreland, of Nance's Mill, (Barbour County) died
recently. He was a brother to J. A. Moreland. He leaves a wife
and children.

Mr. Jos. Roper died at his home in Columbus, Ga., on Wednesday. His wife is a sister of Mesdames Rhodes and Simpson, of
Eufaula.

Thurs. Mar. 24, 1887
Mrs. J. S. Frazer, of Clayton, died Tuesday. She had lived
most of her life in Russell County, a year ago she moved to
Clayton where she could be with her daughter, Mrs. Fred Long.
She leaves five children. Burial in Hurtsboro, her old home.

Mrs. J. H. Washington, nee Alberta Lamar, died Tuesday in

229

Macon, (Ga.) at her father's home. She leaves a baby only a few days old.

Sun. Mar. 26, 1887
     Mr. J. K. Hawley, age 23, died at his home at White Pond in Barbour County on Thursday.

Thurs. Mar. 31, 1887
     Dr. A. Lane, formerly of this county, died a few days ago in Birmingham. He was a guest of his son-in-law, Richard Williams, Esq.

Sat. Apr. 2, 1887
     Mrs. Hiram Kay, an old resident of the county, died at her home near Eufaula on yesterday.

Tues. Apr. 12, 1887
     Dr. Jas. Rutherford, of Quitman County, (Ga.) died at his home near Georgetown yesterday. He was in the neighborhood of 80 years old.

Wed. Apr. 13, 1887
     Mr. Jesse Trohlichstein, an old citizen of Mobile, died suddenly in that city on Thursday last.

     Mr. A. T. Amos, of Cuthbert, Ga., died suddenly on last Monday.

Thurs. Apr. 14, 1887
     Mrs. R. H. Walker, of Columbia, (Ala.) died Monday. She leaves a husband and children.

Tues. Apr. 19, 1887
     Mr. Ransom Covington, age 76, died at his residence near Clopton, Ala., on Saturday last.

Thurs. Apr. 21, 1887
     Savannah, Apr. 18. - Frank M. Fonda, Superintendent of the Savannah & Atlanta division of the Central R. R., was accidentally shot and killed yesterday.

     Lincoln, Neb., Apr. 19. - Congressman A. J. Weaver died at his home in Falls City last night.

Sat. Apr. 23, 1887
     Mrs. W. J. Roberts, nee Miss Balkum, of Quitman County, (Ga.) died at her home yesterday.

Wed. Apr. 27, 1887
     At Beauford, S. C., Capt. J. L. Strong, of the schooner Carrie Strong, shot himself accidentally while hunting, inflicting a fatal wound.

Thurs. Apr. 28, 1887
     The funeral of Alexr. Mitchell took place in Milwaukee, Wis., recently from the St. James Church.

Sun. May 1, 1887
     Grenada, Miss., Apr. 29. - The funeral of Rev. C. F. Stiver, who was shot on Wednesday, took place last night from the Episcopal Church, of which he lately had charge.

     George Douglas, infant son of Mr. and Mrs. Geo. W. Stovall, died in this city Friday and was buried in the Roquemore burial ground 12 miles north of here.

Tues. May 3, 1887
    Rev. Jesse Robson, former Baptist preacher of Clayton and who moved to Texas a few years ago, but after the death of his son-in-law, L. K. Faulk, Esq., he moved to Montgomery where he died recently.

Wed. May 4, 1887
    Irby Hughes, three year old son of Mrs. Fannie Irby Hughes, died in Byron, Ga., and will be buried from the residence of Mr. L. E. Irby in Eufaula this morning.

    Mrs. Minnie Wallerstein* age 73, died at Ft. Gaines, Ga., on Monday. Burial in the Hebrew Cemetery in Efuaula. *(Given name supplied from grave stone in Eufaula.)

Sat. May 7, 1887
    Jackson, Miss. - The death of R. D. Gambrill, editor of the Sword and Shield, occurred in this city on Wednesday.

Sun. May 8, 1887
    L. J. Teague, of Henry County, died recently. -Columbia (Ala.) Enterprise.

Tues. May 10, 1887
    Mr. Wm. G. Malone, age about 30, formerly of Eufaula, died on Apr. 4th in Pomona, Calif. The announcement of his death reached his mother, Mrs. Julia T. Malone, of Eufaula about two days ago. He was a brother of Mrs. T. C. Doughtie.

Thurs. May 12, 1887
    Mrs. E. Courtney, age 75, died yesterday at the home of her son, W. H. Courtney, in Eufaula. She was the mother of Mrs. G. W. Barfield, and Mrs. W. H. Harrison.

Fri. May 13, 1887
    Mrs. W. M. Motley, of Greenville, (Ala.) wife of Rev. Motley, died a few days ago. Burial in Union Springs, (Ala.).

Sun. May 15, 1887
    Mrs. Emmie Bowers, nee Miss Emmie Riddle, died in Columbus a few days ago.

    Senoia, Ga., May 13. - The deaths of W. L. Couch and T. N. Burdette occurred on Wednesday.

Thurs. June 2, 1887
    Hamilton Wellborn, three year old son of Mrs. M. B. Wellborn, of Eufaula, died yesterday.

    Three children of Mr. Jno. L. Cumbie, of Quitman County, (Ga.) died in about ten days.

Wed. June 8, 1887
    Col. P. T. Sayre, the aged landmark of Montgomery, died a few days ago in that city. He was in the years 1852-53 editor of this journal. He was prominent in politics in Barbour County.

Thurs. June 9, 1887
    Mrs. Nancy Barwick, aged 79, died on the 2d inst. She had born to her nine children, four of whom are still living. -Abbeville (Ala.) Age.

    The 17 year old son of Mr. T. J. Galloway drowned in the

Choctawhatchie River on the 29th of May.

Fri. June 10, 1887
    Mr. Geo. W. Sparks, age 41, died at his home near Eufaula
yesterday. Burial at Pine Grove Church. He was born in 1847 in
Muscogee, Ga., and moved to Alabama in 1851. He married Miss
Sallie E. Castellow on Oct. 1879. Survivors are his wife and
four children. (Early data from July 27th issue of Times.)

Sat. June 11, 1887
    Greensboro, (Ala.) June 9. - Jas. G. Mallory, a student of
the University, died unexpectedly this evening. He lives at
Harris, Ala. *His body was excorted home by the President of the
University and three of his fraternity brothers, of the Kappa
Alpha fraternity. *(Harris later changed to Comer.)

Sun. June 12, 1887
    Mrs. Samuel Sappenfield, of Birmingham, formerly Miss Ida
Herring, of Eufaula, died yesterday at the residence of Mr. Jno.
Powell.

Sat. June 18, 1887
    Gen. A. C. Gordon died at his home in Abbeville, (Ala.)
yesterday. He was born in Georgia about 1811. He came to Henry
County in his early boyhood, we believe about 1817. He was soon
afterwards stolen by the Indians, with whom he remained several
months. He learned to speak their language, which he always
remembered. He clerked in a store at Franklin, and was very
useful to his employer in trading with Indians. He married Miss
Hudspeth and settled at Ward's X Roads, four miles north of
Abbeville, and later moved to Abbeville. He served as State
Senator, and was often Chairman of the Executive Committee. He
served in the Indian War of 1836. The widow of the late Col.
Lightfoot and Judge Dan Gordon are all of his family that survive him.

Tues. June 21, 1887
    Mr. Chauncey L. Rhodes, age 26, died yesterday. He leaves
his father, mother, brothers and sisters.
    Mrs. Ellen Barnett, relict of Capt. E. P. Barnett and
mother of Mr. Albert Barnett, died Sunday at her residence in
Eufaula. Deceased was a sister of Alderman Clarence E. Glenn.

Thurs. June 23, 1887
    Miss Carrie Wells died at the residence of her father Judge
Wells, in Fort Gaines, Georgia on Sunday. -Abbeville (Ala.) Age.
    Mr. Patrick Brady, an old citizen of Henry County, (Ala.)
died at his home on Monday. Burial in Americus, Ga., where he
formerly lived.

Sat. June 25, 1887
    Mrs. Catherine Heilman, of Cincinnati, died recently.
    Wm. Diehl was killed by Indians while herding cattle sixty
miles north of Benson, Ariz.

Tues. June 27, 1887
    Conductor A. W. Mitchell, age between 35 and 40 years, was
killed on the Southwestern railroad yesterday. He was the son
of the late Policeman Robt. G. Mitchell, of Columbus, Ga. He
leaves a wife and two children who resides in Macon. Burial in
Macon. -Columbus (Ga.) Enquirer-Sun, 26th.

232

Thurs. July 7, 1887
    Mr. Eugene Granberry, editor-in-chief of the Columbus, (Ga.)
Enquirer-Sun died recently.

Fri. July 8, 1887
    Hon. Duncan F. Kenner, a prominent citizen of New Orleans,
died recently.

    Mr. Wm. Burrus, formerly of Eufaula, but for the past few
years a member of the police force of Columbus, Ga., died there
on the 5th.

Tues. July 12, 1887
    Lexington, Ky., July 6. - The death of Craig Tolliver
occurred at Moreland in Rowan recently. He descended from the
family of Taliaferro, well known in Virginia, the Carolinas and
Georgia.

Wed. July 1, 1887
    Mrs. Mary Archer, sister of Mr. W. T. Simpson, died at her
home in Greenville, Ala., on June 30th.

    Mr. Jas. Cassiday died at his home in Hoboken in Barbour
County yesterday. He leaves a wife. Burial from the Catholic
Church.

    Mr. Hiram Kay, aged 80 years, died yesterday at his home a
few miles from town.

Sun. July 17, 1887
    Mrs. J. W. Stacey died in Dallas, Texas, recently. She was
reared in Eufaula. Survived by her husband.

Wed. July 20, 1887
    Mr. J. L. Daniels, an old citizen of Americus, (Ga.) died
there recently.

    Mr. Meritt Walker, an old citizen of Bullock County, (Ala.)
formerly of Barbour, died at his home near Union Springs on
Monday.

Thurs. July 21, 1887
    Mr. Matt Ryan, Atlanta's first chief of her paid fire
department, died suddenly on the 18th.

    George Tisdale, 13 years old, son of Mr. Geo. H. Tisdale
drowned while swimming in the river. -Montgomery Star, 19th.

    Henry, 12 year old son of Jno. T. Gibson, of Georgetown,
(Ga.) died yesterday.

Fri. July 22, 1887
    Mrs. Catherine Van Buren Seaman, age 108 years old, died in
the Presbyterian Home of aged Women in New York, last week.

Sat. July 23, 1887
    Mr. Newt Trammell, of Stewart County, Ga., died of typhoid
fever on Thursday.

Sun. July 24, 1887
    Mr. W. S. Warren, comparatively young, and keeper of the
poor house, died at his home near Clayton on Tuesday last.
Burial in the Clayton Cemetery.

Thurs. July 28, 1887
    Dr. Moses Padget, age 74, of Wilcox County, died at Allenton

last week. He was a Methodist minister, and a former resident of this place. -Abbeville (Ala.) Age.

Fri. July 29, 1887
    Mobile, July 27. - Mrs. Florence Kennedy Huntley, died last night at Healing Springs. She was an actress, the daughter of Judge Jas. A. Kennedy, who moved to this city from Mississippi when Florence was a small child. Her mother was a Miss Johnson, of N. C. Her first husband was Leon Prevost, a music teacher in this city. She was separated from him and afterwards married Mr. Jas. H. Huntley, who like herself, was devoted to the stage. She leaves two children.

Thurs. Aug. 4, 1887
    Mr. Chas. A. Starke, a New Orleans drummer who has been coming to Eufaula for years, died recently.

Fri. Aug. 12, 1887
    Mr. H. S. Perkins died in Georgiana, Ala. He was a brother-in-law of Mr. Jesse Searcy, of Eufaula. Burial from the Methodist Church in Eufaula this afternoon.

Sun. Aug. 14, 1887
    Mr. J. J. Norton, of near Clayton, died at his home on Tuesday last.

Tues. Aug. 16, 1887
    Elisha A. Welch, the original "Yankee clock" man, died Monday at Forestville, Conn., aged 78.

    Atlanta, Ga., Aug. 14th. - Henry Siggs, grape grower near Ayersville was killed by lightning yesterday. He is one of the Swiss colony who settled near Toccoa a few years since. He leaves a mother, wife and several children, none of whom can speak a word of English.

    Miss Lou Jenkins, of Midway, (Ala.) was buried Saturday.

    Mr. Ed. Thornton, of Midway, (Ala.) died at Jernigan. He was a brother-in-law of M. L. Cliat. Burial in the Baptist Cemetery at Midway.

Thurs. Aug. 18, 1887
    Mrs. Sarah Hutto, age 70, died Sunday last at the home of her son, Mr. Z. H. Hutto. -Abbeville (Ala.) Age.

Fri. Aug. 19, 1887
    Mr. J. E. Thomas, age 43, died Wednesday at his home near Eufaula. Survivors are his wife and five children. Burial was at Epworth Church.

Thurs. Aug. 25, 1887
    Atlanta, Ga., Aug. 22. - Andrew J. Ford, engineer, died this morning at the home of his brother in Atlanta.

Fri. Aug. 26, 1887
    Mr. J. C. Reynolds died at his home in Clopton, (Ala.) on Wednesday. He was the father of Hon. R. J. Reynolds, of Henry County.

Thurs. Sept. 1, 1887
    Mrs. E. M. Causey, age about 40, died at her home near Balkum, in Henry County, (Ala.).

    Mr. Jas. R. Lisenby, a young man, died at the home of his

234

father, Mr. J. S. Lisenby, near Cureton's Bridge. (Henry County, Ala.).

Fri. Sept. 2, 1887
      Rev. Dr. Hardie Brown, pastor of the First Methodist Episcopal Church South, in Birmingha, died recently.

Sat. Sept. 3, 1887
      Mrs. Joe White died recently in Montgomery. Burial in Clayton.

Thurs. Sept. 8, 1887
      Thos. B. Holland, age 77, died at his home near Brackin in Henry County, on the 5th inst. -Abbeville (Ala.) Age.

Sun. Sept. 11, 1887
      Birmingham, Ala., Sept. 9. - T. C. Jowers fell into the Alice Furnace this morning, resulting in cremation. He leaves a wife and five children.

Tues. Sept. 13, 1887
      Mr. Chas. Gillis, aged 70, died on Monday last. He resided in Reeder's Mill Beat, (Barbour County). -Clayton Courier.

Thurs. Sept. 15, 1887
      Mr. Levi McCoy, age 65, died at his home near Abbeville, (Ala.) on last Friday.

      Mrs. Lizzie Tiller, age 25, wife of City Marshal, Mr. J. Tiller, died on the 7th inst., a wife of less than a year. She was buried at Sardis. It only wanted three days to make three years since Mr. Tiller lost his first wife, a sister to the deceased.

Sun. Sept. 18, 1887
      Mrs. Polly Walls, age 83, died on last Sunday. -Clayton Courier.

      Miss Sallie Whitfield Clark, daughter of Col. Whit Clark by his first wife, Elizabeth Cox, died on the 11th inst. She was the last living of her mother's children, and with her death, the family is ended. -Clayton Courier.

Tues. Sept. 20, 1887
      Capt. E. G. Phelps, age about 43, died at the residence of his father-in-law, Capt. Jno. C. McNab, in Eufaula on yesterday morning. For many years he was a Mississippi River steamboat captain. He married Miss Fannie McNab, of Eufaula. Survivors are his wife and two children.

Tues. Sept. 22, 1887
      Mr. Eugene L. Pounds, brother of the proprietor of the Macon (Ga.) News, died recently.

Tues. Sept. 27, 1887
      Mrs. Martha Bray, wife of Mr. Wells Bray, died at her home in Eufaula yesterday. Burial from the Presbyterian Church.

Thurs. Sept. 29, 1887
      Mrs. Forrest Wright, age about 20, died on the 21st inst., at her home near Wright's Church in Beat 13, a wife of one year. She leaves her husband and an infant. -Abbeville (Ala.) Age.

      Rev. D. Rogers, of Shorterville (Henry County) died recently. -Abbeville (Ala.) Age.

Fri. Sept. 30, 1887
Mr. Edwin H. Wood, who lived near Troy, brother to Mrs. T. H. Stout, died yesterday. Deceased married Miss Beauchamp, cousin to Mr. Geo. Beauchamp. He leaves a wife and two children.

Wed. Oct. 5, 1887
Hon. Jas. M. Russell, lawyer of Columbus, Ga., died suddenly at his home on Monday.

Thurs. Oct. 6, 1887
Jas. B. Powell, lawyer and ex-mayor of Union Springs, (Ala.) died recently.

Tues. Oct. 11, 1887
Maj. T. J. Burnett, of Greenville, (Ala.) was buried there on Sunday.

Wed. Oct. 12, 1887
Mrs. M. A. Huguley, wife of Mr. W. A. Huguley, of Eufaula, died at her home on Sunday. She came to Eufaula several years ago and was married about two years ago in this city. She leaves a husband and a daughter, Mrs. L. Wells. Burial in Columbus, Ga.

Thurs. Oct. 13, 1887
Mr. Hilliard Spinks, who spent his childhood at this place, afterwards moving with his step-father, Mr. Jake Davis, to Georgia, died from injuries from an accident in Baker County, Ga., recently. -Abbeville (Ala.) Age.

Sat. Oct. 15, 1887
Mrs. M. A. Hinkle, of Montgomery, died in that city yesterday.

Tues. Nov. 1, 1887
Mrs. Eva Doles died at the home of her father, Mr. Chas. Fuller, near Crawford, Ala., last Friday. She was the widow of Ivey Doles. She leaves five children. Her twin sister, Mrs. Jones, widow of Tom Jones, died about three weeks ago, leaving five children. They too, made their home with Mr. Fuller, now he has the charge of ten orphan children.

Thurs. Nov. 3, 1887
Died at his home near Union Hill Church, Thursday last, Mr. Jas. Ryals, aged about 32 years. He leaves a wife and five children. -Abbeville (Ala.) Age.

Sat. Nov. 5, 1887
Mr. J. Asbell Mathews died today. He leaves a wife and two children. He had lived in this city during the winter for several years. He was from Ozark, (Ala.).

Fri. Dec. 2, 1887
Mrs. Wiley Cargill, aged 26 years, died recently. She leaves a husband and three children.

Wed. Dec. 7, 1887
John S. Bird, age 94, of Charleston, S. C., died recently.

Thurs. Dec. 8, 1887
Birmingham, Dec. 6. - John King, formerly proprietor of the

Columbus (Ga.) Enquirer-Sun, died at the Richard Hotel in this city this morning. Burial in Columbus.

Fri. Dec. 16, 1887
Mr. Wash Whidden, of Smithville, Henry County, (Ala.) died recently.

Sun. Dec. 18, 1887
Mr. Aaron Harrison, son of Mr. Thos. H. Harrison, was accidentally killed while duck hunting last Saturday at Harrison's Mill near Clayton. He leaves a wife and six children. -Clayton Courier.

Mrs. Susan W. Williams, of Columbus, (Ga.) died on Tuesday. She was the widow of the late Seaborn Williams, Esq., of Tuskegee, Ala.

Wed. Dec. 21, 1887
New Orleans, Dec. 17. - Judge J. E. Timble and Jas. A. Ramsey of Farmsville lost their lives by shooting each other after a dispute. Both men leave families.

Montgomery, Ala., Dec. 19. - The funeral of the late Rev. A. J. Briggs will take place at Robison Springs, in Elmore County, (Ala.) tomorrow. He died Saturday. He was once pastor of the M. E. Church in Montgomery, but for the past two years had been on the Verbena and Clanton Circuit. He was the father of Rev. G. Waverly Briggs, of Texas.

Mr. Jas. Tucker, aged 87 years, died at White Oak (Barbour County) on Saturday. He had been a resident of this county for fifty years. Member of the M. E. Church.

Thurs. Dec. 22, 1887
Mr. Z. Taylor Zorn, age 38, died last week. He was unmarried.

EUFAULA WEEKLY TIMES AND NEWS

1887

Thurs. Feb. 3, 1887
Mr. W. G. Hepburn died recently at the home of Mr. H. Opert. -Clayton Courier.

Thurs. May 26, 1887
Miss Willie Tye, of Quitman County, (Ga.) died yesterday. Burial at Sharon Church.

Thurs. June 2, 1887
Dr. Chas. Bedell, of Columbus, Ga., died there recently.

Mrs. M. L. Long, age about 50, of Hurtsboro, (Ala.) died yesterday. She was the mother of Mr. Ed. T. Long, of Eufaula.

Mr. Lewis Holmes, an old citizen of Barbour County, died at his home near Eufaula on Friday.

THE CLAYTON COURIER

1888

E. H. Quillin & Son.

Sat. Jan. 7, 1888

Jno. B. Smoot, mayor of Alexander, Va., age 58, died
recently.

Sat. Jan. 14, 1888
Mr. Jos. C. Jepson, age 65, of Columbus, Ga., died recently.

Sat. Jan. 21, 1888
F. M. Talley, sheriff of Harris County, Ga., died recently
at his home near Hamilton.

Mrs. Martha Fayard, age 106, died near Biloxi, Miss.,
recently.

Sat. Jan. 28, 1888
Mr. Wm. M. Farrior, an aged citizen of Clayton, died Friday.
He leaves a large family.

Sat. Feb. 11, 1888
Mrs. Thos. Gregory died Thursday at the home of her son-in-
law, Mr. J. F. Vinson. Survivors are four grown children.

Judge Jno. H. Hull, of Sylvania, Ga., died recently at the
home of his sister, Mrs. Scarlett, in Camden County.

Mr. Geo. Waddell died at his home in the west recently. He
was formerly of Barbour County.

Mr. W. A. Barnett died in Eufaula yesterday. Survivors are
his wife and three children. -Eufaula Mail.

Mrs. Cary Lilly died yesterday. Survivors are her husband
and three children. (Barbour County death).

Sat. Feb. 18, 1888
Mrs. Carrie Grubbs, an old citizen of Clayton, died last
Saturday.

Col. Chas. E. R. Drayton, editor and proprietor of the
Aiken, S. C. Recorder, died recently.

Capt. Fletcher Barnes, of Mt. Pleasant, Maury County, Tenn.,
died recently. He served in the CSA in Biffie's regiment.

Mrs. S. E. Pynes, wife of C. C. Pynes, a former citizen of
Barbour County, died on Feb. 7th at her home near Mt. Vernon, in
Franklin County, Texas.

Sat. Feb. 25, 1888
Mrs. Thos. Hulen died at her home near Star Hill (in Barbour County) on Saturday.

Sat. Mar. 10, 1888
Mr. Thos. Strickland, age 69 years, died at his home near
Texasville (Barbour County) on Saturday.

Sat. Mar. 17, 1888
Mrs. S. A. Williams, of Troy, (Ala.) sister to Mr. Bass,
died last Saturday.

Mrs. Lucinda Warren, one of the oldest women in this section,
mother of Mrs. G. Smart and Mr. J. B. Warren, died on Saturday
last.

Col. E. B. Cash died recently at his home in Chesterfield
County, South Carolina.

Sat. Mar. 24, 1888
One mile of Blackshear, Pierce County, Ga., the train known

as the "West India Mail" plunged 50 feet from the Hurricane trestle killing the following passengers: C. A. Martin, Bridgeport, Ohio; W. B. Geiger, Savannah; C. A. Fulton; T. M. Smith; Jno. T. Ray, Blackshear; Jno. H. Pate, Hawkinsville, Ga.; E. P. Thompson, New York; Mrs. G. W. Kelly, Palatka, Fla.; W. A. McGriff, Columbia, Ala.; Mrs. W. A. Shaw and daughter, Jacksonville, Fla.; M. A. Wilbur and son of E. P. Wilbur, Bethlehem, Pa.; J. H. Hurlbut, Philadelphia, Pa.

Miss Maggie Martin, age about 18, daughter of Mr. Murdock Martin, living near Pea River Presbyterian Church, died last Friday. (Barbour County).

Sat. Apr. 7, 1888
Mr. Adam Grubbs, age 87, died at his home near Louisville, (Ala.) Wednesday. He had been a resident of Barbour County for over 50 years.

Sat. Apr. 14, 1888
Daniel Sayre, aged 82, died in Montgomery, Ala., recently.

Clay Shown, lawyer of Rheatown, Green County, Tenn., died recently. Survivors are his wife and four children.

Sat. Apr. 21, 1888
Rev. Dr. J. H. Campbell, age over 80 years, Baptist preacher of Georgia, died at his home in Columbus. He was the father of Rev. A. B. Campbell, of Americus, and Rev. Chas. Campbell, of Augusta, Ga.

Hon. Z. W. Leitner, Secretary of the State of South Carolina, died at his home in Columbia. Survivors are his wife and five children. He was born in Fairfield County, near Winnsboro, Sept. 23, 1829.

Sat. Apr. 22, 1888
Mr. F. J. Cobia, * an old citizen of near Lawrenceville, (Henry County) died last Monday. -Abbeville (Ala.) Times.
*(Eufaula Times of Apr. 26th: F. J. Cobin.)

Sat. May 5, 1888
Oliver Bevins, age 77, died at New Orleans, La., recently. He was born in Monroe County, West Virginia, and went to New Orleans in his youth.

Sat. May 19, 1888
Mrs. Carrie Judd, wife of Mr. A. W. Judd, of Chattanooga, Tenn., died recently while visiting her sister, Mrs. H. K. Holman, in Fayetteville.

Sat. May 26, 1888
Geo. Washington Ewing, age 80, member of the Confederate Congress, died at his home near Adairsville, Ky., on Monday.

Jos. R. Anderson, age 68, President of the Bristol Bank, died Saturday at his home in Bristol, Tenn.

Sat. June 2, 1888
Mrs. Martha E. Frink, mother of Drs. L. F. and L. M. Frink, was killed Monday by lightning at Jasper, Fla.

Miss Juliet Earle, daughter of Rev. T. J. Earle of Gowenville, S. C. died recently. She was sister to Theron Earle.

J. D. Williamson, residing in Birmingham, Ala., died recently. He was mail inspector with headquarters in Atlanta.

Michael Duffy, the oldest member of the Montgomery (Ala.) police force, died on Monday. He was a native of Ireland, and has been in the service of the city for thirty years, except when he was in the Confederate Army.

Edward Perkins, pilot of the steamer Fulton, died on Thursday at Paso A. Houtre, (La.) from an explosion on the boat.

Annette Maness, daughter of W. M. Maness, farmer of Darlington County, S. C., died recently.

Died in a fire at the Mundine Hotel in Rockdale, Tex., Monday were Mrs. Brooks, the wife of Dr. W. A. Brooks, the proprietor, her four children, and Pemberton Pierce, of Philadelphia.

Mrs. Lewis L. Wingo was killed by lightning at her home in Spartanburg, S. C. on Thursday. Her husband and children survive.

Judge N. B. Meade, of the corporation court of Alexandria, (Va.) died recently at Marshall, Farquier County, Virginia.

Died on Wednesday, a child, age 5 years, of Mr. Wesley Morrison, living near Hortman's Mill in Barbour County.

Mrs. Margaret E. Knight, age 70, died at her home in Eufaula on Apr. 26, 1888. She was an active member of the Baptist Church for many years.

Sat. June 16, 1888
Wm. T. Wilson, of Atlanta, Ga., died recently. He leaves a wife and several children.

Franklin Stearns, age 74, of Richmond, Va., died on Sunday. He was a native of Vermont, but had lived in Richmond for fifty years.

Geo. Dyson, who for 25 years has been Ordinary of Wilkes County, (Ga.) and Clerk of Superior Court, died recently at the age of 74.

Rev. Wm. Coolson, Baptist preacher of Paulding County, (Ga.) died near his home at Villa Rica on Thursday.

Sheriff Jno. Raines and his son were killed at Jacksboro, Texas, recently.

Mrs. Geo. Rollings, of Cotton Hill, (Barbour County) died Sunday. Survivors are her husband and four children.

Sat. June 30, 1888
W. D. Hartley and Geo. L. Edwards, of near Viola, in Blount County, Ala., were killed by lightning Saturday.

Mr. Wright Faulk, age nearly 80, died at his home in Faulk's Beat on Monday. He had been living in Barbour County over 60 years.

W. H. Parsons, of Atlanta, Ga., died recently at Gainesville, (Ga.) while on a fishing trip.

Harry F. Griscom, age 32, of Chattanooga, Tenn., formerly postmaster, died Sunday.

Mrs. Matilda Miller died at her home in Mt. Andrew (Barbour County) on Thursday last.

Sat. July 14, 1888
E. J. Acosta, widower of Birmingham, Ala., formerly of Savannah, Ga., died Monday at the Palace Royal Hotel. Survivors are his two children.

C. C. Gordon, a teacher in Augusta, Ga., died recently.
He was a member of the Confederate Survivors' Association.

Capt. Wm. S. Swann was killed recently at Wilmington, N. C.
when a pile of lumber from a railroad car fell on him.

Moses M. Camp, age about 50, proprietor of the Camp Hotel at
Navasota, Tex., died Sunday. He leaves a family.

Mrs. J. B. Hooten, of near Clayton, the daughter of Mr.
Council Bush, died Saturday. Survivors are her husband and
several small children. (Aug. 11th, Clayton Courier: Mrs. Rhoda
Hooten was a member of the Mt. Olive Baptist Church.)

Capt. P. W. Bailey, an old citizen of near Sylvan Grove,
in Dale County, died last Tuesday. -Newton (Ala.) Messenger.

Sat. July 21, 1888
Col. Jno. N. Dunn, of Atlanta, Ga., died recently. He was
born in Benton County, Ala., Jan. 2, 1835, but at an early age
of seven moved to Bardley County, East Tenn., where he spent his
early life. He was educated at Hiwassee College, practiced law
at Cleveland, Tenn. He moved to Georgia just after the war, and
lived in Quitman. He went to Atlanta in 1870 to practice law,
but was forced to quit due to bad health. He organized the
Atlanta and Hawkinsville Railroad and served as president until
his death.

Hon. Pat Darden died Tuesday at his home in Jefferson
County, Mississippi.

Col. Jas. L. Davis was killed Saturday near Windsor, South
Carolina, by a train.

C. C. Casey, of Savannah, Ga., contractor and builder, died
Sunday. He was a member of the Chatham County Commissioners.
He was born in New York State 63 years ago.

Mr. Jno. W. Johnston died at his home near Sandy Point on
Monday. (Barbour County).

Sat. Aug. 11, 1888
Robt. Linden, of near Cowpens, S. C., and his wife were
killed by lightning on Saturday. Survivors are five children.

Dr. F. H. Glover died Tuesday at his home in Charlotte,
N. C. He was a native of South Carolina, but for 25 years he
had lived in Charlotte.

Jno. T. McKinnon, merchant of Wadeville, Montgomery County,
N. C., was found dead recently in his store.

Sat. Aug. 25, 1888
Capt. F. M. Trimmer, for the last twenty years Clerk of the
Court, died at Spartanburg, S. C.

W. H. Inman, of New York, died at Tate Springs, Tenn., on
Monday. He was a native of Dandridge, and a brother of Shade
and Walker P. Inman, and the uncle of Jno. H., Samuel M., and
Hugh T. Inman, of Atlanta, Ga. Mr. Inman removed to New York
shortly after the close of the war.

Rev. Jno. L. West, Baptist minister, died at his home near
Scott Station, in Perry County, (Ala.) last Saturday.

Mr. J. C. Willis died at his home in Midway, Ala., on
Friday of last week.

Mrs. Wm. Hale died at her home at Iola, Fla., last week.
She formerly lived at Clayton, and is the sister of Mrs. Jno. C.

Williams. Survivors are her husband and children.

The death of Miss Ida Fulton, age about 17, occurred at Brewton, Ala., recently.

Miss Mattie Harvey and Miss Mattie Lane, of San Felipe, Texas, drowned in the Brazos River recently.

Miss Effie Williamson, age 18, of Fairfax County, Va., was killed by a train near Long Branch Station on Wednesday.

Sat. Sept. 8, 1888
William Fletcher, of Durham, N. C., died recently.

Rev. Dr. Fordyce M. Hubbard, age 80, died at his home in Raleigh, N. C. recently. He was a native of Mass., where he married the daughter of U. S. Senator Bates, of that state. Fifty years ago he went to Newbern, N. C., and in 1849 became professor of Latin in the State University, remaining there until 1868. He then went to New York State as rector of the Episcopal Church at Manlius.

Maj. R. A. Willis, of Walterboro, S. C., died Tuesday.

Sat. Sept. 15, 1888
Mrs. W. H. McEachern died at her home near Clayton on Thursday. She was the daughter of Mr. Bob Andrews. She leaves a husband and children.

Sat. Sept. 22, 1888
Mrs. Mary J. Slaughter, widow of the late G. W. Slaughter, died at her home on Tuesday.

W. D. Crow, of Butler County, Ala., an employee of the Secret Service Division of the Treasury Dept., died in Washington on the 16th inst.

Mr. Robt. H. Richards, business man of Atlanta, Ga., died recently while on a visit to Asheville, S. C.

Sat. Sept. 29, 1888
Henry D., son of M. and M. C. Liliernstern, died Sept. 11th at Mt. Pleasant, Tex. Burial at Tyler, (Tex.). He is survived by his father, mother, brothers and sister. -Titus Texas Times. The Liliernstern family were formerly of Clayton, Ala.

Sat. Oct. 13, 1888
Alex Farrar, who for many years has been the crier of the U. S. Court, died at Charleston, (S.C.) on Sunday.

Sat. Oct. 20, 1888
Jno. W. Nevitt, of Athens, Ga., 73 years old, a former resident of Savannah, died in Athens recently.

Jno. Chaffee, age 73, one of the largest cotton planters in the U. S., died on Monday in New Orleans, La.

I. A. Procher, for many years a professor in the Charleston College, (S.C.) died Monday, aged 82 years.

Rev. F. McNanghan, age 72, died recently at Surry County, N. C., where he had been invited to preach.

Mr. Anderson Bond, of near Clayton, died on Monday last.

Sat. Oct. 27, 1888
Mr. Stephen Hart, age 110, of near Abbeville, (Henry County, Ala.) died on Friday. He had lived in Henry County for 72 years,

having moved there in 1816.

Mrs. Elizabeth Frayer, wife of a prominent farmer, was killed recently by a train near Chattanooga.

Sat. Nov. 3, 1888
National Watts, age 93, died recently in Baltimore, Md. He was an Old Defender and one of the patriots who, Sept. 12, 1814, repulsed the British attack upon Baltimore.

W. Y. Yates, editor of the Home Democrat for 37 years, died at Charlotte, N. C. on Thursday.

Julius Ochs, age 63, treasurer of the Times Printing Company, died recently at Chattanooga, Tenn.

Dr. Jas. S. Hamilton, one of the oldest citizens of Athens, (Ga.) died recently. He was president of the Princeton Factory Company.

Mrs. Laura Barnes, age 48, of Mobile, Ala., died recently. She was the daughter of the late Rev. Joseph Ingraham.

Sat. Nov. 10, 1888
Ben T. McAden, secretary & treasurer of McAden Mills, in Gastonia County, (N.C.) died Tuesday.

Sat. Nov. 17, 1888
Col. Jno. Knapp, age 72, of the Missouri newspaper, Republican, died at St. Louis, Mo., on Monday.

Mrs. Ira T. Jordan, age 70, died at his home in Midway, Ala., on Thursday of last week.

Sat. Dec. 1, 1888
Rev. R. D. Thomas, age 71 years, the devine of the Welsh Congregational Church, died in Knoxville, Tenn., recently. He was a scholar and poet in Wales, and a leading minister of his church in America.

Sat. Dec. 8, 1888
Hon. Thos. Settle died at his home in Greensboro, North Carolina on Sunday.

Sat. Dec. 15, 1888
Jno. P. Vernum, formerly a journalist in Florida, and editor of the Times of Jacksonville, Fla., recently died at Avon, Mass.

Mrs. C. H. Jones, wife of the editor of the St. Louis, (Mo.) Republic, formerly of Jacksonville, Fla., died recently. She was Elizabeth C. Abernathy. She leaves a daughter sixteen years of age.

Sat. Dec. 22, 1888
The death of Jno. J. Tippen, merchant and planter, occurred at Courtland, (Ala.) on Tuesday. He leaves a wife.

Travers Daniel, who had just moved to Nashville, Tenn., died there recently. He formerly lived in Montgomery, Ala.

EUFAULA WEEKLY TIMES AND NEWS

1888

Thurs. Feb. 2, 1888
Mr. W. C. Hart, of Eufaula, died Saturday at Glennville,

243

Ala. He was the youngest brother of the late Capt. Henry C. Hart. He married about twelve years ago to a daughter of Mr. Jno. McGough, of Glennville. Survivors are his wife and daughter. Burial in Glennville.

The death of Mr. Oscar F. Knox, of Troy, Ala., occurred last Thursday. He was a brother of Messrs. J. B. and J. C. Knox, Miss Julia Knox, of Troy, and Mrs. C. C. Preacher, of Decatur.

Thurs. Feb. 9, 1888
Mrs. Lewis Livingston, of Dawson, Ga., died Feb. 1st. She was a sister to Mrs. Sarah A. Toney and Miss Eliza Bass.

Thurs. Feb. 16, 1888
Mr. T. Heilborn, age 93, died Wednesday in Cuthbert, Ga. He was the father of Mrs. H. Bernstein, of Eufaula. He went with Napoleon to Moscow in 1812, and in 1815 was in the battle of Waterloo, where he was wounded by a Cossack soldier. Burial in the Hebrew Cemetery in Eufaula.

Thurs. Feb. 23, 1888
Mrs. M. A. Pearce, of Quitman County, (Ga.) died on Sunday. Survivors are several children.

The funeral of Mrs. Eliza E. Ricks will be held this morning in Eufaula and burial in Clay County, (Ga.). The survivors are Mrs. Alpheus Baker, Mrs. A. J. Locke and Misses Eliza and Leila Ricks.

Thurs. Mar. 1, 1888
Montgomery, Ala., Feb. 24. - Capt. W. H. Tanner, an old citizen of Montgomery, died at his home this morning. He was a brother of Col. Jno. T. Tanner.

Thurs. Mar. 8, 1888
Mrs. Sarah E. Saulsbury, age 67, of Batesville, (Ala.) died Saturday. She was the mother of Messrs. Levy and Preston Saulsbury.

Mr. Jno. D. Etheridge, formerly of Eufaula, was killed recently in a railroad accident at Antonio, Tex., where he was a citizen.

Thurs. Mar. 15, 1888
Mrs. M. E. Mathews, of Glennville, (Ala.) died recently at the home of her son-in-law, Judge Lumpkin, in Georgia. Burial in Montgomery.

Thurs. Mar. 29, 1888
Mr. W. J. Brannon died at his home in Eufaula Sunday. His brothers are T. J., A. W., and A. H. Brannon.

The funeral of Mr. Thos. Robinson, who died in Columbia, (Ala.) took place from the home of Capt. W. F. Robinson in Eufaula today.

Thurs. Apr. 5, 1888
Mrs. J. Schwed, formerly of Eufaula, died in Anniston, (Ala.) Saturday. Burial in Montgomery.

Mrs. J. H. Wood, of Troy, daughter of Hail (or Hall?) Talbot, of Pike County, (Ala.) died Monday. She was a sister-in-law to Mrs. T. H. Stout, of Eufaula.

Hon. Wm. E. Johnston, member of the Legislature from Chilton County, (Ala.) died at his home at Clanton recently.

Mr. C. B. Raines, father of Dr. Raines, of Quitman County, (Ga.) died at his home there on Tuesday.

Mr. Ursus Ramser died Jan. 20, 1888, in Eufaula. He was born in Switzerland Dec. 1, 1807, came to Eufaula in 1843 and entered the cabinet business. He never married.

Thurs. Apr. 12, 1888
Mr. P. A. McDaniel, Sr., an old citizen of Henry County, (Ala.) died recently. He was the father of P. A. McDaniel, Esq. Burial in Abbeville, Ala.

Thurs. Apr. 19, 1888
Hon. J. Eason Smith, age about 60, Judge of the County Court of Quitman County, Ga., died at his home in Georgetown Sunday.

Thurs. Apr. 26, 1888
Mr. Ambrose Brannon, age 76, resident of Columbus, Ga., for half a century, died at his home there on Tuesday. He was the father of Mr. M. M. Brannon, of Eufaula.

Thurs. May 3, 1888
Pratt, Kan., Apr. 27. - Mrs. Wm. Fisher was killed on Sunday when a cyclone struck this city.

Mrs. Peggy Knight, age about 80, died yesterday at the home of her daughter, Mrs. Jula Bedell, in Eufaula. Burial in Henry County, Ala.

Thurs. May 16, 1888
Birmingham, May 11. - Capt. Mat Moor died here this evening. He was formerly from Greensboro, Ala., and came here about four years ago.

Mr. Whit Balkum, age about 60, died at his home in Henry County, (Ala.) Monday. Survivors are his children.

Thurs. June 14, 1888
Mrs. R. W. Williamson, formerly of Eufaula, died in Columbus, Ga., yesterday.

Thurs. July 12, 1888
Mrs. Joe Coxwell, nee Miss Trudie Alday, died Wednesday at Clayton. She was the daughter of Mr. Frank Alday. Burial in Eufaula.

Joel, infant son of Mr. and Mrs. Joel Crawford, died in Gainesville, Fla. on Thursday. Mrs. Crawford was Miss Anna Ramser, daughter of Mr. Jacob Ramser of Eufaula. Burial in Eufaula.

Thurs. July 19, 1888
Mr. Enoch Proctor died at his home in Eufaula recently. Survivors are his wife and three children.

Thurs. Aug. 9, 1888
Jas. O. Harrison, age 84, of Lexington, Ky., died yesterday.

Nashville, Tenn., Aug. 1. - Mr. Jno Kirkman died here to-night. He is survived by his wife and daughters, Miss Jennie Kirkman, Mrs. H. C. Pritchard, Mrs. C. D. Berry and Mrs. Wm. Baxter, of Knoxville, and his son, Mr. Norman Kirkland, of Calif.

Mrs. Isabella McNab, age 80, of Eufaula, died yesterday at the home of her son-in-law, Mr. J. E. Tucker. She was the mother of Capt. Jno. C. McNab. She was born in N. C. in 1808, but has been a resident of this place since 1848.

Mr. Robt. McCadden died at his home near New Salem, N. C., on the 1st inst. He leaves a wife, a son and a step-daughter, Mrs. J. C. Neely, nee Miss Annie Nelson. Mrs. McCadden is a sister of Mrs. A. J. Slaughter and Mrs. A. Miles, of Union Springs. -Union Springs (Ala.) Herald.

Miss Cordie Powers, age 13, died at the home of her step-father, Mr. R. E. L. Martin, in Eufaula on yesterday.

Mrs. L. H. Wimberly, wife of Dr. R. S. Wimberly, died at her home in Eufaula Friday last. Survivors are her husband and children.

Thurs. Aug. 23, 1888

Anniston, (Ala.) Aug. 15. - The funeral of Dr. Samuel Noble took place today from the Grace Church and burial at Hillside Cemetery.

Clarkson, Ky., Aug. 16. - Will Johnson and Alice Sylvester died Tuesday. They were driving to the minister's home to be married when their buggy fell into a ravine causing their deaths.

Mr. Pope Jordan, age about 21, died at his mother's home in Georgetown, (Ga.) yesterday.

Mr. Benj. B. Davis, of Eufaula, died yesterday in Philadelphia while visiting his brothers and sisters and where he grew to manhood. He came south as a young man and in LeGrange, Ga., about 35 years ago he married Miss Mary Callaway, who survives him with his sons, Mr. W. A. Davis, of Anniston, Mr. Geo. B. Davis, Eufaula, two daughters, Mrs. J. E. Fitzgerald and Miss Jennie Davis.

Thurs. Aug. 30, 1888

Mr. Hosea Bailey, age over 80, died at his home in Eufaula yesterday. Burial in Clayton.

Mrs. Alpheus Baker, Jr., died at her home near Cochran (Barbour County) Thursday. Survivors are her husband and infant babe.

Thurs. Sept. 7, 1888

Mrs. Mary Bush, age about 64, wife of Mr. J. A. Bush, died yesterday in Barbour County. Burial at Epworth Church.

Thurs. Sept. 13, 1888

Mr. M. I. Reed, formerly of Barbour County, but now South Carolina, had the misfortune to lose two babes by death, one four years and the other 11 months, only a few weeks ago. His wife died in this county about a year ago.

Thurs. Sept. 27, 1888

Mrs. S. A. Solomon, formerly of Eufaula, died recently at Sneads, Fla. She was the mother of Messrs. R. A. and Wiley Solomon and Mrs. Lydia Griffin.

Thurs. Oct. 11, 1888

Edwin Martin, editor of the Jacksonville (Fla.) Times, died Sunday. Survivors are his mother, wife and three children.

Dr. W. G. Gill died in Decatur, (Ala.) last Saturday, and Dr. R. V. Williams died Sunday. Dr. Gill had been a physician in Decatur for 38 years.

Mr. Robt. A. McTyer, age 87, a citizen of Barbour County for 40 years, died yesterday at his home near Eufaula. The funeral will take place from the Presbyterian Church.

Thurs. Oct. 18, 1888
Mr. A. Holt Brannon, age about 42, died at his home near Eufaula yesterday. Survivors are his wife and four children.

The funeral of J. Craddock, age about 31, took place from his home in East Corsicana, Texas, on the 23rd ult. He was a brother to Messrs. T. H. and L. Craddock, of Dallas, Texas. He was well known in Henry and Barbour Counties. He leaves a wife and an infant.

Thurs. Nov. 1, 1888
The remains of Manche, age 3, daughter of Mr. and Mrs. Orlanda Cargill, formerly of Eufaula, but now of Anniston, (Ala.) were brought to Eufaula Monday for burial.

Mrs. Elizabeth Doswell, age 83, died at her home near Abbeville last Friday. -Abbeville (Ala.) Age, 30th.

Thurs. Dec. 20, 1888
Mr. Geo. Singer died at his home in Eufaula yesterday. Burial in Lumpkin, Ga.

EUFAULA DAILY TIMES

1888

Fri. July 6, 1888
Boston, July 4. - Henry C. Skinner, aged 60, died yesterday. He leaves a wife and four children.

Sun. July 8, 1888
The death of Hon. Peyton Bailey, of Newton, Dale County, (Ala.) occurred last Tuesday, aged about 65.

Tues. July 10, 1888
Mr. Sterling Davis, an old citizen of Eufaula, died at his home last night.

Thurs. July 12, 1888
Tuscumbia, Ala., July 10. - The death of Mr. Oscar Cooper occurred near Town Creek, Lawrence County, yesterday. He leaves a wife and two children.

Sat. July 21, 1888
Judge Bulin A. Blakely, of Lawrenceville, Ga., died on the 18th inst.

Mrs. P. J. Tulley died on the 20th inst., at Lockport, N.Y., where she was visiting. She was Miss Lillie Stephens, of Macon, Ga. (Thurs. July 26th issue of Times: Mrs. Tulley was buried at Lockport, N. Y.)

Thurs. July 26, 1888
Mr. Levi Bridgon died in Quitman County, Ga., on the 19th inst. Burial at Union Church.

Sat. July 28, 1888
Mrs. Emanuel Garner, living three miles from town, died on Tuesday. -Ozark (Ala.) Star.

Thurs. Sept. 6, 1888
Mr. Henry Dawson died at his home a few miles from Union Springs last Saturday. He was a brother to Marshal J. F. Dawson, of Eufaula. -Union Springs (Ala.) Herald.

Sat. Sept. 8, 1888
Lynchburg, Va., Sept. 6. - Gen. Wm. Terry, of Wytheville, was accidentally drowned last night.

Sat. Sept. 15, 1888
Mrs. S. A. Woods died yesterday in Savannah, a bride of one year.

Sun. Sept. 16, 1888
J. H. Swoyer died in Wilkes Barre, Pa., on Monday. He went there in 1857.

Sat. Oct. 20, 1888
Mr. Napoleon B. Mitchell, age 58, of Russell County, died in Montgomery on the 16th, at the residence of a nephew. Burial in Glennville, Ala.

Tues. Oct. 23, 1888
The death of Mr. Clarence Beall, Lumpkin, Ga., occurred recently.

Sun. Oct. 30, 1888
Ed. Edwards died at his home in Rocky Head on Thursday. He leaves a family. -Ozark (Ala.) Star.

Sat. Nov. 3, 1888
Mrs. Sue Cato Murphy, age 32, of Glennville, (Ala.) died last Thursday. She was the daughter of the late Lewis L. Cato, Esq., of Eufaula. She leaves a husband and an infant. Burial in Eufaula.

Thurs. Nov. 8, 1888
Mr. Robt. M. Hardwick, of Hardwicksburg (Henry County, Ala.) aged 78, died on the 5th inst. Burial at County Line Church.

Mon. Nov. 13, 1888
Mrs. Neal Andrews, formerly a resident of Eufaula, died Sunday in Montgomery, aged 66. Her remains were accompanied here by her son, W. A. Andrews and his sister, for burial.

Sat. Nov. 17, 1888
Mr. David Janes, age 90 years, died in Eufaula Tuesday. Burial in Dawson, (Ga.). Survivors are J. D. Janes, Esq., of Dawson, Mrs. H. G. Lamar and Misses Eliza and Corrinne Janes, of Eufaula.

Tues. Nov. 27, 1888
Mr. Thos. K. Wynne died at his home in Columbus, (Ga.) on Saturday last.

Mr. Wm. Lewis died at his home near Georgetown, Ga., last Sunday, aged 79 years.

Sun. Dec. 2, 1888
Died Friday at the residence of Mr. S. R. Pinkston, in Quitman County, Mr. Jno. Ogletree, aged 52. He was brother to Dr. and Mrs. Sam Olgetree. Burial at County Line Church in Quitman County, Ga.

Tues. Dec. 4, 1888
    Mr. Jas. Carter, age under 30, formerly of Eufaula, died at
his home in Macon, Ga., on Sunday. Burial in Eufaula.

Wed. Dec. 5, 1888
    Mr. Wm. Link died yesterday at his residence in Eufaula.
He was born Nov. 30th, 1822 in Wartembery, Germany. He came to
Eufaula about 35 years ago. He leaves a wife.

    Columbia, S. C., Dec. 3. - The death of Furman Jordan, of
Chester County, S. C., occurred yesterday.

    The death of Hinton Turney occurred in Spartanburg County,
S. C. on yesterday.

Sun. Dec. 9, 1888
    The death of Mr. T. W. Kirksey, age 27, of Lumpkin, Ga.,
occurred at Rankin House. He was the son of E. T. Kirksey, of
Lumpkin, and brother-in-law of Rev. Jno. T. Lowe, of Butler. He
leaves five brothers and two sisters. Burial in Lumpkin.

Sun. Dec. 22, 1888
    Mr. Alexr. Bryant died on the 10th inst., at his home in
Dothan, (Ala.). He leaves a wife and five small children.

Tues. Dec. 25, 1888
    Dr. J. R. Barr, aged about 45, died at his home in Eufaula
yesterday. He was a brother of Dr. J. M. Barr. His wife survives him.

Sat. Dec. 29, 1888
    Mrs. Henry Hilliard died in Atlanta last Sunday. Survivors
are her daughters, Mrs. R. T. Dow and Mrs. E. C. Spalding.

    Mrs. Martin Miller died at Lodi last Wednesday, aged 90
years old. (Lodi in Barbour County).

1889

Sat. July 13, 1889
    Mrs. J. J. Murphy, age 40 years, died in Birmingham. She
leaves a husband.

Fri. July 19, 1889
    The death of T. D. Reid, of Barbour County, occurred at
Slidell, La., on July 4th. Burial in Mobile beside his wife.
He leaves five children.

Tues. July 23, 1889
    The death of Judge Jno. T. Clark, of Cuthbert, Ga., occurred
yesterday at Smithville, Ga. (Wed. July. 24th Times: He was born
in Eatonton, Putnam County, Ga., Jan. 1834, married May 2d, 1885
to Miss Laura F. Fort, was ordained minister of Baptist Church
in 1858. He was a brother to Judge Marshall J. Clark, Mrs. E. E.
Rawson, the late Mrs. Sidney Root, Mrs. J. P. Logan, and Miss
Clark. He leaves a wife and one son, Welborn Clark.)

Sun. Aug. 4, 1889
    The death of C. M. Hall, of the Bolivar County, (Miss.)
Democrat, occurred last Friday.

    Mr. A. Weaver, aged 87, died Friday at Harris Station,
(Barbour County).

Thurs. Aug. 8, 1889

Mrs. Jane Brown, aged 63, wife of W. J. Brown, and mother of Mrs. W. M. Tennille, of Eufaula, died here Tuesday. Burial in Georgetown, Ga.

Wed. Aug. 21, 1889
Ex-Gov. Jno. C. Brown, of Tenn., died at Gallatin on Saturday.

Hon. Louis Arnheim, of Albany, Ga., died in Atlanta last Sunday.

Fri. Aug. 30, 1889
Mr. Wm. S. Paullin, aged 80, died yesterday in Clayton at the home of his daughter-in-law, Mrs. J. Stratton Paullin. Funeral from the Baptist Church in this city, and burial in the Eufaula Cemetery.

Tues. Sept. 3, 1889
Mrs. R. T. Hudspeth died Sunday at her home near Clopton, (Ala.). Survivors are her husband and two children.

Mr. Jas. B. Calhoun, age 33, son of Mrs. C. Calhoun, died at New Orleans. Also, Mrs. Em. H. Calhoun, age 23, of Canton, Tex. She leaves a husband and three children. Both were from Barbour County.

Sat. Sept. 21, 1889
Jas. Peoples, of Texasville, Barbour County, died on Thursday night.

Sun. Oct. 6, 1889
The death of Mrs. Lancy Loftless occurred Wednesday in Green's neighborhood, Barbour County. -Clayton Courier.

Fri. Oct. 18, 1889
Solom A. Welborn,* aged 69, died in Eufaulay yesterday. He was born in Washington, Wilks County, Ga., in 1820. He moved to this section in 1836, and in 1850 came to Eufaula. Burial in Eufaula. *(Sat. Oct. 19th issue of Times: Solon B. Welborn.)

Fri. Nov. 1, 1889
Atlanta, Oct. 30. - Mr. Robt. W. T. Denham died at his home on the Green Ferry Road today.

Sat. Nov. 9, 1889
The death of Col. W. C. Falkner occurred at his home at Ripley, Miss., on the 7th inst.

The death of Deputy Sheriff Wm. Weaver, of Birmingham, occurred on the 7th inst.

Sun. Nov. 10, 1889
Lewis, young son of Dr. W. L. Scaife, of Hurtsboro, Ala., was accidently killed on Thursday.

Thurs. Nov. 14, 1889
Mrs. Jeff McGilvary died Sunday. She was the daughter of Walker Williams, of Lodi, (Barbour County). Survivors are her husband and four children.

Fri. Nov. 22, 1889
Mrs. Jas. Fillingame died at Springvale, Ga., on Monday. Burial in the cemetery near the village.

Sat. Nov. 23, 1889
    Died yesterday in Eufaula, Mrs. Emily Flournoy, age 53, the
daughter of the late Judge J. S. Williams. The survivors are a
son, Jno. Flournoy, three brothers and a sister.

Sun. Nov. 24, 1889
    Died at his home near Eufaula on Friday last, Mr. Seth
Brigham, an aged citizen.

Thurs. Nov. 28, 1889
    Capt. A. B. Peck died in Montgomery, Ala., Nov. 25th.

    W. G. Williams, town Marshal of Trenton, Ky., died two
weeks ago.

    The death of Amos Lunsford occurred recently near Ashville,
N. C.

Wed. Dec. 11, 1889
    Trenton, (N. J.) Dec. 8. - Jno. Hitchkash, age about 40,
died here recently. He leaves a family.

EUFAULA WEEKLY TIMES AND NEWS

1889

Thurs. Jan. 3, 1889
    Mr. Jas. S. Wilson, age about 55, died at his home near
Eufaula yesterday. Survivors are his wife and five children,
besides a sister, Mrs. M. L. Foy.

    Mr. Walter K. Stokes, son of Capt. Jas. W. Stokes, died
Tuesday at his home in Henry County. -Abbeville (Ala.) Age.

Thurs. Jan. 10, 1889
    Mr. Joseph A. (Asbury) Sylvester, age 30 years, died
suddenly Tuesday in Eufaula. He leaves a father, mother, sister,
and several brothers.

    Salem, Miss., Jan. 4. - Rev. Fielder Isreal, aged 62,
minister of the First Unitarian Church, died here this evening.
He had been pastor of the First Church since 1887, coming from
Baltimore.

Thurs. Jan. 17, 1889
    Mr. Drewry M. Davidson, age 65, died at his home in Stewart
County, Ga., on Sunday. Survivors are his children, Mr. Monroe
Davidson, of Georgetown, Ga., Mrs. Shelton, of Atlanta, Mrs.
C. M. Weaver, of Cuthbert, and an unmarried daughter.

    Mr. J. W. Young, formerly of Eufaula, died at his home in
Newark, N. J., recently. Survivors are his wife and one child,
Mr. Chas. A. Young, and his brothers and sisters.

    Mr. Chas. F. Simonton, age 38, formerly of Abbeville, Ala.,
died recently in Eatonton, Ga., where he had lived for the past
ten years. He was a brother of Henry Simonton, of Eufaula.
-Abbeville (Ala.) Age.

    Mr. Jno. W. Norris, age about 65, died Saturday last at his
home near Smithville, Henry County. -Abbeville (Ala.) Age.

    Mrs. O. C. W. Olive and Mr. W. O. Martin, both of Bullock
County, died recently. -Bullock County (Ala.) Reporter.

    Mrs. Nannie Pauline, wife of Mr. W. S. Pauline, died last
week. -Clayton Courier.

251

Thurs. Jan. 24, 1889

Mrs. M. Crews died at her home near Lodi (Barbour County) last Friday. She was a sister to D. J. and J. J. Walker, of that neighborhood.

The remains of Joshua Lacy, who was killed by falling from a train near Butte City, Mont., have been brought to Tarleton, Ohio, for interment.

Mr. J. A. B. Besson, age 62, who lived in Eufaula for about 40 years before moving to Montgomery about four years ago, died yesterday at his home in that city. Survivors are his wife and two grown sons and a daughter. He was a brother to Mrs. J. G. L. Martin, of Eufaula.

Mrs. Harry C. Copeland, daughter of Mr. Jno. Hardy, of Eufaula, died at her home in Prescott, Ark., on Thursday. Survivors are her husband and one child.

Mrs. Reubin Martin died at her home near Ozark (Ala.) last week.

Washington, Jan. 24. - Congressman Jas. Nelson Burns of Missouri died this morning. He was born in Indiana on Aug. 23, 1832. His parents moved to Platte County, Mo., in 1837.

Thurs. Feb. 7, 1889

Little Rock, Feb. 1. - Jno. M. Clayton, whose death occurred last Tuesday, was buried at Pine Bluff, (Ark.) today. Survivors are his wife and five or six children.

Mrs. M. Keels died at her home in Abbeville, (Ala.) Sunday. She was the mother of Mr. J. H. Laborus, editor to the Abbeville Age.

Dr. J. T. Stovall died at his home in Columbia, Ala., on Wednesday. Survivors are his wife and three children.

Capt. A. R. Godwin, merchant and farmer, of Cottondale, Fla. died on Sunday last.

Thurs. Feb. 14, 1889

Mrs. Jas. Seay, wife of the section master at Ozark, (Ala.) died at that place Saturday and was buried at Hatcher's Station, Ga. She was the daughter of Mr. T. C. Lancaster. Survivors are her husband and three children.

Thurs. Feb. 21, 1889

St. Louis, Mo., Feb. 16. - Mrs. Wm. G. Pettis, age 80, widow of the first Secretary of the State of Missouri, died last night. Three hours later, Mrs. Chas. Parson, her daughter, died at her home nearby.

Mr. Daniel Creel, of Lodi, (Barbour County) died a few days ago. He was a member of the Primitive Baptist Church.

Millersburg, Ky., Feb. 16. - Frank Grundy, age 50 years, a farmer near Head Quarters, four miles from this place, died recently.

Richmond, Tex., Feb. 16. - Joseph Jones, farmer of this county, died this morning.

Thurs. Feb. 28, 1889

Mr. J. A. Bush, a resident of Barbour County for forty years, died at his home near Eufaula Sunday. Burial from the Epworth Church.

Col. Jas. T. Flewellen died in Washington Sunday. Burial in

Eufaula. He was the father of Mrs. Dr. Copeland.

Mrs. Davis Wood died at her home near Savannah, Ga. Burial in Eufaula. She was Miss Vining who was reared near Eufaula and whose mother now lives here.

Col. Lucicus M. Lamar died at Macon, Ga., on Monday.

Thurs. Mar. 7, 1889
The funeral of Mrs. Julia Young Barnett was held at the home of her mother, Mrs. M. M. Young, yesterday.

Mrs. F. M. Bledsoe died at her home in Georgetown, Ga., on Thursday. Deceased was a sister of Mrs. Mercer, and Col. Samuel Goode, formerly of Eufaula. Burial in Georgetown.

Mr. Wm. Howard, formerly of Eufaula, died in Columbus, Georgia on Friday. Burial in Eufaula.

Thurs. Mar. 21, 1889
Charleston, S. C., Mar. 14. - The death of Capt. F. W. Dawson occurred near his home about Mar. 12th. He was the editor of the News and Courier.

Mr. J. C. Craig, of Jernigan, (Ala.) died at his home there on Monday.

The funeral of Mr. J. S. Ramser, age 34, took place yesterday from his father's home in Eufaula.

Thurs. Apr. 4, 1889
Birmingham, Mar. 24. - The murderer of Mrs. Mary Hargrove, of Cobb County, Ga., which occurred last Jan. has been identified in Birmingham.

Thurs. Apr. 11, 1888
Mr. Jacob Arnold, formerly of near Abbeville, Ala., died at Cypress, Fla., on the 2nd inst. Survivors are his wife and several small children, besides his three brothers and a sister. -Abbeville (Ala.) Age.

Mrs. Effie Williams, age 81, widow of Judge Jno. S. Williams died at her home in Eufaula Thursday. Burial in Clayton, Ala.

Miss Mary Griffin, age about 15, daughter of Mr. J. E. Griffin, of Eufaula, died recently. Burial in Midway, Ala.

Thurs. Apr. 25, 1889
Mrs. Patsey Moneyhan, age 83 years, died at her home in Eufaula Wednesday. She was the consort of Wm. Moneyham, who died near Eufaula in Apr. 1864. Two daughters and two sons survive her.

Mrs. D. T. Parker, wife of the president of the First National Bank of Anniston, (Ala.) died there recently.

Thurs. May 2, 1889
Mrs. Herman Bechter, wife of Prof. Bechter, died in Eufaula Sunday at the Union Female College. Burial in Dawson, Ga.

Mr. Jno. Green, planter, age over 60 years, died at his home in Georgetown, Ga., yesterday. Survivors are his wife and a son and a daughter, the latter the wife of Mr. Marion Gay.

Mr. A. H. Wood, age over 60, planter of Quitman County, Ga., died Tuesday. He had a large family of grown children.

Mrs. M. S. Baynard, age 85, living at Chattanooga, Tenn., died on 23rd inst. She was the mother of ten children, and among

253

them were Mrs. T. H. Willingham, and Mrs. W. L. Pickard, of
Eufaula, a grand-daughter.

Thurs. May 9, 1889
Mr. Jno. J. Price died at his home in Belcher (Barbour
County) on Monday last. His father died last week.

Mr. Abner Wilkerson, age 71, died Mar. 23, 1889, at his
home near Cateston, (Barbour County).

Capt. Wm. C. Wallace, formerly of Eufaula, died at his home
in Gainesville, Ga., on Friday. Survivors are his wife and six
children.

Thurs. May 16, 1889
Mr. J. E. B. James, age 62 years, died at his home at
Poston's Mill (Barbour County) on Monday. Burial at Bascomb
Church.

Thurs. May 23, 1889
Dr. R. B. Crawford, age 49, of Eufaula, Presiding Elder of
M. E. Church, died Saturday. He was born in what was then
Russell County, now Lee, on Nov. 15th, 1841. He leaves a wife,
five boys and one girl.

Thurs. May 30, 1889
The death of Mr. Lewis Pugh, an old citizen, occurred at
his home near Pine Level in Montgomery County, (Ala.) on Monday.

Mrs. R. P. Andrews, an old citizen, died at Newtopia on
Monday. Burial in Clayton.

Mr. D. M. Gugel, Jr., died at his father's residence in
Macon, (Ga.) recently.

Mrs. E. R. King died at her home in Quitman County, Ga.,
yesterday. Her son, Mr. Wesley King was buried Tuesday.

Mrs. W. T. Methvin, of Quitman County, (Ga.) died on Thursday. She was a Miss Castellow. Survivors are her husband and a
ten days old babe.

Thurs. July 4, 1889
Mr. B. Frank Hart, age about 47 years, died Sunday in
Eufaula. Survivors are his wife, a daughter of Maj. H. B. Price,
of Clayton, three sons and a daughter.

Mr. Benj. Leroy, age about 70 years, died at his home in
Barbour County on Wednesday.

Thurs. July 11, 1889
Columbus, Ga., July 2. - Mrs. R. M. Hill, of Brownsville
(near Columbus) was accidentally killed today by a runaway horse.
She leaves some children.

Dr. W. G. Allen, formerly of Eufaula, died Monday at Birmingham, Ala. Burial in Eufaula. He was born in Elbert County, Ga.,
in 1818. For twenty-five years he practiced medicine in Georgia,
and from 1860 to 1882 in Clay County, moving to Eufaula in 1882
and to Birmingham in 1887. Surviving sons are: Dr. T. M.,
Sanford H., and Sam W. Allen, all of whom are residents of
Birmingham.

Ozark, Ala., July 4, 1889. - Hon. Elisha Matthews died at
his home here this morning. He came to this country when a
young man, from Darlington, S. C.

Thurs. July 18, 1889

W. E. Mauldin, Esq., of Dale County, Ala., died last Saturday. His wife died last year and a few months before several of his children.

Mr. G. W. Grier died at her home in Eufaula yesterday. Survivors are her husband and five small children. Burial in Tallassee, Ala.

Thurs. Aug. 1, 1889
Mrs. Ellen Cassady, age 35, died at her home near Eufaula yesterday. She moved to Eufaula from New York about four years ago, and since that time five members of her family have died. She was the sister of Mrs. J. C. Hickey and an aunt of Mrs. W. H. Courtney. Funeral will take place from the Catholic Church.

Thurs. Aug. 15, 1889
Mrs. Jno. Temple Graves died on the 12th inst., at her home in Rome, Ga. She was a niece of Capt. W. T. Simpson, of Eufaula.

Dr. Hugh Black died Aug. 8, 1889, at the home of his sister-in-law, Mrs. M. J. Black in Eufaula. He was born in Glasgow, Scotland, Nov. 25, 1817. He came with his parents to Canada in 1820. He served his apprenticeship as pressman in Montreal and in New York City. He came to Eufaula in 1845, bringing the printing material for the Eufaula Democrat, June 25, 1845. He never married.

Thurs. Aug. 29, 1889
Savannah, Ga., Aug. 21. - Dr. R. R. Parsons, dentist, died at his home in this city today. He was born in Northhampton, Mass., in 1806. In 1833 he came to Savannah.

Judge Geo. Andrews, lawyer, S. T. Powers, merchant, and Alexander Reeder, politician, all of Knoxville, Tenn., were killed Thursday in a train accident near Knoxville.

Dr. O. B. Bowen, an old resident of Henry County, (Ala.) died in Ozark on Sunday.

Mr. Thos. Renfroe, merchant of Ft. Gaines, Ga., died on Monday last.

Mr. J. H. Blair, age about 50, of White Oak Springs, (Barbour County) died yesterday. Survivors are his wife and eleven children.

Mr. Martin Miller, age 78, of near Eufaula, died at his home yesterday. He had several children by his first wife, all of whom are grown. His second wife survives him. Burial at Bethel Church, near White Pond. (Barbour County).

Thurs. Sept. 12, 1889
Maj. H. Wechsler, formerly of Eufaula, died at Brunswick, (Ga.) on the 4th inst.

Thurs. Sept. 19, 1889
Mr. M. M. Glenn, age 77, died yesterday at Glennville, Ala. He was the father of Mr. H. C. Glenn, of Eufaula; Mr. E. H. Glenn, of Seale; Mr. E. M. Blenn, of N. Ala. Conference; Mrs. Dowling and Mrs. Birch, both of North Ala., and Miss Lucy Glenn.

Thurs. Sept. 26, 1889
The funeral of Mrs. Lila Godwin O'Brien was conducted Sunday. She was the wife of J. E. O'Brien and died in Gainesville, Ga. She married on the 17th of Jan. last. Survivors are her husband, three brothers and a sister. Burial in Eufaula.

Mrs. Jane Andrews, age 72, died at the home of her son-in-law, Mr. E. Priest, yesterday. Survivors are three children, Mr. J. D. Andrews, Mrs. W. B. Gorton and Mrs. E. Priest.

Mr. Allie Weston died at his home in Girard, (Ala.) on Saturday. -<u>Columbus</u> (Ga.) <u>Enquirer</u>.

Mr. Luther Bush, youngest son of Mr. Council Bush, died at his home near Clayton on Monday. -<u>Clayton Courier</u>.

Thurs. Oct. 3, 1889*
<u>Miss Maggie Snead</u>, age 36, died at the home of her mother, Mrs. Daniel Snead, near Cateston (Barbour County) on Thursday last. *(The name of the paper changed to: <u>Eufaula Times and News</u>.)

Thurs. Oct. 10, 1889
Mr. Geo. M. Danzey, age 63 years on the 23rd of Apr. last, died at his home near town on the 2nd inst., and was buried at the family burying ground on his premises. He was born in S. C. and moved to this county with his parents when he was five years old. He lived and died on the same farm where his father settled. Survivors are his wife and children. -<u>Abbeville</u> (Ala.) <u>Age</u>.

Mr. W. H. Key died recently at his home in Randolph County, Georgia.

Miss Julia, age 13, daughter of Mrs. Sallie McCormick, died at the home of her grand-father, Dr. S. B. Hawkins on Tuesday. Burial in Oak Grove Cemetery. -<u>Americus</u> (Ga.) <u>Recorder</u>.

Thurs. Oct. 17, 1889
Gen. Henry D. Clayton died Sunday in Tuskaloosa. He was President of the University of Alabama. Burial in Clayton, Ala. He was born in Pulaski County, Ga., on Mar. 7th, 1827. Survivors are his wife, Misses Helen and Mary, Mrs. Walthour and Mrs. Wiley Williams, Joseph, Thomas, Bertram, Jeff, Junius, Lee, and Henry Clayton.

Mobile, Oct. 13. - Rev. Jas. Saunders Rencher, pastor of the Franklin Street M. E. Church, died today. He leaves a family. (From the <u>Times</u>: Rev. Rencher of Louisville, Ala. is a brother of Rev. Jas. S. Rencher, of Mobile.)

Miss Fannie McRae, age 17, daughter of Mr. and Mrs. Jno. McL. McRae, died Thursday at her home in Eufaula.

Thurs. Nov. 7, 1889
Mr. W. L. Bryan, of Austin, Tex., died there Saturday. Survivors are his wife, the daughter of Capt. J. C. McNab, of Eufaula, and one son.

Mrs. Jonah Clark died at her home in Eufaula yesterday. Survivors are her husband and several children.

Thurs. Nov. 14, 1889
Mrs. M. Wellborn, formerly of Eufaula, now of Baltimore, Md., died last Sunday at the home of her son, Rev. Dr. Barron, pastor of the Fulton Avenue Church in Baltimore. She was a sister to Dr. W. W. Evans, of Union Springs, and Mrs. M. Dutton of Eufaula.

Thurs. Nov. 21, 1889
Mr. Jno. Stark died in Columbus, (Ga.) on Tuesday last.

Mrs. Albert Collins, age 23, daughter of Mr. Warren Clark, died at her home near Cotton Hill (Barbour County) Thursday.

Survivors are her husband and two small children, one only a few weeks old.

Thurs. Dec. 5, 1889
    Mr. Jno. H. Hamilton, an old citizen of Columbus, (Ga.) died last Monday.

    Dr. J. W. Clark, formerly of Clayton, who had been visiting in Texas, became exhausted at Harris (Barbour County) and left the train where he died on Sunday.

    Mr. Billy James, age 35, died on Nov. 30th at his home near Eufaula. Survivors are his wife and two children.

    Mrs. Henry W. Baker died at her home in Eufaula yesterday. She leaves a son and three daughters.

Thurs. Dec. 12, 1889
    Mr. L. A. Blanton, a former Clayton merchant, recently a citizen of Ozark, (Ala.) died Tuesday. He leaves a family.

Thurs. Dec. 19, 1889
    Mr. H. T. Turner, age 62, of near Eufaula, died Sunday. Survivors are his wife and a daughter. Burial at Pleasant Hill.

    Mrs. Dr. W. A. Johnson, nee Lula Spurlock, died at the home of her mother near Eufaula yesterday.

    Elijah Reynolds, an old citizen of Dale County, died at his home near Newton last week. -Ozark (Ala.) Star.

    Mr. J. G. L. Martin died at his home in Eufaula Wednesday. He had been a resident here since 1826, having moved from Randolph County, Ga. Survivors are his wife and Eugene C.; R. E. L.; J. H. G.; C. A.; Victor, of Birmingham; and Clarence Martin, of Texas; Mrs. Tyson and Miss Del Martin.

Thurs. Dec. 26, 1889
    Henry Woodfin Grady, of Atlanta, journalist, died on Tuesday. He was born in Athens, Ga., in 1851. Burial in Oakland Cemetery, Atlanta.

    Mrs. M. C. Snead, of near Clayton, died recently. She was the daughter of Dr. Bennett, deceased. Survivors are her husband and family. -Clayton Courier.

THE CLAYTON COURIER

E. R. Quillin & Son.   1889

Sat. Jan. 5, 1889
    Jacob Peter, age 74, an ex-President of the First National Bank of Louisville, Ky., died recently. He was a native of Switzerland.

    Hon. Moses Mordecai, age 85, ex-U. S. Senator from S. C. died recently in Baltimore.

Sat. Jan. 12, 1889
    Col. Jno. Ashford, who was injured by an explosion of the boiler at his factory at Clinton, N. C., died on Tuesday. His two sons died the day of the accident.

    Col. Jno. G. Blue, of Marion, S. C. died recently at the home of relatives in North Carolina.

    The death of Jas. W. Goldsmith, age 65, occurred at Stone Mountain, Ga. on Sunday. He was born, reared, and married in the town where he died.

Sat. Jan. 19, 1889
        The funeral of Col. P. C. Gaillard took place in Charleston,
S. C. recently.

Sat. Jan. 26, 1889
        The remains of Rev. J. P. Boyce were buried at Cave Hill
Cemetery at Louisville, Ky., on Sunday. He died at Cannes,
France three weeks ago.

Sat. Feb. 16, 1889
        Mr. Jerry (Jeremiah)* Whittington, a young man living near
Mt. Andrew (Barbour County) died last Saturday. He was the son
of Mr. Obediah Whittington. *(The given name "Jeremiah" appeared in the next issue of the Courier.)

        Mrs. N. A. Simonton died last Saturday. She was a member
of the Baptist Church.

Sat. Feb. 23, 1889
        Judge Asa M. Jackson, age 74, who for 40 years was Ordinary
of Clarke County, died recently in Athens, Ga.

Sat. Mar. 2, 1889
        Col. A. B. Culberson died recently at his home in West End.
He was born in Troup County, Ga., and when a young man removed
to LaFayette, Walker County, where he studied law. On Feb. 23,
1847 he married Miss Margaret Caldwell. He represented Walker
County in the legislature and was mayor of West End.

        U. S. Marshal Lucius Lamar, age 55, died in Macon, Ga., on
Monday. He was born in Putnam County. He leaves a wife and
several children.

        Mr. W. I. Weems, Tax Collector of Henry County, (Ala.) died
on Friday.

Sat. Mar. 16, 1889
        Mrs. Mattie Beasley, wife of Mr. C. W. Beasley, died at her
home near Solomon's Mill (Barbour County) on Thursday. She had
been married about a year.

Sat. Mar. 23, 1889
        Frederick S. Pinckery, editor of the American Angler, died
recently in Jacksonville, Fla. He went there to write up the
health situation for the New York Times.

        Capt. W. H. R. Workman, the oldest member of the Camden,
S. C. Bar, died recently.

        Mr. Asa Vaughn was killed by a train near Midway, Ala., one
day last week.

Sat. Mar. 30, 1889
        Hon. Jno. R. Neal, member of Congress from the 3d district,
died on Tuesday at his home in Rhea Springs, Tenn.

        Mr. A. J. Heath died at his home near Ozark on Saturday.
-Ozark (Ala.) Star.

Sat. Apr. 13, 1889
        Mr. N. P. Wilson died last Saturday at his home in Ozark.
He leaves a wife. -Ozark (Ala.) Star.

Sat. Apr. 20, 1889

Judge C. E. Stuart, of the Corporation Court of Alexandria, Va., died Wednesday. He was speaker of the House of Delegates for two terms.

Sat. Apr. 27, 1889
The funeral of Mrs. Theodore B. Lyman, wife of the Episcopal Bishop, was held at Raleigh, N. C. on Monday. Burial in Baltimore, Md.

Sat. May 11, 1889
Col. J. D. Alexander, postmaster at Thomasville, Ga., died on Saturday.

Maj. Jno. N. Edwards, an editor of the Kansas City Times, died in Jefferson City, Mo., on Saturday.

Sat. May 18, 1889
Rev. Chas. Phillips, D. D., professor in the University of North Carolina for 50 years, died suddenly at Birmingham, Ala. He was the son of Rev. Jas. Phillips, D. D., of England.

Mr. Jno. Smithwick, who moved to Texas with his family, died at his home near Cameron last week.

Sat. May 25, 1889
Rev. A. M. Thigpen, pastor of the M. E. Church at Carrollton, Ga., died Saturday.

Mrs. Victor Petty died in Huntsville, Ala., last week. Mr. Petty formerly lived in Clayton.

Sat. June 1, 1889
Rev. Geo. W. Murry, age 75, Baptist minister, died recently in Wilcox County, Ga.

The death of Dr. P. H. Cronin, of Ireland, and a resident of Chicago, Ill., occurred a few days ago.

Sat. June 8, 1889
Mr. Josiah Cole, age about 90, living near Star Hill in Barbour County, died last Tuesday. He leaves four daughters.

Sat. June 15, 1889
E. B. Davenport, of Richmond, Va., died Sunday. He was a senior member of an importing and grocery house.

Frank Smith, of Smith Station, Ga., was killed by lightning on Tuesday. He leaves a wife and several children.

Col. Chas. C. Langdon, Secretary of the State of Alabama, died at his home in Mobile on Friday. He was born in Southington, Conn., in 1807, and at the age of 20 came to Ala.

Sat. June 22, 1889
Zacharias McDaniel, aged 102, of Rockingham County, Va., and a pensioner of the War of 1812, died near Elkton, Va., on Tuesday.

Sat. June 29, 1889
Mr. Jno. W. Helms, formerly of Clayton, died at Columbia, (Ala.) last Friday.

Mrs. Katie Lane, wife of Judge L. M. Lane, died at her home in Greenville on last Monday. Survivors are her husband and children. -Greenville (Ala.) Advocate. Mrs. Lane was the daughter of Mrs. A. S. Green, of Clayton.

Sat. July 6, 1889
Mrs. Ann M. Pierce, age 78, wife of the last Bishop Geo. F. Pierce, died at "Sunshine", near Sparta, Ga., on Wednesday.

Sat. July 13, 1889
Mrs. Rebecca Wilkinson, living near Clayton, died last Wednesday.

Sat. Aug. 3, 1889
W. H. Heyward, age 72, planter, died recently at Charleston, S. C.

Judge A. L. Milligan, lawyer of Ozark (Ala.) died at his home in that place last week.

Sat. Aug. 17, 1889
The death of Dr. J. B. Wortham, a citizen of Winchester, Va., occurred on Monday.

Matthew Gibbs, age 108, died at his home near Center, N. C. on Monday.

Sat. Sept. 7, 1889
The funeral of Mrs. Julia Jackson Christian, daughter of Gen. Thos. J. (Stonewall) Jackson, who died on Friday in Lexington, Va., took place on Sunday at the Presbyterian Church in Lexington.

Sat. Sept. 14, 1889
Mr. David Bonnetheau, aged 75, died in Charleston, S. C. on Tuesday. He was the last of an old Huguenot family of that name.

Congressman S. S. Cox died at New York on Tuesday. He was born at Zanesville, Ohio, Sept. 30, 1824.

Sat. Sept. 21, 1889
Dr. J. W. Owen, age over 80, died at his home in Stephens City, Va., on Sunday.

Sat. Sept. 28, 1889
Mrs. Malissa Farrior, wife of Mr. Frank Farrior, died Friday of last week. (Barbour County). She leaves a husband and children.

Sat. Oct. 26, 1889
Mr. Ferdinand Phinizy, age 71, died at his home in Athens, Ga., on Sunday.

Sat. Nov. 9, 1889
Mrs. Sue Flournoy, wife of Mr. Walter Flournoy, living near Louisville, (Ala.) died Wednesday.

Sat. Nov. 23, 1889
Col. Locke Winn, age about 50, died suddenly at his home in Decatur. He leaves a wife and two daughters. Burial from Decatur Presbyterian Church. -Atlanta Journal. Col. Winn was a brother of Dr. J. J. Winn and Rev. P. P. Winn, of Barbour County.

Sat. Dec. 14, 1889
Col. J. H. Rathbone, founder of Order of Knights of Pythias, died at Lima, Ohio on Monday.

Mrs. Anna Dent, wife of Mr. J. H. Dent, died at her home on Tuesday. She was born and reared at Clayton. She leaves a husband and five children.

Sun. Jan. 5, 1890
Mrs. Sarah Cox, age 84, wife of Emanuel Cox, died on 21st of Dec. 1889. She was the daughter of Jno. McNeil, who moved from N. C. in 1821 or 1822, and settled near Pea River Church. He died the year following his arrival. Mr. Cox came from Georgia about 60 years ago. Eleven children were born to this union, only three survive. Mrs. Cox is buried in Clayton. -Clayton Courier.

Judge Samuel F. Rice, age 74, died at his home in Montgomery, Ala., on Friday.

Thurs. Jan. 9, 1890
Dr. Geo. B. Weedon, age 60, died at his home in Quitman, Ga., Monday. He was the brother of Dr. H. M. Weedon in Eufaula. Survivors are his wife and adopted child.

Tues. Jan. 14, 1890
Mr. Bradford Johnson, age 86, died at his home in Henry County on Sunday. He leaves a wife and a number of children.

Tues. Jan. 21, 1890
Mrs. Geo. Flowers, age 30, of near Bush Postoffice, (Barbour County) died last Sunday. She leaves a husband and one child.

Wed. Jan. 22, 1890
Rome, Ga., Jan. 20. - The death of Mr. D. F. Allgood, of Trion, Ga., in Chattanooga County, occurred here today.

Fri. Jan. 24, 1890
Mr. Jas. Sultive, age 40, of Ft. Gaines, Ga., died on Monday last. -Fort Gaines (Ga.) Advertiser.

Tues. Jan. 28, 1890
Mr. Albert L. Smart, age about 38, died in Clio, (Ala.) Sunday. Survivors are his wife and three or four children. Burial in Louisville, Ala.

Mr. Horace Nolen, a printer, died in Montgomery, on Saturday. Survivors are his wife and two children.

Fri. Jan. 31, 1890
Mr. Richard Stokwell, age 74, formerly of Eufaula, died at his home in Columbus, Ga., on last Tuesday.

Sun. Feb. 2, 1890
Mr. Chas. B. Woods, formerly of Eufaula, died at his home in St. Louis on Friday.

Thurs. Feb. 6, 1890
Mr. Edward Franklin, age 80, who has been a resident of this county for forty years, died at his home near Eufaula on Tuesday.

Mr. Asa Byrd, age 85 years, died at his home in Barbour County, near Malone's Chapel, on Monday and was buried there.

Sat. Feb. 8, 1890
Mr. Duncan McGilvary, age 80 years, died at his home near

Cox's Mill (Barbour County) on Wednesday.

Sun. Feb. 9, 1890
        Mr. S. H. Driggers, age 73, died at his home in Belcher
(Barbour County) yesterday. He leaves a wife. Burial in Eufaula.

Tues. Feb. 11, 1890
        Mrs. H. Wright, an aged citizen of Clopton, (Ala.) died at
her home Friday.

Wed. Feb. 12, 1890
        The death of Mr. Robt. B. Gullatt, of Russell County, (Ala.)
occurred recently. He is survived by his wife.

Thurs. Feb. 13, 1890
        Mrs. E. M. McDowell, age 74, mother of Messrs. C. S. and
J. L. McDowell, died suddenly at her home in Eufaula Tuesday.
She had been a resident here since 1872, having moved here from
Tenn.

Fri. Feb. 14, 1890
        Mr. Jas. A. Clendinen, age 65, lawyer of Abbeville, Ala.,
died there recently. Survivors are his wife and several children.

Tues. Feb. 18, 1890
        Mr. Richard Scaif, formerly of Eufaula, son of Mr. J. F.
Scaif, died in Birmingham recently. Burial in Eufaula.

        Mr. Jno. McNab died at his home in Eufaula on Sunday.
Burial from the Presbyterian Church. He was born in Scotland in
1807, and came to this country at the age of eleven, and settled
in Fayetteville, N. C. In 1837 he moved to Eufaula, where he
has resided since.

Wed. Feb. 19, 1890
        Mr. Jordan Gilbert, of Robert's Mill died on Sunday. Sur-
vivors are his wife and one child.

Thurs. Feb. 20, 1890
        The death of Mr. Jack Hilliard, of Coleman, Ga., occurred
Tuesday.

Fri. Feb. 21, 1890
        Mr. Baldwin Miles, age 81, a former resident of White Oak,
Barbour County, died at Eddy, Texas, on the 15th. He was a
brother-in-law of Col. A. J. Locke.

Tues. Feb. 25, 1890
        Mr. Carter D. Grandbury, age 18, living near Columbia, (Ala.)
lost his life recently by a falling tree. He was the son of Mr.
W. H. Grandbury and brother to T. L. Grandbury, of Eufaula.

Wed. Feb. 26, 1890
        Miss Mollie Allen died at her home in Lawrenceville
yesterday. (Henry County, Ala.).

        Mrs. Roxana Wellborn, age 89, a resident of Eufaula for half
a century, died at her home last night. Burial will take place
from the Methodist Church. She was the relict of Dr. Levi T.
Wellborn. She came here in 1837 from Taliaferro County, Ga.
Dr. Wellborn died in 1841.

Fri. Feb. 28, 1890

Mr. E. C. Joyce, nearly 80 years of age, died at his home about 20 miles from Dallas, Tex., on the 19th of Feb. He leaves a wife and five sons. Burial in Lee Cemetery near Seagoville. He was formerly of Eufaula.

Mrs. Jas. Goodson died at her home near Crittenden's Mill (Dale County) on last Thursday. -Ozark (Ala.) Star.

Sat. Mar. 1, 1890
Mrs. Amelia Graddy, wife of Mr. Jas. Graddy, died at her home near Georgetown, Ga., on Thursday. She was 50 years old. Survivors are her husband and eleven children.

Fri. Mar. 7, 1890
Miss Emma Morgan, age 17, daughter of Rev. T. E. Morgan, of Honoraville, (Ala.) died Monday. -Greenville (Ala.) Advocate.

Thurs. Mar. 13, 1890
Mr. Wilson Stern, an aged farmer, died at his home near Glennville, (Ala.) on Wednesday.

Wed. Mar. 19, 1890
Dr. Erbert B. Johnstone died at his home in Eufaula yesterday. Funeral will take place from the Presbyterian Church. He was born in Tuskegee in 1859, and came to this city twelve or fifteen years ago. In 1886 he married Miss Lula Bedell, who survives him.

Mr. Alex Farmer died at his home in Shorterville, (Henry County, Ala.) on last Wednesday.

Sun. Mar. 23, 1890
Mrs. Jesse W. Barnes, of Ozark (Ala.) died there on Friday. Burial in Bay Minette, Miss. Survivors are her husband and two small children, one only a few weeks old.

Tues. Mar. 25, 1890
Mrs. Sophia Miller, age 62, wife of Mr. Irwin L. Miller, died at her home in Eufaula yesterday. She was the daughter of Gen. Jno. L. Hunter, a sister to Mrs. Pugh, Mrs. Clayton, and Mrs. Merrill. She was born in S. C. and came to Eufaula at an early age, lived here for several years and went to Texas, where she remained until after the war. Then Mr. Miller and family went to Brazil where they lived until three or four years ago, when they returned to Eufaula, leaving several members of the family in Brazil. Burial from the Episcopal Church.

Sun. Mar. 30, 1890
Mrs. C. R. Henderson, of Cedartown, Ga., died there yesterday. She was a sister of Mr. E. T. Long and Mrs. A. H. Stevens, of Eufaula. Burial in Hurtsboro, Ala.

Anniston, Mar. 28. - Mr. Duncan T. Parker died tonight. He was formerly of Mobile, Ala. He recently lost his wife and one or two of his children. (Apr. 3rd issue of Times: The daughters are Misses Minnie and Dollie Parker, and Mrs. Stringfellow.)

Dr. J. L. Baker died in Eufaula at the Arlington Hotel Sunday. His remains were carried to Beuna Vista, (Ga.) his old home, for burial

Mr. Edward Lee Butler, age 22, died at the home of his father, Mr. A. C. Butler, near Eufaula, on Sunday. Burial from the residence of his grandmother, Mrs. M. J. Black, in Eufaula.

Mr. W. A. Huguley, formerly of Eufaula, died at the home of his daughter, Mrs. Kate Riley, in Birmingham on Apr. 18th, and burial at Barnesville, Ga. Survivors are Messrs. J. M., Crum, Judge Huguley, Mrs. Riley, and Mrs. Sappenfield.

Mrs. Estelle Long, wife of Mr. Jno. Long, died at her home at Harris Thursday. (Barbour County). She was the sister of Dr. Judson Davie and Mr. Bunyan Davie. She left two little children, the youngest a mere babe.

Thurs. Apr. 24, 1890
Dr. W. H. Blair, age 35, died at Louisville, (Ala.) last Monday. He leaves a wife.

Fri. Apr. 25, 1890
Mrs. Azalla Brannon died at the residence of her son-in-law, Mr. Daniel Riley, near Echo, Dale County, (Ala.) on the 15th.

Sat. Apr. 26, 1890
Mrs. R. D. S. Bell, formerly of Eufaula, died in Russellville, (Ala.) recently and will be buried in Birmingham on Apr. 26th.

Mr. Wm. F. Castellow, age about 42, of near Georgetown, (Ga.) died Monday. Burial in Georgetown. Survivors are his wife, two children, and his aged parents.

Mr. A. I. Young, of Columbus, (Ga.) died recently. Burial in Columbus.

Sat. May 3, 1890
Moses Burton, Sr., and Lewis Wilson, both of Walker County, Ala., died recently.

Sun. May 4, 1890
Jas. R. McCalley died Friday at the home of his kinsman, Dr. W. H. Hooper, in Huntsville, Ala.

Mr. E. H. Cohen died at his home in Eufaula yesterday. Survivors are his wife and four children.

Mrs. J. O. Green, of near Clayton, died Monday. Survivors are her husband and child. -Clayton Courier.

Thurs. May 8, 1890
Mr. Edwin O'Neal, age 87, of Florence, Ga., died recently.

Mr. Jas. Blackman, of Troy, formerly of this county, died at his home last Saturday. -Ozark (Ala.) Star.

Mrs. Jas. S. Edwards, of Newton, (Ala.) died last Sunday. (May 4th issue of Times: Mrs. Edwards was the daughter of Mr. and Mrs. E. B. Kelly, of Newton. Survivors are her aged father, mother, her husband and children. -Ozark (Ala.) Star.)

Fri. May 16, 1890
Mr. Josiah Bass, age 84 years, living near Louisville, (Ala.) died several days ago.

Sun. May 18, 1890
Dr. F. F. Gage, physician of Huntsville, (Ala.) died recently.

Mr. Madison Rasberry, age 82, of the Jemison neighborhood, died last week. -Chilton (Ala.) View.

Thurs. May 22, 1890

Mr. O. P. Allen, of Alexandria Valley, died recently at his home on Cane Creek, (Ala.).

Dr. Bruce H. Mitchell, of Mobile, died Sunday. He was born in Milledgeville, Ga., in 1809 and has lived in Mobile since 1867.

Sun. June 1, 1890
Mrs. Martha Dozier, age 65, of Opelika, (Ala.) died recently.

Fri. June 13, 1890
Mr. Geo. Cade died at his home near Batesville, in Barbour County, last week.

Sun. June 15, 1890
Mrs. Mary Gullens died in Eufaula yesterday. Funeral will take place from the home of Mr. Byrd today.

Wed. June 18, 1890
Hon. C. C. Shorter, of Eufaula, died on June 16th. He was born Feb. 1, 1856, in Eufaula. He leaves a widowed mother, a brother and a married sister.

Thurs. June 19, 1890
Mrs. Milton Smith, wife of Col. Milton A. Smith, of Henry County, was buried at White Oak Tuesday. She was a sister of Mr. Jno. Poston.

Sun. June 22, 1890
Mr. Joseph Hampshire, of Selma, (Ala.) died on Wednesday.

Dr. J. M. Hudson, physician of Scottsboro, (Ala.) died recently.

Tuskaloosa, June 20. - Maj. T. D. Cory, about 60 years of age, of Autauga died in this city this morning. He was a member of the State Legislature of 1884-86. Survivors are his wife and several children, Mr. Chappell Cory, of the Birmingham (Ala.) Age-Herald, being one of his sons.

Thurs. June 26, 1890
Wm. R. Ashford, of Greenville, (Ala.) died yesterday.

Sat. June 28, 1890
The funeral of Mrs. Mary E. Maughon took place from her home in Eufaula yesterday. She leaves two sons and two daughters. One of her sons is a lawyer in Ozark, and the other is a dry goods salesman in Eufaula.

J. M. Bowden and A. C. Zimmerman lost their lives in a train wreck on the Alabama Midland railroad at Josephine, near the Chattahoochee River on Wednesday.

Wed. July 2, 1890
Capt. Thos. McKenna, age 70, formerly a resident of Eufaula for many years, died in Mobile recently. Burial in Eufaula.

Mrs. Sarah Chesnut, age 73, died at Belcher (Barbour County) on yesterday.

Mr. Jno. M. Stone, formerly of Selma, (Ala.) died recently in Florida. Burial was at his old home.

Col. D. C. Anderson, lawyer of Mobile, died recently.

Thurs. July 3, 1890

Mr. Benj. Farmer, age about 90, was buried at Creel's grave yard. (From: Lodi, Barbour County).

Sun. July 6, 1890
Mr. Jos. Singleton, age 89 years, died at his home near Clayton in the Star Hill Beat on July 1st.

Friday evening Mr. J. T. Barton was killed in an explosion at a saw mill near Elamville. He left a family. -Clayton Courier.

Fri. July 11, 1890
Mrs. Elizabeth F. Hamill, age 67 years, sister of our townsman, Dr. W. W. Evans, died Saturday last. -Union Springs (Ala.) Herald.

Sun. July 13, 1890
Mr. Wm. T. Ramser, age 42 years, died at the home of his parents in Eufaula. He was the senior son of Mr. Jacob Ramser, and brother to Messrs. Tom and Major Ramser.

Thurs. July 17, 1890
Dr. W. W. Evans, age 69 years, died on the 14th inst., at his home in this city. -Union Springs (Ala.) Herald. Dr. Evans was a brother of Mrs. Dutton, of Eufaula.

Tues. July 22, 1890
Atlanta, July 20. - Dr. R. C. Word, physician of Decatur, Ga., died this morning.

Wed. July 22, 1890
Mr. R. H. Brumby died at the home of his father-in-law, Major Smith ("Bill Arp") in Cartersville, (Ga.) yesterday. -Americus (Ga.) Recorder.

Thurs. July 24, 1890
Mrs. J. J. Byrd died at her home near Ozark last Thursday. Survivors are her husband and children. -Ozark Star, 23rd.

Wed. July 30, 1890
Mrs. Nelson H. White died in Moulton (Ala.) recently. She was born in Richmond, Va., July 13, 1806. At an early age she came with her parents to Russellville, (Ala.) where she married Mr. White, who for many years was editor of the Moulton Advertiser. She was the mother of sixteen children, of whom only three daughters and two sons are now living. Her sons, Messrs. D. C. and Jourd White are editors of the Moulton Advertiser.

Thurs. Aug. 7, 1890
Mr. Will Wells, business man of Daleville, (Ala.) died recently.

Mr. Jno. C. McLennan, formerly of Alabama, now a resident of Vernon, Texas, died recently. He leaves a wife and five children. -Newton (Ala.) Messenger.

Fri. Aug. 8, 1890
Col. Wm. T. DeWitt, age 87, an old citizen of Barbour County, and formerly a resident of Eufaula, died at the home of his son, Mr. Jno. M. DeWitt, in Geneva on Jly. 21st.

Tues. Aug. 12, 1890
Mrs. Fred Oliver, of Macon, (Ga.) cousin to Mr. Whit Oliver, of Eufaula, died at her home Saturday.

Mr. Lucien H. Snead, age about 40, died at his home in
Pulaski City on Sunday. He had long been a resident of this
city, having been connected with the firm of Lee & Taylor Bros.,
in the capacity of salesman from 1868 to 1876, when he removed
to Ala. to accept the agency of the Southern Express Co., at
Eufaula. He married Miss Lizzie D. Christian, daughter of the
late Mr. Edward D. Christian, by whom he is survived. Burial in
this city from the Court Street M. E. Church. Interment at
Spring Hill Cemetery. -Lynchburg (Va.) News of July 25th.

Fri. Aug. 22, 1890
Mr. Jos. M. Ennis, age 28, son of Mr. W. H. Ennis, died at
Bush (Barbour County) on the 20th. Burial at the Mt. Pleasant
Church.

Esq. E. E. Sellers, age 72 years, died at his home near
Cottonwood, Henry County, on Tuesday last. He leaves a wife and
a large family of children. -Columbia (Ala.) Recorder, Cottonwood, Ala., Aug. 14, 1890.

Sun. Aug. 24, 1890
Mr. William King, an old citizen of near Clayton, died on
Monday last. -Clayton Courier.

Tues. Aug. 26, 1890
Mrs. Lucy Newton, nee Flewellen, daughter of Col. Flewellen,
and sister of Mrs. Dr. Copeland, and who formerly resided here,
died at her home in Washington, D. C. on Saturday.

Tues. Aug. 26, 1890
Col. Jos. H. Thornton died at Oxford, Ala., yesterday. He
came to Anniston from New York several years ago and about a
year ago he went to Oxford to live. -Anniston (Ala.) Hot. Blast.

Fri. Aug. 29, 1890
Mr. Jeff Lewis, brother-in-law of Mr. A. J. Locke, died at
his home in Perote, Bullock County, (Ala.) yesterday. His wife
and two or three children survive him.

Sun. Aug. 31, 1890
Miss Stella Massey died at the home of her father, Hon. C.
F. Massey, north of Eufaula on yesterday.

Died at his home at Louisville, (Ala.) on last Sunday, Mr.
Jourd Grubbs, age 72. He came to this county when he was four
years old, and has been living in and around Louisville for 78
years. -Clayton Courier.

Tues. Sept. 2, 1890
Dr. R. S. Wimberly, who lived awhile in Eufaula two or
three years ago, died in Bluffton, Ga., on Aug. 20th.

Mr. Frank Heidt, age about 35, died Saturday from injuries
he received in an accident at Lodi. (Barbour County). He left a
wife and five children.

Wed. Sept. 3, 1890
Mrs. Mamie Poston Powell, wife of Mr. R. D. Powell, died
recently at the home of her father, Mr. Jno. H. Poston on the
Abbeville road. Burial at White Oak Church, (Barbour County).

Thurs. Sept. 11, 1890
Dr. W. F. Hodnett, oldest resident of Tuskegee, (Ala.) died
on Monday last. He came to Macon County, (Ala.) when he was 25

years old and has resided there since.

Sat. Sept. 13, 1890
Dr. E. J. Roach, physician of Atlanta, Ga., died on Thursday last.

Tues. Sept. 16, 1890
Mr. B. F. Wilder, citizen of Albany, Ga., was thrown from a buggy on Friday, the injuries from which caused his death on Saturday.

Mrs. Lucy Richards, age 85, died at her home in this county near Belcher on Sunday last. She has been a resident of Barbour County for over 60 years. She married Thos. Richards on the 21st of Aug. 1825, and was the mother of eight sons and two daughters. She had six sons in the Confederate Army, the three oldest of whom were killed in battle. She leaves four sons and one daughter. She had been a member of the M. E. Church for about thirty years.

Wed. Sept. 24, 1890
Mr. Thos. G. Crusselle, age 68, citizen of Atlanta, died on Sunday.

Sat. Sept. 27, 1890
Col. Geo. H. Pardee, editor of the Sheffield (Ala.) Daily Enterprise, died on Thursday last.

Sun. Sept. 28, 1890
Mr. W. R. Robinson, of Clanton, Ala., died Thursday last. Survivors are his wife and several small children.

Mrs. W. J. Oliver, of Shellman, Ga., died on Wednesday. She was a sister-in-law to Mrs. W. B. Blackman, of Eufaula.

Mr. Jno. D. Glass, age about 45 years, living on the Daleville road, died yesterday. The funeral takes place at Liberty Church near his late residence.

Tues. Sept. 30, 1890
Mrs. Thos. Reaves, age between 60 and 70 years, living near Eufaula, died yesterday.

Wed. Oct. 1, 1890
Mr. W. H. Turner, one of Selma's ablest inhabitants, died on Sunday last.

Fri. Oct. 3, 1890
Mr. Ben C. Ford, age 57, died at his home in Nashville last Saturday. He married in Eufaula about twenty years ago, to Miss Stella Pope. He is survived by his wife and five children.

The death of Mr. Jno. F. Thompson, age about 40, son of the late Judge Benj. Thompson, of Tuskegee, occurred last Wednesday at Ashford, (Henry County, Ala.). Burial at Tuskegee. He leaves a wife, but no children. Mr. W. I. R. Thompson is his brother.

Sun. Oct. 5, 1890
Mrs. Jas. Caley, age 110 years, died on Friday last in Connecticut.

Sat. Oct. 11, 1890
Rev. Jas. Stringfellow, rector of the Episcopal Church died recently at Tuskaloosa, (Ala.).

Mr. J. Thos. Tanton was assassinated Thursday at his home near Warthen, Ga.

Fri. Oct. 17, 1890
Mr. Chas Hollis, Jr., merchant of Newton died Saturday. Survivors are his wife and two children. -Ozark (Ala.) Star, of the 15th.

Sat. Oct. 18, 1890
Tuskaloosa, Oct. 16. - Mr. F. R. Williamson, age 75, of Monroe County, Ga., died on the train at the depot. He and his wife were on a visit to children in Rushton, La.

Sun. Oct. 19, 1890
Mrs. G. Dallas Richards died at her home on Friday, near Lawrenceville. She was one time a resident of Eufaula.

Mrs. S. W. Dickson, formerly of Eufaula, and Americus, (Ga.) died recently at her home in Texas. She leaves a husband and children.

Wed. Oct. 22, 1890
Mrs. R. R. Gwathney was killed in Sheffield, (Ala.) last Saturday by a runaway of the horse she was driving to a buggy.

Fri. Oct. 24, 1890
Maj. Geo. B. Clitherall, age 80 years, died at Mobile on the 21st.

Sun. Oct. 26, 1890
Mrs. W. H. Hortman died Tuesday last. She was the oldest daughter of Wm. Blair, deceased. -Clayton Courier.

Mr. W. R. Hillman, age about 42, who lived near Hatcher's Station, in Quitman County, Ga., died on Wednesday.

Mrs. Jas. Tucker, age about 75, died at the home of her son-in-law, Mr. N. K. Stevens, at Louisville, Ala., on Friday. She leaves seven children, Mr. J. E. Tucker, of Eufaula; Mrs. N. K. Stevens, of Louisville; Mrs. Jaines Gholston, of Selma; Mrs. Horgan, of Texas; Mrs. Doster, of Dale County; and Messrs. Reuben and Andrew Tucker. Burial at White Oak, (Barbour County) where she formerly lived.

Tues. Oct. 28, 1890
Mrs. Chas. C. Jones, Jr., of Augusta, Ga., died at her home in that city Friday. She was the wife of Georgia's honored historian.

Wed. Oct. 29, 1890
Mrs. Allen West died at her home on Saturday last, burial took place at Bethel Church near White Pond (Barbour County). She was a Miss Dykes. Survivors are six children. (From Oct. 31st issue of Times: Mrs. West was 40 years old, married in 1869).

Fri. Oct. 31, 1890
Mrs. E. McNeil, mother of the late Mrs. B. H. Screws, died Wednesday last at the home of her son-in-law, Capt. B. H. Screws, in Montgomery.

Sat. Nov. 1, 1890
Col. S. M. Gunter, of Jasper, Ala., died Monday last.

Sun. Nov. 2, 1890

Greenville, (Ala.) Oct. 31. - Mrs. Dora Royal, sister of Hon. H. A. Herbert, died yesterday.

Talladega, (Ala.) Oct. 31. - Mrs. Hannah E. Reynolds, relict of the late Walker Key Reynolds, died at her home near Rendalls (Talladega County) on the 28th inst.

Mrs. Elizabeth Reaves, wife of Thos. Reaves, and daughter of Godfrey and Rosanna Stephens, was born in Quincy, Fla., Feb. 29, 1833, and died near White Oak Church in Barbour County, Ala., Sept. 29th. Her first husband, Jas. Cawthon, died in the army.

Fri. Nov. 7, 1890
Mrs. Sallie Tillman, wife of Mr. Jno. P. Tillman, an attorney of Birmingham, and daughter of Mr. H. H. Hunt, Sr., of Marion, Ala., died last Wednesday. Burial in Marion.

Sun. Nov. 9, 1890
Mrs. Nora Vinson, wife of Mr. R. Vinson, died on Friday last. -Clayton Courier.

Mr. Henry C. Thomas died at his home in Clayton on Tuesday. -Clayton Courier.

Fri. Nov. 14, 1890
Mr. Geo. Shealy, age about 80, died at his home near La-Fayette, Chambers County, (Ala.) last week.

T. Colbert Dawson, age about 42, formerly of Russell County, Ala., son of Maj. W. C. Dawson, of Eufaula, died in Columbus, Ga., yesterday. Burial in Glennville, Ala. Survivors are his wife, the former Miss Ruth Howard, of Columbus, his father, sisters, Mrs. T. P. Graves, of Eufaula, and Mrs. Griffith, of Glennville, Ala.

Sun. Nov. 16, 1890
Mr. W. S. Jackson died at Tuskegee, (Ala.) on Friday last.

Miss Lizzie Butt died Friday at her home in Eufaula.

Tues. Nov. 18, 1890
Mrs. Thomas Threwits, of Columbus, Ga., sister of Maj. W. C. Dawson, of Eufaula, died in Columbus on Sunday last. (Nov. 19th issue of Times: Mrs. Ann Threwits, widow of T. P. P. Threwits, was born in Greene County, Ga., Apr. 19, 1814. She was the daughter of the late Gen. Thos. Dawson. All of her children preceded her to the grave. She leaves three grand-children, one a daughter of Dr. J. C. Moffett, of St. Lewis, Mo., one a son of Judge David Clopton, of Montgomery, and a son of Mr. C. E. Beach, of Columbus. -Columbus (Ga.) Enquirer-Sun, 18th inst.)

Mr. Jesse Crummey, planter of Appling County, Ga., died Saturday.

Wed. Nov. 19, 1890
Mrs. Ira A., bride of Gaston A. Robinson, Esq., and daughter of Mr. and Mrs. J. D. Alexander, of Laundsdale, (Ala.) died at Selma on Monday.

Tues. Nov. 25, 1890
Mr. W. J. May, of Pike County, Ala., died on last Saturday.

Bishop Jno. Waltrous Beckwith, age 60, of the Episcopal diocese of Georgia, died at his home in Atlanta on Sunday. He had been a Bishop of Georgia since 1868.

Wed. Nov. 26, 1890
     Capt. Wm. H. Homer, age 68, of Mobile, died on Monday. He
was born in Nantuckett, R. I. He served throughout the Mexican
War.

Thurs. Nov. 27, 1890
     Mrs. Thos. J. Judge, widow of Justice Thos. J. Judge, of
the Supreme Court, died in Anniston on Tuesday last. She was
buried in Greenville, (Ala.).

Sat. Nov. 29, 1890
     Meridian, Miss., Nov. 26. - T. H. B. Gough, age 65, of
Neshoba County was robbed and killed near Meridian last night.
His son fled to the woods, which saved his life.

Thurs. Dec. 4, 1890
     Hon. T. M. Furlow, age 76, of Americus, Ga., died in Atlanta
on Tuesday last.

Fri. Dec. 5, 1890
     Mr. E. S. Powers, an old citizen of Columbia, (Ala.) died
at his home in that place on Monday last.

     Col. Lewis Friersen, of Birmingham, died last night.
-Birmingham (Ala.) News.

Fri. Dec. 12, 1890
     Mr. R. H. Dawkins, age 60, of Lawrenceville, (Henry County,
Ala.) died last Monday. Survivors are four daughters and one
son. Among his children are Mrs. Clark of Lawrenceville, and
Mrs. J. J. Kilpatrick, of Eufaula.

Sun. Dec. 14, 1890
     Jno. Frenkel, merchant of West Point, Miss., and a resident
of Mobile, died on Thursday.

Tues. Dec. 16, 1890
     Mr. T. T. Moses, of Girard, (Ala.) died on Saturday.

Fri. Dec. 19, 1890
     Dr. W. O. Dobbins, age 38, of Ft. Gaines, (Ga.) was buried
yesterday. Survivors are his wife and three or four children.
He was reared in Eufaula.

Sun. Dec. 21, 1890
     Mrs. H. J. Bland, of near Georgetown, (Ga.) died on Monday.
Burial in the Pataula Church Cemetery. -Cuthbert (Ga.) Liberal.

     Mr. L. A. Smith, sheriff of Randolph County, Ga., died
Friday.

Tues. Dec. 23, 1890
     Mrs. Laworia Lamar, living in Rutland District of Bibb
County, Ga., near Macon, died last Saturday.

     Mr. J. R. Walden, age about 25, of Ozark, (Ala.) died Sunday.
Survivors are his wife and one child. (From the Dec. 28th issue
of Times: Name of the deceased was Reuben F. Walden.)

Wed. Dec. 24, 1890
     Troy, (Ala.) Dec. 22. - Two citizens of the county died
Friday, Ben Stripling, age 64, and Joel Carter, age 80. Both
has spent most of their lives in Pike County.

271

Tues. Dec. 30, 1890

Mrs. Orlando Cargill, of Eufaula, died Sunday last. She is survived by her husband and infant of about five months old.

C. J. Callut, ex-policeman, died in Norfork, Va., on Christmas.

Mr. Jas. W. Lister, an old citizen of Etowah, (Ala.) died on the 25th near Gadsden, (Ala.) while on a visit to his sister.

Wed. Dec. 31, 1890

M. A. Dauphin, age 53, President of the Louisiana State Lottery Company, died at his home in New Orleans on Monday last. He was a native of Alsace Lorraine.

273

277

279

280

. W.R. 42	HAUSMAN,JOSHUA 192	. JIMMIE SMITH 48
. WASH 214	HAWKINS,A.N. 53	. JOHN 51
. WILLIAM L. 109	. MARGUERETT E. 18	. JOHN W. 259
. WILLIE 58	. NANNIE J.	. JULIA ANN McCRACKIN 28
HARRISON, 180	. WORTHINGTON 53	. KANSAS 79
. A.T. ANGLIN 8	. NATHANIEL 218	. MARY JANE PHILLIPS 51
. AARON 237	. S.B. 12,256	. MARY PEEPLES 45
. CHARLES 133	. SALLIE 12	. MOSES W. 3,183
. E.L. 65	. T.A.J. 25	. P.L. 45
. FLORA 43	HAWLEY,J.K. 230	. SALLIE WESTMORELAND 9
. GEORGE P. 59	HAWTHORNE,J.B. 75	. SCOTT 52
. GEORGE W. 158	HAY,JOHN 179	. T.A. 9
. J.F. 8	HAYDEN,W.B. 185	. T.C. 79,183,203
. J.L. 26	HAYES,	. WILLIAM A. 48
. JAMES O. 245	. BLANCH V. POWELL 26	HELTON,M.W. 22
. L.C. 3,7,95	. H.A. 26	P.E. WHATLEY 22
. LULA 54	. HENRIETTA O. 88	HENDERSON,A.S.J. 54
. M.A. 149	. HOMER 42	. ANNIE MAYO 54
. MAMIE 86,92	. J.A. 177	. C.R. 263
. MATTIE LIGON 59	. JOHN 65	. CHARLES 69
. THOMAS H. 237	. JOHN L. 164	. FOX 24
. VISA GRANGER 61	. JOHN R. 222	. H.G. 186
. W. POTTS 11	. LEVIE OLIVE 42	. JAMES E. 85
. W.H. 61,149,231	HAYGOOD,A.W. 203	. LAURA 91
HART,ALICE J. 44	. APPLETON 3	. MARY 42
. B. FRANK 254	. EUGENIA 203	. MATTIE HILLIARD 85
. BEALL 90	. H.G. 175	. SALLIE WILKERSON 24
. H.C. 19	HAYNES,	. THOMAS 127
. HENRY C. 56,132,179	. EDDIE C. WILLIAMS 18	. W.D. 170
. 244	. JOHN R. 18	HENDLEY,GEORGIA 40
. MARY E. 102	HAYS,A.P. 74	. LAURA 84
. PARILEE RICKS 132	. C.E. 98	. MELLIE 84
. SALLIE 19,56	. CALVIN 103	. R.D. 84
. SALLIE R. 19	. MAHALA 103	HENDLY,LELA 43
. STEPHEN 125,242	. SUSIE WALKER 74	HENDREE,J. 187
. THOMAS 192	. THOMAS E. 98	HENDRICKS,
. W.C. 243	. W.W. 163	. DARTHULA HARDIE 30
HARTLEY,W.D. 240	. WILLIAM AUGUSTUS 103	. LENNARD 30
HARTMAN,NANNIE H. 31	HAYWOOD,WILLIAM F. 200	. MONROE 227
. VERNA 64	HEAD,J.J. 95	HENDRIX,B.N. 157
HARTUNG,ELLA 127	HEARD, 1	. BEN C. 225
. F.J. 127	. FRANKLIN C. 98	. GEORGE W. 49
. FERD. J. 36	. J.A. 1	. JOHN 157
. JOHN 117	HEATH, 50	. MAMIE 73
. JOSIE HEUER 36	. A.J. 258	. MARY LOU 38
HARTZ,S. 148	. FANNIE 204	. SALLIE LOU McREILI 49
HARVELL,QUEEN 67	. GEORGE W. 199	. W.B. 157
HARVEY,ALBERT 185	. J.D. 79	HENLEY,J. 36
. MATTIE 242	. SALLIE JONES 79	JENNIE 36
HARWELL,IRENE 83	HECHT, 37	HENRY,ANNIE MAE 81
. J.H. 194	HEIBRON, 149	. BETTY 19
. J.R. 194	. FREDDIE 37	. ELIZABETH BALLART 68
. W.F. 74	. SAMUEL 134	. GUS 172
. WALTER 83	HEIDT,DAVID 215	. GUSTAVUS A. 172
HARWOOD,MAMIE 81	. FRANK 267	. I.M.P. 71
HASSELTON,	. MARIA A. CARGILL 215	. JAMES 198
. FANNY MAY MILLER 57	. SARAH A.B. 2	. JAMES J. 205
. JOHN 57	HEILBORN,JULIA 46	. JOHN 68
HASTY,LOLA HALL 90	. SAMUEL 130	. KATE 49
. W.H. 90	. T. 244	. W.J. 150
HATCH, 17	HEILMAN,CATHERINE 232	HENSON,F.J.C. 190
. ALFRED 134	HEISEL,ADAM 14	HENTZ,CAROLINE LEE 105
. PARKER 226	. GEORGIA LINDLEY 14	HEPBURN,W.G. 197,237
HATCHETT,CLARA 37	HEISKELL,	HERBERT,DORA 270
HATCHIE, 17	. AUGUSTA LAMAR 26	HERNDON,BEAL 86
HATFIELD,A.R. 169	. T.H. 26	. BENJAMIN 15
. JAMES 40	HELMS, 32	. DABNEY 113
. MARY 155	. A.C. 183	. MARY A. 60
. ROBERT 40	. AARON 35,180	. THOMAS H. 178
HATHAWAY,E.R. 146	. CHARLES 133	HERON,CAROLINE 102
HAUGHTON,J.W. 16	. FANNY CAMPBELL 52	. E.M. 102
. VINA RONEY 16	. G.D. 28	HERRING,B.L. 65

290

292

296

298

```
McMILLEN,SOPHIE        50    . EVA FIELDS           197    . LUCY MICOU              23
McMULLAN,JOHN S.      127    . J.F.                  93    . SAMUEL                 246
McNAB,FANNIE          235    . LIZZIE C. THOMPSON    93   NOBLES,JANE              135
. IDA                  18    . MAGGIE                12    . MORRIS                 219
. ISABELLA            245    . ROBERT A.            247    . WESLEY V.              180
. J.C.                256    . S.B.                  45   NOLAND,W.W.              142
. JOHN            110,262    . SUMP               50,69   NOLEN,HORACE             261
. JOHN C. 91,223,235,246    . TERESA               188    . MARY BERRY              43
. LIZZIE               12    . TOM                   32    . McNAUGHTON              43
. MARY A.              11   McTYRE,S.B.              66   NORMAN,FRED            55,58
. MITTIE               69   NALL,ROBERT             212    . NILLA                   18
. ROSA                 91   NANCE,B.A.              216   NORRED,SIMON K.          185
McNAIR,ALICE KEILS     11    . BEN                   88   NORRELL,JAMES N.         103
. C.M.                 86    . H.H.                  21   NORRIS,DELLA LAMPLEY      80
. E.                  7-8    . K.D.                  54    . J.A.                    80
. EVANDER           7,214    . L.F.                 216    . JOHN W.                251
. MALCOLM              11    . LYDIA                 54    . SUSAN PARKER           131
. W.N.                 80    . R.F.                  77    . WILLIAM                207
. WILLIE R. McCALL     86    . ROBERT F.         26,135   NORTHERN,T.H.             75
McNAMEE,WILLIAM H.    118    . ROSA BELLE SCOTT      77   NORTON,ADDIE          14,125
McNANGHAN,F.          242    . SARAH                141    . AQUILLA CLARKE          36
McNEESE,HENRIETTA      18   NAPPER,ABB               77    . EMMA M. McKENZIE        18
McNEIL,E.             269    . JOHN                 190    . J.J.                   234
. JANE                114    . SARAH SAUNDERS        77    . JAMES                  225
. JOHN                261   NASH,P.G.               185    . M.E.                    94
. JOHN C.             114   NASON,GEORGE             23    . MASON                   28
. SARAH               261    . MINNIE PRYOR          23    . S.J. McCRANEY          205
. WILLIE A.           170   NEAL,JOHN R.            258    . SARAH JANE McKRANEY 25
McNEILL,ANGIE          18   NEELY,ANNIE NELSON      246    . STEPHEN                 36
. FLORA               226    . EFFIE                 92    . THOMAS                 205
. NEAL D.             200    . J.C.                 246    . THOMAS C.               25
. S.E.                 18   NELSON,ANNIE            246    . W.K.                   125
McNULTY,CALEB J.       97   NESTOR,JOHN             142    . WEST                   152
. M.A.                206   NETTLES,J.H.            201    . WILLIAM H.              18
McPHERSON,H.H.         39   NEVITT,JOHN W.          242    . WILLIAM K.              25
. MAMIE LITTLE         39   NEWBERRY,JOHN A.         71    . WILLIE PETTY            28
. MATTIE WALLACE       19    . NICEY LOGAN           71   NORWOOD,MINNIE            74
. WALLACE              19    . W.P.R.               155    . ROSA                    24
McRAE,                 19   NEWELL,                       . W.B.                   127
. BETTIE P.            11    . CALEDONIA ALEXANDER    1   NUNN,FANNIE               14
. CHRISTIAN            75    . R.J.                   1   NUNNALLY,              68-69
. CLARA                41   NEWMAN,                 162    . G.A.                 57,66
. DANIEL              106    . ANNIE                 39    . SALLIE                  75
. DUNCAN               28    . CLARA                 71   NUNNELEE,MARY             45
. FANNIE           65,256    . JAMES R.              81   NUTTING,C.A.             168
. G.W.                129    . LARKIN               149   OAKLEY,JOHNNIE DAFFIN 55
. GILBERT             187    . NANCY WILLIAMS        81    . N.J.                    55
. JABEZ               111    . NORA                  16    . NANCY                  186
. JACK                 68   NEWTON,B.F.              92    . ROXIE                   30
. JENNIE            65,76    . DAVID                139   OATES,ED                  16
. JOHN McL.           256    . LUCY FLEWELLEN       267    . EPHRAIM                 49
. JULIA          49,53,76   NICHOLLS,JOSEPH         128    . JAMES WYATT             31
. MARY                 28    . WILLIAM M.           176    . MAGGIE                  16
. MARY McRAE           28   NICHOLS,E. FARLEY        95    . MATTIE A. SOLOMON       31
. MOLLIE               20    . ELIZABETH             2    . PINK SAUNDERS           49
. PEARLA               55    . WILLIAM H.            95    . SALLIE A. TONEY         39
. TEXANNA CHAMBERS     68   NICOLL,GEORGE A.        137    . W.C.                    31
. WASH                 20   NISBET,F.A.             204    . WILLIAM C.           39,45
McRANEY,DANIEL        179   NISBETT,ALICE BONNELL 76   OATTIS,M.A.              140
McREE,                155    . JAMES T.              76   OBERLY,
. CHRISTIAN McRAE      75   NIX,ALICE               228    . ELVIRA CAMPBELL         39
. J.D.                 75    . CARRIE L. MABRY       77    . R.                      39
. MOLLIE               34    . CHARLES EDWARD        77   OBRANNON,WILLIS          201
. SUSAN WALLER        186    . ED                    55   OBRIEN,ALFRED             74
McREILI,SALLIE LOU     49    . JIM                   58    . J.E.                   255
McSWAIN,ELI           186    . JOE                   44    . JAMES E.                79
. LEOLA               186    . NORA                  85    . LILA GODWIN             79
McSWEAN,ELI            40    . W.H.                 228    . LULA GODWIN            255
. LEONORA JOHNS        40   NOBLE,ADDIE              69    . M.J.                    79
McTYE,TERESE W. HUNTER 7    . EDWARD F.             23    . MATTIE J. THOMAS        74
. WILLIAM A.            7    . GEORGIA HAMBRICK      42   OBRYNE,J.E.              135
McTYER,EMILY CAMPBELL 32    . JAMES                 42    . JULIA WHEELER           89
```

. M. 148-149
. P.O. 89
OBYRNE,LARY 28
. LILLIS BATES 28
. MARY A.T. 30
OCHS,JULIUS 243
OCKENDEN,ALBION 71
OCONER, 79
OCONNER,M.P. 154
OCONOR,CHARLES 201
ODOM,HUSON 157
. M.C. 5
OFFUTT,TOM H. 171
OGLESBY,JULIA 68
OGLETREE,A. 76
. ABBIE 61,65,74,76
. CAMILLA 22
. CARRIE 56
. JOHN 248
. S.R. 56
. SAM 248
. SAMUEL R. 22
OHARA,CYNTHIA COBB 168
OKEEFE,MAUD 75
OLDHAM,CORA SPARKS 80
. W.E. 80
OLIVE,LEVIE 42
. O.C.W. 251
OLIVER,ANNIE 72
. C.W. 47
. CARRIE OGLETREE 56
. DORA CALLOWAY 50
. EDGAR 56
. ELIZABETH 3
. FRED 266
. IDA 93
. J. EASON 25
. LUCY PYE 25
. M.C. 85
. M.D. 7
. M.W. 220
. MOLLIE BOUIE 85
. PARRIE E. RICKS 7
. SAMUEL W. 145
. SARAH 3
. W.J. 268
. WHIT 266
. WILEY 3
. WILLIAM 50
OMEN,GEORGE 48
. JULIA JAMES 48
ONEAL,ANNIE SLATON 23
. EDWIN 264
. JOHNNIE McLEOD 57
. LOU 23
. MARY C. 60
. SEABORN 137
. SIMON 20,214
. W.L. 57
OPP,
. ADDIE BELLE GARDNER 90
. HENRY 90
OPPENDYKE,
. SARAH THOMAS 59
. WILLIAM 58
OPPERT,H. 74
. SQUIRE 33
OREILLY,HENRY 224
ORMOND,ROBERT M. 87
  WILLIA A. MITCHELL 87
ORR,J.M. 71
. JAMES 70,80,88

. MATTIE LEE 71
OSBORN,JOEL 127
OSMER,R.A. 152
OSULLIVAN, 58
OTIS,HENRY 157
OTT,E.S. 219
. ED S. 205
OTTENSASSER,LOUIS 37
OTTENSOSSER,
. BERTHA BODENHEIMER 51
. DAVID 51
. FANNY LESSER 73
. L. 73
OWEN,CATHERINE 176
. J.W. 260
. WILLIAM 176
OWENS,A.D. 225
. AGNES 93
. ALBERT M. 94
. CALLIE EVERETTE 32
. ELLA 161
. FRANKLIN L. 142
. GUSTAN B. 22
. HICKSON C. 98
. J.E. 20
. LEILA H. 170
. MARY SKIPPER 22
. MILLARD 16
. WILLIAM 32
. Z.A. 171
PACE,J. AUGUSTUS 12,95
PADGET,MOSES 233
PADGETT,LAURA RUSSELL 91
. LEVI 91
PAGE,LEONARD 156
PAINE,ROBERT 177
PALMER,H.L. 178
. N.J. 74
. PHILLIP 142
PAPPOT,G.W. 173
. MARIE CAMPBELL 173
PARAMORE,NOAH H. 206
PARDEE,GEORGE H. 268
PARISH,ED 58
. ELLA 58
. FANNIE CREEL 35
. IDA 33,41
. J.E. 33,41,48
. KATE 33
. KATIE 41
. LIZZIE 48
. MAY 58
. SARAH 172
. Z.T. 35
PARK,H.S. 217
. J.T.S. 5
. KATIE 94
. R.H. 118
. WILLIAM 67
PARKE,C.D. 220
PARKER, 55,74,85,88,90
. ALIDA M. COURIC 11
. CORA WINDHAM 82
. D.T. 253
. DOLLIE 263
. DUNCAN T. 263
. ELLA LOCKE 57
. FRANK 72
. HENRY H. 57
. J.J. 82
. J.W. 45,83,124
. MARCENA R. 11

. MARGARET A. 18
. MARY A. 58
. MINNIE 263
. NELLIE ELMORE 72
. ROBERT 156
. S.D. 223
. STEPHEN D. 224
. SUSAN 131
PARMER,BENJAMIN 103
. JANIE 67
. JOHN T. 70
. MARTHA 187
. NANCY 103
. SALLIE J. SIMS 70
PARSON,CHARLES 252
PARSONS,R.R. 255
. W.H. 240
PARTRIDGE,DANIEL 190
. JOHN A. 6
. SARAH J. WHATLEY 6
PASCHAL,E.C. 21
. EVA 25
. MINNIE 25
PASSMORE, 136
. GEORGE 159
PATE,JOHN H. 239
PATRICK,ELLA DOHN 38
. M. 38
PATRON,JOHN B. 200
PATTERSON,A.M. 202
. ANGELINA 7
. CARNELIA 10
. ESTELLE 92
. F.M. 46
. G. 15
. JOHN L. 189
. JOSIAH 98
. LUCRETIA 189
. M.A. 2
. M.B. 45
. MATTIE LIVINGSTON 46
. P.B. 30,36,41,51
. S. 160
. T.D. 10
. TURNER D. 57,121
. W.F. 130
. W.G. 170
. W.H. 17,20,23,26-27
.   30-31,39,46,51,53-54
.   55-59,61,63,73-75,80
. 95
PATTILLO,ELIZABETH C. 81
PATTON,ELIZABETH J. 209
. J.O. 209
. M.M. 136
. R.M. 204
PAUL,L.M. 74
PAULINE,NANNIE 251
. W.S. 251
PAULLIN,
. ANN HELEN BRANNON 107
. ELIZA 173
. EMILY S. McKLEROY 13
. FLORENCE B. 76
. J. STRATTON 9,11,25
.   173,250
. J.S. 13,18,28,41,173
. JAMES S. 8,107
. STRATTON H. 218
. WILLIAM S. 173,250
PAYNE,A.E. 163
. BUCKNER H. 187

306

BENJAMIN BOSWORTH 201
. BILL ARP 217,266
. BRIDGES 205
. C. 16
. CAROLINE A. 217
. CHARLES 132
. CHARLES A. 50
. D.L. GILFORD 87
. DELACY 67
. E.L. 93
. ELAND EASLEY 19
. ELECTRA 62
. ELIZABETH 102,198
. ELLA 87
. EUGENE Q. 38
. FANNIE NUNN 14
. FIDELIA WHETSTONE 24
. FRANCIS SHIRLEY 75
. FRANK 259
. GEORGE E. 51
. H.C.A. 211
. HENRY 57
. IDA 87
. ISAAC 15
. ISHAM 41
. J. EASON 245
. J.E. 20
. J.G. 72
. J.J. 75
. J.M. 30,48
. J.Q. 168
. J.R. 55,123
. J.T. 8,209
. J.W. 25
. JACK 123
. JACOB 228
. JALANEY JANE 6
. JAMES 157
. JENNIE 87,173
. JERE 183
. JIMMIE 48
. JODIE BURNES 93
. JOHN 65
. JOHN G. 36,83,215
. JOHN J. 123
. JONAS 124
. KATIE WOOD 38
. L. 51
. L.A. 271
. L.D. 87
. L.M. 140
. LOUISE M. 22
. LOULA F. CORY 55
. LULA 41
. LYDIA BERRY 30
. M. FANNIE 149
. M.J. KIRKLAND 36
. M.V. WHIGHAM 6
. MARGARET SAULSBURY 8
. MARTHA 15
. MARTHA LOCKE 65
. MARY LAWSON 200
. MILTON 212,228,265
. MILTON A. 55,200,265
. MINNIE B. THREEFOOT 70
. MOLLIE M. 13
. MORGAN H. 14
. N.A. 19
. OLIVER E. 70
. OLIVER T. 38
. OLLIE 215
. OTIS 3

. PHANEY KENNEDY 48
. R.C. 1
. R.E. 149
. ROSA B. CRANE 50
. ROSA L. SAUNDERS 51
. SALLIE 40
. SALLIE E. FLEWELLEN 38
. SENIE THOMSON 15
. SHEROD 77
. SUSAN 42
. SUSAN O. 215
. T.J. 47
. T.M. 239
. T.T. 215
. W.J. 36
. WILLIAM F. 86
. WILLIAM J. 213
. WYATT W. 178
. YANCEY 82
. Z. 51
. ZEKE 67
SMITHA,MINNIE 40
. WILLIAM 202
SMITHWICH,JOHN 215
SMITHWICK,JOHN 259
SMOOT,JOHN B. 238
SMYLY,JOHN 1
. SUSANNAH 1
SNEAD,ANNIE 92
. CLEMMIE 92
. DANIEL 256
. JOHN 92
. L. HESTON 47
. LIZZIE CHRISTIAN 47
. LIZZIE D.
.   CHRISTIAN 267
. LUCIEN H. 267
. M.C. 257
. MAGGIE 256
SNEED,DANIEL 157
SNELL,WILLIAM 143
SNIDER,ANNIE DAWSON 206
. C.R. VEAL 48
. D.B. 48
SNIPES,JOHN D. 134
 MARION 198
SNODGRASS,FANNIE 22
SNOW,C.W. 1
. EMILY E. LOVELACE 1
SOLLY,SEABORN 146
SOLOMON,BELLE 53
. BELLE CHITTY 167
. C.L. 88
. EMMETT 16
. EVA LIDDEN 56
. FANNIE 55
. FANNY 53
. J.W. 18
. JAMES 61
. JOHN Z. 56
. LILLIAN LEWIS 88
. LINA BELL
.   THREADGILL 53
. LUDIE 41
. LYDIA 246
. M.S. 31
. MACK CHITTY 42
. MANIE ALLEN 16
. MATTIE A. 31
. MOLLIE 16
. PEARL REYNOLDS 61
. R.A. 42,167,246

. S.A. 246
. SAM H. 53
. THOMAS 16
. WILEY 246
SOUTHER,G. 185
SOUTHERLAND,JIM 91
SOUTHWICK,D.L. 172
SOWYER,J.H. 248
SPAIN,CLIFFORD 186
. CLIFFORD E. 27
. JAMES 27
SPALDING, 89
. E.C. 249
. EUGENE 54
. VAN HILLIARD 54
SPANN,ANNIE 83
. JOHN 85
SPARGER,WILLIAM 68
SPARHAWK,CHARLES K. 113
SPARKS,CORA 80
. G.W. 84
. GEORGE W. 23,232
. NELLIE H. 84
. SALLIE CASTELLOW 232
. SALLIE E. CASTELLO 23
. WILLIAM H. 164
SPAULDING, 65
. E.W. 73
. ERASTUS W. 86
SPEAR, 55
. B. FRANKLIN 101
. W.R. 199
SPEER,MARY F. 185
SPEIGHT,MINNIE 94
. NELLIE 75
SPENCER,JAMES 42
. JOSEPHINE GOSA 42
. PERRY 82
. SAMUEL 30
SPIDLE,J.M. 116
SPIERS,CARRINGTON 133
SPIES,AUGUST 68
. VAN ZANDT 68
SPINKS,HILLIARD 236
SPIVEY,WILLIAM 143
SPIVY,ELLA 66
. JOHN H. 66
SPORMAN,CHARLES F. 10,45
.   183
. CHARLES H. 144
. HENRY 151
. MATTIE M. PRICE 45
. VASSIE L. 183
. VASSIE L. ANDREWS 10
SPRINGER,F.J. 172
SPURLOCK, 65
. ANNIE FREEMAN 83
. ANNIE NEWMAN 39
. ELLA S. 42
. EULA 42,65
. J.M. 42,83
. JAMES M. 42,191
. JOHN 39
. OSBORN R. 83
STACEY,J.W. 233
. JAMES 164
. JOHN 164
. MINERVA C. 164
STACKS,JOHN 131
STALLINGS,
. BELLE McALLISTER 72
. ELLA C. McALLISTER 44

314